D1422904

THE
ROYAL AIR
FORCE
DAY BY DAY

This book is dedicated
to all the men and women who have served in the Royal Air Force.
Remembering in particular those who
'Failed to Return'.

THE
ROYAL AIR FORCE
DAY BY DAY

AIR COMMODORE GRAHAM PITCHFORK

FOREWORD BY AIR CHIEF MARSHAL SIR GLENN TORPY
KCB CBE DSO ADC BSc(Eng) FRAeS FCGI RAF
Chief of the Air Staff

SUTTON PUBLISHING

First published in the United Kingdom in 2008 by
Sutton Publishing, an imprint of The History Press
Cirencester Road · Chalford · Stroud · Gloucestershire · GL6 8PE

Copyright © Air Commodore G.R. Pitchfork MBE, BA, FRAeS, 2008

All rights reserved. No part of this publication may be reproduced, stored in a retrieval system, or transmitted, in any form, or by any means, electronic, mechanical, photocopying, recording or otherwise, without the prior permission of the publisher and copyright holder.

G.R. Pitchfork has asserted the moral right to be identified as the author of this work.

British Library Cataloguing in Publication Data
A catalogue record for this book is available from the British Library.

ISBN 978-0-7509-4309-3

Typeset in Photina MT.
Typesetting and origination by
The History Press.
Printed and bound in England.

LUNA HABITALIS

The time will come when thou shalt lift thine eyes,
To watch a long drawn battle in the skies,
And aged peasants too amazed for words,
Stare at the Flying Fleet of won'drous birds.
England, so long the Mistress of the Sea
Where wind and waves confess her sovereignty.
Her ancient triumphs yet on high shall bear
And reign, the Sovereign of the conquered air.

Written by the poet Thomas Gray (1716–71)

FOREWORD

Air Chief Marshal Sir Glenn Torpy KCB CBE DSO ADC BSc(Eng) FRAeS FCGI RAF
Chief of the Air Staff

In comparison with our sister services, the Royal Air Force is still very young – a mere 90 years old. Despite that, the impact that the Service has had on the conduct of modern warfare has been vast. Building on the initial successes of the Royal Flying Corps and the Royal Naval Air Service, the Royal Air Force was formed on 1 April 1918 as the world's first independent Air Force. By the end of the First World War, it had convincingly demonstrated the critical importance of air power. No major conflict would ever again be conducted solely in two dimensions.

Flexibility, speed, reach and the exploitation of technology became the key features of Royal Air Force operations during the next twenty years, with the Service involved in long-term aerial policing and peace-keeping in several overseas territories. The Second World War brought the 'Junior Service' its greatest and most significant challenge – the Battle of Britain. Without the untiring efforts and bravery of 'The Few' – and all who supported their endeavours – the freedom of the Western world could easily have been lost. The members of Bomber Command, who valiantly spearheaded offensive operations deep into enemy territory, also displayed these same characteristics in abundance. Eventually, the tide was turned and peace restored. But, even as one threat was defeated, others emerged. Throughout the Cold War, the Royal Air Force played a vital role in both defending the United Kingdom's airspace and providing a robust and capable deterrent capability alongside other NATO allies. Since then, hardly a year has passed in which British Forces have not been involved in some conflict – and the Royal Air Force has played a key role in each and every operation.

Achievement and success in battle has shaped the rich heritage of the Royal Air Force, and I am delighted that Air Commodore Graham Pitchfork has taken the time to chronicle so painstakingly the history of the Service that I am extremely proud to lead. Whether you use *The Royal Air Force Day by Day* as a serious reference book or simply as a reminder of the many exploits of the Service, I am sure you will unearth fascinating gems of information as well as reminders of truly great events. I commend this book to everyone with an interest in the history of aviation and, in particular, in the world's oldest Air Force.

ACKNOWLEDGEMENTS

When this project to commemorate the ninetieth anniversary of the formation of the Royal Air Force was first considered, the then Chief of the Air Staff, and now Chief of the Defence Staff, Air Chief Marshal Sir Jock Stirrup, gave it his full support. His successor, Air Chief Marshal Sir Glenn Torpy, endorsed the project and kindly agreed to write the Foreword. I am grateful to them for their staunch support.

In compiling this record of RAF activities it has been my policy to use primary sources where they existed and could be traced. Much of the research has been carried out at the Air Historical Branch where the Head of the Branch, Sebastian Cox, has given me wise counsel and guidance in addition to allowing me complete access to the comprehensive records held in the Branch. Among his helpful staff, Clive Richards gave me expert advice, opinion and a great deal of his time, and Graham Day and Flight Lieutenant Mary Hudson were most helpful. Without the support of the staff of the Air Historical Branch, this book would not have been possible.

Mr Chris Hobson, the Head Librarian at the Joint Services Command and Staff College, Watchfield, gave me a very great deal of help and advice and full access to the College's excellent library where he allowed me to spend many hours. At the RAF Museum, Hendon, Peter Elliott and Andrew Cormack responded to all my requests and provided a great deal of information. I am also indebted to the Keeper of The National Archives at Kew where I consulted a wide variety of sources, the major documents being listed in the Bibliography.

Many individuals have given me specialist advice and I want to thank them all. Group Captain Chris Morris has been an immense help, providing much information and checking the narrative. Others who have made significant contributions are: Paul Baillie, Professor Dugald Cameron, Alan Carlaw, Wing Commander Colin Cummings, Stephen Davies, Ray Deacon, Flight Lieutenant Tom Draper, Air Vice-Marshal Peter Dye, Peter Green, Stuart Haddaway, Wing Commander Martin Hooper (RAF Regiment Museum), Wing Commander Jeff Jefford, Bill Jordan, Air Chief Marshal Sir Michael Knight, Air Commodore Ben Laite, Group Captain Min Larkin (Halton Aircraft Apprentices Association), Stuart Leslie, Sergeant Rick Mellor (RAF Cottesmore), Roy Nesbit, Group Captain Kingsley Oliver, Tom Patterson, Tim Pierse (RAF College Cranwell Library), Group Captain Jeremy Saye, William Spencer, Roger Stanton, Squadron Leader Andrew Thomas, Air Commodore Philip Wilkinson. At the Ministry of Defence, Squadron Leader Brian Handy has been my point of contact and has been most helpful.

Many of the photographs are from the Air Historical Branch and the Ministry of Defence and I am indebted to the MOD's Intellectual Property Rights Group for permission to include Crown Copyright images. Andy Renwick, Keeper of Photographs at the RAF Museum, gave a great deal of help and advice, and I am also grateful to the Photographic Department of the Imperial War Museum. Many individuals and organisations have helped with photographs and I trust that they will accept the acknowledgement accompanying each photograph as a token of my thanks for their help. Every care has been taken to trace copyright holders. However, if I have omitted anyone, I apologise and, if informed, will make corrections in any future edition.

Finally, I want to thank the staff at Sutton Publishing, in particular Jonathan Falconer, Jane Hutchings, Glad Stockdale and Catherine Watson for their untiring efforts in ensuring that this book was published.

INTRODUCTION

The Royal Air Force was formed on 1 April 1918 when the Royal Naval Air Service and the Royal Flying Corps were combined to form the world's first independent Air Force. Although this landmark date marks the beginning of the recording of events and activities in *The Royal Air Force Day by Day*, it would be entirely inappropriate to ignore the key milestones that led to this momentous event and, therefore, they have been included for completeness.

Many of the major events that feature in this book will be well known to the reader. However, the rich tapestry of the history of the Royal Air Force is made up of countless other less publicised aspects that also contribute to the traditions and ethos of the Service. These have been included where it has been possible to attribute a specific date. All serve to highlight that the Royal Air Force is never 'off duty'.

The history of the Service is not only about aircraft and operations. People are the essence of a fighting service and so their gallantry, dedication and achievements are given prominence. Inevitably, the famous appear more frequently but the service and exploits of the countless 'many' have made all the entries in this book worth recording. Traditions and ceremonial also play a key role in the history and heritage of the Royal Air Force and they too are given prominence.

By cataloguing such a wide spectrum of events, anniversaries and directives, I hope to stimulate interest and further research. In carrying out my own investigations, I came across a number of anomalies. Even in some official accounts, a surprising number of events have been attributed to different dates. Where this has happened, I have sought additional references and made a judgement on the most reliable or appropriate date.

LIST OF ABBREVIATIONS

A&AEE	Aeroplane and Armament Experimental Establishment	BD	Bomb Disposal
AASF	Allied Air Striking Force	BEF	British Expeditionary Force
AC 1	Aircraftman First Class	BFTS	British Flying Training School
ACA	Air Crew Association	BMEWS	Ballistic Missile Early Warning System
ACFE	Allied Command Far East	CALTF	Combined Airlift Task Force
ACM	Air Chief Marshal	CAS	Chief of the Air Staff
ACSEA	Allied Command South-East Asia	CAS	Close Air Support
ADGB	Air Defence of Great Britain	CATOR	Combined Air Transport Operations Room
ADIZ	Air Defence Identification Zone	CB	Companion of the Order of the Bath
AEAF	Allied Expeditionary Air Force	CENTO	Central Treaty Organisation
AEW	Airborne Early Warning	CFE	Central Fighter Establishment
AFC	Air Force Cross	CFS	Central Flying School
AFM	Air Force Medal	CGM	Conspicuous Gallantry Medal
AG	Air Gunner	C-in-C	Commander-in-Chief
AHB	Air Historical Branch	CLE	Central Landing Establishment
AHQ	Air Headquarters	CND	Campaign for Nuclear Disarmament
AHQNEI	Air Headquarters Netherlands East Indies	COMSEC	Communication Security
		CRE	Central Reconnaissance Establishment
ALARM	Air Launched Anti-Radar Missile	CRO	Civilian Repair Organisation
ALBM	Air Launched Ballistic Missile	CTO	Communist Terrorist Organisation
AM	Air Marshal	CTTO	Central Trials and Tactics Organisation
AMDGW	Air Ministry Directorate-General of Works	DAF	Desert Air Force
		DCI	Defence Council Instruction
AMO	Air Ministry Order	DFC	Distinguished Flying Cross
AMSO	Air Member for Supply and Organisation	DFM	Distinguished Flying Medal
		DSO	Distinguished Service Order
AMTC	Aero Medical Training Centre	DWI	Directional Wireless Installation
AMWO	Air Ministry Weekly Order	DZ	Dropping Zone
ANZUK	Australia, New Zealand, United Kingdom	EANS	Empire Air Navigation School
AOC	Air Officer Commanding	EATS	Empire Air Training Scheme
AOP	Air Observation Post	EFA	European Fighter Aircraft
APC	Armament Practice Camp	EFTS	Elementary Flying Training School
ASR	Air Sea Rescue	EGM	Empire Gallantry Medal
ASR	Air Staff Requirement	EWOSE	Electronic Warfare Operational Support Establishment
ASV	Air-to-Surface Vessel		
ATA	Air Transport Auxiliary	FEAF	Far East Air Force
ATD	Air Transport Detachment	FGA	Fighter Ground Attack
ATFERO	Atlantic Ferry Organisation	FIDO	Fog Investigation (Intensive) Dispersal Operation
ATS	Auxiliary Territorial Service		
AVM	Air Vice-Marshal	FOB	Forward Operating Base
AWTI	Air Weapons Training Installation	FTS	Flying Training School
BAFF	British Air Forces in France	**GC**	George Cross
BAFO	British Air Forces of Occupation	GCI	Ground Control Interception
BCAIR	British Commonwealth Air Forces	GDR	German Democratic Republic
BCATP	British Commonwealth Air Training Plan	GM	George Medal
		GOC	General Officer Commanding

GPO	General Post Office	RAE	Royal Aeronautical Establishment
GPTN	General Purpose Telephone Network	RAF	Royal Air Force
HMAFV	His (Her) Majesty's Air Force Vessel	RAFRU	Royal Air Force Rugby Union
HMS	His (Her) Majesty's Ship	RAFVR	Royal Air Force Volunteer Reserve
HQ	Headquarters	RAPWI	Release of Allied Prisoners of War and Internees
HSL	High Speed Launch		
IFF	Identification Friend or Foe	RATG	Rhodesian Air Training Group
IRA	Irish Republican Army	RAuxAF	Royal Auxiliary Air Force
IRBM	Intermediate Range Ballistic Missile	RCAF	Royal Canadian Air Force
JARIC	Joint Air Reconnaissance Intelligence Centre	RCM	Radio Counter Measure
		RDF	Radio Direction Finding
JHQ	Joint Headquarters	REAF	Royal Egyptian Air Force
KBE	Knight of the Order of the British Empire	RFC	Royal Flying Corps
		RMAF	Royal Malayan Air Force
LAA	Light Anti-Aircraft	RN	Royal Navy
LAC	Leading Aircraftman	RNAS	Royal Naval Air Service
LACW	Leading Aircraftwoman	RNZAF	Royal New Zealand Air Force
LNSF	Light Night Striking Force	ROC	Royal Observer Corps
LRDU	Long-Range Development Unit	RP	Rocket Projectile
LRMP	Long-Range Maritime Patrol	R/T	Radio Telephony
LS&GC	Long Service and Good Conduct Medal	S of TT	School of Technical Training
LST	Landing Ship Transport	SAAF	South African Air Force
MAMS	Mobile Air Movements Squadron	SAC	Strategic Air Command
MBF	Medium Bomber Force	SAC	Senior Aircraftman
MC	Military Cross	SACEUR	Supreme Allied Commander Europe
MDAP	Mutual Defence Aid Programme	SAM	Surface-to-Air Missile
MEAF	Middle East Air Force	SBA	Sovereign Base Area
MEDME	Mediterranean and Middle East	SCC	Supply Control Centre
MFH	Mobile Field Hospital	SCU	Servicing Commando Unit
MI	Military Intelligence	SD	Special Duties
MM	Military Medal	SEATO	South-East Asia Treaty Organisation
MPBW	Ministry of Public Buildings and Works	SH	Support Helicopter
MRAF	Marshal of the Royal Air Force	SHAEF	Supreme Headquarters Allied Expeditionary Force
MRS	Mobile Receiving Station		
MSFU	Merchant Ship Fighting Unit	SHORAD	Short Range Air Defence
MSM	Meritorious Service Medal	SIB	Special Investigation Branch
MU	Maintenance Unit	SIS	Secret Intelligence Service
NAEW	NATO Airborne Early Warning	SNCO	Senior Non-Commissioned Officer
NATO	North Atlantic Treaty Organisation	SOAF	Sultan of Oman's Air Force
NCO	Non-Commissioned Officer	SOE	Special Operations Executive
NEAF	Near East Air Force	SU	Signal Unit
OBE	Officer of the Order of the British Empire	TA	Territorial Army
		TACEVAL	Tactical Evaluation
OCU	Operational Conversion Unit	TAF	Tactical Air Force
OTU	Operational Training Unit	TASMO	Tactical Air Support of Maritime Operations
PFF	Pathfinder Force		
PGM	Precision Guided Munition	THUM	Thermometer and Humidity
PIU	Photographic Intelligence Unit	TIALD	Thermal Imaging and Laser Designation
PJI	Parachute Jumping Instructor		
PMRAFNS	Princess Mary's RAF Nursing Service	TLP	Tactical Leadership Programme
POW	Prisoner of War	TNKU	North Kalimantan National Army
PR	Photographic Reconnaissance	TRE	Telecommunications Research Establishment
PRU	Photographic Reconnaissance Unit		
QRA	Quick Reaction Alert	TTTE	Tri-National Tornado Training Establishment
RAAF	Royal Australian Air Force		

UAS	University Air Squadron	VSTOL	Vertical and Short Take Off and Landing
UE	Under Establishment	WAAF	Women's Auxiliary Air Force
UKADR	United Kingdom Air Defence Region	WO	Warrant Officer
USAAF	United States Army Air Force	WOM	Wireless Operator Mechanic
USAF	United States Air Force	WOM/AG	Wireless Operator Mechanic/Air Gunner
USN	United States Navy		
USS	United States Ship	WOP	Wireless Operator
VC	Victoria Cross	WOP/AG	Wireless Operator/Air Gunner
VCP	Visual Control Post	WRAF	Women's Royal Air Force
VHF	Very High Frequency	WSO	Weapon System Operator
VLR	Very Long Range		

1 JANUARY

1920 The RAF Police School (Flt Lt F.E. Bishop) was established at RAF Halton.

1925 A new formation encompassing all units of the RAF's Home Defence Force, Air Defences of Great Britain (later renamed Air Defence of Great Britain) was formed. This in turn was subdivided into Wessex Bombing Area, which controlled all regular bombing squadrons, Fighting Area, which controlled all regular fighter squadrons and an Air Defence Group (later No. 1 Air Defence Group), which consisted of the cadre and auxiliary squadrons. The first Air Officer Commanding-in-Chief was AM Sir John Salmond.

1927 ACM Sir Hugh Trenchard was created as the first Marshal of the Royal Air Force (MRAF).

The Imperial Defence College was opened, commanded successively by an officer from each of the fighting services.

1929 Control of the Observer Corps was transferred from the War Office to the RAF. See 1 March 1929.

1930 ACM Sir John Salmond was appointed as Chief of the Air Staff in succession to MRAF Sir Hugh Trenchard who was created Baron Trenchard of Wolferton on his retirement. On 4 February 1936 he was created a Viscount.

Far East Command was formed. The first RAF airfield, Seletar on Singapore Island, was officially opened.

1931 'Air Ministry Orders' (AMO) were instituted to replace the existing Air Ministry Weekly Orders and Air Ministry Technical Orders. The AMO was divided into three main sections:
- Administrative orders – prefix 'A'.
- Equipment orders – prefix 'E'.
- Temporary orders and notices – prefix 'N'.

1933 The rank of Sergeant Major was abolished in the RAF leaving Warrant Officer Class I and Class II as the only Warrant rank. During the early years of the Second World War, the Warrant Officer Class II rank was abandoned.

1939 The nucleus of four Groups in Maintenance Command was established at RAF Andover, each assuming executive control of a number of Maintenance Units (MUs) during March and April:
- No. 40 Group, an Equipment Group providing all forms of equipment except bombs and explosives.

RAF Service Police, with Flt Lt F.E. Bishop, stationed at RAF Halton Park in 1920. *(Steven Davies Collection)*

1

- No. 41 Group, an Aircraft Group responsible for the receipt, storage, equipping, maintaining while in store, allotting and despatching aircraft to flying units.
- No. 42 Group, an Ammunition and Fuel Group.
- No. 43 Group, a Repair and Salvage Group responsible for the repair, modification and salvage of aircraft and engines.

At the end of August 1939, approximately 2,500 aircraft were held in No. 41 Group MUs with deliveries to service units of 250 per month. Largely civilian manned, No. 41 Group played a key role and in August 1940 issued 1,420 aircraft, the majority Hurricanes and Spitfires. By the end of 1943, the Group had grown to more than twenty MUs storing 9,000 aircraft. No. 43 Group had thirteen depots by 1944 and employed 18,000 technical personnel. A total of 3,687 aircraft were repaired during 1944, the rebuilding of Lancasters being the largest commitment. By the end of the Second World War 385 MUs had been formed.

1940 Coding was introduced on IFF to identify Bomber, Coastal and Fighter Command aircraft. VHF R/T installations were completed in eight fighter sectors.

1941 The first mobile GCI station was sited and manned at RAF Sopley, Hampshire. Four more were sited by the end of the month.

1945 Operation Bodenplatte (Baseplate): the Luftwaffe launched over 800 fighters and

Wreckage of a Typhoon at Eindhoven following the Luftwaffe's audacious attacks against Allied airfields on New Year's Day 1945. *(N. Franks)*

fighter-bombers, predominantly Focke-Wulf Fw 190s and Messerschmitt Bf 109s, in a low-level surprise attack on Allied advanced airfields in Belgium and the Netherlands. Surprise was complete, although the attacks on some airfields were ineffective. Nevertheless, 224 Allied aircraft were destroyed (144 RAF) with a further 84 damaged beyond unit repair. Despite this, Bodenplatte proved to be a pyrrhic victory. Allied pilot losses were minimal, and the aircraft destroyed were replaced within two weeks. By contrast, the Luftwaffe lost 300 aircraft during the course of the operation to Allied airfield defences, German anti-aircraft units that had not been warned of the planned assault, and accidents. The Luftwaffe lost 237 pilots including some of Germany's most experienced fighter leaders.

RAF Regiment LAA Squadrons at eleven RAF airfields in Holland and Belgium fired over 7,500 rounds of 40mm ammunition and 5,000 rounds of .303-inch ammunition, shooting down forty-three enemy aircraft and damaging a further forty-two.

VC: Flt Sgt George Thompson, a wireless operator of No. 9 Squadron saved the lives of members of his Lancaster crew despite suffering severe burns. He died of his wounds on 23 January. (*London Gazette*, 20 February 1945, posthumous award)

1946 MRAF Sir Arthur Tedder was created Baron Tedder of Glenguin and appointed as Chief of the Air Staff.

1947 The RAF Secretarial, Provost and Catering Branches were formed.

1950 ACM Sir John Slessor was appointed Chief of the Air Staff.

1951 The star system of denoting Air rank replaced the rank pennants introduced on 6 January 1927.

1953 ACM Sir William Dickson was appointed Chief of the Air Staff.

1955 The name Central Gunnery School was abolished and the School became two units:

MRAF Sir William Dickson (1898–1987). *(AHB)*

the Fighter Weapons School and the Coastal Command Gunnery School. The former trained fighter pilots as pilot attack instructors and the latter trained air gunners as free gunnery instructors.

1956 MRAF Sir William Dickson became the first holder of the appointment of Chairman, Chiefs of Staff Committee. He remained in post after the appointment was converted to Chief of the Defence Staff, a position he held until 16 July 1959.

ACM Sir Dermot Boyle was appointed Chief of the Air Staff and became the first RAF College Cranwell graduate to fill the highest appointment in the Service.

1959 The Second Tactical Air Force (2nd TAF) was renamed RAF Germany.

1960 ACM Sir Thomas Pike was appointed Chief of the Air Staff.

No. 38 Group (AVM P.G. Wykeham) was reformed as a specialist tactical group within RAF Transport Command.

RAF Police provide security for a Vulcan bomber on QRA.
(G.R. Pitchfork Collection)

1962   The strike QRA commitment in Bomber Command commenced with one aircraft per squadron holding fifteen-minutes readiness. This brought the Medium Bomber Force (MBF) state of readiness into line with that of Valiants under SACEUR.

1969   Signals Command was disbanded and formed as No. 90 Group within Strike Command.

1993   MRAF Sir Peter Harding was appointed Chief of the Defence Staff. He resigned on 13 March 1994.

2 JANUARY

1918   An Order in Council defined the composition and duties of members of the Air Council and a separate Air Ministry was formed in London. The following day the first Air Council was created when Lord Rothermere was appointed the first Secretary of State for the Air Force (re-titled Secretary of State for Air from March 1918).

1919   The rank titles for non-commissioned personnel were defined in AMWO 24/19. In order of seniority they were:
  • Warrant Officer 1

  • Sergeant Major 1st Class
  • Warrant Officer 2
  • Sergeant Major 2nd Class
  • Flight Sergeant
  • Sergeant
  • Corporal
Below these Warrant and NCO ranks was the common denomination of Aircraftman with the three classifications of Leading Aircraftman, Aircraftman 1st Class and Aircraftman 2nd Class.
    See 22 August 1950.

Capt Lang and Lt A.W. Blowes, flying a DH 9, established a world height record of 30,500ft. Lang was subsequently placed under open arrest for divulging details of the flight.

1935   Twelve Hart aircraft of No. 11 Squadron left Risalpur in India on a Long Distance Training Flight to Singapore to test the efficiency of the revised scheme for the reinforcement of Singapore. Eleven aircraft arrived on 8 January and returned to Risalpur on the 24th. This was the first time the reinforcement route had been exercised by a complete squadron.

1963   The air electronics flying badge was worn by ex-air signallers who were redesignated air electronics operators after further training, and from 1965 by newly qualified non-commissioned personnel (AMO A.6/1963).
    See 9 January 1957.

2004 MRAF Sir John Grandy, former Chief of the Air Staff, died.
See 1 April 1967.

2005 A C-17 Globemaster II of No. 99 Squadron landed at Banda Aceh, northern Sumatra, with the first British aid following the Tsunami disaster.

3 JANUARY

1924 The Air Ministry announced the introduction of the Short Service Commission Scheme for 400 officers for flying duties.

1942 Fifty-one crated Hurricane fighters and twenty-four pilots arrived in Singapore with the advance parties of Nos 17, 135, 136 and 232 Squadrons.

4 JANUARY

1944 An air interdiction campaign commenced against the Italian railway and road system in support of the Allied amphibious landings at Anzio. The Air Directive outlined the aim as 'to attack enemy communications in such a manner as to impose maximum disruption to enemy supply lines to the battle area and to support the ground and naval operations by every means possible from the air'.
See 19 March 1944.

1964 Operation Nutcraker: air operations in support of ground forces commenced in the western part of the Radfan in the Aden Protectorate. Hunters of the Khormaksar Wing flew ground-attack sorties and Belvedere and Wessex helicopters provided airlift to remote areas. The initial phase was completed by 15 January.
See 29 April 1964.

1998 An RAF Chivenor-based Sea King (captain Flt Lt A. Potter) and two Nimrods from RAF Kinloss were scrambled to assist the Spanish fishing trawler *Sonia Nancy*. The vessel with ten fishermen on board was sinking 200 miles south-west of Ireland in

A Wessex of No. 78 Squadron positions a 75mm Howitzer in a firing position in the Radfan. *(AHB. CMP 1518)*

atrocious weather conditions. A Nimrod dropped life rafts and survival stores and monitored the situation until the arrival of the Sea King, which winched all of the men to safety, the winchman sustaining injuries during the rescue. The first Nimrod on the scene was struck by lightning but the crew elected to continue in the hope of saving the trawler crew and providing safety cover to the helicopter. Awards were made to the Sea King and Nimrod crews for their brave and determined efforts.

5 JANUARY

1936 The Air Ministry bought Bawdsey Manor on the Suffolk coast near Felixstowe for £25,000 to become the first radar station in the world. It began as a research establishment and served as one of the five stations guarding the air approaches to London at the outbreak of war in 1939.

1968 The phasing out of the Hastings transport aircraft began after the aircraft had given twenty years of service.

6 JANUARY

1927 Masthead distinguishing rank flags were authorised for station flag masts and cars. They were also applied unofficially to RAF aircraft (AMWO 8/27).

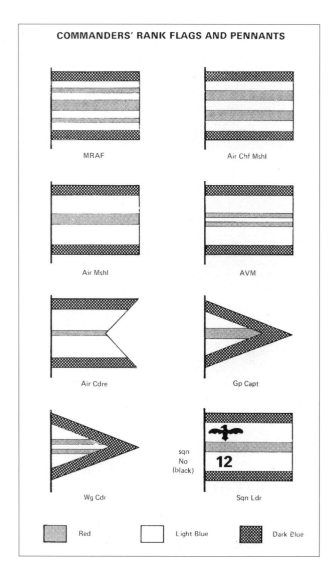

COMMANDERS' RANK FLAGS AND PENNANTS

MRAF

Air Chf Mshl

Air Mshl

AVM

Air Cdre

Gp Capt

Wg Cdr

sqn No (black) 12

Sqn Ldr

Red　　Light Blue　　Dark Blue

1942 The Royal Warrant was signed announcing the impending formation of the RAF Regiment as a specialised airfield defence 'corps' formed as an integral part of the RAF.
See 1 February 1942.

1944 The signaller flying badge was introduced for WOP/AGs and WOM/AGs. The pattern was the same as the air gunner badge with 'S' in the laurel. It was superseded by the air electronics operator badge in 1963 but reinstated solely for No. 51 Squadron linguists in 1970 (AMO A.36/1944).
See 2 January 1963.

1959 A bomb disposal team, led by OC 6209 BD Flight (Flt Lt J.M. Waters) defused the largest bomb ever tackled by the RAF, a 12,000lb 'Tallboy' bomb, dropped by Bomber Command on 15 October 1944 on an operation against the Sorpe Dam. The bomb was discovered when the dam was partially drained.

1982 The Tornado GR1 entered operational service with No. 9 Squadron at RAF Honington.

7 JANUARY

1917 **VC**: Sgt Thomas Mottershead of No. 20 Squadron RFC, the only Victoria Cross to be won by a non-commissioned officer of the RFC during the First World War, for recovering his burning aircraft, a FE2d, from a fighting patrol in Ploegsteert Wood in France and for saving the life of his observer. He died of his extensive injuries on 12 January 1916. (*London Gazette*, 12 February 1917, posthumous award)

1926 From this day, the word 'aerial' was only to be used in connection with wireless telegraphy. Otherwise, the word 'air' in place of the word 'aerial' was to be adopted as the standard expression, e.g. air gunner and air reconnaissance in place of aerial gunner and aerial reconnaissance.

1941 **GC**: Sqn Ldr John Noel Dowland for bomb disposal.

Masthead distinguishing flags authorised in 1927. *(RAFM)*

1942 The first RAF reinforcements reached Burma when sixteen Blenheim IVs of No. 113 Squadron (Wg Cdr R.N. Stidolph) arrived at Toungoo from the Middle East. They attacked Bangkok docks the following day.

1944 The crew of a No. 157 Squadron Mosquito (Fg Off P. Huckin and Flt Sgt R. Graham) were forced to ditch 200 miles south of the Scilly Islands in very bad weather. After surviving a grim ordeal in the dinghy they boarded a lifeboat dropped by a Warwick of No. 280 Squadron (captain Flt Lt G. Chesher). They had been afloat for four days and sailed north almost 200 miles before being picked up 30 miles from Land's End. They were in excellent condition, due to the good use made of the equipment they found in the lifeboat. This was the longest recorded rescue using an airborne lifeboat. Huckin and Graham were awarded an immediate DFC and DFM respectively.

1945 Reversion to red, white and blue roundels on the upper surfaces of all British aircraft except those involved in night flying and on aircraft in South-East Asia and the Pacific areas.

1948 The RAF School of Education was established at RAF Wellesbourne Mountford.

1949 Four Spitfires of No. 208 Squadron conducted a tactical reconnaissance sortie over the Egypt–Israel border following an Israeli ground incursion. Israeli anti-aircraft fire shot one down. Israeli Air Force Spitfires mistook the three other RAF Spitfires for Egyptians and shot them down. One pilot was killed, Bedouin tribesmen picked up one, and Israeli soldiers captured two: they were released on 23 January.

1974 The RAF College of Air Warfare became embedded within the RAF College, Cranwell, to become the RAF College's Department of Air Warfare.

8 JANUARY

1928 'Akforce' (Air Cdre T.C.R. Higgins) was formed at Ur Junction, Southern Iraq, for operations against the Akhwan tribes of Najd. Operations were conducted by DH 9As of Nos 55 and 84 Squadrons, Victorias of No. 70 Squadron and two sections of armoured cars. These continued until May and the RAF force was disbanded on 3 June.

A DH9A of No. 84 Squadron, part of Akforce.
(G.R. Pitchfork Collection)

A Shackleton AEW 2 of No. 8 Squadron. *(Andrew Thomas Collection)*

1929   The Far East Flight was redesignated No. 205 Squadron (Sqn Ldr G.E. Livock) to become the first permanent RAF flying unit based in Singapore.
       See 1 November 1928.

1940   A Wellington equipped with a Directional Wireless Installation (DWI) – a mine exploding ring – exploded a mine near the Tongue lightship, north of Margate, the first success for this anti-mining operation.

1955   The first V-bomber squadron, No. 138 Squadron (Wg Cdr R.G.W. Oakley), received its first Valiant at RAF Gaydon.

A Wellington equipped with a mine-exploding ring. *(AHB. CM 5315)*

1972   No. 8 Squadron was formed as the RAF's first airborne early warning (AEW) squadron operating the Shackleton AEW Mk 2 at RAF Lossiemouth.

1981   Security at all RAF stations was reviewed and gate controls introduced following the explosion of an IRA bomb at RAF Uxbridge, which caused serious damage but no casualties.

9 JANUARY

1957   The air electronics officer flying badge was introduced. It was the same design as the air gunner badge with 'AE' in the laurel. Until 1963 it was worn only by commissioned officers (AMO A.18/1957).
       See 2 January 1963.

10 JANUARY

1919 A regular London to Paris air service was started by No. 1 (Communications) Squadron flying DH4s.

1941 The Telecommunications Research Establishment (TRE) handed over the first GCI Station, at Durrington, to the RAF.

The first major 'blitz' against Malta started when the airfields at Luqa and Halfar and the aircraft carrier HMS *Illustrious* came under concentrated attack. Heavy dive-bombing attacks occurred on the 19th. By the 20th, when the attacks tailed off, the island's defenders had accounted for forty aircraft destroyed.

Wellington bombers operating from Malta bombed the Italian Fleet at anchorage at Naples. The battleship *Giulio Cesare* was badly damaged. The Italian Navy withdrew its remaining battleships further north to Genoa.

The first 'Circus' operation – daylight raids by small numbers of bombers with large fighter escorts against short-range 'fringe' targets, with the aim of bringing enemy fighters to battle – was flown over occupied Europe. Blenheims of No. 114 Squadron, supported by nine squadrons of fighters, attacked targets in the Forest of Guines.

1944 The newly formed Allied Expeditionary Air Force (AEAF) Bombing Committee (Air Cdre E.J. Kingston-McCloughry) considered the first draft of a strategic bombing plan, 'Air Attacks on Rail and Road Communications'. In due course, this formed the basis for the 'Transportation Plan' implemented in the build-up to the Allied invasion of France (Operation Overlord).
See 15 April 1944.

1969 A disbandment parade was held at RAF Akrotiri, Cyprus, for the squadrons of the Canberra-equipped NEAF Strike Wing. (Nos 6, 32, 73 and 249 Squadrons). Subsequently, a new CENTO-dedicated Strike Wing was formed with Nos 9 and 35 Squadrons equipped with the Vulcan.

1978 Gen William Evans, Commander Allied Air Forces Central Europe, formally opened the Tactical Leadership Programme (TLP) at Fürstenfeldbruck air base near Munich. The need for an international tactical leadership training course was first expressed by MRAF Sir Andrew Humphrey when the Chiefs of Air Staff of the Central Region met at Ramstein in April 1976. RAF aircrew were among the first members of the directing staff.

11 JANUARY

1944 The air operations designed to support the Allied invasion of France (Operation Overlord) commenced. They fell into four phases:
- **Preliminary**: January–February 1944. In many respects, these were a continuation of the Bomber Command attacks against submarine construction yards, aircraft industry, transportation, oil industry and 'others in the war industry', and Coastal Command's crucial anti-submarine patrols in the Atlantic to protect the vital convoy routes.
- **Preparatory**: March–May 1944 when the main weight of attacks was to be directed against invasion targets including railways, early warning radar sites and coastal gun emplacements.
- **Assault**: D minus Two to D plus One.
- **Follow-up**: D plus Two onwards.
See 14 April 1944.

12 JANUARY

1919 No. 221 Squadron arrived at Petrovsk on the Caspian Sea in preparation for air operations with a mixture of DH4s, DH9s and DH9As in support of White Russian forces. In March No. 266 Squadron, equipped with Short 184 seaplanes, arrived as reinforcements. Both units were disbanded on 1 September.

1931 Three Victorias of No. 216 Squadron flew from Heliopolis, Egypt, to Cape Town and back completing the 11,242-mile flight on 11 March; the longest 'cruise' to date by heavy transport aircraft.

A Short 184 seaplane arrives at Petrovsk. *(RAFM)*

1940 Whitleys of No. 77 Squadron, operating from Villeneuve in France, dropped leaflets on Prague and Vienna.
  See 7 March 1940.

1957 The Central Reconnaissance Establishment (CRE) was formed at RAF Brampton.

1962 Exercise Lifeline: a seven-day exercise for the new concept in airborne support was launched. No. 38 Group, Transport Command, supplied and supported two brigade groups of the strategic reserve with 200–250 tons of supplies per day over 200 miles. This was the first exercise for the Gnome-Whirlwind helicopters and fighter ground attack (FGA) Hunters.

Hudsons of No. 48 Squadron. *(G.R. Pitchfork Collection)*

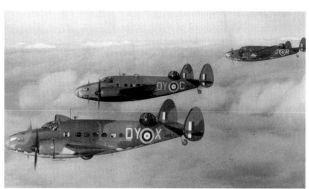

13 JANUARY

1940 The first air-to-surface vessel radar sets (ASV Mk 1) were installed in twelve Coastal Command Hudsons by a working party from No. 32 Maintenance Unit.
  See 4 September 1937.

1964 Indonesian Confrontation: the British government authorised the C-in-C Far East to carry out offensive patrols across the border into Kalimantan to a depth of 10,000yd.

14 JANUARY

1919 Winston Churchill was appointed to the post of Secretary of State for War and the Royal Air Force within the new Lloyd George administration.

1943 Bomber Command was instructed, in a Directive from the Air Ministry, to undertake bombing raids against the U-boat bases on the west coast of France at Lorient and St Nazaire. This turned out to be both an error and a tragedy. The Germans had by then built enormously strong concrete shelters for the submarines and their essential facilities and the bombing had little

military effect. The French population suffered heavy casualties. This campaign against the U-boats continued until the spring, and was later extended to include submarine construction yards in Germany.

1991 Operation Granby: a reconnaissance detachment of six Tornado GR1As, drawn from Nos 2 and 13 Squadrons, was established at Dhahran.

15 JANUARY

1920 The RAF Rugby Union (RAFRU) was formed under the chairmanship of Air Cdre C. Lambe. Wg Cdr A.W. Morris (later Air Cdre), a former England international, was appointed sole selector and treasurer. He held the latter post for the next forty-two years until his death.

1942 The Japanese army crossed into Burma from Siam and commenced a ground offensive up the Kra Isthmus towards Moulmein and Rangoon.

Armourers arming Hurricanes with rockets in Burma.
(AHB. C 1992)

1946 Operation Sunburn: aircraft based in Palestine commenced searches for shipping carrying illegal immigrants to Palestine.
See 17 January 1946.

1951 A Sunderland of No. 88 Squadron (captain Flt Lt H.J. Houtheusen) landed 200yd off the enemy-held harbour of Wonsan, North Korea, to pick up a US Navy pilot who had ditched. Houtheusen was awarded the DFC.

1952 RAF Wildenrath, the first of the four 'Clutch' stations west of the River Rhine, was opened. The other stations were at Geilenkirchen (opened on 24 May 1953), Bruggen (opened in May 1953) and Laarbruch (opened on 15 October 1954).

1953 HRH Prince Philip, Duke of Edinburgh, was promoted to Marshal of the Royal Air Force.

1963 The first WRAF to be formally enrolled as aircrew received their quartermasters flying badge.

The crew of a Tornado GR1 strap themselves into their aircraft prior to a night strike over Iraq. *(RAFM)*

16 JANUARY

1936　An order was issued authorising unit badges subject to the approval of the RAF Inspector of Badges (J.D. Heaton-Armstrong). The design and criteria for unit badges have remained in existence ever since (AMO A.8/1936).

　　See 18 June 1936.

1943　Target indicator bombs (250lb) were used for the first time during a raid on Berlin.

1946　A Lancaster B.1 (PD 328) 'Aries I' (captain Wg Cdr C.M. Dunnicliffe) of the Empire Air Navigation School flew from RAF Thorney Island to Cape Town. With a forty-minute refuelling stop at Cairo, the aircraft covered the 6,900 miles in 32 hours 21 minutes for a new record.

　　See 30 April 1947.

1968　Sweeping defence cuts were announced including the cancellation of an order for fifty General Dynamics F-111s ordered for the RAF. British forces were to be withdrawn from the Far East and Persian Gulf by December 1971. The phasing out of the RN's fixed-wing carrier fleet was to be accelerated with the Fleet Air Arm's fixed-wing aircraft transferred to the RAF.

17 JANUARY

1939　The Auxiliary Air Force Reserve was formed to allow ex-members of the Auxiliary Air Force to serve with Auxiliary flying squadrons in an emergency.

1944　No. 46 Group (Air Cdre Fiddament), equipped with five squadrons of Dakotas, was formed within Transport Command for airborne operations and tactical resupply by air.

1946　AHQ Levant brought all RAF units to a state of maximum defence readiness in anticipation of reprisal attacks by underground terrorist organisations in Palestine. Attacks against RAF units commenced a few days later.

　　See 25 February 1946.

1991　Operation Desert Storm: the Coalition air assault on Iraq began in the early hours.

During the opening phase of the assault, four airfield attacks were carried out by twenty Tornado GR1s armed with the Hunting JP233 airfield denial weapons and two others with ALARM (Air Launched Anti-Radar Missile). Victor tankers supported the attacks. A Tornado was shot down and the crew ejected and were taken prisoner. During the day, Jaguars attacked a variety of targets in Kuwait including supply dumps, surface-to-air missile sites, enemy artillery positions and naval targets.

18 JANUARY

1918 Maj Gen Sir Hugh Trenchard was appointed as the first Chief of the Air Staff. Maj Gen J. Salmond succeeded him as GOC of the RFC in France.

1940 **GC** (ex-EGM): Cpl John McIntosh McClymont for rescue operations in the fuselage of a burning aircraft that crashed in a snowstorm. (*London Gazette*, 19 July 1940)

1952 The first two United States Lockheed P2V maritime patrol aircraft, given the name Neptune in the RAF, arrived at RAF St Eval. The following day No. 217 Squadron was re-formed to operate the aircraft.

1965 The Air Force Board Standing Committee decided to withdraw the Valiant force from service following the discovery of metal fatigue in a wing structure.

19 JANUARY

1939 The trade of aerial gunner – ground tradesmen who had voluntarily undertaken such duties in addition to their full trade – was established as the full-time aircrew category of 'air gunner' (AMO A.17/1939).
See 21 December 1939.

An LAC air gunner, serving with a Whitley squadron, wears the distinctive 'winged bullet' insignia on his sleeve. Shortly afterwards, the badge was replaced by the new air gunner brevet. *(AHB)*

MRAF The Viscount Trenchard (1873–1956). *(AHB. CHP 864)*

Wellington air gunners prepare belts of .303mm ammunition prior to arming the Browning machine guns in the rear turret. *(ACA Archives)*

1945 Stalag Luft VII at Bankau was evacuated in blizzard conditions and Allied POWs commenced marching to the west on what became known as 'The Long March'.
See 27 January 1945.

20 JANUARY

1938 The Air Ministry announced that the RAF Display at Hendon would be discontinued, giving the reason that the airfield was too small for modern aircraft.

1942 Hurricanes based in Singapore shot down eight of a formation of twenty-seven unescorted Japanese bombers over Singapore.

1944 ACM Sir Arthur Tedder assumed duties as Deputy Supreme Commander Allied Expeditionary Force. US Gen Dwight D. Eisenhower had taken up the post of Supreme Commander on 16 January 1944.

1946 Airmen at RAF Mauripur, Karachi, dissatisfied with conditions and the slow rate of demobilisation, held a demonstration and went 'on strike'. After AM Sir Roderic Carr addressed the airmen, they returned to work on the 25th. The disaffection spread to other RAF units in Ceylon and Singapore, where the Commander-in-Chief, ACM Sir Keith Park, addressed a mass parade. The problem rumbled on for a number of months.

21 JANUARY

1920 The RAF's first 'Little War', commenced when 'Z Force', equipped with twelve DH9 aircraft, began operations against the 'Mad Mullah' (the tribal leader Mohammed bin Abdullah Hassan) in British Somaliland in co-operation with the Camel Corps. Operating from a disguised base in Berbera, 'Z Force' succeeded in destroying three Dervish forts in five days. The squadron subsequently provided air support and communications for the ground forces. The RAF contingent, under the command of Gp Capt R. Gordon, were 'the main instrument and decisive factor' in the overthrow of the 'Mad Mullah', who had defied British military power since 1900.

1936 HM King Edward VIII was promoted to Marshal of the Royal Air Force.

1941 **GC**: Flt Lt Wilson Hodgson Charlton for dealing with 200 unexploded bombs.

GC: AC1 Vivian Holloway of No. 14 Service Flying Training School for carrying out rescue duties at the sites of two crashed aircraft.

1943 The Casablanca Directive was issued by the Combined Chiefs of Staff defining the primary objectives of the Combined Bomber Offensive:
• German submarine yards.
• German Air Force industry.
• Transportation targets.
• Oil targets.
• Other targets in enemy war industry.

1991 Operation Desert Storm: with the achievement of air superiority, and the departure of the majority of the Iraqi Air

A casualty of 'Z Force' is loaded into a DH9 prior to evacuation (see 1 February 1920). *(AHB. H 96)*

Force, the Tornados abandoned their low-level tactics and commenced attacks from medium level.

22 JANUARY

1944   Operation Shingle: Allied amphibious landings took place at Anzio, Italy, in an effort to outflank German positions. Allied air forces made heavy attacks on airfields and lines of communication, dropping 12,500 tons of bombs in three weeks. The early success by the ground forces was not exploited.

The official formation of the RAF Mountain Rescue Service was announced. The Service was based on the voluntary organisation established in May 1942 by Flt Lt G. Graham, the station medical officer at RAF Llandwrog, Caernarfon. He and his team attended many crashes in North Wales and were responsible for saving numerous lives.

23 JANUARY

1963   The last National Service airman serving in the RAF, SAC J. Wallace (Mech Gen) left RAF Kinloss on demobilisation. To mark

the occasion, AVM R.B. Thomson, AOC No. 18 Group, presented him with a scroll, and an engraved station crest. After the ceremony SAC Wallace lunched in the Airmen's Mess with friends of his section before being piped aboard a Shackleton aircraft of No. 120 Squadron and flown by the AOC to Renfrew airport. On arrival, he was taken by staff car to his home in Glasgow. The event received full press and TV coverage.

Flt Lt G. Graham, who established the first voluntary mountain rescue team at RAF Llandwrog. *(AHB)*

24 JANUARY

1935 The term 'air pilotage' was replaced by 'air navigation'. This involved the change of numerous titles. e.g.:
- Air Pilotage School to be Air Navigation School.
- *Manual of Air Pilotage* (AP 1234) to be *Manual of Air Navigation, Vol 1.*
- Air pilotage officers to be termed 'navigation officers'.

1941 The Secretary of State for Air gave approval for the establishment of the Directorate of Sea Rescue Services (later Air Sea Rescue). The new Directorate (Air Cdre L.G.LeB. Croke) took up its duties on 6 February 1941.

1944 AM O.T. Boyd escaped from a villa near Florence and made his escape to England. Sadly, he died of natural causes on 5 March 1944.
See 20 November 1940.

Above: Air Cdre L.G. Croke, the first Director of Sea Rescue, with Lt The Lord Rossmore RNVR. *(AHB)*

Below: ACM Sir Andrew Humphrey prepares to take off in a Jaguar at RAF Coltishall. *(AHB)*

The certificate awarded to those of the
Path finder Force. *(ACA Archive)*

ROYAL AIR FORCE

PATH FINDER FORCE

Award of
Path Finder Force Badge

This is to certify that

1604589 FLIGHT SERGEANT MARCHANT, T.C.

having qualified for the award of the Path Finder Force Badge, and
having now completed satisfactorily the requisite conditions of
operational duty in the Path Finder Force, is hereby

Permanently awarded the Path Finder Force Badge

Issued this 20ᵗʰ day of JUNE in the year 1944

Air Officer Commanding, Path Finder Force.

1977 MRAF Sir Andrew Humphrey, the Chief of Defence Staff, died in post.
See 1 April 1974, 24 October 1976.

1996 Wg Cdr R.A.B. Learoyd **VC** died.
See 12 August 1940.

25 JANUARY

1943 The Pathfinder Force was elevated to Group status as No. 8 (PFF) Group (Air Cdre D.C.T. Bennett) with headquarters at Huntingdon.
See 15 August 1942.

1956 Six Canberra bombers of No. 9 Squadron left RAF Binbrook for West Africa, visiting the Gold Coast, Sierra Leone, Gambia and Nigeria. The Squadron's presence in Nigeria coincided with a state visit by HM The Queen.

1964 Following a mutiny by men of the five battalions of the King's African Rifles, Belvedere helicopters of No. 26 Squadron embarked on the aircraft carrier HMS *Centaur* landed Royal Marine commandos at the Colito Barracks, Tanganyika. Beverleys of No. 30 Squadron flew 450 infantrymen into Entebbe from RAF Eastleigh, Nairobi, to suppress the mutiny in Uganda.

26 JANUARY

1923 The RAF badge was registered at the College of Arms after HM King George V had approved it.
See 15 September 1949.

1942 Twelve Vildebeest torpedo bombers, from a force of thirty-six of Nos 36 and 100

A Vildebeest of No. 36 Squadron over Singapore.
(AHB. H 361)

27 JANUARY

Squadrons, were lost attacking the Japanese landings at Endau in southern Malaya.

1962 No. 38 Support Unit was formed at RAF Odiham to provide communications for operational deployments and field exercises. Over a period of years the unit changed title and locations before becoming the Tactical Communications Wing in 1969, moving to RAF Brize Norton in 1976.

1976 No. 2 Squadron, RAF Regiment, established a long-term Regiment presence (followed by other squadrons on roulement) at RAF Aldergrove to meet the increasing threat posed by the IRA.

1991 Operation Desert Storm: the first of twelve Buccaneers drawn from Nos 12 and 208 Squadrons and No. 237 OCU departed for Muharraq, Bahrain, where they provided a laser designation capability for the Tornado force using the Pave Spike laser-designating pod.

1921 The RAF Nursing Service was established as a permanent branch in the RAF.

1942 The first of forty-eight Hurricane Mk IIa fighters, flown by pilots of Nos 242, 258 and 605 Squadrons, took off from HMS *Indomitable* to reinforce the defences of Singapore.

1945 Late at night, the POWs at Stalag Luft III at Sagan were roused and given less than one hour to gather their belongings and evacuate the largest German POW camp, so began The Long March.

1953 Flt Lts L.M. Whittington and J.A. Brown in a Canberra PR3 set up a point-to-point record between London and Mauripur in Karachi covering the 3,921 statute miles in 8 hours 52 minutes 28 seconds. The following day they continued the flight to set up a new London to Darwin point-to-point record of 22 hours 21 seconds.

THE LONG MARCH

An unknown POW captures the ordeal of The Long March. *(RAFM)*

On 27 January 1945, as the Soviet Army advanced rapidly into Poland and Germany, thousands of POWs were sent out into the night in freezing conditions to begin a journey to camps in the west that would involve marching some 400–500 miles and taking some eighty-six days. The men often had to fend for themselves. Twelve camps were evacuated and about 60,000 men were on the move. On 17 February, the Red Cross reported that 'the evacuation towards the west is being carried out in most difficult conditions, on foot, without food, in severe cold'. Hundreds died of exhaustion, exposure and malnutrition. On 19 April, Allied fighters attacked a column and over sixty POWs were killed. As men arrived at the camps in the west, massive overcrowding caused further intense hardship. The Red Army liberated the last camp at Luckenwalde on 12 May. As POWs were released, a major repatriation operation (Operation Exodus) was put in force.

See 3 April 1945.

28 JANUARY

1935 The Committee for the Scientific Survey of Air Defence, chaired by Mr H.T. Tizard, held its first meeting. The Air Ministry had established the committee to 'consider how far recent advances in scientific and technical knowledge can be used to strengthen the present methods of defence against hostile aircraft'.

29 JANUARY

1920 An order announced the opening of an Air Navigation School at RAF Calshot in April 1920. Graduates were awarded a certificate as an 'Air Navigator' (AMWO 96/20).

1941 A United Kingdom Delegation (AVM J.C. Slessor) arrived in Washington to conduct discussions with the Americans, which

Three Tornado GR1s of the TTTE fly over RAF Cottesmore. *(RAF Cottesmore)*

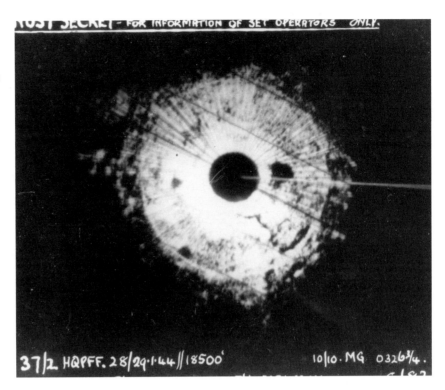

The screen of an *H2S* radar set showing a built-up area where a lake and river can be identified. *(RAFM)*

resulted in joint recommendations to exchange Military Missions.

See 22 April 1941.

1951 In response to the outbreak of the Korean War, the Prime Minister, Clement Attlee, announced plans to improve the UK's military preparedness. Proposals included the recall of reservists for training and the call up of the Royal Auxiliary Air Force fighter squadrons for refresher courses.

Under a bilateral agreement to train RAF aircrew, the first pilot trainees arrived at RCAF Gimli for flying training. The first navigators arrived at RCAF London on 12 March before moving to RCAF Summerside for navigator training. Entries of twenty-five, a mixture of regular and National Service officers, arrived at each training school at six-week intervals. A NATO scheme, embodying the RAF scheme, came into being in 1953 and ended with a ceremony in Winnipeg on 19 July 1958.

1971 The first Westland/Aérospatiale Puma helicopter was delivered to Air Support Command. Forty-eight Pumas were built for the RAF and No. 33 Squadron was the first to be equipped, forming at RAF Odiham in June 1971.

1981 The Chiefs of Air Staff of the RAF, the German Air Force, the Italian Air Force and the Chief of Naval Staff, German Navy, officially opened the Tri-National Tornado Training Establishment (TTTE) at Cottesmore.

See 8 May 1978.

30 JANUARY

1940 Coastal Command achieved its first success against a U-boat when a Sunderland of No. 228 Squadron (captain Fg Off E.J. Brooks) shared with two Royal Navy escorts in the sinking of *U-55* off Ushant.

1943 The RAF made its first daylight attacks on Berlin when Mosquitos of Nos 105 and 139 Squadrons bombed to coincide with speeches made by Goebbels and Goering at the tenth anniversary celebrations of Hitler's regime.

The *H2S* navigation and bombing radar aid was used operationally for the first time when Stirlings of No. 7 Squadron and Halifaxes of No. 35 Squadron of the Pathfinder Force marked Hamburg, the target for 148 bombers.

1952 RAF forces in the Canal Zone were reinforced as the Anglo/Egyptian political situation deteriorated. Lincolns of No. 148 Squadron arrived at Shallufa from RAF

RAF servicing commandos refuel a Spitfire. *(AHB. CL 79)*

Upwood and Vampires of Nos 6 and 73 Squadrons deployed from their bases in Iraq and Malta. RAF Regiment armoured car and anti-aircraft squadrons arrived from Jordan and the United Kingdom.

1985 MRAF The Lord Cameron, former Chief of the Defence Staff and Chief of the Air Staff, died.
See 7 August 1976, 31 August 1977.

31 JANUARY

1942 The Air Ministry gave instructions to form three Servicing Commando Units (SCU) whose role was to occupy advanced landing grounds and provide ground servicing and support for fighter squadrons.
See 8 November 1942.

1945 Operation Haycock: Mosquito PRXVIs of No. 544 Squadron commenced a courier service for the Yalta Conference from RAF Benson flying via San Severo in Italy to Saki in the Crimea with some flights terminating in Cairo and Athens. The flights continued until 20 February.

1946 The Spitfires of No. 273 Squadron were withdrawn from Saigon leaving a small RAF station headquarters with No. 2963 RAF Regiment Squadron and a staging post remaining for a few more months.
See 19 September 1945.

1950 The Royal Observer Corps medal was instituted for officers and observers who had completed twelve years of satisfactory service.

1953 Operation Floodlight: following devastating flooding in East Anglia helicopters and Ansons dropped supplies to the worst hit areas. Fourteen Hastings and six Valettas shuttled millions of sandbags from Europe to contain the waters. Over 100,000 photographs were taken to prepare maps of the devastation and to identify breaches in the defences.

1962 The Air Minister announced that the NORD AS.30 air-to-surface missiles would be acquired for the RAF Canberra force to help extend the life of the aircraft until TSR-2 entered service.

1972 No. 1 Flight Safety Officers' Course assembled at Tavistock Square, London.

1 FEBRUARY

1913 The RFC flying badge for pilots was introduced. It was worn when pilots were certified as competent by CFS. It was superseded by the RAF pilot's badge in 1918.

1920 The first aeromedical operation by a specifically converted RAF aircraft involved a DH9 of 'Z Force'. Capt F.J. Goodman, of the Somaliland Camel Corps, was flown to a base hospital at Berbera, saving a three-day camel trek.
See 21 January 1920.

1922 RAF Iraq Command was formed. The first AOC was AVM Sir John Salmond.

1929 The RAF Cadet College at Cranwell assumed the name RAF College.

1934 The Armament Group was formed at RAF Eastchurch. The AOC was responsible for all air armament training and assistance in the development of the tactical application of air armament.

1939 RAF Reserve Command was formed (AM C.L. Courtney).

No. 1 School of Cookery – formed in 1919 – gained independent status from No. 1 S of TT, Halton.

1942 The RAF Regiment was established by Royal Warrant as an integral part of the RAF with Maj Gen C.F. Liardet, 'loaned' from the Army, in command of the new formation composed of the existing 150 Defence Squadrons.
See 6 January 1942.

The Luftwaffe's onslaught against the island of Malta continued throughout February. During the course of the month, 2,447 sorties were flown against the island, the airfield at Luqa was attacked no fewer than 142 times, Takali 37 times, Halfar 23 times and the 'Q' (decoy) site at Krendi 20 times.

The Mingaladon Wing (Wg Cdr F.R. Carey) was formed for the defence of Rangoon, Burma.

The Air Training Corps was formed (Commandant, Air Cdre J.A. Chamier).

Maj Gen C.F. Liardet inspects the RAF Regiment.
(AHB. CH 5914)

1943 To reduce the visibility of Coastal Command general reconnaissance aircraft to U-boat crews, white was made the main colour of these aircraft. Some variations were required for particular areas and roles.

1944 The *London Gazette* announced that Wg Cdr L.F.W. Cohen had been awarded the DFC. Cohen, who had fought in the Matabele and Boer Wars and the First World War, when he was awarded the DSO and MC, had flown sixty-nine operations as an air gunner with Coastal Command squadrons. The day following the announcement of his award he celebrated his seventieth birthday.

1949 The Women's Royal Air Force (Air Comdt Felicity Hanbury) was established, replacing the Women's Auxiliary Air Force (WAAF) and marking the formal creation of

Left: A bomb-scarred Takali Airfield on the island of Malta. *(AHB. CF 4182)*

Below: An Auster 6 of the Antarctic Flight. *(RAFM)*

women's branches within, rather than as an adjunct to, the RAF.

A Whitley in the low-visibility Coastal Command scheme. *(AHB. CH 7047)*

Sisters of the PMRAFNS were granted commissions.

1950 An Auster of the Antarctic Flight carried out the first reconnaissance off Queen Maud Land. During the next six weeks, two Austers made nine sorties off the sea and forty equipped with skis and flying off the ice. During the expedition, Cpl L. Quar lost his life when a snow tractor sank through the sea ice.

See 23 November 1949.

1951 The Air Ministry equipment and engineering staffs were brought under control of one Member of the Air Council by combining the Department of Air Member for Supply and Organisation and the Air Council Member for Technical Services under the title of the former (ACM Sir William Dickson).

The first RAF aircrew were posted to serve with No. 77 Squadron, Royal Australian Air Force (RAAF), during the Korean War.

They were initially attached in order to convert RAAF pilots from the P-51 Mustang to the Meteor F8. Subsequently, the Squadron flew ex-RAF Meteor F8s in action from June 1951 to the end of the war. A total of thirty-two RAF pilots served with No. 77 Squadron in Korea. Four were killed in action, one was killed in a flying accident and one was made a prisoner of war. Four RAF pilots were awarded the DFC.

See 13 February 1952.

1953 The FEAF Casualty Evacuation Flight at RAF Sembawang, Singapore, was re-formed as No. 194 Squadron (Sqn Ldr G.R.G. Henderson) with Dragonfly Mk 4s. This was the first operational RAF helicopter squadron.

1957 RAF control of the Aden Protectorate Levies was handed over to the Army in order to begin establishing the Federal Regular Army prior to South Arabian independence.

A Gnat T1 of the Central Flying School at RAF Little Rissington. *(AHB. PRB 22457)*

2 FEBRUARY

1962 The first Gnat trainer was delivered to the Central Flying School at RAF Little Rissington.

1991 Operation Desert Storm: Buccaneers flew their first operations when they provided laser designation for two Tornados attacking a bridge over the River Euphrates

Buccaneer S2s and a Tornado GR1 train over the desert before commencing operations over Iraq. *(Sqn Ldr N. Browne)*

at Al Samawah. Six Paveway bombs destroyed the bridge.

1996 No. 34 Squadron, RAF Regiment, was withdrawn from Cyprus, ending the Regiment's presence on the island after forty years.

3 FEBRUARY

1922 The first entry of aircraft apprentices entered training at RAF Halton. During February 1920 the first three-year boy mechanics' course had started at RAF Cranwell, a temporary location until all the

U-boat under attack in the Bay of Biscay. (AHB)

necessary facilities at RAF Halton had been built. In due course, the boy mechanics of the four entries to Cranwell became known as aircraft apprentices and the first Halton course was re-designated No. 5 Entry.

1969 Communications squadrons were given squadron number plates to replace unit or regional titles.

2002 A Sea King (captain Flt Lt A. Gear) of No. 202 Squadron rescued eighteen fishermen from the French trawler *Le Perrain* 250 miles west of the Hebrides. Nimrods maintained visual contact with the listing ship as the Sea King lifted the survivors two at a time before landing at Stornoway with minimum fuel. Operating in winds of 70mph and at extreme range, the rescue was described as 'epic'.

4 FEBRUARY

1920 Lt Col P. van Ryneveld and Flt Lt C.J. Quinton-Brand (later AVM) left Brooklands in a civil Vickers Vimy 'Silver Queen' to fly to South Africa. The Vimy crashed at

Korosko, near Wadi Halfa, on 11 February. The flight was continued in an RAF Vimy, departing Cairo on 22 February and crashing at Bulawayo on 6 March. The flight was completed in a DH9, arriving at Cape Town on 20 March, thus achieving the first journey by air from England to South Africa. Both pilots were knighted for their feat.

1943 Operation Gondola: the first of a series of operations mounted to attack U-boats transiting the Bay of Biscay from French ports to the Atlantic. The 'Battle of the Bay' intensified in May when U-boats were ordered to transit on the surface in daylight and remain submerged at night because of the increasing threat posed by Coastal Command aircraft equipped with the Leigh-Light searchlight.

1953 Aircraft from Transport Command in Britain and Second Tactical Air Force in Germany were sent to take part in rescue operations in flooded areas in Holland.

1964 The Secretary of State for Air (Mr H. Fraser) announced that the V-Force was equipped and trained to attack targets from low level.

Above: Graduates of the first entry of officer cadets at the RAF College Cranwell. *(RAF College Cranwell)*
Below: No. 1 Helicopter Course. *(AHB)*

5 FEBRUARY

1920 The RAF Cadet College at Cranwell opened (Commandant Air Cdre C.A.H. Longcroft). RAF Headquarters Cranwell was granted command status with the opening of the College. An initial entry of fifty-two cadets entered the College.

1941 A Royal Warrant established the Air Training Corps when it absorbed the Air Defence Cadet Corps, which had been formed in 1938 by the Secretary-General of the Air League.

1945 The RAF's first helicopter unit, the Helicopter Training Flight, No. 43 OTU (Sqn Ldr B.H. Arkell), was formed at RAF Andover with Sikorsky R-4 (Hoverfly I).

Balloon Command was disbanded.
See 1 November 1938.

1952 During a meteorological reconnaissance climb over Hong Kong, Flt Lt E. Powles reached 51,550ft (true) in a Spitfire Mk 19 of No. 81 Squadron.

In this air-sea rescue exercise, a Walrus alights to pick up a 'survivor' as a Lysander orbits the scene.
(R. Nesbit Collection)

6 FEBRUARY

1933 A Fairey Long-Range Monoplane, flown by Sqn Ldr O.R. Gayford and Flt Lt G.E. Nicholettes, took off from Cranwell for South Africa. The aircraft landed with fourteen gallons of fuel at Walvis Bay (south-west Africa), to establish a world distance record of 5,309 miles in 52 hours 25 minutes.

1941 The recently approved Directorate of Sea Rescue (Air Cdre L.G.LeB. Croke) took up its duties for the first time. Its title was soon changed to 'Air Sea Rescue' (ASR) to differentiate it from the contemporary Naval Sea Rescue Service. From this date, until the end of the war, 5,772 RAF and USAAF aircrew were saved by the ASR organisation in the waters around the United Kingdom. Overseas units rescued at least 3,200 – a conservative figure since complete records were not kept in some theatres in the early days. In addition, 4,665 soldiers, sailors and civilians were saved.

1942 Japanese air attacks against the airfields at Palembang, Sumatra, commenced. Over the next eight days the RAF lost thirty Hurricanes – most of which were destroyed on the ground on 7 February. Subsequently, six enemy transports were sunk for the loss of seven aircraft on 14 February.

1975 ACM Sir Keith Park, AOC No. 11 Group during the Battle of Britain, died in his native New Zealand.

7 FEBRUARY

1924 The first in-flight refuelling trials took place when the Royal Aircraft Establishment, Farnborough, conducted the first of eleven test flights using Bristol F2Bs as tanker and receiver.
See 7 August 1930.

1945 **GC**: Flt Sgt Stanley James Woodbridge of No. 159 Squadron was captured on 31 January 1945 by the Japanese after his Liberator had crashed in the jungle. He resisted repeated interrogation and torture before he was beheaded. (*London Gazette*, 28 September 1948, posthumous award)

2007 HRH The Princess Royal opened the Cold War Exhibition at the RAF Museum, Cosford.

Above: The Gnome & Rhone aero-engine factory at Limoges after the attack by No. 617 Squadron. *(R. Nesbit Collection)*

Below: A rocket-firing Typhoon is serviced in Holland during the harsh winter of 1945. *(AHB. CL 1797)*

A Beaufighter of No. 144 Squadron at RAF Dallachy after crash-landing on return from Norway on 'Black Friday'. *(F.S. Holly)*

8 FEBRUARY

1942 Following heavy air bombardment Japanese forces landed on Singapore Island capturing RAF Tengah airfield.

1944 Twelve Lancasters of No. 617 Squadron attacked the Gnome & Rhone aero-engine factory at Limoges. The squadron commander, Wg Cdr G.L. Cheshire, marked the target from very low level and the remaining Lancasters dropped 12,000lb Tallboys, severely damaging the factory. This was the first use of such low-level marking techniques by No. 5 Group.

1945 In preparation for the Allied operations to cross the River Rhine, fighter-bombers of 2nd TAF carried out extensive armed reconnaissance and attacks on enemy headquarters, bridges and trains.

1956 Six Hunters of the Day Fighter Leader School at RAF West Raynham were lost in the space of eight minutes when bad weather closed the airfield. One pilot was killed, four ejected and one carried out a forced landing in a field. The remaining two in the formation of eight landed at RAF Marham.

9 FEBRUARY

1923 RAF Reserve of Officers was formed.

1945 Thirty-two Beaufighters of the Dallachy Strike Wing, with an escort of ten Mustangs of No. 65 Squadron, attacked shipping near Sognefjord, Norway. The aircraft attacked in the face of intense flak and as they left the target area were intercepted by Focke-Wulf 190 fighters. Within minutes, nine Beaufighters and one Mustang were shot down. Many of those that did get back crash-landed and were written off. The day became known as Coastal Command's 'Black Friday'.

1951 Hastings of No. 47 Squadron began the 'Japan Shuttle' between RAF Changi and Iwakuni, Japan, in support of the Korean War and for casualty evacuation.

1959 Operations in Central Oman ceased after almost eighteen months of RAF support. Venoms of No. 8 Squadron flew 1,315

Above: A Shackleton MR2 of No. 37 Squadron over Oman. *(Andrew Thomas Collection)*
Below: Sqn Ldr J.W. Gillan (right). *(RAFM)*

10 FEBRUARY

sorties and Shackletons of No. 37 Squadron flew 429 bombing sorties providing the main weight of attack.
See 24 July 1957.

1998 Operation Bolton: Tornados of No. 14 Squadron deployed from RAF Bruggen to Ali Al Salem Airbase, Kuwait, flying the 3,500 miles non-stop. No. 34 Squadron, RAF Regiment, provided airfield defence.

1938 Sqn Ldr J.W. Gillan, CO of No. 111 Squadron, made headline news when he flew a Hurricane from Edinburgh to RAF Northolt in forty-eight minutes at an average speed of 408.75mph. Flying at 17,000ft without oxygen, the evening flight benefited from a strong tail wind; the speed from overhead Turnhouse to overhead Northolt was 456mph.

1941 The RAF's first four-engined bombers operated for the first time when three Stirlings of No. 7 Squadron joined a larger force to attack oil-storage tanks at Rotterdam.

Operation Colossus: the first operation by British airborne forces was carried out by thirty-eight men of 'X' Troop, No. 11 Special Air Service Battalion, against two aqueducts at Traqino in southern Italy. Six Whitleys of No. 78 Squadron, operating from Malta and led by Wg Cdr J.B. Tait, dropped the troops. Two further aircraft mounted a diversionary raid on Foggia; one failed to return. The paratroopers succeeded in destroying a pier of the Traqino Viaduct, but were captured before reaching a pick-up rendezvous.

The body of MRAF The Viscount Trenchard lies in state.
(AHB)

1942   Kallang airfield on Singapore was evacuated and the last eight Hurricanes of No. 232 Squadron left for Sumatra.

1944   After the Japanese had surrounded the 7th Indian Division at Sinzweya – known as the 'Admin Box' – in the Arakan, the four Dakota squadrons of No. 177 Wing (Gp Capt G.F.K. Donaldson) kept the Division resupplied, dropping some 2,000 tons of supplies in the critical period up to 6 March.

1956   MRAF The Viscount Trenchard of Wolferton died at his home in London at the age of 83. He was buried in the Battle of Britain Chapel, Westminster Abbey.

1991   Operation Desert Storm: Tornado GR1s equipped with Thermal-Imaging and Laser-Designating (TIALD) pods carried out their first mission, an attack on hardened aircraft shelters, thought to contain mobile Scud launchers at the H3 Southwest airfield in Western Iraq.

The body of MRAF The Viscount Trenchard lies in state.
(AHB)

11 FEBRUARY

1942   Operation Fuller: the 'Channel Dash' by the German battlecruisers *Scharnhorst* and *Gneisenau* and the cruiser *Prinz Eugen*. After repeated attacks by Bomber Command against the ships in the ports of western France, the German High Command decided to withdraw the three capital ships to Germany. In parallel, the Luftwaffe drew up a plan to provide a massive fighter screen to protect the ships en route through the English Channel. Under cover of poor weather, the ships sailed from Brest at 2245hr. Misfortune dogged the comprehensive surveillance established by the RAF to detect the German capital ships as soon as they sailed and standing patrols failed to detect the force as it left Brest. It was twelve hours before the force was positively sighted. In response six Swordfish of No. 825 Squadron Fleet Air Arm at RAF

A Catalina of No. 259 Squadron drops a practice bomb over the Indian Ocean. *(Andrew Thomas Collection)*

Manston launched a torpedo attack. All six aircraft were destroyed and the leader of the force, Lt Cdr E. Esmonde RN, was posthumously awarded the **VC**. Subsequently, attacks in appalling weather by RAF Beaufort torpedo bombers and Hudsons of Coastal Command failed to hit the warships, as did any of the 242 aircraft despatched by No. 5 Group, Bomber Command. However, both *Scharnhorst* and *Gneisenau* detonated air-dropped mines previously laid by the RAF. *Scharnhorst* shipped 1,000 tons of water and could only limp into Wilhelmshaven.

1944 Seven Catalinas combed the Indian Ocean to locate the German supply ship and oil tanker *Charlotte Schliemann*. Flt Lt R. Dutton and his crew of No. 259 Squadron sighted the ship with a U-boat in company 900 miles east of Mauritius. HMS *Relentless* was homed to the scene and sank the German ship. Dutton landed after a 21-hour flight with just 120 gallons of fuel remaining. He was later awarded the DFC.

1985 Seventeen members of the RAF Germany Band and an RAF policeman were killed when their coach crashed near Munich. Two members of the band died later from their injuries. The Director of Music, Sqn Ldr R. Tomsett, was among those killed.

12 FEBRUARY

1919 The Department of Civil Aviation was established within the Air Ministry.

1935 Mr R.A. Watson-Watt, Superintendent of the Radio Department at the National Physical Laboratory, submitted to the Air Ministry his historic paper 'Detection and Location of Aircraft by Radio Methods'. Thus was born 'RDF' (Radio Direction Finding), later called 'radar'.

13 FEBRUARY

1945 Bomber Command despatched 805 bombers to attack Dresden, causing devastating damage. The death toll may, according to some historians, have exceeded 50,000, although the figure remains disputed.

1952 Following the conclusion of an informal bilateral agreement between the RAF and USAF, a group of four pilots led by Wg Cdr J.R. Baldwin – a highly successful fighter pilot during the Second World War – arrived in Korea. Wg Cdr Baldwin and Flt Lt R. Knight were attached to the 51st Fighter Interceptor Wing at Suwon; Sqn Ldr W. Harbison and Flt Lt B.J. Spragg were attached to the 4th Fighter Interceptor Wing at Kimpo. Both units were equipped with the North American F-86 Sabre. By the end of the Korean War, twenty-one RAF officers had served with either the 4th or the 51st Wings. Four had failed to return from operational sorties; these included Wg Cdr Baldwin, who was declared missing in action on 15 March 1952. Sqn Ldr G.S. Hulse was credited with destroying two MiG 15s in combat before failing to return from a sortie on 13 March 1953. A further five pilots were credited with one kill.

See 1 February 1951.

1953 Operation Sandbag: Hastings and Valettas of Transport Command, flew several million sandbags from the Continent to the United Kingdom to repair breaches in sea defences caused by severe floods from Lincolnshire to Kent.

See 31 January 1953.

1958 The Defence White Paper stated that the USA would supply Thor Intermediate Range Ballistic Missiles (IRBMs) and specialised equipment to Britain and would provide training assistance.

See 22 February 1958.

Flt Lt K. Williamson (later MRAF Sir Keith Williamson) in Korea with his Meteor F8 of No. 77 (RAAF) Squadron. *(AHB)*

Above: Sandbags being loaded on to an RAF Hastings. *(RAFM)*

Below: A Lancaster bomber prepares to taxi for an operation. *(G.R. Pitchfork Collection)*

14 FEBRUARY

1928 The Air Ministry announced a new scheme for promotion of officers in the General Duties branch. The guiding principle was a system of antedates, by means of which seniority was weighted to give earlier promotion to officers who had acquired certain specialisations and other service qualifications, and to officers specially recommended. The scheme took effect after the promotion list of 1 July 1928.

1942 The Air Ministry issued the 'area bombing' Directive to Bomber Command, which specified: 'It has been decided that the primary objective of your operations should now be focussed on the morale of the enemy civil population and in particular of the industrial workers.'

The King's Flight was absorbed by No. 161 (Special Duties) Squadron on the Squadron's formation at RAF Newmarket as the RAF's second special duties squadron.

Japanese paratroopers landed at Palembang P 1 airfield in Sumatra and the remnants of the remaining RAF squadrons withdrew to a landing strip (P 2) south of the city to continue the fight.

Fg Off M. Taute and eighty-six ground gunners fought a fierce battle with Japanese forces parachuted onto Palembang P 1 airfield, Sumatra. Taute was subsequently captured and became a POW. In 1946 he was awarded the MC, making him the first RAF Regiment officer to receive the award and the last wartime recipient to be gazetted.

15 FEBRUARY

1924 Plt Off N. Vintcent of No. 8 Squadron became the first former Cranwell cadet to be awarded the DFC. Flying a DH9A in Iraq when 'having been forced to land owing to engine failure, he beat off an attack by hostile tribesmen with great courage and determination'.

1942 Singapore capitulated to Japanese land forces. The AOC, AVM C.W.H. Pulford, was authorised to evacuate himself on 5 February 1942 but he opted to remain. He and his naval counterpart, Rear Admiral Spooner, were among the last to leave. Unfortunately their motorboat was hit and

Groundcrew worked under difficult conditions in the Far East campaigns. *(G.R. Pitchfork Collection)*

An escorting Hurricane flies over a small dropping zone in Burma after a supply drop by Dakotas. *(IWM. CI 602)*

forced to run aground on a malaria-ridden island in the Juju group. The survivors managed to hold out for two months before being forced to surrender to the Japanese, but Pulford and Spooner were not among them, both having died of exhaustion and malaria shortly before. Although he was reported missing in 1942, the situation in the Far East was such at the time that Pulford's death did not become known until after the Japanese surrender in 1945. He was posthumously mentioned in despatches for his service in the Far East.

1943   The First Chindit Operation: Dakotas of No. 31 Squadron and Hudsons of No. 194 Squadron commenced supply dropping to the seven columns of Chindits, led by Brig O. Wingate, which had crossed the Irrawaddy two days earlier with orders to create alarm and confusion. By 5 May the two squadrons had flown 178 sorties and dropped 303 tons of supplies. Wingate commented during the campaign: 'Throughout the campaign the RAF supply

dropping has been nearly perfect and capable of astonishing performances.' See 28 April 1943.

1944   The heaviest attack on Berlin was made when 891 aircraft dropped 2,643 tons of bombs.

1970   ACM The Lord Dowding, Commander-in-Chief of Fighter Command during the Battle of Britain, died.

16 FEBRUARY

1940   A Hudson of No. 220 Squadron patrolling off the Norwegian coast located the German supply ship *Altmark*, carrying 299 British merchant seamen on board, the crews of five ships sunk by the *Graf Spee*. HMS *Cossack* pursued the ship into a Norwegian fjord when a boarding party released the prisoners after a short fight.

1941   A new Area Combined Headquarters was established at Derby House, Liverpool, to exercise operational control of the Battle of the Atlantic. To create the necessary air partnership, No. 15 Group was transferred from Plymouth to work alongside the newly formed naval Western Approach Command. A new Group, No. 19, was established at Plymouth.

17 FEBRUARY

1922 Royal Air Force Ireland (Gp Capt I.M. Bonham-Carter) was formed. The life of this command was short and it was disbanded in 1923.

1938 The post of Assistant Chief of the Air Staff (ACAS) was created in the Air Ministry. (AVM W. Sholto-Douglas).

1972 Gp Capt G.S.M. Insall **VC**, MC died.

18 FEBRUARY

1942 Surviving RAF aircraft fell back on Java in the face of intense Japanese attacks on Sumatra. The force had been reduced to eighteen Hurricanes and an attack force of eighteen Blenheims and Hudsons.
See 8 March 1942.

MRAF The Lord Douglas (1893–1969). *(AHB)*

1943 Mediterranean Air Command (ACM Sir Arthur Tedder) was formed with the HQ at Algiers. The Command comprised the Middle East Command, RAF Malta, and the North-West African Air Forces.

1944 Operation Jericho: eighteen Mosquitos of Nos 21, 464 and 487 Squadrons were tasked to breach the walls of Amiens jail in an attempt to release French prisoners. The first wave (No. 487 Squadron) succeeded in breaching the eastern wall. Two aircraft failed to return, including that flown by Gp Capt P.C. Pickard and Flt Lt J.A. Broadley. Five days after the raid a message was received from the French Resistance thanking the crews for the attack, which allowed many prisoners to escape, including twelve who were due to be executed the following day.

1954 The Annual Statement on Defence included the words: 'We intend as soon as possible to

Coastal Command Operations Room. *(AHB. CH 1366)*

39

A model of Amiens jail made to brief the Mosquito crews before their attack. *(AHB. CH 4742)*

build up in the RAF a force of medium bombers capable of using the atomic weapon to the fullest effect . . . the RAF has major deterrent role . . . atomic weapons are in production in this country and delivery to the forces has begun.'

1969 A UNIVAC 1106 computer, the size of four filing cabinets, was introduced at RAF Innsworth to process the payments of the entire RAF (over 100,000 strong) in only four hours. At the time, it was the fastest commercial computer of its type in the world; the only one comparable was dedicated to the Apollo moon shot programme.

19 FEBRUARY

1917 The first recorded 'casevac' was made when a trooper of the Imperial Camel Corps, whose ankle had been smashed by a Bedouin bullet at Bir-el-Hassana in the Sinai desert, was flown to safety in the observer's cockpit of an unspecified aircraft. The forty-minute flight saved an overland journey of three days. In Egypt during the last year of the First World War, experimental stretcher installations were made in various aircraft including the DH6, DH9 and FK8. Flight trials with a stretcher fitted to a DH6 are believed to have been carried out, but there is no record of any operational aero-medical flights.

1952 The first British-designed helicopter (Bristol Sycamore) was delivered to Coastal Command at RAF St Mawgan.

1955 The South-East Asia Treaty Organisation (SEATO) was formed. Original signatories were the United Kingdom, Australia, France, New Zealand, Pakistan, the Philippines, Thailand and the United States.

20 FEBRUARY

Valiants of No. 214 Squadron. *(AHB)*

1945 This was the first of thirty-six consecutive nights when Mosquitos of the Light Night Striking Force (LNSF) attacked Berlin. The series ended on the night of 27/28 March.

1958 Valiants of No. 214 Squadron (Wg Cdr M.J. Beetham) commenced operational development of air-to-air refuelling (AAR), including support for several long-distance unofficial record flights. No. 214 Squadron became one of the first RAF tanker squadrons in April 1962.

1959 The Memorandum accompanying the 1959–60 Air Estimates stated that: 'A contract is being let for the development of the TSR-2 to operate in NATO and overseas commands. The TSR-2 will be a versatile aircraft with advanced operational and technical ideas. It will meet the exacting requirements in the 1960s of army support and other tactical roles.'

See 6 April 1965.

1961 The Memorandum accompanying the 1961–2 Air Estimates stated: 'Subject to

the successful completion of its development programme [the Government] plan to introduce Skybolt . . . in the mid-1960s. Production weapons will be bought outright and will be carried by the Vulcan 2. They will be fitted with British warheads.' It was also believed that the current level of expenditure on the British strategic nuclear deterrent, inclusive of capital and running costs of V-force, its airfields, nuclear weapons and R and D, together with the running costs of the Thor IRBM force, represented about '10 per cent' of the Defence Budget.

See 21 December 1962.

21 FEBRUARY

1923 The first RAF troop lift was completed. Ten Vernons of Nos 45 and 70 Squadrons lifted 333 troops and 30,000lb of ammunition from Kingerban to Kirkuk in a successful operation to pre-empt an attack on the north Iraqi town.

A Gladiator ready for a delivery flight from the Gloster Aircraft Company factory at Brockworth. *(B. Mabbett)*

Rail traffic in Soltau station comes under attack by Mosquitos. *(IWM. CL 2011)*

1927 All six squadrons based in India (Nos 5, 20, 27, 28, 31, 60) staged a grand Air Display at the Delhi Race Course before a distinguished audience including the Viceroy and senior Indian and Army officials. Described as a 'mini Hendon', the event provided an impressive display of air power.

1928 Following an incursion into Aden by Yemeni forces and Zeidi tribesmen, DH9As of No. 8 Squadron commenced operations against the Zeidi. A truce was agreed and operations ceased.

1951 A Canberra B2, flown by Sqn Ldr A.E. Caillard, Flt Lt E.A.J. Haskett and Flt Lt A.J.R. Robson made the first non-stop, un-refuelled transatlantic crossing by a jet bomber from RAF Aldergrove to Gander, Newfoundland in 4 hours 40 minutes at 449mph.

1958 A Memorandum to the Air Estimates 1958–9 stated that Canberras of Bomber Command and 2nd TAF were being given a nuclear capability.

MRAF Sir Arthur Harris (1892–1984). *(ACA Archives)*

22 FEBRUARY

1937 The RAF's last biplane fighter, the Gloster Gladiator, entered service with No. 72 Squadron at RAF Tangmere.

1940 Army Council Instruction No. 152 of 1940 announced the details of a scheme allowing Army officers to become pilots in the RAF. The object of the scheme was to fill 50 per cent of the pilot establishment of RAF Army Co-operation Squadrons. Surplus numbers were employed in bomber squadrons. Those joining were granted temporary commissions in the RAF.

1942 AM A.T. Harris succeeded ACM Sir Richard Peirse as C-in-C Bomber Command, a post he held for the remainder of the war.

1945 Operation Clarion: in preparation for the crossing of the River Rhine, large-scale heavy and medium bomber attacks were made on rail bridges and viaducts, road and rail traffic and marshalling and repair yards along a line from Bremen southward to Koblenz with nearly 9,000 Allied aircraft involved.

1958 An agreement was concluded between the UK and the USA to install sixty Thor Intermediate Range Ballistic Missiles (IRBMs) in eastern England for a five-year period. Under the terms of the agreement, the USA furnished the missiles and warheads with the UK providing operating sites and associated installations. The missiles were to be operated and maintained by RAF personnel; launching the missiles was to be via a 'dual key' system involving RAF and USAF officers.

23 FEBRUARY

1944 For the first time, Mosquitos dropped 4,000lb HE bombs when No. 692 Squadron attacked Dusseldorf.

1945 **VC**: Capt Edwin Swales DFC, SAAF, captain of a No. 582 Squadron Lancaster, was master bomber of a 374-aircraft raid on Pforzheim. His bomber was severely damaged by enemy action and he remained at the controls to allow his crew to bale out. He was the only member of the SAAF

Armourers load a 4,000lb 'cookie' onto a Mosquito of No. 692 Squadron. *(G.R. Pitchfork Collection)*

to receive the supreme award. (*London Gazette*, 24 April 1945, posthumous award)

1999   Further details of Joint Force 2000 (JF2000) were announced. The new land- and carrier-based force would be located at the RAF bases of Wittering and Cottesmore and combine the RAF Harrier fleet and the Royal Navy's Sea Harrier aircraft under one headquarters located at RAF Strike Command, High Wycombe.

24 FEBRUARY

1922   The Duke of York opened the RAF Club's permanent home at 128 Piccadilly, London, which, in the early eighteenth century had been the site of the Running Horse Inn.
See 30 October 1918.

1942   The crew of a No. 42 Squadron Beaufort (captain Sqn Ldr H. Cliff) were rescued from the North Sea after spending twenty-four hours in their dinghy. A successful search was mounted after 'Winkie', one of two pigeons carried on the aircraft, returned to its loft near RAF Leuchars.

1945   'Tiger Force' (AM Sir Hugh Lloyd) was formed from squadrons in Bomber Command for the strategic bombing of Japan from airfields on Okinawa.
See 31 October 1945.

1956   The Javelin delta-wing night fighter entered RAF service with No. 46 Squadron at RAF Odiham.

1991   Operation Desert Storm: the Allied coalition air forces undertook an intensive bombing campaign in advance of the ground offensive to liberate Kuwait, which began at 0400hr.

25 FEBRUARY

British dependants prepare to board a Victoria transport aircraft at Kabul. *(AHB. H1195)*

1926 In response to Navy and Army pressure for their own air arms, Prime Minister Stanley Baldwin announced in the House of Commons that the government had no intention of reviving the question of the need for a separate air arm, adding 'It is in the interests of the fighting services that controversy upon the subject should now cease.'

1929 The evacuation of the Kabul Legation was completed when seven Victorias of No. 70 Squadron and a Hinaidi brought out the last of 586 evacuees.
See 23 December 1928.

1936 In response to the expansion of the German Air Force, the Cabinet approved Expansion Scheme F. Its notable features were the strengthening of the air striking force by eliminating the light bomber and substituting the medium bomber, and making adequate provision for war reserves. Scheme F, provided the Metropolitan Air Force with 124 squadrons with 1,736 front-line aircraft, an overseas strength of 37 squadrons of 468 aircraft and a Fleet Air Arm with the equivalent of 26 squadrons and 312 aircraft. This was the longest-lived of all the expansion schemes and the only one to be fully implemented.
See 18 July 1934, 25 March 1935, 10 November 1938.

1943 Bomber Command began 'round-the-clock' bombing of targets in Germany and occupied territories.

1946 As part of a series of terrorist attacks against British military installations, members of the Jewish Irgun organisation raided the RAF stations at Petah Tiqva, Qastina and Lydda at night. Seven Spitfires of Nos 32 and 208 Squadrons were destroyed or seriously damaged at Petah Tiqva. Six Halifax VIIs of No. 644 Squadron were destroyed at Qastina with five Halifax IXs subsequently written off as beyond economic repair. Two Ansons were destroyed at Lydda.

1970 The concept of the Military Salary was approved by Parliament.

Above: Irgun terrorists destroy a Spitfire of No. 208 Squadron at Petah Tiqva. *(Wg Cdr R. Bowie)*

Below: A Hercules drops famine aid in Nepal. *(AHB)*

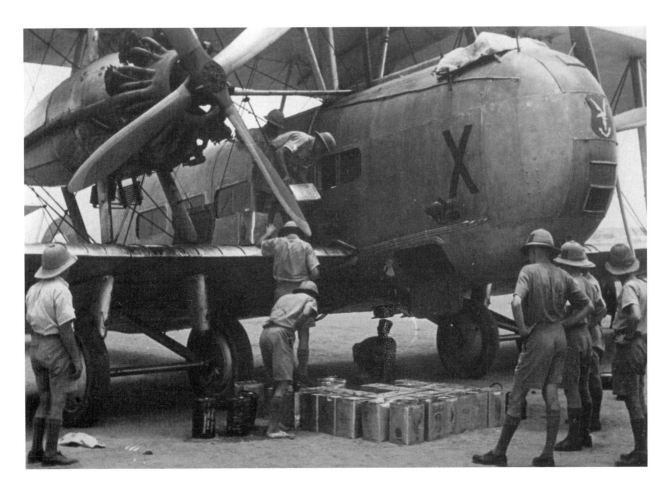

A Valentia of No. 216 Squadron is refuelled during the flight to South Africa in support of the reinforcement exercise of 1934. *(G.R. Pitchfork Collection)*

1973 Operation Khana Cascade: a Hercules detachment (Wg Cdr M.J. Hardy) commenced a famine relief operation, air-dropping rice, wheat and grain to the starving people in the remote and less accessible areas in the mountain regions of western Nepal. By the end of the operation on 11 April, 1,964 tons of aid had been dropped.

26 FEBRUARY

1919 The first RAF representative rugby match was played at Richmond when the RAF was beaten 0–10 by a team from the RN Depot, Devonport. The RAF team finished with thirteen players and the *Daily Telegraph* reported 'the RND invested their work with a roughness and disregard for the safety of their opponents which surprised everybody'. A member of the RAF team was Capt W.W. Wakefield, who later became captain of the RAF, Combined Services, Harlequins and England teams, gaining thirty-one caps for England – a record at the time. Later as Lord Wakefield of Kendal he became President of the Rugby Football Union.

1925 The Staff College qualifying examination was introduced.

1934 In response to South African concerns of Italian territorial ambitions in the area, No. 45 Squadron mounted a reinforcement exercise from Helwan, Egypt, to Pretoria. The five Fairey IIIFs, accompanied by Valentias of No. 216 Squadron, arrived at Pretoria on 8 March.

1935 Following proposals put to the Committee for Scientific Survey of Air Defence, the first practical demonstration of the use of radio to detect aircraft was demonstrated. Signals generated by a 10-kilowatt transmitter at Daventry were reflected off an RAF Handley Page Heyford enabling the aircraft to be detected by staff from the Slough Radio Research Station using experimental apparatus erected at Weedon in Northamptonshire. An estimated maximum detection range of 8 miles was achieved during the trial.

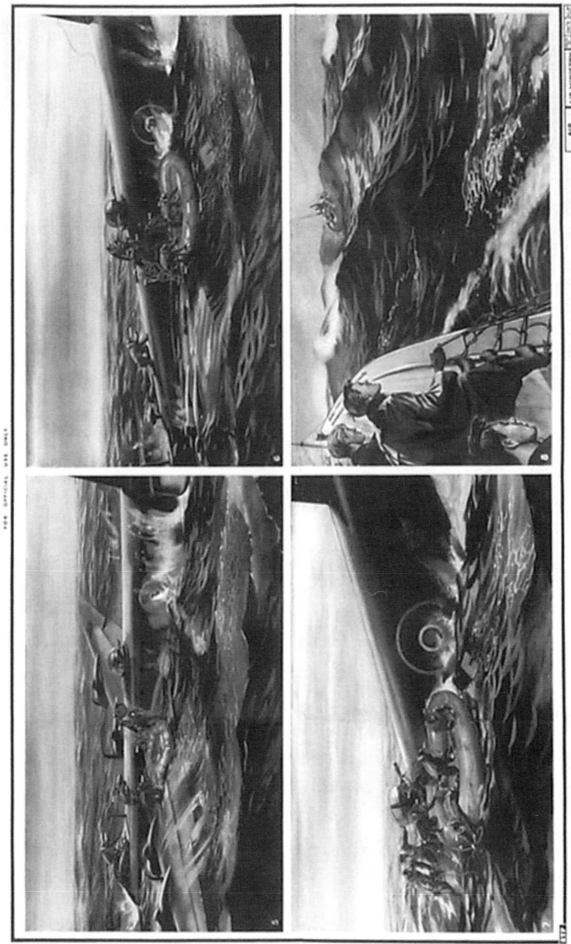

ABANDONING BY DINGHY – STIRLING I & II

A poster used to educate aircrew on air-sea rescue techniques. *(RAFM)*

The CO of a Hurricane squadron briefs his pilots at a Burma airstrip. *(IWM)*

1943 The School of Air Sea Rescue was formed at RAF Squires Gate, near Blackpool.

1944 The Japanese called off their attacks in the Arakan. For the first time British and Indian troops successively withheld a major Japanese offensive by staying put and fighting, relying on extensive air support and air resupply.

1992 No. 26 Signals Unit (SU) at Teufelsberg, Berlin, closed at midnight after twenty years of continuous operation.

27 FEBRUARY

1942 Operation Biting: Whitleys of No. 51 Squadron, led by Wg Cdr P.C. Pickard, took off from RAF Thruxton carrying 6 officers and 113 men of 'C' Company, 2nd Bn the Parachute Regt (Maj J.D. Frost), together with RAF RDF (radar) specialist, Flt Sgt C.W.H.

Cox. This assault force was dropped near the Luftwaffe *Würzburg* radar station at Bruneval, near Le Havre, and successfully seized the station. Flt Sgt Cox dismantled elements of the radar, which were brought back to the United Kingdom for examination, together with three prisoners, when the force withdrew by sea. The assault was brilliantly successful, with all of the objectives achieved, at a cost of three members of the attacking force killed, two missing and seven wounded. Cox was awarded the MM.

1943 RAF Lindholme, a bomber airfield near Doncaster, became the first recipient of the 'Joliffe Trophy' awarded to the best RAF dining hall. Lord Sherwood (Under-Secretary-of-State for Air) presented the trophy, which has been competed for annually ever since.

1944 Allied air operations against targets in Italy assumed overriding priority in the Mediterranean theatre.

The marshalling yards at Naples after a heavy attack. *(AHB. C 5922)*

A Lysander of No. 208 Squadron. *(AHB. H 1664)*

28 FEBRUARY

1911 An Army Order was signed authorising the formation of the Air Battalion of the Royal Engineers to take effect on 1 April. A headquarters was established at South Farnborough with No. 1 (Airship) Company at Farnborough and No. 2 (Aeroplane) Company at Larkhill. The latter were later to become Nos 1 and 3 Squadrons, Royal Flying Corps (RFC), respectively. The commanding officer, Maj Sir Alexander Bannerman of the Royal Engineers, had 14 officers, 23 non-commissioned officers, 153 men (Royal Engineers) and 2 buglers under him. The unit had 4 riding horses, 32 draught horses, 5 aeroplanes and a miscellaneous collection of kites, balloons and airships. A Reserve was also established.

1941 Nos 11 and 113 Squadrons (Blenheims), No. 33 Squadron (Hurricanes) and No. 208 Squadron (Lysanders) arrived in Greece to reinforce the RAF contingent there.

1955 A Canberra B2 piloted by AVM J.R. Whitley, AOC No. 1 Group, flew from RAF Scampton to Nicosia, Cyprus, to set a new point-to-point record of 4 hours 13 minutes.

1991 Operation Desert Storm: on the orders of United States President George Bush, offensive operations against Iraq ended at 0500hr local time.

29 FEBRUARY

1984 With the withdrawal of No. 16 Squadron from Laarbruch, thirty years of Hunter operations in Germany came to an end.

A Hunter T.7 of the Laarbruch Wing escorts a Buccaneer of No. 15 Squadron over the hills south of Hamm, Germany. *(G.R. Pitchfork Collection)*

A formation of Jaguars en route to a target in Kuwait. *(Peter March)*

FIRST GULF WAR

During the First Gulf War (17 January–28 February 1991), many RAF units were involved and provided significant detachments in the operational area. The main offensive contribution was in the ground-attack role provided by over forty Tornado GR1s and GR1As, a squadron of Jaguars and a squadron of Buccaneers, all flying at intensive rates. They dropped some 3,000 tons of ordnance, which included approximately 100 JP 233 runway denial weapons, 6,000 bombs of 1,000lb or greater, together with 100 ALARMs and 700 air-to-ground rockets. Six Tornado GR1s were lost in combat with five aircrew killed in action and seven captured to become POWs. They were later released.

Tornado F3 operations formed part of the integrated, tri-national Saudi/US/UK overland air defence system. The tanker force of Victors, VC10s and Tristars played a crucial role in theatre and on routes between the UK and the Gulf. In the six-week air war these aircraft flew 730 sorties and off-loaded 13,000 tons of fuel to almost 3,000 aircraft. Just before the air campaign began, the nature of Nimrod operations changed from the search for vessels seeking to break the embargo to the direct support of Allied warships operating at the northern end of the Gulf.

The air transport force established an air bridge to the theatre on the first day of Operation Granby and a sizeable force operated in theatre. By the end of the conflict, these aircraft had logged over 50,000 flying hours and carried over 30,000 tons of freight and 66,000 passengers.

The largest overseas deployment of RAF helicopters ever operated by day and night in support of 1st (British) Armoured Division and Special Forces. In addition to the flying squadrons and the RAF Regiment, whose strength rose to 1,000 men in theatre, the Tactical Supply Wing, Tactical Communications Wing, Mobile Catering Support Unit, Aeromedical Evacuation Squadron and the Mobile Air Movements Squadron were heavily committed throughout Operation Desert Storm/Granby.

1 MARCH

1926 Led by Wg Cdr C.W.H. Pulford, four Fairey IIIDs left RAF Helwan for Cape Town on the first RAF Cairo–Cape flight. They returned on 27 May to be equipped with floats before proceeding to Lee-on-Solent, arriving on 21 June, having completed a 14,000-mile flight.

See 15 February 1942.

1929 Air Cdre E.A.D. Masterman became the first Commandant of the Observer Corps. The Corps consisted of volunteers, enrolled as special constables, who were recruited to observe, identify and report hostile aircraft within visual range. Following experience gained during the First World War, Observer Corps personnel were to man posts at 5-mile intervals around the UK. They were tasked with observing and reporting by telephone the course and height of all aircraft seen or heard to group centres, which in turn reported to RAF Fighting Area Headquarters and adjacent sector operations rooms.

1935 The Office of the Chester Herald was appointed as Inspector of RAF Badges, and from this date unit devices were regulated and gradually the informal unit emblems disappeared.

1953 No. 275 Squadron re-formed at RAF Linton-on-Ouse, becoming the first RAF search and rescue helicopter squadron. The squadron was equipped with the Bristol Sycamore HR13/HR14.

1955 Operation Milage: the first detachment of Canberra B.6 bombers left for Butterworth to participate in the Malayan Emergency (Operation Firedog). Aircraft and crews for the first detachment were drawn from No. 101 Squadron. Additional detachments of six to eight aircraft were later drawn from Nos 9, 12 and 617 Squadrons. The final detachment ended on 31 August 1956.

1963 Two Belvedere Mk I helicopters of No. 26 Squadron (Sqn Ldr P.F. Hart) arrived at

A Fairey IIID of the Cape Flight. *(AHB. H 1614)*

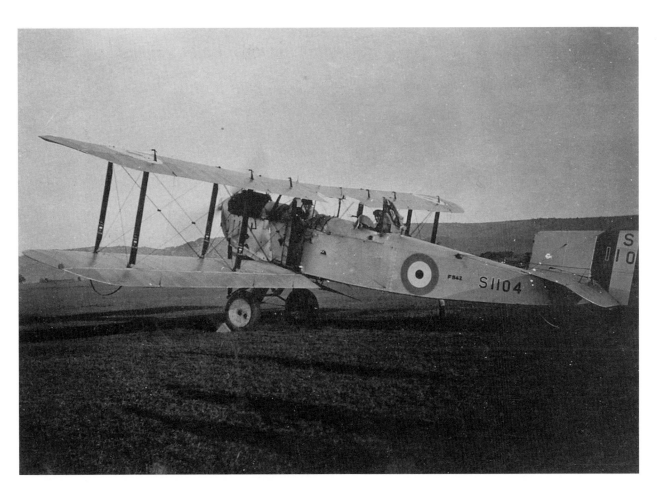

A Sycamore of No. 275 Squadron. *(P.H.T. Green Collection)*

Khormaksar, Aden, after ferrying direct from El Adem, Libya – a distance of 2,260 miles – the longest overseas flight by RAF helicopters to date. The Belvederes had flown from RAF Odiham to El Adem in January to take part in a series of exercises.

1964 Centralised engineering service was introduced on the V-bomber stations.

1991 Fg Off Anne-Marie Dawe graduated at No. 6 FTS, Finningley, as the RAF's first female navigator.

2 MARCH

1960 The Secretary of State for Air (Rt Hon. George Ward) announced that four V-bombers could be airborne in less than four minutes from warning of a potentially hostile attack.

Gibraltar-based Shackletons of No. 224 Squadron flew aid to Agadir, Morocco, after an earthquake had killed 12,000 people.

3 MARCH

1942 The few remaining Allied aircraft began to evacuate Java. RAF and Dutch fighters continued to provide fighter cover until 7 March.

Four Lancasters of No. 44 Squadron laid mines in the Heligoland Bight, the first operational sortie by the RAF's most successful wartime bomber.
See 10 March 1942.

Some 220 RAF aircraft attacked the Renault factory at Billancourt, Paris. It was recognised as one of the most accurate attacks against a single target at that stage of the war.

1945 In a surprise attack, approximately 200 German night-fighters mounted their

Four Vulcans prepare to scramble. *(J. Falconer Collection)*

Operation Gisella, a series of intruder sorties to attack returning bombers over England. Twenty bombers were shot down for the loss of three fighters. One German fighter crashed near RAF Elvington, York, and was the last to crash on English soil during the war.

2000 The Joint Forces Air Command Headquarters reached initial operating capability at RAF High Wycombe.

2000 Operation Barwood: four Puma helicopters of No. 33 Squadron were delivered to Mozambique to provide rescue and relief supplies following a devastating cyclone and flooding. The Pumas flew a gruelling 350 hours, airlifted 563 people to safety and distributed 425 tons of vital supplies before leaving on 20 March.

4 MARCH

1964 The Ministry of Defence was established with three single service departments, thus signalling the end of the Air Ministry after forty-five years.

5 MARCH

1941 The first twelve Army pupils for glider pilot instruction arrived at the Glider Training Squadron, RAF Thame.
See 4 November 1941.

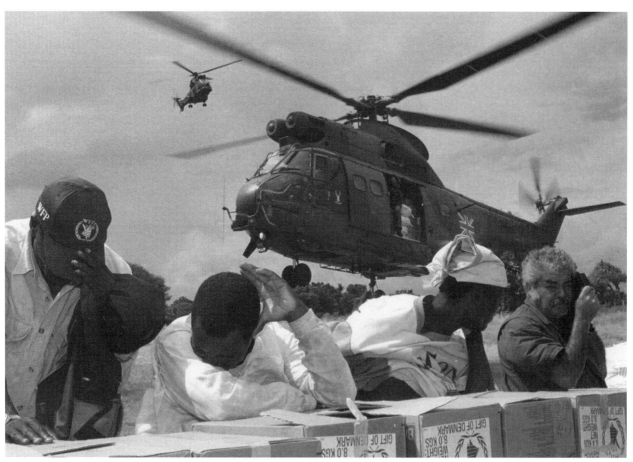

Pumas deliver aid during the Mozambique flood disaster. *(MOD)*

Part of the
Krupps factory
badly damaged
during the raid
on Essen. *(ACA
Archives)*

1941 The American-built Catalina flying-boat entered RAF service with No. 240 Squadron.

1943 The Battle of the Ruhr opened with an attack on Essen by 442 aircraft supported by *Oboe* marking by Mosquitos.

1944 Operation Thursday: RAF and USAAF transport aircraft commenced the fly-in of the leading elements of two Long Range Penetration Chindit brigades (Maj Gen O. Wingate) to landing zones deep behind the Japanese lines east of the River Chindwin in Burma. On the second night AVM J.E.A. Baldwin, AOC 3rd TAF, piloted one of the Dakotas landing on the Broadway jungle strip. The initial phase was completed by 11 March, by which time the RAF and USAAF had landed 9,052 men, 1,362 mules and 254 tons of stores by glider, aircraft and parachute; such a large assault was only possible due to the high degree of air superiority established. RAF transport squadrons (Nos 31, 62, 117 and 194) continued to resupply the force until its withdrawal in April.

See 2 June 1944.

An RAF wireless unit with the Chindits. *(IWM. CF 126)*

1949 The red equilateral triangle, with 9in sides and pointing downwards, was adopted as a standard safety marking below the cockpit on aircraft fitted with ejector seats. It was first used on the Meteor F8.

1991 Operation Granby: six of the seven Tornado aircrew shot down during operations in January were released from Iraqi captivity. The seventh was released the following day.

6 MARCH

1936 The RAF's first operational 'modern' monoplane, the Avro Anson, equipped with a retractable undercarriage, entered service with No. 48 (General Reconnaissance) Squadron at RAF Manston.

1941 Prime Minister Winston Churchill declared, 'We must assume that the Battle of the Atlantic has begun.' He issued a Directive ordering that until further notice absolute

Above: Ansons of No. 48 Squadron. *(AHB. H 1190)*

Below: A patrolling aircraft supports an Atlantic convoy. *(AHB. CH 801)*

Men of the RAF Regiment assemble their anti-aircraft gun, watched by a crowd of Burmese. *(AHB)*

priority had to be given to overcoming the U-boat and the Focke-Wulf aircraft (FW 200) threat.

1944 Bomber Command commenced a trial bombing offensive against rail centres in northern France in preparation for the invasion. A raid by 261 Halifaxes dropped 1,258 tons of bombs on the marshalling yards at Trappes, south-west of Paris.
See 15 April 1944.

The North-East Atlantic Chain of *Loran* (Long-Range Aid to Navigation) came into operation. Liberators of No. 59 Squadron and Halifaxes of No. 518 Squadron first used it operationally on 1 May 1944 on patrols over the Atlantic.

1945 No. 1307 Wing, RAF Regiment, with three Field Squadrons and an LAA Squadron, landed at Meiktila, Burma, to defend the airfield. In fierce fighting during the three-week 'Battle of Meiktila Airfield' OC 1307 Wing, Wg Cdr C.M. Landers, was killed leading a patrol at dawn on 24 March. During this crucial battle the besieged garrison was resupplied almost entirely by

the RAF's Dakota squadrons with L-5 light aircraft used for casualty evacuation.

1963 With the end of National Service, a revised trade structure, known as 'The 1964 Trade Structure', was announced. Its main features were:
- The combination of the skilled and advanced trades and the command and technician ladders to provide a single avenue of advancement.
- The introduction of promotion examinations, testing both trade and general service knowledge, to qualify airmen for promotion to NCO ranks.

The revised trade structure was introduced on 1 April 1964 (AMO A.80/1964).
See 22 August 1950.

1969 A soldier of the Parachute Regiment made the millionth parachute descent of No. 1 Parachute Training School when he jumped from a Hercules of No. 30 Squadron at RAF Weston-on-the-Green, Oxfordshire.

Spitfires take off for Malta from the aircraft carrier *Eagle*.
(IWM. A 9583)

7 MARCH

1929 A decision was promulgated that in all future service types of aircraft in which the pilot does not sit in the fore-and-aft line, the pilot's seat would be placed on the port side.

1940 Whitleys of No. 77 Squadron, flying from Villeneuve, dropped leaflets on Poznan, the first to be dropped on Poland.
See 12 January 1940.

1942 The first Spitfires reached Malta, when fifteen aircraft were flown off the aircraft carrier USS *Wasp* and completed the 400-mile flight to RAF Takali. The first squadron on Malta to re-equip with the Spitfire, No. 249 Squadron, became operational on 10 March.

Wg Cdr J.R. Jeudwine, OC No. 84 Squadron, and ten members of his squadron commandeered a ship's lifeboat, which they named *Scorpion* after the squadron's badge, and sailed from Tjilatjap, Java, to escape the advancing Japanese forces. Forty-seven days later they came ashore on the remote coast of north-west Australia. Jeudwine was awarded the OBE but was killed in a flying accident in 1945, having also been awarded the DSO and DFC for bomber operations.

2001 European Helicopter Industries Merlin HC3 delivered to No. 28 Squadron at RAF Benson.

8 MARCH

1942 Hostilities ceased in Java. A very small number of RAF personnel managed to avoid capture but thousands were taken including AVM P. Maltby, AOC Java, and the most senior RAF officer to be made a prisoner.

Japanese forces entered Rangoon. The remnants of No. 221 Group RAF moved north to Magwe and Akyab Island where they formed into the Burwing and Akwing.

The *Gee* radar navigation aid was first used in full strength by Bomber Command during a raid on Essen by 211 aircraft including 74 equipped with *Gee*. The aid gave coverage of

A Merlin of No. 28 Squadron refuels at Shaibah, Southern Iraq. *(Maj P.R.G. Pitchfork)*

400–500 miles. *Gee* had been tested operationally in July 1941 but CAS ruled that to prevent enemy 'jamming', it was not to be used again until sufficient aircraft were equipped to operate in strength.

1954 The Central Flying School Helicopter Development Flight formed as a lodger unit at RAF Middle Wallop with two Dragonfly Mk 4s before taking up residence at RAF South Cerney on 14 June.

1956 The new aircrew category of air electronics officer was created (AMO A. 54/56).

1971 HRH The Prince of Wales commenced training at the RAF College Cranwell. His flying instructor was Sqn Ldr R.E. Johns (later ACM Sir Richard Johns and CAS).

See 20 August 1971.

1996 HQ No. 2 Group at Rheindahlen closed, marking the final demise of an RAF headquarters in mainland Europe.

The survivors of No. 242 Squadron captured in Java, after their release from a Japanese POW Camp after three and a half years' captivity. *(IWM. CF 703)*

A Dragonfly of the Central Flying School.
(P.H.T. Green Collection)

9 MARCH

1918 An Order was promulgated directing the Air Council to transfer and attach those personnel belonging or attached to the Royal Naval Air Service and the Royal Flying Corps to the RAF on formation on 1 April 1918.

1925 Bristol Fighters from Nos 5, 20 and 31 Squadrons and DH9s from Nos 27 and 60 Squadrons were despatched to airstrips at Miranshah and Tank, under the command of Wg Cdr R.C.M. Pink, in an effort to control the Mahsud tribesmen of South Waziristan attacking Army posts. Air action began against mountain strongholds and an 'air blockade' was established. Bristol Fighters of No. 31 Squadron flew night sorties, and operations continued over the next few weeks in what was dubbed 'Pink's War' in honour of the senior RAF commander.
See 1 May 1925.

1937 The Whitley bomber entered service with No. 10 Squadron at RAF Dishforth.

1941 With the prospect that Britain faced the possibility of its absolutely vital ocean links with the Americas being severed, the Prime Minister issued a simple instruction. For the next four months, Bomber Command's main operational effort was to be directed towards those targets that housed the sources of the threats to British shipping. The Air Ministry passed on these orders to Bomber Command in a Directive with the initial emphasis on the U-boat and long-range aircraft threats. The targets included the U-boat shipbuilding yards at Kiel, Hamburg and Bremen, the cities of Mannheim and Augsburg with the marine diesel-engine factories in addition to the U-boat bases and the Focke-Wulf Kondor airfields.

1959 Colonel Grivas, the EOKA leader in Cyprus, reluctantly ordered a ceasefire. His forces had tied down 40,000 British troops and killed 99 since the outbreak of violence on 1 April 1955. In the last six months, Chipmunks of No. 114 Squadron played a leading role flying anti-terrorist patrols.

A Bristol F2B Fighter of No. 31 Squadron patrols India's North-West Frontier. *(AHB)*

Chipmunks of No. 114 Squadron on security patrol of the Kyrenia Mountains in Cyprus. *(AHB. CMP 10145)*

63

A Halifax Mk I awaiting delivery to the RAF. *(P.H.T. Green Collection)*

10 MARCH

1941 The first bombing operation by the Halifax was mounted when No. 35 Squadron took part in a raid against Le Havre.

1942 The first bombing operation by the Lancaster was mounted when Essen was the target for No. 44 Squadron Lancasters. They had been used operationally for the first time on the night of 3/4 March on a minelaying operation.

1944 Gen Eisenhower, the Supreme Commander, issued the Directive for the invasion of Europe: 'the object of Operation "Overlord" is to secure a lodgement area on the Continent from which further offensive operations can be developed'. The Directive outlined a strategic air plan and a tactical air plan.

1957 All Royal Auxiliary Air Force flying squadrons and Royal Auxiliary Air Force Regiment Squadrons were 'stood down' as a result of the sweeping defence cuts announced in the 'Sandys' White Paper.

1975 In the final hours of the Vietnam War, RAF Hercules were used to evacuate civilians from Phnom Penh, Cambodia.

11 MARCH

1940 The first U-boat was sunk during the war by an RAF aircraft without the assistance of surface vessels. A Blenheim (captain Flt Lt M.V. Delap) of No. 82 Squadron identified *U-31* on the surface near Borkum. The low-level attack resulted in the Blenheim sustaining damage, but it returned safely. Delap was awarded the DFC. The U-boat was subsequently raised and was eventually scuttled in May 1945.

GC (ex-EGM): Fg Off Anthony Henry Hamilton Tollemache of No. 600 Squadron for his attempt to rescue a fellow crew member from a burning Blenheim at RAF Manston, during the course of which he was severely burned. (*London Gazette*, 6 August 1940)

1941 House Resolution HR1776, passed by the United States Congress, authorised the 'Lend-Lease' programme. This allowed United States-manufactured aircraft ordered by the British Purchasing Commission for the Royal Air Force after March 1941 to be provided via Lend-Lease.

A Beverley of No. 47 Squadron with rear freight doors removed approaches RAF Abingdon. (*W. Grundy*)

12 MARCH

1921 A conference in Cairo reviewed existing policy and future proposals for the maintenance of British control in the Middle East Mandates. Air Staff proposals to adopt a policy of 'air control and responsibility' for the defence of a particular region by the RAF were approved.

1930 Wg Cdr W.G. Barker **VC**, DSO & Bar, MC & 2 Bars, RCAF died in an aircraft accident in Canada.
      See 27 October 1918.

1940 **GC** (ex-EGM): LAC Michael Campion and AC1 Ernest Ralph Clyde Frost of No. 90 Squadron displayed 'great courage' during the rescue of an unconscious pilot from a burning aircraft at RAF Upwood. (*London Gazette*, 5 July 1940)

1942 The Empire Central Flying School (Gp Capt H.H. Down) was formed at RAF Hullavington from the Central Flying School.

1945 Dortmund was bombed by 1,108 aircraft, the largest number of RAF aircraft to attack a single target during the Second World War, and 4,851 tons of bombs were dropped – another record.

1953 MiG15 fighters shot down a Lincoln of the Central Gunnery School after it strayed into East German airspace. The crew of seven were killed.

1956 The Beverley entered service with No. 47 Squadron. At the time it was the largest aircraft to enter service with the RAF and the first specially designed for dropping heavy Army equipment.

13 MARCH

1962 Sqn Ldr P. Howard of the Institute of Aviation Medicine made the first airborne ejection in the new Martin-Baker rocket-assisted seat. The test ejection took place from the company's airfield at Chalgrove from a modified Meteor 7.

14 MARCH

1923 The Secretary of State for Air, Sir Samuel Hoare, said of the RAF, 'We must keep it a *corps d'elite*, highly trained, well equipped and capable, so far as possible, of quick expansion.'

1945 A Lancaster (captain Sqn Ldr C.C. Calder) of No. 617 Squadron made the first operational drop of the 22,000lb 'Grand Slam' bomb. It was dropped on the Bielefeld railway viaduct, which collapsed as a consequence of the attack.

Sir James Martin greets Sqn Ldr P. Howard after the first airborne test of the rocket-assisted ejection seat. (Martin-Baker Co.)

MARTIN-BAKER EJECTION SEAT

Martin-Baker Aircraft Company started as an aircraft maker in 1934 by Capt (later Sir) James Martin and Capt Valentine Baker. The company soon started to investigate ejection seats, some four years before Germany and Sweden, and concluded that an explosive-powered ejection seat would be the best solution. After completing studies to find the human tolerance for upward acceleration, Bernard Lynch, a fitter at the company, volunteered to make the first experiments. He made the first 'live' ejection from a modified Meteor on 24 July 1946 over Chalgrove Airfield in Oxfordshire.

The first use of an ejector seat in a real situation was made on 30 May 1949 when J.O. Lancaster, an Armstrong Whitworth test pilot, ejected from the AW42 experimental wing aircraft at 3,000 feet. Martin-Baker was a leading pioneer in expanding the operational envelope of the ejection seats so that they could be used at low altitudes leading eventually to a 'zero-zero' capability. Over 69,000 seats have been provided and by August 2007 had saved 7,196 lives of aircrew from ninety-three Air Forces.

Sir Samuel Hoare, Secretary of State for Air. (RAF Museum)

A 22,000lb 'Grand Slam' bomb is taken from the bomb dump. (AHB. CH 15369)

15 MARCH

Gp Capt J.E. Fauquier (OC No. 617 Squadron) poses with a 22,000lb 'Grand Slam' bomb. (G.R. Pitchfork Collection)

1913 King George V approved *Per Ardua ad Astra* as the official motto for the Royal Flying Corps. It was promulgated in Army Order No. 3 in the following April – a motto without a meaning. It has been variously translated as 'Through Struggle to the Stars' and 'Through Difficulties to the Skies'. The Air Ministry, in a final effort to establish a translation appealed to the College of Arms, but that high authority could only confirm, 'No authoritative translation is possible'.

1940 No. 1 Air Ministry Works Area (France) Supervisory Unit landed at Le Havre to supervise the construction of airfields in the Tours/Orleans area. The rapid advance of German forces resulted in the abandonment of the project after three months.

See 22 July 1940.

1943 The Iraq Levies were renamed the Royal Air Force Levies (Iraq). In recognition of their gallantry at Habbaniya in April 1941, NCOs and men of the force were authorised to wear the RAF eagle arm badge.

See 1 July 1928, 1 October 1955.

1944 Flt Sgt N. Alkemade, a rear gunner with No. 115 Squadron, jumped from his burning Lancaster over Germany after his parachute had been destroyed by fire. He fell 18,000ft before crashing through pine trees into a snowdrift. He survived, regained consciousness after three hours and was captured. Initially disbelieved, the German authorities found his parachute harness and officially corroborated his story. Alkemade remained a POW until the end of the war.

1991 The Bonn Convention and the Quadripartite Agreement were formally terminated following the reunification of Germany, thus signalling the beginning of the rundown of RAF forces in Berlin.

See 26 February 1992, 7 September 1994.

16 MARCH

1922 The recommendation of the Geddes Committee of National Expenditure that the RAF be retained as a separate service was approved by Parliament.

1953 The first six Canadair Sabre F4s arrived at RAF Wildenrath. The conversion flight formed on 1 April and the first two squadrons, Nos 3 and 67, formed during May.

1966 Three Shackletons, drawn from Nos 37 and 38 Squadrons, arrived at Majunga, Madagascar, to commence patrols in support of the Royal Navy's blockade of the port of Beira, Mozambique, following the imposition of sanctions against Rhodesia. The 'Beira Patrol' was maintained until 17 March 1972 by Shackleton detachments from Nos 37, 38, 42, 204 and 210 Squadrons.

1996 Flt Lt Rory Underwood, a pilot with No. 100 Squadron, played his eighty-fifth (a record at the time) and final rugby game for England. He made his debut against Ireland on 18 February 1984 and was England's premier winger for the next twelve years scoring forty-nine tries, a record that still stands. He was the first to play fifty times for England and he also made six appearances for the British Lions on tours to South Africa and New Zealand.

2004 HM The Queen dedicated a tribute and commemorative feature in the South Cloister at Westminster Abbey to those who had served with Coastal Command and its successor formations. The book of remembrance contains 10,875 names of those who lost their lives in Coastal Command operations from RAF, Commonwealth and Allied squadrons.

17 MARCH

1927 From this date, aircraft serial identity numbers were to be marked on the wing under-surfaces of all RAF aircraft.

1931 The first seaplane tender (ST200) was received for service trials. The 37.5ft tender was ordered in large numbers and became the standard type in RAF marine service.

1953 HM The Queen, Air Commodore-in-Chief, presented her Colour to the RAF Regiment at Buckingham Palace.

1972 A Shackleton (captain Flt Lt W.P. Hay) of the Majunga detachment flew the last 'Beira Patrol' sortie.

See 16 March 1966.

HM The Queen presents her Colour to the RAF Regiment. *(AHB)*

18 MARCH

2002 Operation Veritas: the Secretary of State for Defence announced the deployment of a Royal Marine Brigade Group to Afghanistan. Chinooks of No. 27 Squadron provided battlegroup mobility. RAF tanker, reconnaissance and surveillance, and transport aircraft, which had commenced operations in October 2001, continued to provide substantial support.

See 24 September 2004.

19 MARCH

1925 The introduction of promotion examinations for officers of the General Duties Branch was announced. The qualifying examination for each rank was:
- To flying officer – examination A
- To flight lieutenant – examination B
- To squadron leader – examination C

The examinations were held for the first time in January 1926 (AMWO 181/25).

1944 Following Japanese Army attacks aimed at isolating British troops at Imphal and Tiddim, Dakotas of No. 194 Squadron and Curtis C-46 Commando transport aircraft of the USAAF airlifted a complete army division to Imphal, a feat accomplished in 748 sorties. Subsequently, during the siege of Imphal Allied transport squadrons, reinforced by units despatched from the Middle East, successfully kept the garrison and RAF fighter units supplied until the siege was lifted on 22 June.

See 22 June 1944.

Operation Strangle: the air interdiction programme began when two squadrons of Bostons and two of Baltimores attacked the rail and road communications system in central Italy. An assessment of the operation, which continued until 11 May 1944, concluded 'it had turned an orderly

Dakotas over Burma. *(AHB. CH 15088)*

Spitfire Vs of No. 253 Squadron are serviced on an Italian airstrip. *(AHB. CAN 3054)*

retreat into a partial rout and temporarily rendered the German army ineffective as a fighting force'.

1945 Lancasters of No. 617 Squadron dropped six 22,000lb 'Grand Slam' bombs on the viaduct at Arnsburg. A 40ft gap was blown in the viaduct.

20 MARCH

1917 **VC**: Capt Frank Hubert McNamara of No. 1 Squadron, Australian Flying Corps, the only Australian airman to be so decorated in the First World War, gained the award for his rescue of a downed fellow pilot after a bombing attack on a railway across Wadi Hesse at Tel el Hesi in Palestine. (*London Gazette*, 8 June 1917)
See 2 November 1961.

1918 Air Ministry Weekly Orders invited applications for permanent commissions in the planned Air Force. The Order stated that 'it would only be possible to accept the permanent services of a few officers'.

1924 The Aeroplane and Armament Experimental Establishment (A&AEE) (Wg Cdr N.J. Gill) formed at RAF Martlesham Heath.

1937 The first Balloon Barrage Group, No. 30 (Air Cdre J.G. Hearon), was formed under the operational control of Fighter Command.
See 1 November 1938.

1942 Some 10 Hurricanes and 9 Blenheims from Magwe attacked Mingaladon, destroying 16 Japanese aircraft on the ground and 11 in the air. In the following twenty-four hours 230 enemy aircraft attacked Magwe, destroying 11 Hurricanes and all but 6 Blenheims.

The Luftwaffe launched a devastating series of raids on the fighter airfield at Takali in Malta, demolishing virtually every building. The Luftwaffe's all-out assault on the airfield was repeated the following morning.

1950 Operation Musgrave: a detachment of Lincoln bombers from No. 57 Squadron arrived at RAF Tengah, Singapore, to support security operations during the

Blenheims on Magwe Airfield after a Japanese attack.
(G.R. Pitchfork Collection)

A TriStar tanker refuels two Tornado F3s during Operation Telic. *(MOD)*

SECOND GULF WAR

Although the first bombs were dropped on 20 March 2003, the air campaign began in earnest the following day. Precision attacks by aircraft and cruise missiles were made against several hundred military targets. As the land battle developed, an increasing number of close air support (CAS) sorties were flown. Tornado GR4s and Harrier GR7s flew 1,353 offensive strike sorties and released 919 weapons, the great majority precision-guided weapons including the first use of the Storm Shadow stand-off missile released by Tornados. All the RAF's main operational air assets were heavily engaged in the operation together with six RAF Regiment squadrons and personnel drawn from fifteen specialist RAF ground support units.

Malayan Emergency (Operation Firedog). The detachment was subsequently relieved by detachments from Nos 61 and 100 Squadrons. Operation Musgrave was suspended on 29 March 1951.
See 26 March 1950.

2003 Operation Telic (Gulf War II): Iraq failed to comply with a series of United Nations Resolutions so Coalition forces commenced military operations. Some 125 RAF aircraft and 8,000 personnel were involved with AM B. Burridge appointed as the British National Contingent Commander.
See 21 March 2003.

21 MARCH

1920 After many months of difficult negotiations with the Treasury, the Secretary of State approved the continued existence of a separate Chaplain's Department of the RAF, which assured the future of the Branch as an integral part of the RAF.

1944 GC: Wg Cdr Forest Frederick Edward Yeo-Thomas, an SOE agent, was betrayed and captured by the Gestapo in Paris. He underwent prolonged torture and was sentenced to death at Buchenwald

VENICE
SOME MINUTES BEFORE
ATTACK BY D.A.F.

M/V. OTTO LEONHAR
3,200 TONS

COASTER 1,000 TO

COASTAL TANKER
1,000 TONS

WAR PARTENOPE T/BOATS
649 TONS

INACTIVE SHIPPING

concentration camp from where he eventually escaped. (*London Gazette*, 15 February 1946)

The docks at Venice moments before the attack during Operation Bowler. *(M. Walters)*

1945 Seventeen Mosquitos of Nos 21, 464 and 467 Squadrons, escorted by Mustangs of No. 64 Squadron, destroyed the main building of the Gestapo HQ in the Shellhaus building in Copenhagen. Tragically, one Mosquito crashed on a nearby school causing heavy loss of life. Pilot of one of the Mosquitos was AVM B. Embry (AOC 2nd TAF) who flew as 'Wg Cdr Smith'. He had flown on numerous low-level sorties and was awarded the DFC to add to the four DSOs he had already earned.

Seventy-two Kittyhawks and Mustangs of No. 239 Wing (Wg Cdr G. Westlake) successfully bombed shipping and storage areas in Venice harbour, the only Allied bombing attack against the historic city.

2003 Operation Iraqi Freedom: the air campaign against Iraq opened at 0234hr GMT. A Tornado GR4 made the first operational release of the Storm Shadow long-range, highly accurate missile against a key regime target. The air campaign continued until 18 April.

Boeing B-29s, given the name Washington by the RAF, over the North Sea. *(AHB. PRB 1658)*

22 MARCH

1941　Training in the United States of the first course of RAF observers commenced at Miami, Florida, with Pan American Airways. By the end of the scheme in October 1942 1,177 observers had been trained in addition to a further 538 trained by the US Navy at Pensacola, Florida, under the 'Towers Scheme'.

1950　The first four of seventy US B-29 Bombers (named Washington in RAF service) provided to the RAF under the Mutual Defence Assistance Programme (MDAP) arrived at RAF Marham.

1961　The first issue of the *RAF News* went on sale, priced 3*d*.

23 MARCH

1944　The follow-on phase of the Second Chindit operation began when a brigade was flown into the clearing 'Aberdeen' by Dakotas of No. 194 Squadron. RAF aircrew with a signals section accompanied the columns to

provide control of close air support operations.

1953　No. 1340 Flight moved from Thornhill in Rhodesia to RAF Eastleigh, Nairobi, to commence intensive anti-terrorist operations in Kenya in support of the British Army. The flight was equipped with Harvard IIb advanced trainers (previously used by the Rhodesian Air Training Group) armed with 20lb fragmentation bombs.

24 MARCH

1921　The Royal Air Force Ensign was established by Order of Council.

1941　No. 95 Squadron, equipped with Sunderlands operating from Freetown, Sierra Leone, commenced anti-submarine patrols off West Africa. The Squadron was disbanded on 30 March 1945 when the U-boat threat in the area had disappeared.

1944　RAF prisoners in Stalag Luft III POW Camp at Sagan in Poland staged a mass breakout. Using a tunnel codenamed 'Harry', seventy-six prisoners escaped before it was detected. Fifteen of the POWs were recaptured and returned to the camp, but the escape so incensed Hitler and Himmler that fifty others

A jeep manhandled aboard an RAF Dakota during the second Chindit operation. *(AHB. CF 145)*

Airmen return after servicing a Sunderland at Bathurst, Gambia. *(AHB)*

Tunnel 'Harry' used during the Great Escape from Stalag Luft III at Sagan. *(RAFM)*

were handed to the Gestapo following their recapture and were subsequently shot in cold blood. Those murdered included the leader of the escape, Sqn Ldr R.J. Bushell. Eight POWs were detained by the Gestapo and sentenced to death but were not shot. Three escapers succeeded in evading the massive German manhunt and escaped to neutral territory. This exploit later served as the inspiration for the film, *The Great Escape*. Postwar, RAF war crimes investigators traced and brought to trial eighteen former members of the Gestapo responsible for the murders.

See 3 September 1945.

In the last major raid of the 'Battle of Berlin', 811 aircraft of Bomber Command attacked the German capital. Casualties were heavy with the loss of seventy-two aircraft, 8.9 per cent of the attacking force. Although Mosquitos of the LNSF mounted frequent attacks during 1944, the main force did not attack Berlin again until the night of 14/15 April 1945.

1945 Operation Varsity: in support of the amphibious assault across the River Rhine, tug aircraft of Nos 38 and 46 Groups towed 439 gliders to drop zones near Wesel. This followed a heavy air bombardment of the defences and the airborne assault by Nos 3 and 5 Parachute Brigades dropped from aircraft of No. IX US Troop Carrier Command. For a few days prior to the operation, bombers and fighter-bombers attacked rail and road communications and flak batteries. The 2nd TAF provided close air support throughout the day. Gen Sir Bernard Montgomery sent the following signal to HQ Bomber Command: 'My grateful appreciation for the quite magnificent co-operation you have given us in the Battle of the Rhine. The bombing of Wesel was a masterpiece and was a decisive factor in making possible our entry into that town before midnight.'

1978 The Queen's Colour Squadron of the RAF Regiment was assigned a war role as a Field Squadron.

1992 The Open Skies treaty was signed in Helsinki by the sixteen NATO countries, Russia, Belarus, Ukraine, and the five former Warsaw Pact countries.

Operation Varsity: a Halifax tows a Hamilcar glider over RAF Tarrant Rushton. *(G.R. Pitchfork Collection)*

Groundcrew of No. 1(F) Squadron prepare a Thermal Imaging and Laser Designating (TIALD) pod for fitment to a Harrier GR7 at Gioia Colle, Italy. *(MOD)*

1999   Operation Allied Force: following the collapse of diplomatic efforts to achieve a settlement regarding the status of the province of Kosovo, NATO forces embarked upon a systematic bombing campaign against Serbian forces in Kosovo and infrastructure targets in Serbia itself, aiming to force the withdrawal of Serbian troops from the province. Allied Force commenced with cruise missile attacks and NATO air attacks against Serbian military installations and troop positions in Kosovo. During the first night of the operation, six Harrier GR7 aircraft, four armed with Paveway II laser-guided bombs, participated in an attack on an ammunition storage facility used by the Serbian Ministry of Interior Police. E-3D Sentry aircraft of No. 8 Squadron, a Canberra PR 9 of No. 39 Squadron and Tristar tankers of No. 216 Squadron were used to support NATO operations throughout Operation Allied Force. See 27 May 1999.

25 MARCH

1920 The wearing of field boots was made optional for officers of all ranks (AMO 292/1920).

1935 During a visit to Berlin by Sir John Simon (Foreign Secretary), the German Chancellor (Adolf Hitler) claimed that the German Air Force, which had enjoyed an official existence of only a fortnight, was already as strong as the RAF. This caused consternation in the Cabinet and a fresh expansion scheme resulted.

See 25 February 1936.

1943 Transport Command was formed (ACM Sir Frederick Bowhill) and absorbed Ferry Command, which became No. 45 Group.

26 MARCH

1918 'King's Regulations and Orders for the Royal Air Force' for the new service to be formed on 1 April 1918 were issued.

1,000lb bombs arrive for a Lincoln of No. 57 Squadron at RAF Tengah, Singapore. *(AHB. CFP 221)*

1943 Battle of the Mareth Line: a major air offensive commenced involving light and medium bombers and a relay of fighter-bombers, including Hurricane 'tank busters' against the main German defensive line in southern Tunisia at 1530hr. After thirty minutes the infantry attacked as aircraft bombed and attacked ahead of the advance. The enemy was overwhelmed in two and a quarter hours, the Desert Air Force having made 412 sorties at a cost of eleven pilots missing.

1945 Wg Cdr J.N. Stacey (later AVM) led eight Liberators of No. 160 Squadron, based in Ceylon, to drop mines in Singapore harbour. To maintain surprise, the outbound flight of 1,700 miles was flown at low level. The aircraft returned at medium level directly across Sumatra and were airborne for twenty-one hours. Stacey was awarded the DSO.

1950 **GC**: AC1 Ivor John Gillett of the Far East Flying Boat Wing was blown out of an exploding Sunderland but passed his lifebelt to a wounded colleague despite being injured himself. (*London Gazette*, 3 October 1950, posthumous award)

Operation Firedog: Lincolns of No. 57 Squadron commenced bombing operations against Communist positions in Malaya.

1970 The *Gee* navigation system was closed down.

A Hurricane IID of No. 6 Squadron armed with two 40mm cannons for 'tank busting'. (AHB. CM 4957)

27 MARCH

1918 **VC**: 2/Lt Alan Arnett McLeod of No. 2 Squadron, RFC. At 19 years of age, he was the youngest airman to receive this award during the First World War, for action during a bombing mission over Bray-sur-Somme in France and for saving the life of his observer after being shot down in an Armstrong Whitworth FK8. (*London Gazette* 1 May 1918)

See 6 November 1918.

1924 Official titles of RAF squadrons embodied their functional character, e.g. Bombing, Fighter, Army Co-operation. In May 1929, the word 'bombing' was changed to 'Bomber' (AMWO 218/1924).

1927 The RAF's first all-metal fighter, the Armstrong Whitworth Siskin IIIA, entered service with No. 41 Squadron.

A Dakota of No. 31 Squadron evacuates personnel from Myitkynia in April 1942. *(No. 31 Squadron Association)*

1942 The Japanese launched a three-day assault on Akyab, destroying a number of aircraft on the ground. The remainder were evacuated to India. Over 8,600 civilians were airlifted to safety by Dakotas of No. 31 Squadron – the only RAF transport squadron in theatre – and by the USAAF.

1945 AM Sir Peter Drummond (Air Member for Training) and Mr H.A. Jones (Director of Public Relations (RAF)) were posted missing after the Liberator of Transport Command in which they were travelling to attend the ceremony marking the formal closure of the British Commonwealth Air Training Plan in Ottawa, disappeared en route from RAF Northolt to Lagens, Azores.

1952 An Air Ministry Order gave the details of 'The Standard' announced by HM King George VI on 1 April 1943. '"The Standard" will consist of a rectangular silk flag with the appropriate squadron badge centred on a light blue background; it will be fringed and tasselled, with scrolls added as necessary, for recording battle honours. "The Standard" is to be carried on a staff surmounted by a gold eagle.'

The Order announced the RAF operational squadrons to be awarded a Standard and stated that His Majesty had approved that squadrons of the RAF Regiment and Royal Auxiliary Air Force should also be eligible. A list of approved battle honours was contained in an Appendix to the Order. The maximum number of battle honours to be shown on the scrolls was set at eight and authority was given for squadrons that earned a greater number to select the eight which they wished to appear on their Standards (AMO A.177/1952).

1980 The North Sea accommodation platform *Alexander L. Kielland* capsized with 208 people aboard after being hit by a huge wave. A Sea King of 'A' Flight, No. 202 Squadron (captain Flt Lt R. Neville) took off from RAF Boulmer within minutes. In 60-knot winds, winchman Flt Sgt C.M. Yarwood rescued ten men from a life raft and they were taken to another rig. A lifeboat with twenty-six on board was located and, although exhausted, Yarwood was lowered to determine their condition. Nimrods played a significant role co-ordinating activity, but 120 men were lost. Yarwood was awarded the AFM.

28 MARCH

The Standard of No. 1(F) Squadron. *(AHB)*

1942   Bomber Command mounted its first concentrated raid against a German city when 234 aircraft, the majority Wellingtons, attacked Lübeck with a large number of incendiaries. Such was the effect of this and similar raids that the Germans for the first time used the phrase *Terrorangriff* (terror raids) to describe them.

1946   The Air Ministry announced that control of transport formations and services overseas were to be transferred from Transport Command to RAF commands overseas. However, Transport Command retained home-based transport formations and continued to be responsible for the operation of trunk services.

1947   **GC**: Sgt John Archibald Beckett of RAF Ein Shemer. Although badly burned he drove his fuel bowser away from twenty parked aircraft. He died from his injuries. (*London Gazette*, 16 December 1947, posthumous award)

1967   Operation Mop Up: Hunters from RAF Chivenor and RAF West Raynham carried out repeated attacks, using bombs and rockets, in support of Buccaneers of the Fleet Air Arm, to break up the very large crude-oil carrier *Torrey Canyon* aground on the Seven Sisters Reef near Land's End and to destroy the 120,000-ton cargo of oil, which was polluting the nearby Cornish beaches.

1970   RAF El Adem and associated weapons ranges were handed back to the Libyan authorities, bringing to an end the British military occupation of airfields on the North African littoral, which dated from before the founding of the RAF.

The Wellington was able to sustain considerable damage and return to base. This aircraft of No. 428 Squadron lost its rear turret. *(AHB. CH 9868)*

The air traffic control tower at RAF El Adem, Libya. *(G. Tyak)*

29 MARCH

1918   **VC**: Capt James Thomas Byford McCudden of No. 56 Squadron RFC, for 'conspicuous bravery, exceptional perseverance, keenness and very high devotion to duty'. He was credited with destroying fifty-seven enemy aircraft. (*London Gazette*, 29 March 1918)

See 9 July 1918.

1944   Japanese forces cut the Dimapur–Imphal road, thereby isolating the Fourteenth Army who were supplied entirely by air until the siege was lifted on 22 June.

1945   The last *Vergeltungswaffe* No. 1 (the V-1) to fall on England was shot down near Sittingbourne. Of the 3,957 bombs destroyed, fighters accounted for 1,847, guns of Anti-Aircraft Command 1,866, balloons 232 and 12 by guns of the Royal Navy. No. 3 Squadron flying Tempests had the highest score to its credit, accounting for 258. Of the thirty-four pilots credited with destroying more than ten, the list was headed by Sqn Ldr J. Berry of No. 501 Squadron who shot down fifty-nine and shared one. He was awarded the DFC three times but was killed in action flying a Tempest on 2 October 1944.

The rudimentary control facilities at Imphal. *(AHB. CI 763)*

The RAF's island staging post at Gan in the Maldive Islands. (*P.H.T. Green Collection*)

1960 An agreement was reached with the USA for British participation in the Skybolt air-launched ballistic missile (ALBM) development and acquisition programme. The missile was to be carried by modified Vulcan aircraft.

See 21 December 1962.

1976 The RAF presence in the Maldive Islands came to an end with the final withdrawal of personnel from the staging post on the island of Gan, Addu Atoll. The RAF station was formally closed on 1 April and handed to the Maldivian authorities.

30 MARCH

1918 **VC**: Lt Alan Jerrard of No. 66 Squadron, RFC, for gallantry displayed during an offensive patrol over Italy in a Sopwith Camel. (*London Gazette* 1 May 1918)

See 14 May 1968.

1941 Bomber Command began a prolonged bombing campaign against the French port of Brest, with the aim of damaging the German Navy battlecruisers *Scharnhorst* and *Gneisenau* (and subsequently the cruiser *Prinz Eugen*), preventing them from leaving the port to attack shipping in the Atlantic. In the ten months following this date, Bomber Command mounted 2,928 sorties against the port, 171 of which were in daylight. Although few of the weapons dropped hit the ships, the need to defend the port drew away resources, which might have been more profitably used elsewhere. The warships escaped to Germany on 12 February 1942.

See 12 February 1942.

1944 Bomber Command suffered its heaviest loss in a single raid when 795 aircraft were sent

to attack the city of Nuremburg. Against intense night-fighter attacks, ninety-five aircraft were lost, a casualty rate of 11.9 per cent. A total of 545 British, Commonwealth and Allied airmen were killed.

VC: Plt Off Cyril Joe Barton, a Halifax pilot of No. 578 Squadron, came under intense night-fighter attack en route to Nuremburg and three of his crew baled out. He pressed on to the target and returned successfully to England, 'in the face of almost impossible odds', before crash-landing near Durham. Barton died of his injuries but the three remaining crew members survived. (*London Gazette*, 27 June 1944, posthumous award)

1978 After almost thirty years of operations, the RAF's air traffic control radar on the peak of Tai Mo Shan (3,144ft), Hong Kong, closed down when the Crown Colony's Civil Aviation Department's new long-range radar on Hong Kong island became operational.

Halifax bombers attack the German Navy battlecruisers *Scharnhorst* and *Gneisenau* at Brest. *(AHB)*

1983 The Falkland Islands Phantom detachment, formed from No. 29 Squadron after the islands were captured, was disbanded and its place taken by No. 23 Squadron, which was re-formed at RAF Stanley.

1993 RAF Gutersloh in Germany was closed.

31 MARCH

1919 Maj Gen Sir Hugh Trenchard was reappointed Chief of the Air Staff.

1941 The first two 4,000lb HC bombs to be dropped by Bomber Command were delivered by a No. 149 Squadron Wellington (captain Sqn Ldr K. Wass) and a No. 9 Squadron Wellington (captain Plt Off Franks). The target was Emden.

A Hercules tanker with Phantoms of No. 23 Squadron near the Falkland Islands. *(J. Abell)*

The first dedicated anti-submarine aircraft arrived in Iceland when three Hudsons of No. 269 Squadron landed at Kaldadarnes. The first operation, a convoy escort, was flown three days later. The remainder of the squadron arrived during June.
See 27 August 1941.

1945   The British Commonwealth Air Training Plan (BCATP), known as the Empire Air Training Scheme (EATS) prior to June 1942, officially ended. By 30 September 1944, EATS/BCATP had generated a total of 168,662 aircrew in training schools located in Canada, Australia, New Zealand and Southern Rhodesia. Of this total, 75,152 were pilots, 40,452 navigators, 15,148 air bombers and 37,190 belonged to other aircrew categories. Although South Africa was not part of EATS/BCATP, under a parallel agreement, RAF aircrew were trained in SAAF Air Schools.
See 29 April 1940.

1955   Operation Firedog: the record weight of supplies dropped in any single month of the Malayan emergency was achieved when 808,035lb were dropped during 218 sorties – a greater volume than had been dropped during the entire first year of the campaign.

1964   The term 'Air Ministry Roof', used in weather bulletins, was replaced by 'Roof of the London Weather Centre'.

1974   ACM Sir Denis Spotswood was promoted to MRAF.

1976   The Near East Air Force (NEAF) disbanded as part of the continuing draw down of RAF commitments worldwide. AHQ Cyprus, with the status of a Group, was re-formed the following day to control units in the Mediterranean; this AHQ reported to HQ Strike Command.

1977   After a presence of almost fifty years, the RAF withdrew from the airfield at Masirah. Salalah was also vacated and both airfields were handed over to the Sultan of Oman Air Force.

Above: Hudsons over the barren landscape of Iceland. *(AHB. CS 59)*

Below: Newly qualified pilots signal the end of the BCATP scheme. *(AHB)*

A Vulcan displays its large bomb bay.
(G.R. Pitchfork Collection)

1979 RAF Luqa was closed and the RAF withdrew from Malta, ending a sixty-year presence on the island.

1984 The Vulcan was withdrawn from service with the disbandment of No. 50 Squadron at RAF Waddington.

1986 The RAF Marine Branch was disbanded after sixty-eight years of providing marine services. A ship management company assumed responsibility (from 1 February 1986) for the management, operation and maintenance of RAF marine craft.

1993 HRH The Duke of Edinburgh took the salute at a parade held at JHQ Rheindahlen to mark the disbandment of the RAF's last overseas command. The Queen's Colour of the Royal Air Force in Germany was paraded for the last time before being laid up in the RAF church, St Clement Danes in London, on 27 June. With the disbandment

ACM Sir Richard Johns (who served on No. 3 Squadron) takes the salute at RAF Cottesmore as the Typhoon enters operational service with No. 3(F) Squadron, previously equipped with the Harrier GR7.
(RAF Cottesmore)

of RAF Germany, HQ No. 2 Group was re-formed at Rheindahlen to command the remaining RAF units in Germany.

See 16 September 1970, 1 April 1996.

1995 The Balloon Operations Squadron was disbanded at RAF Hullavington marking the end of the military use of balloons, 132 years after the first experiments were conducted at Aldershot.

1998 At midnight the RAF relinquished the nuclear role with the withdrawal of the WE 177 nuclear weapon at RAF Bruggen.

1999 RAF Laarbruch in Germany closed.

2002 No. 72 Squadron disbanded as a helicopter squadron having completed thirty-eight years of detached and permanent service in Northern Ireland, the longest period of sustained operations in one operational theatre.

2006 The Typhoon entered RAF operational service equipping No. 3(F) Squadron.

1 APRIL

1918 **The Royal Air Force was formed following an Order in Council made by His Majesty King George V on 22 March 1918 resulting in the union of the Royal Naval Air Service and Royal Flying Corps.**

On the inauguration of the Royal Air Force, His Majesty the King sent the following telegram to Lord Rothermere, the President of the Air Council:

> *Today the Royal Air Force, of which you are Minister in Charge, comes into existence as a third arm of the Defences of the Empire. As General-in-Chief I congratulate you on its birth, and I trust that it may enjoy a vigorous and successful life.*
>
> *I am confident that the union of the Royal Naval Air Service and the Royal Flying Corps will preserve and foster that esprit de corps which these two separate forces have created by their splendid deeds.*

Officers holding permanent commissions and serving in the RNAS and RFC were attached to the RAF, and all other officers, all warrant officers, petty officers, non-commissioned officers and men who belonged or were attached to the RNAS or RFC were transferred to the RAF. Maj Gen Sir Hugh Trenchard retained the appointment of Chief of the Air Staff.

All RNAS squadrons were renumbered from 201 onwards.

The RAF Record Office was established at Blandford, moving to RAF Ruislip early in 1921.

The Women's Royal Air Force (WRAF) was formed.

The Royal Aircraft Establishment was formed from the Royal Aircraft Factory at Farnborough.

Royal Navy and Royal Air Force officers aboard the aircraft carrier *Argus. (ACA Archives)*

1920   The RAF Central Band (Fg Off J.H. Amers), sixty strong, was formed at the RAF Depot Uxbridge. The RAF (Cadet) College Band, twenty-four strong, was formed at Cranwell with a Warrant Officer Bandmaster.

The WRAF was disbanded. Between the date of its formation on 1 April 1918 and its disbandment, 32,000 women had served in the ranks of the WRAF.

The Meteorological Office absorbed single-service meteorological sections and was attached to the Air Ministry.

1921   No. 4 Flying Training School (FTS) formed at RAF Abu Sueir in Egypt. It was the only regular FTS established overseas and was finally disbanded at RAF Habbaniya, Iraq, in July 1941.
See 30 April 1941.

1923   Existing RAF squadrons with a naval role were disbanded and replaced by flights. Each flight was given a number in the 400 series and normally comprised six aircraft.

1924   RAF Palestine Command formed (Air Cdre E.L. Gerrard).

Marine Aircraft Experimental Establishment formed at Felixstowe (Wg Cdr C.E.H. Rathbone).

The Fleet Air Arm of the RAF was formed, comprising RAF units normally embarked on aircraft carriers and fighting ships. Personnel were drawn from both the RAF and the Royal Navy.

1933   ACM Sir Geoffrey Salmond was officially appointed to succeed his brother MRAF Sir John Salmond as Chief of the Air Staff. However, Sir Geoffrey fell ill before he could assume the post and died on 27 April, Sir John therefore continued to serve as CAS in his brother's stead.

1937   Camouflage was introduced as factory finish on all operational aircraft.

1938   RAF Maintenance Command was formed at Andover (AVM J.S.T. Bradley).

1941   The first edition of *Tee Emm*, the aircrew training publication, was published. Plt Off

PERCY PRUNE, PILOT-OFFICER

Pilot Officer Prune. *(ACA Archives)*

Prune, the RAF's legendary dimwit, was the protagonist of the magazine, which broke with tradition and, using humour as a teaching device, set Prune to demonstrate how not to do it.

1943   To mark the RAF's 25th anniversary, HM The King announced his intention to award a ceremonial flag, to be known as 'The Standard', to twenty-five squadrons on the completion of twenty-five years' unbroken service. (The first presentation was made to No. 1 Squadron on 20 April 1953.)
See 27 March 1952.

The RAF presented Prime Minister Winston Churchill with honorary pilot's wings to mark their 25th anniversary, although he was not a qualified pilot.

Nos 2768 (Sqn Ldr A.G. Vaughan) and 2773 (Sqn Ldr A.S. Cooper) Squadrons of

The RAF Regiment mount guard at Buckingham Palace.
(AHB. CH 9010)

the RAF Regiment took over the guard at Buckingham Palace and St James's Palace until 4 April to mark the 25th anniversary of the formation of the RAF.
　See 12 June 1968.

Works squadrons were renamed airfield construction squadrons and numbered in the 5000 series.
　See 22 July 1940.

1950　The first British operational helicopter unit, the Casualty Evacuation Flight at RAF Seletar, Singapore, was formed with Dragonfly helicopters for work in connection with operations against Communist terrorists in Malaya.

1954　Operation Firedog: the last operational sortie by a Spitfire was flown when Spitfire

PR19s of No. 81 Squadron flew a number of photo-reconnaissance sorties.

1955　A series of bomb explosions throughout the island marked the commencement of the EOKA terrorist campaign in Cyprus.
　See 26 November 1955.

1958　The command structure in the Middle East was once again reformed. AHQ Levant was disbanded and its functions transferred to HQ Middle East Air Force (MEAF). A separate command was established to control RAF units in the Arabian Peninsula, retaining the title HQ British Forces Arabian Peninsula. These changes rationalised the division of command between the Mediterranean and Gulf regions.

1959　RAF Home Command was disbanded; control of the Air Training Corps passed to Flying Training Command and sub-sequently to the Air Ministry.

The Casualty Evacuation Flight at RAF Seletar, Singapore. *(AHB. H 4035)*

Spitfire PR19s of No. 81 Squadron make the last RAF operational flight of the iconic fighter. *(AHB. CFP 846)*

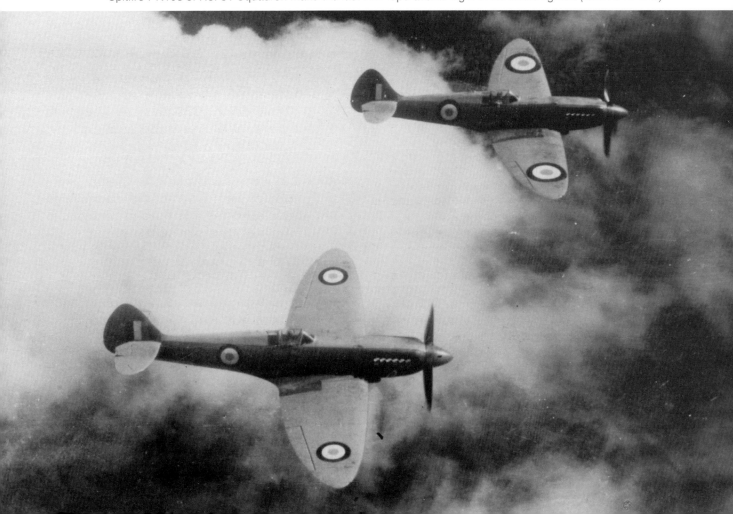

RAF Calshot. *(AHB. H 2429)*

1961 The RAF's last flying-boat station, and scene of the Schneider Trophy successes, RAF Calshot, closed after forty-eight years of service with the RNAS and the RAF.

1962 Nos 90 and 214 Squadrons, equipped with the Valiant, were officially declared as the RAF's first air refuelling tanker squadrons.

1963 The Air Ministry Directorate-General of Works (AMDGW), formed in 1919 as AMWD, became part of the Ministry of Public Building and Works (MPBW).

1964 The unified Ministry of Defence was formed. The Air Ministry became the Air Force Department, the Air Council the Air Force Board, and the Secretary of State for Air the Minister of Defence for the RAF.

1966 The Airfield Construction Branch was disbanded with personnel transferring to the Royal Engineers or to other RAF branches.

1967 ACM Sir John Grandy was appointed Chief of the Air Staff.

1968 The 50th anniversary of the Royal Air Force was celebrated by parades and fly-pasts throughout Britain and overseas, and an Air Force Board Banquet and Reception at Lancaster House was attended by the Queen, Duke of Edinburgh, the Queen Mother, Princess Margaret, Duchess of Gloucester and Princess Marina.

1971 ACM Sir Denis Spotswood was appointed Chief of the Air Staff.

1974 ACM Sir Andrew Humphrey was appointed Chief of the Air Staff.

1993 HM The Queen presented a new Colour to the RAF to mark the 75th Anniversary of the founding of the Service.

RAF Germany was disbanded thus relinquishing its status as an overseas command. HQ No. 2 Group was formed as a group within RAF Strike Command.
See 31 March 1993.

1994 RAF personnel and logistic staff were removed from London and incorporated with the staff of RAF Support Command to form two new commands:
• RAF Personnel and Training Command (ACM Sir Andrew Wilson – also Air Member for Personnel) at RAF Innsworth.
• RAF Logistics Command (ACM Sir Michael Alcock) at RAF Brampton.

The WRAF was disbanded.

1996 Headquarters No. 2 Group was disbanded at JHQ Rheindahlen and command of the

RAF's remaining flying squadron in Germany passed to HQ No. 1 Group at RAF High Wycombe. Command of the remaining RAF Regiment squadrons in Germany was passed to HQ No. 38 Group, also at RAF High Wycombe.

1997 The RAFVR and RAuxAF were combined into a single reserve force in line with the Reserve Forces Act. This resulted in the integration of members into the RAuxAF and the disbandment of the RAFVR after sixty years of service.

The Operations Support Branch was formed by bringing together the existing air traffic control, fighter control, intelligence and RAF Regiment specialisations. A fifth specialisation – flight operations – was created within the new branch.

1998 The last edition of the traditional *Air Clues* was published. It was superseded by two new quarterly publications, *Air Power*

sponsored by the Director of Defence Studies (RAF) and a new *Air Clues* sponsored by the Inspector of Flight Safety.

2000 Royal Navy Sea Harriers joined the RAF Harrier Force at RAF Wittering to form the Joint Force Harrier (JFH).

2006 Nine Expeditionary Air Wings were formed to support the RAF on deployed operations.

2 APRIL

1918 Miss Sylvia Hodkinson became the first WRAF recruit.

1945 Lt R.H. Veitch (SAAF) of No. 260 Squadron baled out of his Mustang over the north Adriatic Sea after it had been hit by anti-aircraft fire. A Warwick of No. 293 Squadron dropped an airborne lifeboat to

Women were employed in many roles in the WRAF. *(RAFM)*

Members of the Women's Royal Air Force in France.
(AHB)

3 APRIL

him and he was rescued. Two days later he was shot down and was again rescued with the aid of an airborne lifeboat. On 30 April his Mustang was again hit by anti-aircraft fire and he baled out for the third time in four weeks. A US Fortress of the Emergency Rescue Squadron dropped a lifeboat. On each occasion he sailed out of an enemy minefield and was rescued. He was awarded the DFC and made Commodore of the DAF Sailing Club by his AOC.

1982 Argentinean forces invaded the Falkland Islands and were opposed by a Royal Marine detachment of fifty-seven men. After initial resistance the marines were forced to surrender. Plans to recover the islands were started immediately and four Hercules departed for Gibraltar. The operation was given the codename Corporate.

1933 The Houston–Mount Everest Expedition – two converted Wallace aircraft, piloted by Sqn Ldr the Marquess of Douglas and Clydesdale, OC No. 602 Squadron, and his deputy Flt Lt D.F. McIntyre – made the first flight over Mount Everest. Lady Houston funded the expedition after the Air Ministry felt unable to do so. Both pilots were awarded the AFC.

1941 The Iraqi Revolt: pro-Axis Iraqi politician Raschid Ali, backed by four generals, seized power in Baghdad from the regent Abdullah Illah. The latter fled to the RAF station at Habbaniya, 50 miles west of the capital. RAF forces were present at Habbaniya under the terms of the 1930 Anglo-Iraqi Treaty.

A force of Blenheims of No. 14 Squadron, Wellesleys of Nos 47 and 223 Squadrons

and Swordfish of the Fleet Air Arm sank with bombs an Italian Navy flotilla of four destroyers in the Red Sea, the last Italian ships in the region.

Wellesleys of No. 223 Squadron at a desert airstrip *(G.R. Pitchfork Collection)*

1942 To meet the increasing demands on Gibraltar as a staging post and operational

The westerly extension to the runway at Gibraltar. *(AHB)*

97

Allied prisoners of war return to England. *(AHB. CH 15088)*

base in support of Operation Torch, work began to extend the runway on to land reclaimed from the sea. The initial extension to 1,150yd was completed in four months and was described as 'one of the great constructional achievements of the war'. By July 1943 the runway had been extended to 1,800yd.

1944 The first Allied air attacks were carried out on Hungary when the USAAF daylight attack was followed by an attack at night by RAF Wellingtons of No. 205 Group on armament factories and marshalling yards in Budapest.

1945 Operation Exodus: the repatriation of liberated POWs from Germany began. The main airlift was completed on 31 May.
See 25 April 1945.

1948 CAS issued a note on 'Modernisation of the Strategic Bomber Force'.

4 APRIL

1922 The RAF Staff College was opened at Andover (Commandant Air Cdre H.R.M. Brooke-Popham). Of the twenty-nine students on No. 1 Course, six became Commanders-in-Chief, and one – Sqn Ldr C.F.A. Portal – the Chief of the Air Staff.

1940 No. 75 (New Zealand) Squadron was formed at RAF Feltwell, equipped with Wellingtons to become the first Commonwealth squadron in Bomber Command.

1942 A Catalina (captain Sqn Ldr L.J. Birchall RCAF) of No. 205 Squadron sighted a Japanese carrier task force approaching Ceylon. As a report was transmitted – and received – the Catalina was shot down and survivors from the crew spent the rest of the war in captivity. On the following day, 150 Japanese aircraft attacked Colombo harbour but the Royal Navy's Far East Fleet had put to sea. Thirty-six Hurricanes of Nos 30 and 258 Squadrons and Fleet Air Arm Fulmars took off to intercept. The Mitsubishi Zero fighter outclassed them and fifteen Hurricanes and four Fulmars were shot down, but Ceylon was saved. On his release from a Japanese POW camp in August 1945, Birchall was awarded the DFC and dubbed 'The Saviour of Ceylon'.

A Catalina (captain Flt Lt D.E. Hawkins) of No. 240 Squadron conducted a reconnaissance of sea ice conditions

Wellingtons of No. 75 (NZ) Squadron. *(IWM. CH 467)*

between Jan Mayen Island and Spitsbergen. They returned to RAF Sullom Voe, Shetlands, after a flight of 24 hours. This was the first of a series of reconnaissance flights by Catalinas to the high Arctic.

See 6 June 1942.

1949 The North Atlantic Treaty was signed in Washington by twelve nations. It came into force on 24 August 1949.

1955 A mutual defence agreement between the United Kingdom, Turkey and Iraq – the Baghdad Pact – was signed. Subsequently Pakistan and Iran signed and the United States, although not a signatory, was closely associated with the Pact. With the withdrawal of Iraq during the spring of 1959, the Pact was renamed the Central Treaty Organisation (CENTO).

See 20 August 1959.

1957 A Defence White Paper presented by the Secretary of State for Defence, Duncan Sandys, included the statement 'fighter aircraft will in due course be replaced by a ground-to-air missile system'. It also foreshadowed far-reaching changes in the

RAF's strength and role with an all-regular force by 1962, reduction in certain commitments, and the accelerated replacement of aircraft by missiles. The main casualties were the squadrons of Fighter Command and the disbandment of the Royal Auxiliary Air Force squadrons.

1970 The last Dakota retired from the RAF after twenty-seven years' service. In March 1993, the type re-entered service when ZA947 joined the Battle of Britain Memorial Flight.

1993 MRAF The Lord Elworthy, former Chief of the Defence Staff and Chief of the Air Staff, died.

See 1 September 1963, 7 August 1967.

1995 The Armed Forces Minister, Mr Nicholas Soames, announced that the WE 177 free-fall nuclear weapon would be withdrawn from operational service in 1998 without replacement.

See 31 March 1998.

The final loading on a Tornado of a practice WE 177 nuclear weapon. *(AHB)*

1999 Operation Allied Force: operating from RAF Bruggen, and with VC-10 tanker support, Tornado GR1s flew their first sorties when six aircraft attacked bridges and tunnels on the main supply routes between Kosovo and Serbia.

5 APRIL

1921 The dual appointment of Secretary of State for War and Air was relinquished and Capt the Hon. F.E. Guest became the first Secretary of State for Air at the Air Ministry.

1944 Japanese forces completed the encirclement of the Kohima garrison. Ground-attack Hurricane and Vengeance aircraft provided close support and the defenders were maintained entirely by air drops from Dakotas until the garrison was relieved on 20 April. The RAF continued to provide support during the bitter fighting around Kohima, which continued until June.

1965 In response to a Soviet threat to the air corridors into Berlin, Argosy transport aircraft conducted a series of ten probing flights into and out of Berlin between 5 and 10 April. On 4 April an RAF Germany fighter squadron deployed to the Luftwaffe airfield at Celle, previously occupied by the RAF between 1945 and 1957, to escort the flights into Berlin, should that prove necessary. In the event, escorts were not required.

1982 Operation Corporate: two Nimrods of No. 42 Squadron deployed to Wideawake Airfield, Ascension Island, as the first RAF detachment to the South Atlantic. Two days later, one aircraft (captain Flt Lt J.G. Turnbull) flew the first of 111 maritime reconnaissance sorties flown by RAF Nimrods during the operation.

Bombing up Vengeances in Burma. *(AHB)*

1984 MRAF Sir Arthur Harris, Commander-in-Chief of Bomber Command from February 1942 until the end of the Second World War, died.

See 22 February 1942.

Jaguars of No. 2 Squadron and Tornados of No. 15 Squadron exercised off a stretch of autobahn used as an emergency landing strip. Aircraft parking and turn-round facilities were established in a *parkplatz* more usually used by motorists.

6 APRIL

1940 No. 10 Operational Training Unit (OTU), the first of twenty-eight bomber OTUs, was formed at RAF Abingdon equipped with the Whitley. The first fighter OTU, No. 5 (later No. 55), was formed at RAF Aston Down on 6 March 1940 and the first coastal OTU, No. 1, formed at RAF Silloth on 1 April 1940.

1941 **VC**: Fg Off Kenneth Campbell of No. 22 Squadron was the pilot of the sole aircraft to attack the German battle cruiser *Gneisenau* while docked in Brest harbour, releasing his torpedo under intense fire. The *Gneisenau* was hit but Campbell's Beaufort was shot down. (*London Gazette*, 13 March 1941, posthumous award)

The Iraqi Revolt: following a coup in Iraq by Raschid Ali, the AOC RAF Iraq (AVM H.G. Smart) asked for RAF reinforcements.

See 1 May 1941.

1956 The Venoms of No. 6 Squadron left RAF Habbaniya, marking the end of the RAF's operational deployment in Iraq.

1965 The annual Budget Speech announced the cancellation of the TSR-2 strike/reconnaissance aircraft.

Above: Wellingtons of No. 30 OTU at RAF Hixon. *(AHB. CH 18411)*
Below: A Wessex of No. 72 Squadron operating over Oman. *(AHB)*

1974 Four Wessex helicopters of No. 72 Squadron detached to RAF Salalah in Oman to assist in the construction of a new defensive line (the Hornbeam Line). The Sultan of Oman's Air Force (SOAF) tasked the operations for the detachment, which also acted as artillery spotters and forward air controllers. The detachment was withdrawn in November 1974.

7 APRIL

1945 Operation Amherst: forty-six Stirlings of No. 38 Group dropped French paratroops of 2nd and 3rd Regiments de Chasseurs Parachutistes on twenty selected dropping points in northern Holland to support the First Canadian Army in securing airfields, and road and railway bridges. Despite the poor weather, the troops were successfully dropped 'blind' from 1,500ft using the *Gee* navigation aid.

1946 Headquarters Allied Command South-East Asia (ACSEA) moved to RAF Changi. The following day, the Commander-in-Chief, ACM Sir Keith Park, formally opened the airfield (built by the Japanese) and welcomed No. 48 Squadron on its arrival from Kallang. Changi was to remain the location for the various main RAF Headquarters in Singapore and, later, the Far East until October 1971.

1951 The Shackleton entered operational service with No. 120 Squadron at RAF Kinloss.

1975 The first Jaguar arrived in RAF Germany at the start of the programme to re-equip the four Phantom squadrons at RAF Bruggen.

8 APRIL

1920 An Air Ministry Order announced the introduction of a full-dress uniform – 'home' pattern – for officers of the RAF.

A Shackleton MR1. *(G.R. Pitchfork Collection)*

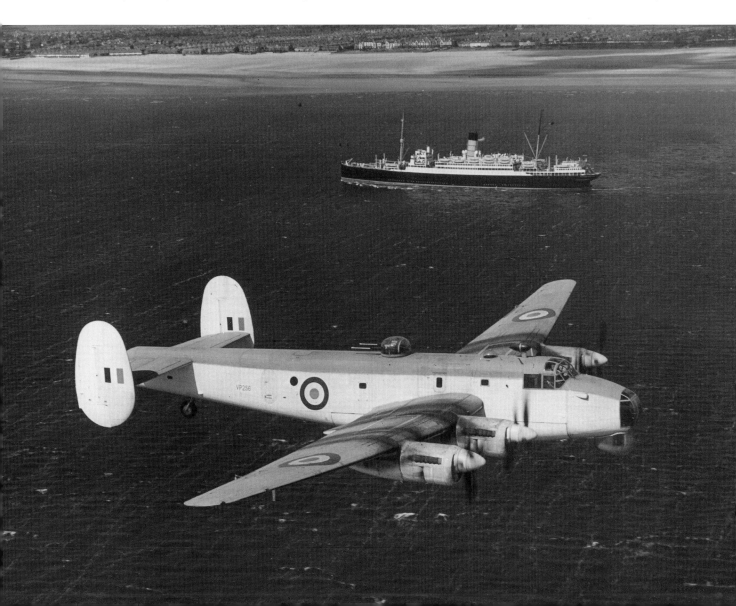

A No. 14 Squadron Jaguar arrives over RAF Bruggen.
(AHB. TN 7342)

A sword of the straight pattern with gilt hilt formed part of the uniform. Until 1926, the head dress was a similar design to the blue service dress. Initially, the provision of the uniform was optional (AMWO 332/1920).

1940 A Sunderland of No. 204 Squadron detected the German cruiser *Admiral Hipper* and escorting destroyers heading towards Trondheim in Norway. The warships were carrying part of a German force that had been assembled for the invasion of Norway, which commenced in the early hours of the following morning.

The Civilian Repair Organisation (CRO) was formed utilising civilian resources for the rapid repair of damaged RAF aircraft, returning them to the frontline without the use of RAF engineering resources. Between

1940 and 1945, the CRO repaired a total of 80,666 aircraft.

1944 Liberators and Wellingtons of No. 205 Group, operating from airfields in Italy, opened the offensive against the River Danube when forty mines were dropped. In ten days the total had risen to 177 and during May a further 354 mines were laid. On the night of 1 July 16 Liberators and 53 Wellingtons dropped a total of 192 mines. The last minelaying operation took place on the night of 4/5 October.

1991 Operation Provide Comfort: Hercules of Nos 47 and 70 Squadrons operating from Incirlik, Turkey, made the first air drop of food and aid to the Kurdish people who had fled for their lives from Iraqi troops loyal to Saddam Hussein and sought refuge on the Iraqi/Turkish border. The RAF dropped more than 450 tons of supplies before the Hercules detachment returned to Lyneham on 3 May.

9 APRIL

1941 HM King George VI approved the change of title of the Observer Corps to the Royal Observer Corps (ROC) in recognition of the Corps' service during the German blitz on British cities.

1945 A force of Lancasters attacked Kiel. The pocket battleship *Admiral Scheer* was hit and capsized. The cruiser *Admiral Hipper* was seriously damaged and scuttled, and the cruiser *Emden* was badly damaged.

Mosquitos of the Banff Wing (Sqn Ldr H.H.K. Gunnis) mounted daylight strikes in the Kattegat, sinking two U-boats (*U-804* and *U-1065*) with rockets. Coastal Command's Strike Wings continued to attack surfaced U-boats until the end of the war, destroying nine and damaging two.

1958 The two-man crew of a Canberra (Flt Lt J. de Salis and Fg Off P. Lowe), operating from RAF Hemswell, made the highest recorded emergency escape from an aircraft when they ejected at 56,000ft using a semi-automatic Martin-Baker Mk IC ejector seat. They descended in free-fall to 12,000ft.

The badge of the Royal Observer Corps.
(G.R. Pitchfork Collection)

A Mosquito of No. 143 Squadron armed with rockets.
(G.R. Pitchfork Collection)

The first Air Course assembled at Farnborough. *(R. Nesbit Collection)*

10 APRIL

1912 Unable to wait for the Central Flying School (CFS) to open, the War Office organised a preliminary military aviation course at Farnborough. Part One of the course included reconnaissance from captive balloons, free balloons and airships, theory of flight and aeroplane design, aviation engines, navigation, instruments and photography. Part Two, which commenced on 10 May, was the flying training phase, including practical work on the erection and rigging of aeroplanes, dismantling and reassembly of engines and propellers, and compass adjustment.

See 19 June 1912.

1940 The Night Interception Unit (later renamed Fighter Interception Unit) was formed with six Blenheims at RAF Tangmere to conduct technical and operational trials on air interception (AI) radar.

1941 The Women's Auxiliary Air Force became part of the Armed Forces of the Crown.

1942 The first 8,000lb bomb was dropped during a raid on Essen by a No. 76 Squadron Halifax (captain Plt Off M. Renaut).

1943 Gp Capt J.R. Whitley, the station commander of RAF Linton-on-Ouse, flew as second pilot of a Halifax of No. 76 Squadron attacking Frankfurt. The bomber was shot down and Whitley parachuted to safety. He made contact with the Belgian-led escape organisation, the Comet Line, was taken down the escape line and crossed the Pyrenees into Spain. He was awarded the DSO. He retired as an Air Marshal in 1962 and became Controller of the RAF Benevolent Fund.

1948 No. 3(F) Squadron based at RAF Wunstorf became the first squadron in BAFO to be re-equipped with jets when Vampire F1s started to replace Tempests.

Vampire F1s of No. 3(F) Squadron. *(Andrew Thomas Collection)*

1997 ACM Sir Richard Johns was appointed Chief of the Air Staff.

The Defence Helicopter Flying School was opened at RAF Shawbury. The school absorbed the flying training element of No. 2 Flying Training School and the Search and Rescue Training School at RAF Valley.

11 APRIL

1918 The RAF Marine Craft Section came into being (Lt Col G. Holmes). An AMWO announced that 192 marine craft were to be transferred to the RAF from the RNAS and RFC with a further twenty-two on loan until they could be replaced. Two Marine Acceptance Depots were formed at Hamble, near Southampton, and at Brough near Hull (AMWO 124/1918).

1940 Six Wellingtons of No. 115 Squadron, with two Blenheims of No. 254 Squadron as fighter escort, were tasked to attack Stavanger/Sola airfield. Three bombers attacked, the first RAF assault on Norway, and the first of sixteen on this airfield over the following days.

1944 Six Mosquitos of No. 613 (City of Manchester) Squadron led by Wg Cdr R.N. Bateson, with Fg Off B.J. Standish as his navigator, attacked the Dutch Central Population Registry in The Hague where the Gestapo were holding key records of Dutch families. The precision attack from very low level against just one building, with delayed-action bombs, was accurate and the records were destroyed. Bateson was awarded the DSO and Standish the DFC. Both were later decorated with the Dutch Flying Cross.

2001 RAF Nordhorn weapons range in Germany was closed (see map opposite).

Herdla Airfield at Stavanger is attacked by RAF bombers. *(R. Nesbit Collection)*

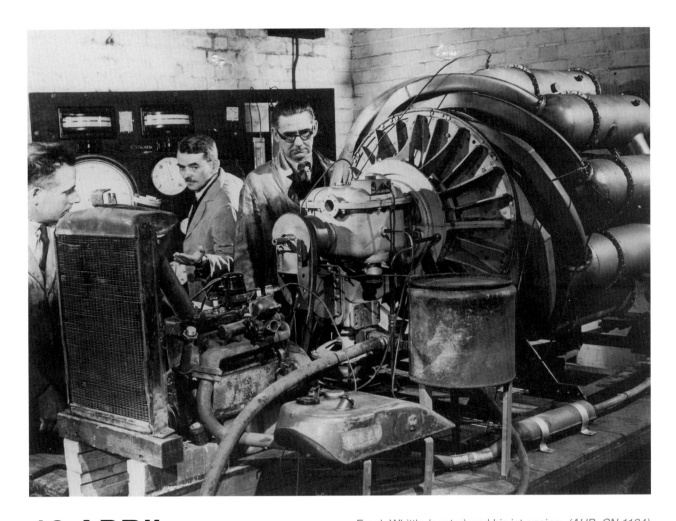

12 APRIL

Frank Whittle (centre) and his jet engine. *(AHB. CN 1124)*

1918 Following a dispute with Lord Rothermere, Maj Gen Sir Hugh Trenchard resigned from the post of Chief of the Air Staff and was succeeded by Maj Gen Sir Frederick Sykes.

Capt H.W. Woollett of No. 43 Squadron flying a Camel shot down six enemy aircraft during two patrols. He was the second pilot to achieve this feat: Capt J.L. Trollope RFC, also of No. 43 Squadron, had shot down six aircraft on 24 March 1918.

1923 Approval was given for the issue of special arm badges in gilded metal to aerial gunners and physical training instructors below the rank of Warrant Officer. The design of the badges was:
- Aerial gunner: a winged bullet.
- Physical training instructor: three arms, each wielding a club, protruding from a centre piece bearing the letters 'PTI'.

The badges were worn on the upper right uniform sleeve (AMO 204/1923).
See 21 December 1939.

1937 Frank Whittle, a serving flight lieutenant studying on a postgraduate year at Cambridge University, ground-tested his first gas-turbine engine. The engine had a single-stage centrifugal compressor coupled to a single-stage turbine.

1940 Heavy daylight losses finally convinced Bomber Command that the self-defending daylight bomber formation theory was not valid and this day marked the end of the pre-war bombing policy; this was the most important turning point in Bomber Command's war.

1967 Spain announced the introduction of a prohibited flying area around Algeciras, forcing aircraft approaching Gibraltar from the west to make a 90° right turn on short finals. Aircraft taking off to the west had to make a similar sharp left turn. On 4 May, two Hunters of No. 54 Squadron arrived to establish a long-term fighter detachment and give visual and audible reminders of the RAF's presence.

A Blenheim MkIV of No. 110 Squadron is bombed up at RAF Wattisham. *(AHB. CH 364)*

Sea mines are prepared for an operation. *(G.R. Pitchfork Collection)*

A VC10 refuels two Tornado F3s during Operation Deny Flight. *(MOD)*

1993 Operation Deny Flight: Tornados of No. 31 Squadron (Wg Cdr A.P.N. Lambert) commenced operations from IAF Gioia del Colle airbase to enforce United Nations Resolution 816, the imposition of a no-fly Zone over Bosnia-Herzegovina. TriStar tankers of No. 216 Squadron and Sentry AEW aircraft of No. 8 Squadron supported the fighters. Jaguars of No. 6 Squadron (Wg Cdr A.D. Sweetman) deployed to Gioia del Colle on 16 July to provide an offensive support capability.

See 31 October 1992.

13 APRIL

1912 A Royal Warrant constituted the Royal Flying Corps. The Corps was to include a Military Wing; a Naval Wing; a Central Flying School; a Reserve; and the Royal (formerly Army) Aircraft Factory at Farnborough. The first commander of the Military Wing was Capt F.H. Sykes.

See 13 May 1912.

1918 The Air Ministry approached the Admiralty 'to obtain the services of Chief Naval Instructor Ivor Curtis RN for the purpose of formulating and organising a scheme for the education of the whole of the Royal Air Force'.

1937 GC (ex-EGM): Plt Off Gerald Charles Neil Close attempted to rescue the crew of a crashed aircraft at RAF Miramshah, India, despite the danger of bombs and ammunition on board the aircraft. (*London Gazette*, 21 December 1937)

1940 Bomber Command mounted the first RAF minelaying operation of the Second World War. Fifteen Hampdens were despatched and fourteen laid mines off the Danish coast. One aircraft failed to return. During the war, the RAF flew 19,917 minelaying sorties and sea mines laid by RAF aircraft sank 638 vessels, at a cost of 450 aircraft lost.

1944 Nos 2771 and 2788 Squadrons, RAF Regiment, were detached to the US 5th Army to reinforce army units in the front line at Monte Cassino, Italy.

1960 The MOD announced the cancellation of the Blue Streak missile and reaffirmed that the British nuclear deterrent would rely on the V-Force and on the procurement of an air-launched ballistic missile – Skybolt.

2006 ACM Sir Glenn Torpy was appointed Chief of the Air Staff.

14 APRIL

1944 A Directive was issued placing Allied strategic bombing forces in the north-west European theatre under the control of the Supreme Commander Allied Expeditionary Force, Gen Dwight D. Eisenhower, for operations in support of the invasion of Europe (Operation Overlord). This was the official date but Bomber Command had made a modest start on the approved target list at the end of March.

1956 The RAF rundown in the Canal Zone was completed when the airfield at Abu Sueir was returned to the Egyptian government, bringing to an end seventy-four years of British military presence in Egypt.

1991 Operation Haven: Chinook helicopters from RAF Odiham and RAF Gutersloh commenced an airlift of humanitarian aid to Kurdish refugees sheltering in Turkey and Northern Iraq. The detachment was increased to twelve aircraft and they operated from a Forward Operating Base (FOB) at Silopi, close to the tri-national border with Turkey, Syria and Iraq. The detachment returned home in early July.

15 APRIL

1940 The Beaufort flew its first operational sortie when nine aircraft of No. 22 Squadron laid mines in the Schillig Roads, the first mining sortie by aircraft of Coastal Command.

1941 Coastal Command came under the operational control of the Admiralty.

1942 The USAAF VIIIth Air Force bomber headquarters was established alongside HQ Bomber Command at RAF High Wycombe.

A Coastal Command Sunderland III of No. 201 squadron on patrol over the Atlantic. *(AHB. CH 15302)*

Men of the RAF Regiment guard the entrance to the Headquarters Middle East at RAF Ismailia. *(AHB)*

Groundcrew of No. 217 Squadron take a tea break before continuing to service their Beauforts. *(R. Nesbit Collection)*

Chambley marshalling yards. *(R. Nesbit Collection)*

1944   The Overall Air Plan in the build-up to Operation Overlord was issued outlining the principal air tasks:

- To attain and maintain an air situation whereby the German Air Force is rendered incapable of effective interference with Allied operations.
- To provide continuous air reconnaissance of the enemy's dispositions and movements.
- To disrupt enemy communications and channels of supply by air attack.
- To support the landing and subsequent advance of the Allied armies.
- To deliver offensive strikes against enemy naval forces.
- To provide airlift for airborne forces.

Following the success of the trial raid against the Trappes railway centre on the night of 6/7 March 1944, the Chiefs of Staff approved the 'Transportation Plan', the attack by Bomber Command and the USAAF against seventy-five railway targets in Belgium and northern France.

See 21 and 25 May 1944.

Ninety-two Wellingtons of No. 205 Group made the RAF's first bombing attack against a Romanian objective when they attacked the marshalling yards and rail facilities at Turnu Severin.

1958   The Victor – the RAF's third V-bomber – entered service with No. 10 Squadron at RAF Cottesmore.

16 APRIL

1942   In recognition of the gallantry of its citizens and defenders, under incessant air attack and in the face of serious food shortages, the island of Malta was awarded the George Cross.

Victor Mk 1s of No. 10 Squadron at RAF Cottesmore.
(MOD)

1945 Sixteen Lancasters of No. 617 Squadron dropped 12,000lb Tallboy bombs to sink the German pocket battleship *Lutzow* at Swinemunde.

1959 The first launching of a Thor IRMB by an RAF crew under training (drawn from No. 98 Squadron) took place at Vandenberg AFB in the USA.

1968 MRAF Sir John Salmond, former Chief of the Air Staff, died.
See 1 January 1930.

17 APRIL

1918 The Air Council decided that medical officers employed exclusively with RAF units would take instructions from the Medical Department of the RAF instead of the Army Medical Directorate (AMWO 75/18). An RAF Women's Medical Service

MRAF Sir John Salmond (1881–1968). *(AHB)*

A Beaufort over the RAF airfield at Luqa, Malta. (*R. Nesbit Collection*)

THE SIEGE OF MALTA

The small island of Malta, half the size of the Isle of Man, lies at the 'crossroads' of the Mediterranean Sea just 60 miles south of the island of Sicily astride the main supply lines from Italy to North Africa and the west–east route from Gibraltar to the Suez Canal in Egypt. The long and dramatic battle for Malta began on 10 June 1940, the day Italy declared war on the Allies, with the Axis Powers determined to subdue the island in order to control the Mediterranean. Thus the island was of great strategic importance and crucial to both the Allies and the Axis Powers – not only in the Mediterranean, but also in North Africa and the Middle East.

The struggle for possession of the island lasted two and a half years, during which time 14,000 tons of bombs were dropped on the defiant population – in April 1942, Malta suffered a greater tonnage of bombs than Britain did in any one month during the Battle of Britain. Meagre RAF resources were faced with overwhelming odds but the enemy was finally deterred from invading by a handful of fighters and the resolute determination and courage of the Maltese people.

The war that saved Malta was fought in the air and on and under the sea. In the early stages, 346 Hurricanes, and later 382 Spitfires, were flown off aircraft carriers in the western Mediterranean to reinforce the depleted RAF forces on the island. Subsequently, the island served as the base for a concentrated assault by RAF and Fleet Air Arm aircraft and Royal Navy submarines against Axis supply lines from Italy to North Africa. These attacks played an important part in hampering Rommel's forces and greatly assisted the Allies' drive for victory in North Africa. The cost was high, for over 7,000 civilians and servicemen died in the defence of the island.

was inaugurated in September to take care of the WRAF.

See 27 August 1918, 13 July 1920.

1919 The apprentice badge or 'wheel' was approved. The four-bladed propeller within a circlet, manufactured in brass, was worn on the sleeve of the left arm to distinguish apprentices from adult airmen 'so as to check smoking and the forgathering of boys with men'.

1941 A 'Starfish' decoy fire site at Hayling Island collected 170 high-explosive bombs, 32 parachute mines and 5,000 incendiary bombs intended for Portsmouth.

1942 Twelve Lancasters of Nos 44 and 97 Squadrons were despatched on a daylight low-level raid on the MAN submarine diesel engine works at Augsburg in southern Bavaria. Although a brilliant feat of arms, seven aircraft were shot down.

VC: Sqn Ldr John Dering Nettleton, commanding officer of No. 44 Squadron, leader of the twelve Lancasters on the daylight low-level raid on the MAN submarine diesel engine works at Augsburg. (*London Gazette*, 28 April 1942)

See 12 July 1943.

1943 The final phase of the air campaign in Tunisia commenced.

1952 Operation Jiu Jitsu: three USAF RB-45C aircraft in RAF markings, flown by crews of a RAF Special Duties Flight (Sqn Ldr J. Crampton), took off from RAF Sculthorpe at night to carry out three reconnaissance flights. After in-flight refuelling the aircraft flew independent routes over northern, central and southern Russia before returning to Sculthorpe after a ten-hour flight. The nine aircrew involved were awarded the AFC or AFM.

See 28 April 1954.

1991 A Shackleton AEW Mk 2 of No. 8 Squadron made the type's final flight in RAF service bringing to a close forty years of service by the Shackleton. The Squadron officially handed over AEW duties to the E-3A Sentry unit at RAF Waddington with a transfer of command on 1 July.

18 APRIL

1942 The North Coates Beaufighter Wing (Wg Cdr H.N.G. Wheeler) carried out the first successful operation by Coastal Command's Strike Wings when it attacked a convoy off the Dutch islands, sinking a large merchant vessel and severely damaging escort ships. This was the prelude to many successful attacks over the next three years.

1943 Spitfires and USAAF fighters intercepted about eighty escorted Junkers Ju52 transport aircraft off Cap Bon, Tunisia. Fifty-nine transports were shot down or forced to crash-land on the beach and this followed the massacre of twenty-four Ju52s on 10 April. On 22 April the Germans committed the giant six-engine Messerschmitt Me 323 transports in a last desperate effort to re-supply their beleaguered troops in Tunisia. Twenty-one transports were shot down in addition to ten fighter escorts. Allied claims for April totalled 432 transports for the loss of thirty-five fighters.

Spitfires on a forward airfield in Tunisia.
(R. Nesbit Collection)

117

Beaufighters of the Dallachy Strike Wing attack a merchant vessel off Norway. *(AHB)*

In November 1942 RAF Coastal Command began to form special Strike Wings to attack heavily defended, and seemingly invulnerable, convoys that brought Germany's vital supplies of iron ore from Scandinavia down the coast of Europe to Holland, and thence to Germany, to feed its war machine. The outcome was a series of air-sea battles fought at close quarters, and with great ferocity, until the last days of the war.

The Wings employed up to thirty-six attacking aircraft, often escorted by fighter wings, with a large element used in the anti-flak role armed with cannons and rockets, with the main attack delivered by torpedo-carrying aircraft. The Germans provided a formidable defence of fighters, intense flak, parachute mines and balloons against the Beaufighter and Mosquito Strike Wings.

Coastal Command-controlled aircraft sank 366 vessels (512,330 tons) and damaged a further 134 vessels, but casualties were some of the highest of all the RAF's operations. Beaufort and Beaufighter Strike Wings also operated in the Mediterranean and Aegean Seas against Axis supply ships.

One of the outstanding Strike Wing leaders was Wg Cdr 'Bill' Sise DSO & Bar, DFC & Bar (left) here with his navigator, Fg Off Evans. *(G.R. Pitchfork Collection)*

1982 Operation Corporate: Victor tankers of Nos 55 and 57 Squadrons deployed to Ascension Island.

19 APRIL

1919 No. 1 School of Navigation and Bomb Dropping based at RAF Andover commenced a series of training flights around the British Isles. Two Handley Page 0/400s, piloted by Capts Stewert and Snook and each with a crew of seven, flew around the coast anti-clockwise refuelling at Waddington and Turnhouse on the first day. Routing via Inverness, they reached Aldergrove during the evening of the second day and the following day flew over Dublin to reach Tenby. On 22 April they flew home routing over Plymouth and Portsmouth. Later in the month, a similar aircraft piloted by Maj K.R. Park (later ACM Sir Keith Park) and Capt Stewert, and which bore the legend LAST DAYS, completed a very similar route of 1,600 miles in 30 hours, averaging 66mph and 450 miles each day.

Victor tankers of the Marham Wing positioned at Ascension Island. *(AHB)*

1927 Bombing and air firing ranges opened at RAF Practice Camps North Coates Fitties, Sutton Bridge and Weston Zoyland.

1936 An outbreak of disorder in Jaffa proved to be the opening of a three-year period of severe disturbances and conflict in Palestine.

A Hardy of No. 6 Squadron over Haifa. *(AHB. H 606)*

119

Nos 6, 14 and 33 Squadrons provided extensive army co-operation and reconnaissance sorties in support of ground forces. Other RAF squadrons provided regular reinforcement detachments.

1948   An Anglo-French military air transport agreement was signed, regularising flights by military aircraft of the United Kingdom and France over both countries and providing for servicing such aircraft at RAF and French Air Force bases.

20 APRIL

1924   A Fairey IIID of HMS *Pegasus* (Flt Lt G.E. Livock) made the first flight by an RAF aircraft from Singapore from the site that became RAF Seletar.

1938   In an effort to strengthen the RAF as rapidly as possible, Air Cdre A.T. Harris visited the USA to examine American aircraft designs with a view to possible procurement. In June orders were placed for 200 Lockheed Hudsons and 200 North American Harvard trainers.
See 22 June 1938.

1951   The Ministry of Supply, on behalf of the RAF, placed an order for twenty-four Valiants, the RAF's first V-bomber.

1982   Operation Corporate: a Victor (captain Sqn Ldr J.G. Elliott) flew the first maritime radar reconnaissance sortie from Ascension towards South Georgia with air-to-air refuelling support, and was airborne for 14 hours 45 minutes.

21 APRIL

1918   Capt Manfred Baron von Richthofen, the 'Red Baron' and the most successful fighter pilot in the First World War, was shot down and killed over the Somme. He landed behind British lines and was buried with full military honours at Bertrangles. Capt A.R. Brown of No. 209 Squadron attacked his aircraft at low level and the two flew through heavy ground fire from an

Australian battery. Who finally shot down von Richthofen has since been the source of long and endless debate.

1943   The RAF bomb disposal (BD) organisation was formally established. It consisted of a Bomb Disposal Wing HQ (Wg Cdr H. Dinwoodie) formed at Eastchurch, with six BD Squadrons and a total of twenty-nine BD Flights. By VE Day, RAF bomb disposal units had dealt with some 84,000 weapons in the UK and 92,000 in mainland Europe.
See 27 August 1940.

1949   A Sunderland of No. 88 Squadron (captain Flt Lt K.H.F. Letford) landed on the River Yangtze with emergency aid for HMS *Amethyst*, which had been shelled by Chinese Communist artillery batteries between Shanghai and Chinkiang, suffering extensive damage and sustaining numerous casualties. An RAF Medical Officer (Flt Lt M.E. Fearnley) and some aid were transferred to *Amethyst* but the Sunderland came under fire and had to make an emergency take-off. Further relief flights were made over the next few days. *Amethyst* eventually broke out and ran the gauntlet of shore batteries and rejoined the Fleet on 31 July. Letford was subsequently awarded a Bar to his DFC, Fearnley received the DSC and the Sunderland crews received the Naval General Service Medal.

2000   ACM Sir Peter Squire was appointed Chief of the Air Staff.

22 APRIL

1923   The RAF Central Band was chosen to be the first military band ever to make a radio broadcast, which was transmitted from BBC Marconi House.

1941   Recommendations by British and American staffs to exchange Military Missions were accepted by the respective governments. The RAF Delegation in Washington was established on 1 June 1941 with AM A.T. Harris as the first Head of the Delegation.

1944   The first of two Yugoslav squadrons, No. 352, was formed within the RAF. Equipped

Above: Flt Sgt D. Simons defusing a booby trap. He is wearing the distinctive 'Bomb Disposal' badge. *(IWM. CL 748)*

Below: The RAF Central Band, October 1920. *(AHB. H 2343)*

121

initially with Hurricanes, it formed at Benina before moving to Italy.

1971 MRAF The Lord Portal of Hungerford, Chief of the Air Staff from October 1940 until the end of the Second World War, died.
See 25 October 1940.

23 APRIL

1931 AVM F. Vesey-Holt, the AOC Fighting Area, Air Defence of Great Britain, was killed in a Moth of No. 24 Squadron following a mid-air collision with an escorting No. 43 Squadron Siskin fighter over RAF Tangmere.

1943 Operation Beggar: in preparation for Operation Husky, the invasion of Sicily, No. 295 Squadron, equipped with Halifax aircraft, was ordered to ferry thirty-six Horsa gliders from RAF Portreath in Cornwall to Tunisia via Sale in Morocco. By the end of June thirty had left and twenty-seven arrived in North Africa after a 9 hours 20 minutes flight, which had routed across the Bay of Biscay. The onward stages over 1,000 miles of mountainous terrain in poor weather were difficult and only nineteen reached Kairouan in Tunisia.
See 9 July 1943.

1946 Twenty Spitfires of Nos 11 and 17 Squadrons arrived aboard HMS *Vengeance* at Iwakuni, Japan, for service with the British Commonwealth Air Forces of Occupation (BCAIR) (AVM C.A. Bouchier). They deployed to Miho Airfield on 6 May and carried out the first surveillance flight on the 15th.
See 15 November 1947.

24 APRIL

1929 Sqn Ldr A.G. Jones-Williams and Flt Lt N.H. Jenkins flying a Fairey Long Range Monoplane from RAF Cranwell to Karachi – a distance of 4,130 miles – completed the first non-stop flight from the United Kingdom to India in 50 hours 48 minutes. They landed with 8 gallons of petrol left.

Six months later, flying the same aircraft, they attempted to fly non-stop from Cranwell to Capetown but were killed when their aircraft crashed south of Tunis.
See 6 February 1933.

1940 Eighteen Gladiators of No. 263 Squadron (Sqn Ldr J.W. Donaldson) arrived off Norway on HMS *Glorious* and flew to the ice-bound Lake Lesjaskog to support British ground forces. Ten were lost in a German bombing attack the following day and the remainder withdrew to Aandalsnes.
See 21 May 1940.

The Air Council decided to establish the Technical Branch, both in the regular and non-regular air forces, for officers employed on the following specialist duties: engineering, signals and armament. By the end of the war, the Branch comprised over 9,000 officers (AMO A.228/1940).

1941 The evacuation of Greece was completed with the withdrawal of the last seven Hurricanes to Crete. The RAF lost almost 200 aircraft in the abortive Greek campaign.

The Iraqi Revolt: 400 men of the King's Own Royal Regiment were flown in Valentias of No. 31 Squadron and requisitioned Douglas DC-2s from RAF Shaibah to RAF Habbaniya to reinforce the armoured cars of No. 1 RAF Armoured Car Company in the ground defence role.

1942 At a meeting of the Air Council, the new aircrew categories of air bomber and navigator were introduced, the latter to replace the observer.
See 17 September 1942.

1944 The air campaign against road and rail communications in Burma reached a climax. Once the Bangkok to Rangoon railway – the infamous Railway of Death – had been completed, it became the chief target for the Liberator force; 2,700 tons of bombs were dropped against the enemy's chief supply line, the greatest weight of bombs against any target in Burma.

1945 Meteors of No. 616 Squadron carried out ground-attack sorties against Nordholz

Airfield, the first operation on the Continent by RAF jet aircaft.

A WAAF flight mechanic, LACW Margaret Horton, had an involuntary flight clinging on to a Spitfire. In windy conditions she was sitting on the tailplane to prevent the aircraft tipping onto its nose as it taxied to the runway at RAF Hibaldstow. Having reached the runway, the aircraft should have paused for the mechanic to drop off. This time the pilot did not pause. The Spitfire climbed to 800ft when the strange shape of the tailplane was noticed from the ground. The emergency services were alerted and the pilot instructed to land without being told the reason. He landed safely and LACW Horton was uninjured.

1953 No. 1 Squadron became the first to receive its Squadron Standard. AVM Sir Charles Longcroft, the Squadron's second commanding officer, presented the Standard at a ceremony at RAF Tangmere when it was 'consecrated'. It was later considered more appropriate that the service of consecration should be changed

Above: Bombs arrive at a Liberator based at Digri, India.
(R. Nesbit Collection)
Below: An all-white Meteor of No. 616 Squadron at
Melsbroek, Brussels. *(AHB)*

Presentation of the Squadron Standard to No. 1(F) Squadron at RAF Tangmere. *(AHB. PRB 6197)*

to one of 'dedication'. This change came into force on 9 October 1953 when No. 7 Squadron was presented with its Standard.
See 1 April 1943.

25 APRIL

1917 **VC**: Capt Albert Ball of No. 56 Squadron RFC, in recognition of his 'most conspicuous and consistent bravery' in the skies over France in an SE5. Twenty-year-old Ball, credited with at least forty-four destroyed, out of control and forced down, was awarded three DSOs and an MC before he failed to return on 7 May 1917. He was buried with full military honours by the Germans. (*London Gazette*, 8 June 1917, posthumous award)

1932 Aircraft of Nos 30, 55 and 70 Squadrons were engaged against a revolt in north-east

Iraq instigated by Sheikh Ahmad of Barzan. Leaflet drops warning villagers of forthcoming attacks presaged RAF raids. Verbal warnings were also broadcast in Kurdish dialect using loudspeakers fitted to Victoria transport aircraft. Sheikh Ahmad surrendered on 21 June.

1941 The Defence (Women's Forces) Regulations of this date declared that all personnel enrolled in the Women's Auxiliary Air Force (WAAF) were members of the Armed Forces of the Crown. The Air Council was empowered to apply the Air Force Act to the WAAF; the Air Council issued instructions on 12 June 1941. Nursing staff in the PMRAFNS were granted emergency commissions and wore officers' rank but were addressed by their professional titles of Matron, Sister, etc.

The first Norwegian squadron, No. 330, was formed within the RAF. It operated from Iceland in the anti-submarine role until January 1943 when it moved to RAF Oban.

1945 Hitler's 'Eagle's Nest' chalet and SS barracks at Berchtesgaden were attacked by 359 Lancasters and 16 Mosquitos.

Fourteen Lancasters carried out the final minelaying operation of the war when they laid mines in Oslo Fjord.

Operation Exodus: the pool of released POWs at Brussels had become excessive and SHAEF requested the assistance of Bomber Command for their evacuation to England. Repatriations reached a peak load of 36,204 on 11 May.
    See 3 April 1945.

The Ministry of Civil Aviation was formed and took over the Civil Aviation Division of the Air Ministry.

1967 The Hercules entered service at RAF Colerne. The first squadron, No. 36, began re-equipping with the Hercules at RAF Lyneham in July 1967.

26 APRIL

1915 **VC**: 2/Lt William Barnard Rhodes-Moorhouse of No. 2 Squadron flying a BE2 on a low-level bombing sortie to Courtrai. Despite being mortally wounded he continued the

Above: Wapiti IIs of No. 55 Squadron and Rolls-Royce armoured cars of an RAF Armoured Car Company. *(C. Morris Collection)*
Below: A wartime poster: 'Join the WAAF'. *(IWM. MH 13647)*

125

Stirlings prepare to repatriate Allied prisoners of war from a Belgian airfield. *(IWM)*

A Belvedere of No. 72 Squadron lowers the flèche onto the roof of Coventry Cathedral. *(AHB)*

attack and managed to return to his airfield. He died of his injuries the next day. This was the first **VC** awarded to an airman. (*London Gazette*, 22 May 1915, posthumous award)

1944 **VC**: Sgt Norman Cyril Jackson, a flight engineer on No. 106 Squadron, climbed onto the wing of his Lancaster in order to extinguish a fire during a bombing operation to Schweinfurt. He subsequently parachuted to the ground to become a POW. (*London Gazette*, 26 October 1945)

1945 The Meteorological Air Observer flying badge was introduced. It was the same design as the air gunner badge with 'M' in the laurel. It ceased to be awarded in 1951 (AMO A.409/1945).

1960 The sixtieth, and last, Thor IRBM for the RAF was delivered to RAF North Luffenham.

1962 A Belvedere helicopter of No. 72 Squadron (Sqn Ldr J.R. Dowling) placed the 80ft flèche and its surmounting sculpture on the roof of the newly reconstructed Coventry Cathedral.

1994 WO N.C. Jackson **VC** died.
See 26 April 1944.

27 APRIL

1939 A new policy was introduced for RAF aircraft markings with roundels changed to blue and red only on camouflaged surfaces of operational aircraft. Squadron identification was to be by code letters (AMO A.154/39).

1967 A Rapier surface-to-air missile destroyed a Meteor drone on its final trial.

28 APRIL

1941 The US War Department confirmed that final approval had been given for the establishment of six British Flying Training Schools (BFTS) in the USA. The schools were under RAF control but were fully financed and operated under the terms of the Lend-Lease Act. Nearly 7,000 RAF pilots graduated under the scheme. Apart from the BFTS operation, two other schemes

Above: The sixtieth and final Thor missile is unloaded from a USAF C-124 Globemaster at RAF North Luffenham. *(AHB. PRB 18563)*

Below: A group of RAF aircrew cadets trained under the Arnold Scheme at Maxwell AFB, Alabama, received USAAF pilot wings on graduation. On arrival in Canada a few days later they exchanged the wings for the RAF flying badge and received their sergeants' chevrons. *(D. Ellis)*

were implemented, the Towers Scheme operated by the US Navy and the Arnold Scheme operated within the South-east Army Air Corps Training Centre, with HQ at Maxwell Field, Montgomery, Alabama.

1943 A Dakota of No. 31 Squadron (captain Fg Off M. Vlasto) landed on a rudimentary strip hacked in a jungle clearing behind Japanese lines east of the River Chindwin to evacuate seventeen wounded and sick soldiers of a Chindit column. Vlasto was awarded an immediate DFC for 'his outstanding piece of flying'.

1954 Operation Jiu Jitsu: the RAF Special Duties Flight flew the second of two reconnaissance sorties over Russia from RAF Sculthorpe. Three RB-45C aircraft in RAF markings flew three routes; the longest, flown by the Flight's commanding officer Sqn Ldr J. Crampton, involved flying 1,000 miles over southern Russia to cover thirty targets.
See 17 April 1952.

Operation Manna: food is loaded onto a Lancaster. *(IWM. CL 2489)*

2006 ACM Sir Jock Stirrup was appointed as Chief of the Defence Staff.

29 APRIL

1929 Lady Maude Hoare (the wife of the then Secretary of State for Air, Sir Samuel Hoare) laid the foundation stone of College Hall, Cranwell.

1940 The Empire Air Training Scheme commenced in Canada, Australia and New Zealand.
See 19 May 1942, 31 March 1945.

1945 Operation Manna: the beginning of food-dropping operations to the starving Dutch population by 250 RAF bombers; the Operation continued until 8 May. Thirty-three squadrons from Nos 1, 3 and 8 Groups Bomber Command flew approximately 3,150 sorties and delivered 6,685 tons of food. The USAAF delivered a further 3,700 tons in 5,343 sorties (Operation Chowhound).

1964 Operation Flamingo: Radforce was established to end the activities of

dissidents in the Radfan region of the Aden Protectorate and to stop the spread of revolt and hold the Dhala road open. Hunters of the Khormaksar Wing played a key role and in May and June they flew 642 sorties and fired 2,508 rockets and 183,900 rounds of 30mm cannon. Shackletons of No. 37 Squadron conducted night attacks on dissident positions and Beverleys of No. 84 Squadron and Belvedere helicopters of No. 26 Squadron provided airlift and tactical support. The main campaign was over by the end of June but sporadic action continued until November.

See 18 November 1964.

1968 Bomber Command was stood down at a parade at RAF Scampton (Gp Capt D.J. Furner), in the presence of the Secretary of State for Defence (Denis Healey). The AOC-in-C Bomber Command (ACM Sir Wallace Kyle) took the salute while fourteen Squadron Standards were marched past as the AOC-in-C's pennant was lowered and a Lancaster flew past.

CEREMONY TO MARK THE STANDDOWN OF BOMBER COMMAND ROYAL AIR FORCE SCAMPTON 29th APRIL 1968

1936 – 1968

Above: The programme to mark the stand-down of Bomber Command. *(ACA Archives)*
Below: A Hunter FR10 of No. 8 Squadron overflies a village in Aden. *(R. Deacon)*

30 APRIL

1936 Changes were announced to the officers' service dress uniforms. Breeches, field boots and puttees were abolished and a new field service cap and blue shirts were introduced (AMO A.93/1936).

1941 The Iraqi Revolt: following the further deterioration of relations between Britain and Raschid Ali's government, Iraqi forces totalling 9,000 troops and 28 pieces of artillery laid siege to RAF Habbaniya from positions overlooking the station. Habbaniya contained only training units, including No. 4 Flying Training School with a large complement of elderly Audax and Gordon biplane trainers, and Oxford twin-engine trainers. Seventy training aircraft were rapidly adapted to carry light bombs, and six Gladiators arrived from Egypt to supplement the three Gladiator trainers on the station. These aircraft were formed into four ad hoc 'bombing' squadrons and a fighter flight.

1942 During April the blitz on Malta reached its height. The Luftwaffe flew a total of 9,599 sorties against Malta, dropping 6,500 tons of bombs. Forty-four RAF aircraft were destroyed on the ground, eighty-two were damaged and a further twenty fighters destroyed in combat over the island. The Luftwaffe lost forty-five aircraft.

1945 The Institute of Aviation Medicine was opened at RAE Farnborough by HRH The Princess Royal.

1947 Sqn Ldrs H.B. Martin and E.B. Sismore, flying a Mosquito PR 34, established a point-to-point record between London and Cape Town in a time of 21 hours 31 minutes 30 seconds for the 6,011 miles. The aircraft made two refuelling stops at El Adem and Kisumu.

1968 Bomber Command and Fighter Command were merged to form RAF Strike Command (ACM Sir Wallace Kyle).
See 1 April 2007.

The Central Trials and Tactics Organisation (CTTO) (Air Cdre D.G. Evans) was established at RAF High Wycombe. It was absorbed into the Air Warfare Centre on 1 October 1993.

1986 RAF Stanley was closed down following the departure to RAF Mount Pleasant of the last RAF units. By this date the new airfield at Mount Pleasant was protected by long-range radar and Rapier SAM units of the RAF Regiment.

1988 After almost thirty years, the last Lightnings were retired from RAF service; the last units to use the type were Nos 5 and 11 Squadrons at RAF Binbrook.

A Lightning F.6 of No. 23 Squadron intercepts a Bear of the Soviet Naval Air Force. *(AHB)*

1 MAY

1918 The RAF flying badge (pilot badge from 1947), which was similar in design to the RFC pattern, was introduced. The RFC observer badge was continued for all non-pilot aircrew, including ex-RNAS balloonists, observers, gun-layers and wireless operators. The latter ceased to be issued after the end of 1918 (AMO 162/1918).
  See 21 October 1937.

1919 The Warrant Officers' and Other Ranks' metal cap badges were introduced and the same basic designs remain in use today (AMWO 545/19).

1925 The Mahsud tribesmen of South Waziristan sought peace, ending 'Pink's War'. Order had been restored at the cost of one aircraft and its crew. This was the first time in India that the RAF had been used independently of the Army. The 46 officers and 214 non-commissioned airmen received the clasp 'Waziristan 1925' to the India General Service Medal, 1908, the rarest for any Indian operational campaign and the only clasp awarded exclusively to the RAF.
  See 9 March 1925.

1941 The Iraqi Revolt: AVM H.G. Smart was instructed to restore the British position in Iraq and therefore decided to attack the besieging Iraqi forces around Habbaniya.

  Malta-based Blenheims of No. 21 Squadron made their first attacks against enemy shipping supplying Axis forces in North Africa.

1942 The airfield at Gibraltar was renamed RAF North Front.

1943 A Beaufighter crew of No. 600 Squadron (Flt Sgt A.B. Downing and Sgt J. Lyons), on attachment to No. 153 Squadron, were on a pre-dawn patrol south of Sardinia when they encountered a force of Junkers Ju52 transport aircraft laden with troop reinforcements for Tunisia. In the space of ten minutes they shot five down. Both were awarded the DFM.

1946 RAF Reserve Command formed (AVM Sir Alan Lees). The Command was primarily concerned with the maintenance and training of reserve organisations.

  The King's Flight was re-formed at RAF Benson with Air Cdre E.H. Fielden appointed as Captain.

  The first edition of *Air Clues*, the successor to *Tee Emm*, was published.
  See 1 April 1998.

1947 Four Royal Auxiliary Air Force Regiment squadrons formed in the Light Anti-Aircraft

The Indian General Service Medal, with the rare clasp of 'Waziristan 1925' for operations in 'Pink's War', and awarded only to members of the RAF. *(G.R. Pitchfork Collection)*

The first edition of *Air Clues. (RAFM)*

Vulcan XM 607 returns to Ascension Island after its long-range bombing attack against Stanley Airfield. *(AHB)*

(LAA) role. Eight further squadrons were formed by the end of the year with a final squadron formed in June 1949.

See 10 March 1957.

1951   The THUM (Thermometer and Humidity) Flight operated by Messrs Shorts and Harland was formed at RAF Hooton Park, Cheshire, equipped with Spitfire XIV aircraft. A Mosquito completed the Flight's final sortie from RAF Woodvale on 1 May 1959.

1961   Fighter Command was assigned to the NATO (SACEUR) air-defence system. This included fighter squadrons, air-defence missile squadrons and the control and reporting system. AOC-in-C, Fighter Command (AM Sir Hector McGregor) assumed the additional title of Commander, UK Air Defence Region (UKADR).

1966   The United Kingdom Mobile Air Movements Squadron (UK MAMS) was granted squadron status when it became an independent unit under the operational control of HQ Air Support Command. Based at RAF Abingdon, its existence had begun in July 1958.

1982 Operation Corporate: British offensive air operations to recover the Falkland Islands commenced with Operation Black Buck I. A Vulcan of the Waddington Wing (captain Flt Lt W.F.M. Withers) dropped twenty-one 1,000lb bombs on Stanley Airfield with one bomb cutting the runway. The Vulcan was supported by sixteen Victor tankers and was airborne for almost sixteen hours, having covered 7,860 miles, the longest bombing

Above: A Viking of the Queen's Flight. *(AHB. PRB 2990)*

Below: The cratered runway at Stanley after the Vulcan attack. *(J. Falconer Collection)*

mission ever carried out by the RAF and the longest by any air force at that time. Withers was awarded the DFC. In addition to the damage to the runway at Stanley, the impact of the raid was wide-ranging and the

133

Argentinians were reluctant to base their high-performance aircraft at Stanley. The raid demonstrated that the RAF had the capability to strike from very long range and targets on the Argentine mainland were vulnerable. Argentinian fighters were redeployed from the combat area in the south of the country to defend Buenos Aires, although there was never a British plan to attack the capital.

2 MAY

1940   The Night Interception Committee decided to fit 100 Blenheim fighters with AI equipment with the highest priority.

1941   The Iraqi Revolt: at 0445hr, ten Wellingtons of No. 70 Squadron flying from Shaibah, Basra, attacked the Iraqi

positions. Soon afterwards Audaxes, Gordons and Oxfords from No. 4 FTS also attacked. The Iraqis responded by heavy shelling of the station and adjacent airfield. Aircraft were forced to take off under observed shellfire and make for an improvised landing ground on the station golf course. A total of 193 sorties were flown during the day, for the loss of two aircraft in the air and one on the ground. Iraqi shelling became noticeably reduced.

1945   Bomber Command mounted its last raid on Germany when a force of 126 Mosquitos attacked Kiel. Two RCM Halifax aircraft supporting the raid were lost. They were the last Bomber Command aircraft to be lost in the war. There were only three survivors.

Wg Cdr E.J.B. Nicolson **VC**, DFC was killed in action when the Liberator he was flying

---

BOMBER COMMAND

From the start of the Second World War on 3 September 1939, Bomber Command operated on 71.4 per cent of all nights and on 52.5 per cent of all days. A total of 8,953 aircraft were lost and of approximately 120,000 aircrew who served in the squadrons and training units, 55,500 were lost on operations and in accidents with a further 18,700 wounded, injured or made POWs. Of those killed, 38,462 were British, 9,919 Canadian, 5,720 from Australia and New Zealand, 929 Polish and 534 others from other Allies including from elsewhere in the Commonwealth.

Unlike those who fought in Fighter Command during the Battle of Britain, and the men of the 1st and 8th Armies in the Desert campaigns, the men of Bomber Command received no official recognition or emblem to mount on their war medals, despite having fought from the first to the last day of the European war.

A tired bomber crew are debriefed after a raid over Germany. *(ACA Archives)*

Allied prisoners of war flood out of Rangoon Jail after the Japanese had left, and are photographed by Wg Cdr A.E. Saunders from his Mosquito. *(AHB. C 5303)*

in as an observer on a bombing operation crashed in the Bay of Bengal on the way to the target.

See 16 August 1940.

Wg Cdr A.E. Saunders, OC No. 110 Squadron, landed his Mosquito at a deserted Mingaladon Airfield. He and his navigator then proceeded to Rangoon to be the first to enter the city. He went to the jail to be met by the Senior British Officer (Wg Cdr L.V. Hudson RAAF), who was dressed only in a loincloth, and 1,400 POWs who immediately set about clearing the debris on the airfield to allow transport aircraft to land.

1955 At a ceremony attended by HM King Feisal of Iraq, command of the RAF stations at

Habbaniya, Basra and Shaibah was handed over to the Royal Iraqi Air Force. The RAF continued to use the airfields as staging posts supported by RAF Support Units until the final unit withdrew from Basra on 8 June 1959.

The RAF Levies (Iraq) were disbanded after thirty-two years under the control of the RAF.

1982 Operation Corporate: the first three Harrier GR3s of No. 1 Squadron flew directly from UK to Ascension in 9 hours 15 minutes. Others followed and on 6 May, six aircraft sailed south on the *Atlantic Conveyor*.

3 MAY

1942 Operation Fritham: a Catalina of No. 210 Squadron (captain Flt Lt D.E. Healy) carried out the first of a series of top-secret reconnaissance flights to Spitsbergen with a view to establishing a flying-boat base to provide support to the Russian convoys. This proved impractical and Russian facilities near Archangel were made available.
See 12 September 1942.

1943 Twelve Venturas of No. 487 (RNZAF) Squadron carried out a daylight raid on an Amsterdam power station. One aircraft turned back and the remainder were shot down.

VC: Sqn Ldr Leonard Henry Trent RNZAF, a flight commander on No. 487 (RNZAF) Squadron, was the leader of the raid against the Amsterdam power station. Despite the loss of all his aircraft, he pressed on to bomb the target before he too was shot down. On the night of the 'Great Escape' on 24 March 1944, a sentry discovered the tunnel as Trent was emerging and he was immediately captured. (*London Gazette*, 1 March 1946)
See 24 March 1944.

1944 During preparations for the Normandy invasion, 346 Lancasters and 14 Mosquitos attacked the German military camp near the French village of Mailly-le-Camp.

Communications difficulties led to a delay in the main bomber force attack during which German night-fighters attacked the bombers. Forty-two Lancasters – some 11.6 per cent of the force – were shot down. The target suffered heavy damage.

After multiple attacks, Wellingtons of Nos 8 and 621 Squadrons drove *U-852* ashore on the coast of Italian Somaliland where it was blown up by the surviving crew. Earlier in the U-boat's cruise, the captain, Kapitanleutnant H. Eck, had ordered the machine-gunning of survivors from one of his victims. After the war the Allies executed him.

1967 The evacuation of service families from Aden commenced following an increase in terrorist activities. It was completed on 31 July.

4 MAY

1924 The AOC British Forces in Iraq (AVM J.F.A. Higgins) ordered troops to be airlifted from Hinaidi to Kirkuk after Assyrian levies and members of the local Muslim community had run amok in the Sulaimaniya region. No. 30 Squadron maintained extensive air reconnaissance of the surrounding district.
See 26 and 27 May 1924.

1941 The Iraqi Revolt: continuous attacks by aircraft of No. 4 FTS suppressed the Iraqi artillery and other forces on the plateau and, their morale broken, the enemy forces decamped during the night of 5/6 May. RAF and British and Empire ground forces then set about restoring the Regent to power.

Indian Airlines civil Douglas DC2 transport aircraft were pressed into RAF service with No. 31 Squadron for the evacuation of non-essential personnel at RAF Habbaniya.

1945 Rocket-firing and cannon-armed Beaufighters of Nos 236 and 254 Squadrons, led by Sqn Ldr S.R. Hyland, sank four U-boats attempting to escape to Norway on the surface.

Nimrod of No. 206 Squadron meets two Royal Navy submarines at the North Pole. *(AHB)*

Nine ad hoc task forces, drawn from eleven RAF Regiment LAA, Rifle and Armoured Car squadrons in NW Germany, moved ahead of the British Army to occupy Schleswig-Holstein up to the Danish border. They seized Luftwaffe airfields and took the surrender of 50,000 German military, naval and air force personnel – including Hitler's successor, Grand Admiral Doenitz.

1988 Two Nimrods of No. 206 Squadron landed at RAF Kinloss after a rendezvous with two Royal Navy nuclear submarines HMS *Superb* and HMS *Turbulent*, which had surfaced at the North Pole the previous day.

5 MAY

1941 The Merchant Ship Fighter Unit (MSFU), equipped with Hurricanes, was formed at Speke, Liverpool.
See 25 May 1942.

1943 The first operational rescue using an airborne lifeboat was completed when a Hudson of No. 279 Squadron (captain Fg Off L.G. Wilson) dropped a lifeboat to the crew of a No. 102 Squadron Halifax that had ditched in the North Sea. The bomber crew successfully boarded the lifeboat and eight hours later were picked up by RAF High Speed Launch (HSL) 2579.

1944 The RAF joined the bombing campaign against the Romanian oil industry when forty-one Wellingtons and seven Halifaxes of No. 205 Group attacked the Steaua Romana refinery plant. The last of four major RAF attacks against oil targets near Ploesti was flown on 17 August.

1958 Canberra squadrons of the RAF's 2nd Tactical Air Force in Germany acquired a nuclear strike capability.

1993 MRAF Sir Dermot Boyle, former Chief of the Air Staff, died.
See 1 January 1956.

An airborne lifeboat is loaded on a Warwick. *(AHB. CA 125)*

6 MAY

1919   Afghanistan declared war on India – the so-called Third Afghan War. The RAF's only squadrons in India, Nos 31 and 114, provided support for the ground forces.
   See 24 May 1919.

1941   The Iraqi Revolt: the rebel forces withdrew from the area around RAF Habbaniya. The training aircraft of No. 4 FTS had dropped well over 3,000 bombs and had fired 116,000 rounds of ammunition. The operations room recorded 647 sorties but there were many more that went unrecorded.

1942   Two Dakotas of No. 31 Squadron, the only transport squadron in Burma at the time, were destroyed on the ground at Myitkyina as they prepared to take off with evacuees. Flights continued later that day when a DC-2 with a capacity of twenty-one seats took off with over sixty passengers. From the outset of the evacuation on 27 April, the squadron's DC-2s and Dakotas lifted over 4,000 people from central Burma before Myitkyina was captured by the Japanese on 8 May.

1944   Air Cdre R. Ivelaw-Chapman, flying as second pilot of a No. 576 Squadron Lancaster, was shot down attacking Aubigne. He had detailed knowledge of the coming Normandy invasion, but the Germans never realised his importance and he was treated in the normal manner.

2006   A Lynx helicopter was shot down over Basra. Among the five on board were Wg Cdr J. Coxen, the most senior officer to be killed during the Iraq conflict, and Flt Lt Sarah Mulvihill, the first servicewoman killed on operations since the Second World War.

7 MAY

1945   The unconditional surrender of Germany signalled the end of the Second World War in Europe.

The last U-boat to be sunk by an aircraft under Coastal Command control – the Type VIIC submarine *U-320* – was attacked by a No. 210 Squadron Catalina (captain Flt Lt K.M. Murray). The submarine subsequently sank with all hands. Between 3 September 1939 and 8 May 1945, aircraft under Coastal Command control had participated in the destruction of 207 U-boats and sunk 513,804 tons of Axis shipping (343 ships). A total of 5,866 aircrew and 1,777 aircraft were lost on operations.

At the end of the war in Europe, the RAF had grown to a strength of 55,469 aircraft (9,200 in the front line) with 1,079,835 RAF, Dominion and Allied officers and men, of whom 193,313 were aircrew.

1946   The Central Flying School was re-formed at RAF Little Rissington (Gp Capt E.A.C. Britton).

1965   The first sortie by a Victor B(K)1 tanker was flown from RAF Honington by an aircraft of No. 55 Squadron. Three Victor squadrons were converted to the air-to-air refuelling role to replace the grounded Valiant force.

1969   The first RAF Phantom squadron, No. 6 Squadron, was formed at RAF Coningsby.

A BE2c of No. 31 Squadron prepares to take off from an airstrip on the North-West Frontier. *(S. Leslie Collection)*

8 MAY

1945   Operation Doomsday: aircraft of No. 38 Group transported 7,000 troops and 2,000 tons of equipment and stores to Oslo, Stavanger and Kristiansands to establish Allied control in Norway. The operation was carried out over a period of five days because of bad weather.

The Royal Observer Corps was stood down and re-formed on a peacetime basis.

1953   On successfully completing his flying training on the Chipmunk and Harvard, HRH The Duke of Edinburgh was presented with his wings by the Chief of the Air Staff, ACM Sir William Dickson.

1959   Operation Globetrotter: a Shackleton Mk 3 (captain Wg Cdr J.G. Roberts) of No. 201 Squadron left RAF St Mawgan on a round the world trip, returning on 19 June after flying 24,300nm in a flying time of 130 hours.

1979   The Memorandum of Understanding was signed at RAF Cottesmore by senior officials

A wartime painting depicts the Royal Observer Corps post at Copythorne, Hampshire. *(AHB. LD 5435)*

of the British, German and Italian governments to create a Tri-National Tornado Training Establishment (TTTE).
See 29 January 1981.

9 MAY

1942 Operation Bowery: sixty-four Spitfires (leader Sqn Ldr S.B. Grant) took off from the aircraft carriers HMS *Eagle* and USS *Wasp* to reinforce Malta. Of the twenty-five reinforcement operations flown from aircraft carriers since the first on 2 August 1940, this involved the largest number of fighters. Pilots were on standby when the Spitfires arrived at RAF Takali and some

were airborne on patrol within fifteen minutes of the arrival of the first flight of aircraft.
See 2 August 1940.

1960 The first course commenced at the Aero-Medical Training Centre (AMTC) established at RAF Upwood.

10 MAY

1918 The Air Council approved in principle the establishment of RAF bands (twenty-four strong) at four locations.
See 1 April 1920.

1940 The German offensive in the west – Fall Gelb (Operation Yellow) – opened at dawn with the invasion of the Netherlands, Belgium and Luxembourg. All three countries were neutral.

Thirty-two Battles of the AASF attacked enemy advance columns. Twenty failed to return and most of the surviving aircraft were damaged. Eight Whitleys of Nos 77 and 102 Squadrons made the first deliberate British bombing attack against the German mainland when they attacked the lines of communication west of the Rhine.

1941 The Iraqi Revolt: armoured cars of No. 2 Armoured Car Company (Sqn Ldr M.P. Casano) overwhelmed the fort at Rutbah and then advanced under constant attack towards RAF Habbaniya, reaching the base on 18 May.

The ROC post at Embleton, Durham, tracked a hostile aircraft as it crossed the coast. Other ROC posts and radars continued to track the aircraft, a Messerschmitt Bf110 fighter, until it crashed south of Glasgow. The pilot, Rudolf Hess, Hitler's Deputy Fuhrer, who was the sole occupant, was captured.

1942 Following the arrival of RAF fighter reinforcements in Malta, the Luftwaffe mounted heavy attacks against the island. Furious air battles were fought over the island resulting in sixty-three enemy aircraft destroyed or damaged by fighters

Sqn Ldr M.P. Casano (OC No. 2 ACC) with his dog Butch who accompanied his master throughout operations in the Middle East until he was killed by enemy gunfire. *(IWM. CM 1553)*

RAF armoured cars in the Middle East. *(AHB. CM 2953)*

The crew of the *Aries I* flight assemble under their modified Lancaster. *(AHB. CH 15243)*

and anti-aircraft fire. The air battle marked the turning point in the defence of Malta.

1944 Attacks commenced against German communication, reporting and radar sites in preparation for Operation Overlord. As a security precaution, for every post attacked in the landing areas two were attacked outside them. The assault was delivered for the most part by Typhoon and Spitfire squadrons of Nos 83 and 84 Groups.

1945 A modified Lancaster B.1 *Aries I* (captain, Wg Cdr D.C. McKinley) of the Empire Air Navigation School (EANS) departed RAF Shawbury to fly to the North Geographic and North Magnetic Poles staging through airfields in Iceland, Greenland and Canada. The crew of eleven returned to Shawbury on 26 May, having flown 19,965 miles in 109 hours 40 minutes' flying time.

Operation Doomsday: a Stirling transport aircraft of No. 190 Squadron deploying troops to Norway to secure the country at the end of hostilities disappeared near Oslo in bad weather. Six crew, two passengers and sixteen troops were killed. One of the passengers was AVM J.R. Scarlett-Streatfield, AOC No. 38 Group. The remains of the aircraft were not discovered until 21 June.

1990 The first two women to fly solo in RAF jet aircraft were Flt Lts Sally Cox and Julie Gibson. Both flew Jet Provosts as part of their flying training at No. 1 FTS, RAF Linton-on-Ouse.
See 14 June 1991.

11 MAY

1916 The Air Board was created, under the presidency of Lord Curzon. The roles of the Board included:
- Discussion of matters of general policy in relation to the air, and in particular combined operations of the Naval and Military Air Services.
- Making recommendations on the types of machine required. If either the

142

Flt Lts Julie Gibson (left) and Sally Cox. *(AHB)*

Admiralty or the War Office declined to act on recommendations of the Board, the President was to refer questions to the War Committee Cabinet.

- Organising and co-ordinating the supply of material, preventing competition between the two departments.
- Organising a complete system for the interchange of ideas between the two Services, and such related bodies as the Naval Board of Invention and Research, the Advisory Committee for Aeronautics and the National Physical Laboratory. See 22 December 1916.

1944 The air campaign against enemy airfields within 150 miles of the Normandy invasion beaches was intensified.

The land offensive in Italy began to break the Gustav line and finally capture Monte Cassino. Medium bombers attacked road and rail communications and fighter-bombers provided direct support for the ground forces. By the beginning of June, there were 124 railway cuts north of Rome of which 47 were major bridge cuts.

1949 In light of the civil war raging in China, Spitfire FR18s of No. 28 Squadron (Sqn Ldr R.D. Yule) left Malaya in order to reinforce the defences of Hong Kong. Apart from a brief period in 1967–8, the squadron remained based in the colony until the British withdrawal in June 1997.

1969 An air race between London and New York was sponsored by the *Daily Mail* to commemorate the 50th anniversary of the first transatlantic air crossing. British military participation in the air race was

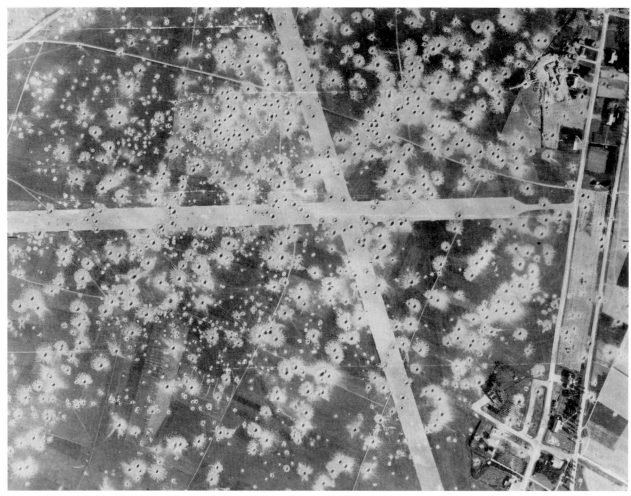

Above: The airfield at Le Culot after a visit by Allied bombers. *(AHB. C4562)*
Below: Baltimores head for the Sulmona railway yards in northern Italy. *(AHB)*

co-ordinated by an RAF team and included a Harrier GR1, Victor tankers of Nos 55 and 57 Squadrons and a Wessex of No. 72 Squadron. Sqn Ldr T. Lecky-Tompson flying a Harrier GR1 achieved the shortest overall time of 6 hours 11 minutes 57 seconds between the Post Office Tower in London and the Empire State Building in New York. He took off vertically from a coal yard at St Pancras, London, and made a vertical landing 5 hours 33 minutes later on New York's Manhattan Island. A Phantom of the Fleet Air Arm, with Victor tanker support, achieved the shortest eastward time. Sqn Ldr G. Williams flew a Harrier GR1 on the eastbound journey and landed vertically at the St Pancras coal yard after flying non-stop for 5 hours 33 minutes. The two RAF Harrier pilots were awarded the prestigious American award, the Harmon International Aviator's Trophy.

12 MAY

1940 **VC**: Fg Off Donald Edward Garland and Sgt Thomas Gray, pilot and navigator of the lead aircraft of a formation of five Battles of

Sqn Ldr G. Williams lands his Harrier GR1 at St Pancras station after completing his flight from New York.
(AHB. PRB 655)

No. 12 Squadron, which attacked the bridges across the Albert Canal at Maastricht. Four aircraft failed to return including Garland and Gray's. These were the first RAF VCs of the war. (*London Gazette*, 11 June 1940, posthumous award)

1943 A Liberator (captain Flt Lt J. Wright) of No. 86 Squadron dropped a Mk 24 acoustic homing torpedo and seriously damaged *U-456*, forcing it to the surface. The submarine was later made to dive by approaching destroyers and then sank as a result of the damage sustained during the Liberator attack. Thus this was the first successful use of an air-dropped precision weapon in air warfare.

1944 A force of thirteen Mosquitos of No. 692 Squadron, supported by Mosquitos of No. 100 Group, laid mines from 300ft at night into the Kiel Canal. As a result of this first Mosquito mining operation, the Canal was closed for seven days. After another three days it had to be closed again for a further three days, causing great disruption.

1945 The Royal Observer Corps was stood down.

1949 Operation Plainfare: the Berlin blockade was officially lifted at 0001hr, although the airlift continued until 6 October to build up stocks in Berlin. Aircraft of twenty RAF squadrons and two OCUs were used during the Operation.
See 28 June 1948, 6 October 1949.

1962 Six hundred veterans of the Royal Flying Corps and Royal Naval Air Service attended an Air Council and Admiralty reception at Lancaster House to mark the fiftieth year of military aviation.

1986 A memorial to the memory of the 244 American and 16 British fighter pilots who served in the three RAF Eagle Squadrons prior to the participation of the United States in the Second World War was unveiled opposite the American Embassy in Grosvenor Square, London.

13 MAY

1912 The Royal Flying Corps (RFC) was formed and took over the Air Battalion of the Royal Engineers. The badge of the RFC derived from that of the Royal Engineers

A Handley Page 0/100 of the Independent Force with an SE5 parked alongside. *(AHB. H 1455)*

and consisted of the monogram RFC ensigned by a crown that broke the laurel wreath encircling the monogram.
See 13 April 1912.

1918 An announcement was made of the formation of the Independent Air Force (IAF) commanded by Maj Gen Sir Hugh Trenchard, as from 6 June 1918. This was the first time that an air force had been formed for the express purpose of conducting war without reference or subordination to Army or Navy Commands. It operated by day and night against industrial targets in Germany and enemy aerodromes. In five months the nine squadrons of the IAF (equipped with DH4s, DH9s, DH9As, FE2Bs, and Handley Page 0/100s and 0/400s with one squadron of Camels for escort work) dropped 550 tons of bombs (390 tons by night). This was the world's first strategic air command, and the historical forerunner of Bomber Command.

1931 Sheikh Mahmud, the rebel leader of the Kurds in Iraq, surrendered following air action against his tribesmen. Going up to the nearest RAF officer, the Sheikh tapped the RAF wings on the officer's uniform and said solemnly, 'You are the people who have broken my spirit . . . but I taught you to bomb.' Iraq had been the first testing ground of Trenchard's policy of 'air control' and had, under the local RAF commanders, been wholly effective and

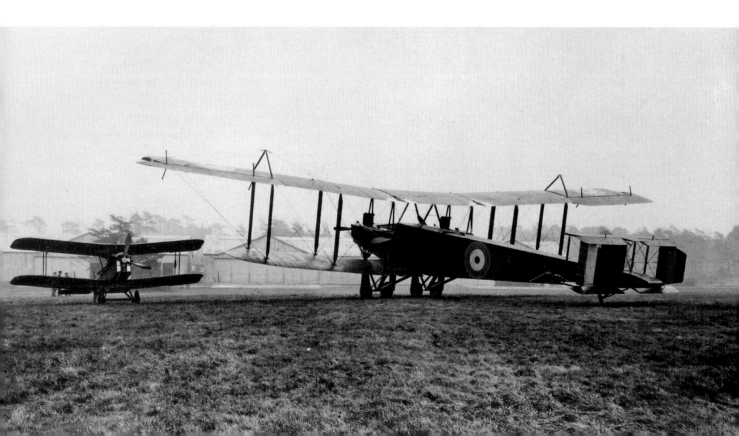

enabled the scheme to be applied to other British mandated territories.

Sheikh Mahmud (centre) with RAF officers after his surrender. *(C. Morris Collection)*

1941 The Iraqi Revolt: German fighters arrived at Mosul in Northern Iraq to support Rachid Ali's revolt. Under constant harassing attack from RAF units in Iraq they achieved little.

1943 The last of the Axis forces in Tunisia surrendered, bringing the campaign in North Africa to an end. During the campaign from 18 February, North-West African Tactical Air Force units completed 59,000 sorties and claimed the destruction of 573 enemy aircraft, more than 500 motor transport vehicles, 23 ships, and during the latter stages, provided the largest weight of air attack ever undertaken in support of a ground battle to that date. The best tribute to the effectiveness of air support is contained in a German report written in 1944: 'The Anglo-American air forces played a decisive part in the enemy operational successes, which led to the destruction of the German–Italian bridgehead in Tunisia.'

1945 No. 1318 Wing RAF Regiment, with three squadrons, landed in Norway and secured and occupied seven airfields.

14 MAY

1940 The German Army broke through the French front at Sedan. All available Battles and Blenheims (seventy-one aircraft) of the AASF were despatched to attack five pontoon bridges and troop columns. Heavy fighter opposition was encountered and forty-one aircraft failed to return, representing a 58 per cent loss rate – the highest ever suffered by the RAF in an operation of this size.

1943 **GC**: LAC Kenneth Gerald Spooner RCAF, a student navigator aboard an Anson when the pilot collapsed. With no piloting experience he took control of the aircraft to allow three other students to bale out. The aircraft crashed killing the pilot and Spooner. (*London Gazette*, 7 January 1944, posthumous award)

1958 US Air Force Strategic Air Command (SAC) aircraft participated in the Bomber Command bombing competition for the first time. Six B-52 Stratofortress aircraft and crews of the 92nd Bomb Wing were

Battles of No. 103 Squadron return to their airstrip in northern France. *(AHB. C 1061)*

detached to RAF Brize Norton for the competition; the detachment won five of the six awards for which it was eligible.

1968   Lt A. Jerrard **VC** died.
See 30 March 1918.

15 MAY

1940   The War Cabinet authorised bombing attacks on Germany east of the Rhine.

The first large-scale Bomber Command attack on German industry took place, with sixteen different targets attacked at night in the Ruhr area (ninety-nine aircraft). Twelve further bombers attacked railways in Belgium, the first time that over a hundred bombers were despatched on one occasion since the war had begun.

1941   The first flight by a British jet-propelled aircraft – the Gloster E28/39 – took place at RAF Cranwell. D.E.G. Sayer, Gloster's chief test pilot, flew the aircraft and the flight lasted seventeen minutes.

1947   Details of aircraft finishes were promulgated for postwar RAF aircraft.

1949   The first of four Sunderlands of No. 88 Squadron flew from Hong Kong to Shanghai to evacuate British nationals as Chinese Communist forces approached the city. Over the next three days, 121 people were evacuated.

1957   Operation Grapple: in the first of a series of tests, Britain's first thermonuclear weapon – a prototype Yellow Sun with a yield of 100–150 kilotons – was dropped over Malden Island in the south-west Pacific from a Valiant (captain Wg Cdr K.G. Hubbard) of No. 49 Squadron.

1958   The Air Council agreed to the assignment of three Valiant squadrons (twenty-four aircraft) to SACEUR in place of a Canberra Force (64 UE).

1959   The last operational flight by an RAF flying-boat was made by a Sunderland of No. 205 Squadron at RAF Seletar, Singapore.

1965   The premier RAF aerobatic team, the Red Arrows (Flt Lt L. Jones), equipped with the Gnat, made their first public display at the Biggin Hill Air Fair.

1972   The Red Arrows (Sqn Ldr I.C.H. Dick) departed from RAF Kemble for their first visit to North America. The nine Gnat aircraft staged through Iceland, Greenland

Above: Britain's first jet-propelled aircraft, the Gloster E28/39. *(AHB)*
Below: Valiants of No. 49 Squadron at Christmas Island for Operation Grapple. *(P.H.T. Green Collection)*

The last Sunderland in RAF service is 'paid off' at RAF Seletar. *(ACA Archives)*

The Red Arrows Aerobatic Team fly a 'diamond nine' in their Gnat aircraft. *(R. Deacon)*

A Nimrod, seen through the rear periscope of a Victor tanker, refuels over the South Atlantic. *(AHB)*

and Canada before arriving at Dulles Airport, Washington, where they gave their first display on 26 May.

1982 Operation Corporate: a Nimrod of No. 201 Squadron (captain Flt Lt J.A. Cowan) flew a long-range surveillance sortie off the Argentinan coast with the support of twelve Victor tankers on a sortie lasting 19 hours 5 minutes.

16 MAY

1940 ACM Sir Hugh Dowding, C-in-C Fighter Command, wrote to the Under-Secretary of State for Air (Harold Balfour) to express his deep concern following orders to send further fighter reinforcements to France. He pointed out that it had previously been agreed that fifty-two squadrons were necessary for the defence of the United Kingdom, but he had only thirty-six available. He wished to know how many squadrons were to be kept at home and concluded that, if his force was drained away further, this would result in 'the final, complete and irredeemable defeat of this country'.

Training Command Operational Order No. 1 outlined a scheme for fitting racks for 20lb bombs on Tiger Moth and Harvard training aircraft based at Flying Training Schools, so that they could be used to attack incoming enemy invasion barges.

1943 Operation Chastise: a force of Lancasters of No. 617 Squadron, led by Wg Cdr G.P. Gibson, took off from RAF Scampton to attack a series of dams in the Ruhr Valley.

VC: Wg Cdr Guy Penrose Gibson DSO & Bar, DFC & Bar, the commanding officer of No. 617 Squadron leader of the Dams Raid, delivered his attack with great accuracy and afterwards circled low for half an hour, drawing the enemy fire to his aircraft to clear the way for the attacks that followed. (*London Gazette*, 28 May 1943)
See 19 September 1944.

OPERATION CHASTISE

The daring attack on the Ruhr dams on 16–17 May 1943 by RAF Lancasters of No. 617 Squadron was one of the most outstandingly successful and gallant attacks during the Second World War. The operation, codenamed Chastise, was only made possible by the unprecedented co-operation of a team of men and women drawn from across the political, scientific and military communities. That it happened at all was largely due to the tenacity and vision of two individuals: Dr Barnes Wallis and ACM Sir Charles Portal. It was Wallis who invented the revolutionary bouncing bomb, and Portal, the Chief of the Air Staff, who saw its potential and overruled the objections of the C-in-C Bomber Command, ACM Sir Arthur 'Bomber' Harris, giving the go-ahead for the operation.

One hundred and thirty-three RAF airmen took off in nineteen specially modified Lancaster bombers on the evening of 16 May, their targets the great dams of western Germany. Only twelve aircraft reached the targets with their Upkeep bouncing bombs – five attacked and breached the Mohne Dam and three breached the Eder Dam. Two aircraft attacked the Sorpe Dam, inflicting minor damage. Floodwaters of massive proportions were unleashed along the Ruhr valley, disrupting transport and industry and claiming the lives of more than 1,200 people.

Fifty-six airmen and eight Lancasters failed to return from Chastise, making it one of the

The breach in the Mohne Dam photographed by a Spitfire the morning after the attack by Lancasters of No. 617 Squadron. *(R. Nesbit Collection)*

RAF's most costly operations of the war. Thirty-five aircrew were decorated.

In the years that have followed the raid, opinion among historians and commentators on both sides about its strategic value has been divided, but the fillip it gave to civilian and service morale was immense.

Wg Cdr G.P. Gibson (right) with his wireless operator, Flt Lt R.E.G. Hutchison. *(AHB. CH 9682)*

152

1962 The air quartermaster flying badge was introduced. It was to the same design as the air gunner badge with 'QM' in the laurel. The air loadmaster badge superseded it in 1970 (AMO A.117/1962).

See 30 September 1970.

1982 Operation Corporate: a Hercules of No. 47 Squadron (captain Flt Lt H.C. Burgoyne) dropped special stores and eight members of the special forces to the Task Force in the South Atlantic on a sortie that lasted 24 hours 5 minutes. Burgoyne was awarded the AFC.

2003 At a graduation ceremony at RAF Cranwell, the first weapon system officer and weapon system operator (WSO) badges were awarded. The design was a single wing with the RAF monogram surmounted by a crown. The navigator, air electronics officer, air electronics operator, air engineer, air loadmaster and air signaller specialisations had been formally merged on 1 April. Those who had qualified previously for the specialist aircrew badges were allowed to continue wearing them. The FC, AT and PJI flying badges continued to be awarded.

17 MAY

1919 Following the outbreak of the Third Afghan War with an attack on the Afghan Army post at Dakka, aircraft of No. 31 Squadron carried out concentrated raids on the Afghan city of Jalalabad on three days (17th, 20th, 24th). Three aircraft were lost.

1940 A force of twelve Blenheims of No. 82 Squadron was tasked to attack an enemy armoured column on the Gembloux road. German fighters attacked the formation and eleven were shot down. The sole survivor returned to RAF Watton, but the aircraft was damaged beyond repair.

The Ministry of Aircraft Production was constituted by an Order in Council with Lord Beaverbrook appointed as the first Minister.

1973 The Second Cod War: Nimrod maritime patrol aircraft began surveillance flights to establish the positions of Icelandic government gunboats and UK trawlers within the 50-mile zone proclaimed by the Icelandic government. In an effort to conserve Nimrod flying hours, a small number of fishery protection sorties were also flown by Britannia transport aircraft from 20 July 1973. The last sortie was flown on 3 October 1973.

See 2 June 1976.

1978 The majority of the RAF presence at Kai Tak, Hong Kong, was relocated to RAF Sek Kong where the HQ RAF (Hong Kong) was collocated with Army Headquarters.

18 MAY

1918 Six DH4 bombers of No. 55 Squadron, led by Capt F. Williams, made the first daylight raid in force on Cologne. Bombing from 14,500ft, they caused considerable damage before returning to their aerodrome at Tantonville after a five-hour flight. Williams, who had already received the MC for a previous long-distance bombing operation, was awarded the DFC.

1929 LAC S. Ferris won the Windsor to London marathon for the fifth consecutive time, completing the course in 2 hours 40 minutes 47 seconds.

19 MAY

1918 The last, and biggest, aircraft night raid by the Germans against England involved forty-three Gotha and Giant bombers sent to attack London. Six Gothas fell to the defences: three to the anti-aircraft gunners, who fired 30,000 shells, and three to aircraft. A seventh bomber crash-landed near Clacton.

See 5 August 1918.

1941 Following intense air attacks by the Luftwaffe, the last RAF airworthy aircraft on Crete were evacuated to Egypt. With complete air superiority, the Germans launched an airborne assault the following day. RAF bombers based in Egypt attacked German positions and airfields but Allied forces were forced to withdraw from the island by 1 June. Sunderland flying-boats of

Sunderlands of No. 230 Squadron evacuate the remnants of British forces from Crete. *(AHB)*

Nos 228 and 230 Squadrons assisted in the evacuation of key personnel but 226 RAF personnel had to be left behind, the majority becoming POWs.

1942 The Ottawa Air Training Conference was convened to review all aspects of aircrew training, which resulted in the introduction of the air bomber and the replacement of the observer by the navigator. It was also agreed to place all the training establishments in Canada under one Canadian organisation and to renew the mandate for the Empire Air Training Scheme for a further two years. The scheme was renamed the British Commonwealth Air Training Plan (BCATP).
See 29 April 1940.

1943 Air Cdre Sir Nigel Norman Bt Commander of No. 38 (Air Co-operation) Wing was killed en route to the Middle East when his Hudson aircraft crashed shortly after taking off from RAF St Eval, Cornwall. He had made a major contribution to the development of airborne forces and glider operations.

1982 Operation Corporate: No. 1(F) Squadron, operating from HMS *Hermes*, flew its first operational sortie when two Harriers, led by the squadron commander (Wg Cdr P.T. Squire, later ACM Sir Peter Squire CAS), were vectored towards a 'bogey' at 30,000ft, but the interception was unsuccessful. The squadron flew its first ground-attack sortie the following day.

Operation Corporate: Flt Lt G.W. Hawkins, attached to the Special Forces, was killed when a Royal Navy Sea King helicopter crashed. He was the only RAF casualty during the Falklands War.

1986 Gp Capt L.H. Trent **VC**, DFC died.
See 3 May 1943.

20 MAY

A Harrier GR3 of No. 1(F) Squadron lands aboard the aircraft carrier *Hermes* in the South Atlantic. *(J. Falconer Collection)*

1917 A 'Large America' flying-boat (Flt Sub-Lt C.R. Morrish) of the RNAS destroyed the first hostile submarine to be sunk by an aircraft without any form of assistance. On patrol from Felixstowe, Morrish sighted the German submarine *U-C36* on the surface near the North Hinder Light Ship and attacked. Destruction of the submarine was confirmed in January 1919.

1927 A modified Hawker Horsley torpedo bomber flown by Flt Lts C.R. Carr (later AM Sir Roderick Carr) and L.E.M. Gillman departed from RAF Cranwell in an attempt to establish a new distance record. After a flight of 34 hours 45 minutes they ditched in the Persian Gulf, having flown 3,400 miles. Their attempt was overshadowed the next day when Charles Lindbergh landed at Paris after crossing the Atlantic, a distance of 3,590 miles.

1937 The single-engine Battle bomber, which was to suffer such severe losses in France in 1940, entered squadron service with No. 63 Squadron at RAF Upwood.

1939 The last Empire Air Day took place when sixty RAF stations and eighteen other airfields were open to the public, attracting about 1,000,000 spectators.

1970 A Phantom FGR2 of No. 54 Squadron (Sqn Ldrs G.H. Arkell-Hardwick and D.C. Read) landed at RAF Tengah, Singapore, after a non-stop flight from RAF Coningsby, Lincolnshire, in a point-to-point record time of 14 hours 14 minutes. The Phantom made nine in-flight fuel transfers from Victor tankers. A second Phantom diverted to RAF Gan after its Victor tanker became unserviceable. A second pair of Phantoms arrived the following day, clipping five minutes off the record.

21 MAY

1928   The Far East Flight left RAF Seletar, Singapore, to circumnavigate Australia, the second stage of their cruise, returning on 15 September.
See 17 October 1927, 1 November 1928.

1940   Gladiators of No. 263 Squadron returned to northern Norway, flying off the aircraft carrier HMS *Furious* to the airfield at Bardufoss near Narvik and were soon in action. Hurricanes of No. 46 Squadron (Sqn Ldr K.B.B. Cross) joined the force on 26 May.
See 8 June 1940.

1941   A Spitfire of the PRU (Plt Off M. Suckling) flying from RAF Wick, photographed the *Bismarck* at anchor near Bergen, thereby providing intelligence for the ultimately successful chase and eventual sinking of the German battleship.

1944   As an extension to the 'Transportation Plan', attacks by Allied fighters and fighter-bombers commenced over France and Belgium against locomotives and rolling stock.
See 15 April 1944.

The photograph of the German battleship *Bismarck* at anchor near Bergen, taken by a Spitfire of the PRU. *(AHB. CS 159)*

Seventy-four Horsa gliders landed in twelve minutes on a small landing zone near Netheravon during the last large-scale exercise at night before D-Day.

1957 The RAF/USAF Memorandum of Understanding on supply of atomic weapons and co-ordination of nuclear strike plans was signed.

The Vulcan entered squadron service with No. 83 Squadron at RAF Waddington.

1982 Operation Corporate: Flt Lt J. Glover's Harrier was shot down during an armed reconnaissance of Port Howard. Glover ejected, was wounded and taken prisoner to become the only British POW of the war. He was released on 8 July 1982.

22 MAY

1925 Snipes of No. 1(F) Squadron, supporting a force of levies and cavalry en route to Halebja, annihilated a large body of Sheikh Mahmud's followers caught in the open.

1933 ACM Sir Edward Ellington was appointed Chief of the Air Staff.

1935 Proposals were announced to increase the strength of the Royal Air Force to 1,500 aircraft by 1937.

1940 Seven Lysanders of No. 16 Squadron dropped supplies to a besieged Allied garrison at Calais. Over the course of the next two weeks more than thirty Lysanders from five squadrons were lost on these operations.

1945 ACM Sir Sholto Douglas was appointed AOC-in-C British Air Forces of Occupation (BAFO) Germany.

1948 Royal Egyptian Air Force (REAF) Spitfires attacked an RAF detachment of Nos 32 and 208 Squadrons at Ramat David, destroying a number of their Spitfires and a Dakota. Pilots of No. 208 Squadron and gunners of No. 52 (Rifle) Squadron RAF Regiment repulsed two further attacks and

Snipes of No. 1(F) Squadron in formation near Baghdad.
(AHB. H 802)

157

Top: A Lysander of No. 16 Squadron.
(P.H.T. Green Collection)
Above: Chief Tech D. Carol and Cpl R. Bail on the
summit of Mount Everest. *(RAF Sports Board)*

shot down five REAF Spitfires. Four RAF
personnel were killed on the ground. The
Egyptian pilots had assumed that Israeli

forces had occupied the airfield. The REAF
Spitfire shot down by Fg Off T. McElhaw is
the last occasion an RAF pilot in an RAF
aircraft shot down another aircraft in an
air-to-air engagement.

2001 Chief Tech D. Carol and Cpl R. Bail became
the first RAF personnel to reach the
summit of Mount Everest.

23 MAY

1940 The first combats took place between Spitfires and Messerschmitt Bf109s. Among the RAF pilots shot down and taken prisoner was Sqn Ldr R. Bushell, who was later to mastermind the 'Great Escape' from Stalag Luft III.
See 24 March 1944.

1943 During a heavy raid on Dortmund, the total weight of bombs dropped by Bomber Command on Germany reached 100,000 tons. To mark the occasion, the AOC-in-C Bomber Command, ACM Sir Arthur Harris, sent this message: 'In 1939, Goering promised that not a single enemy bomb would reach the Ruhr. Congratulations on having delivered the first 100,000 tons of bombs on Germany to refute him.'

Scottish-born Sgt S.N. Sloan, a bomb-aimer on No. 431 (RCAF) Squadron, was awarded the Conspicuous Gallantry Medal for flying his Wellington back from Dortmund after two members of the crew, including the only pilot,

had baled out after the bomber had been damaged by anti-aircraft fire. He landed the aircraft safely at RAF Cranwell. Later in the war he was trained as a pilot and awarded a DFC for operations on a Halifax squadron.

1963 The RAF V-Force was formally assigned to SACEUR for targeting, planning, co-ordination and execution of nuclear strikes. For national operations the Force remained under British national control.

2001 The C-17 Globemaster III heavy-lift transport aircraft entered RAF service with No. 99 Squadron at RAF Brize Norton.

24 MAY

1919 The Handley Page V/1500 four-engine heavy bomber, 'Old Carthusian' (captain Capt R. Halley), successfully bombed the Amir Ammanulla's palace in Kabul,

Bomber Command's response to Goering's boast. *(RAFM)*

159

Above: Sgt S.N. Sloan is congratulated on the announcement of the award of CGM. On his left are Fg Off J. Bailey (WOP) and Sgt G.C.W. Parslow (navigation) who were awarded the DFC and DFM respectively for their part in the recovery of their aircraft. *(G.R. Pitchfork Collection)*

Below: Student pilots in Southern Rhodesia. *(AHB. CM 1173)*

Parachutists jump from a Virginia at an Empire Air Day at RAF Henlow. *(G.R. Pitchfork Collection)*

Afghanistan, dealing a major blow to Afghan morale and helping to ensure a quick settlement of the conflict.

See 13 December 1918.

1934 The first Empire Air Day took place. RAF stations were opened to the public with all proceeds from the day donated to the RAF Benevolent Fund.

1939 Administrative control of the Fleet Air Arm was transferred from the RAF to the Admiralty.

1940 The first RAF aircrew commenced training at No. 25 EFTS at Belvedere, near Salisbury, Southern Rhodesia. The scheme stemmed from a bilateral agreement to establish the Rhodesian Air Training Group (RATG), which was given Air Ministry support and a UK Treasury promise to pay later. This was the first of the Empire Air Training Schemes to be implemented. Ten RATG air stations were eventually established and trained 10,000 aircrew, of which 7,600 were pilots.

25 MAY

1942 The Merchant Ship Fighting Unit (MSFU) achieved its first success when a Hurricane was catapulted from the foredeck of the specially adapted merchant ship *Empire Morn* escorting the westbound convoy QP 12 from Murmansk. Fg Off J.B. Kendall shot down a Junkers Ju88 attacking the convoy 220 miles east of Jan Mayen Island. He returned to the ship and baled out but his parachute only partially deployed and he died of his injuries.

A Hurricane on the catapult of a merchant ship. *(ACA Archives)*

De Havilland DH9s of No. 55 Squadron at Sulaimaniya, Iraq. *(G.R. Pitchfork Collection)*

1944 The final element of the 'Transportation Plan' commenced with attacks against bridges. By D-Day all twenty-four major bridges over the Seine between Paris and Rouen, plus a further twelve significant bridges, had been collapsed.

See 15 April 1944.

1951 The RAF's first jet bomber, the Canberra, entered service with No. 101 Squadron at RAF Binbrook.

See 28 July 2006.

1960 A Valiant of No. 214 Squadron (captain Sqn Ldr J.H. Garstin) made the first non-stop flight from the United Kingdom to Singapore, a distance of 8,110 miles in 15 hours 35 minutes, at 623mph. The aircraft refuelled in the air over Cyprus and Karachi.

1962 Following a Pathet Lao offensive, six Hunter FGA9s of No. 20 Squadron deployed from RAF Tengah to Don Maung, Bangkok, as part of a SEATO multinational Joint Task Force. The detachment – then ten aircraft strong – later transferred to Chieng Mai in northern Thailand. The detachment ceased on 15 November 1962.

1982 During air combat training over Germany, a No. 92 Squadron Phantom inadvertently released a Sidewinder missile and shot down a No. 14 Squadron Jaguar. The Jaguar pilot ejected safely.

Canberra B2s of No. 101 Squadron at RAF Binbrook.
(AHB. PRB 4141)

26 MAY

1918 The Rev H.D.L. Weiner, who had served as a naval chaplain for sixteen years, was lent to the RAF by the Admiralty to organise and draw up a scheme for the Air Force Chaplain's Department.

See 11 October 1918.

1924 Following the troop deployment of 4 May, Sheikh Mahmud declared a Jihad (a holy war) against the British and began to gather a large force. He failed to respond to an ultimatum air-dropped by the RAF indicating that Sulaimaniya would be bombed should he fail to comply. Forty-two aircraft from Nos 6, 8, 30, 45, 55 and 70 Squadrons gathered at Kingerban and Kirkuk prior to commencement of operations the following day, when RAF aircraft dropped 28 tons of bombs on the town. The population had been forewarned and there were no civilian casualties, but extensive damage was caused.

Sheikh Mahmud fled to nearby caves, returning on 1 June.

1940 Operation Dynamo: the evacuation of British and French forces from Dunkirk

Top: A Coastal Command Hudson on patrol off Dunkirk during the evacuation of the BEF. *(AHB. C 1715)*
Above: A Hurricane of No. 46 Squadron is loaded onto a lighter prior to embarkation on HMS *Glorious*. *(Andrew Thomas Collection)*

began. Some 200 Hurricanes and Spitfires of Fighter Command, operating from the south-east of England, provided cover throughout the operation. During the nine days of the evacuation, the RAF flew 651 bomber, 171 reconnaissance and 2,739 fighter sorties in direct support of the operation.

See 4 June 1940.

Eighteen Hurricanes of No. 46 Squadron (Sqn Ldr K.B.B. Cross) took off from the aircraft carrier HMS *Glorious* and landed at Skaanland, northern Norway.

See 8 June 1940.

1941

A Catalina of No. 209 Squadron (captain Fg Off D.A. Briggs) relocated the *Bismarck*

The Catalina of No. 209 Squadron that located the *Bismarck. (R. Nesbit Collection)*

550 miles west of Land's End steaming at reduced speed for Brest. Catalina aircraft remained shadowing the battleship until torpedoes and naval gunfire sank it at 1036hr on 27 May.

Wg Cdr G. Nottage (OC No. 177 Squadron) and his navigator Fg Off N.A. Bolitho were rescued from behind Japanese lines by Flt Lt J.D. Dunbar flying an L-5 Sentinel light aircraft. They had evaded capture for thirty-one days after their Beaufighter had been shot down. Dunbar was awarded the DFC.

1951 HRH Princess Elizabeth, on behalf of HM King George VI, presented the first King's Colour for the Royal Air Force in Hyde Park.
See 27 December 1947.

27 MAY

1920 An Air Ministry instruction notified the introduction of the 'Starter, aeroplane engine, Hucks, Ford'. It was made mandatory to use these devices for all aircraft engine starting except the Avro 504Ks with the 100hp Monosoupape engine.

1940 Wg Cdr B.E. Embry (later ACM Sir Basil Embry) was shot down when leading No. 107 Squadron Blenheims attacking St Omer. He was captured but soon escaped and travelled through France, crossed the Pyrenees and returned to England ten weeks later.
See 21 March 1945.

Training Command was disbanded to create Flying Training Command and Technical Training Command. Reserve Command was disbanded.

The Directorate of Ground Defence was formed at the Air Ministry (Air Cdre A.P.M. Sanders).
See 1 February 1942.

Above: A Hucks Starter prepares to start the engine of a Bristol F2B Fighter. *(AHB. H27)*
Below: ACM Sir Basil Embry (1902–77). *(AHB)*

1940 Airmen mustered as WOP/AG or air gunners were automatically granted the rank of sergeant on completion of training. The order was not published until 27 June.

1965 HM The Queen, accompanied by HRH The Duke of Edinburgh, flew along the air corridors to RAF Gatow, Berlin, in an Andover of the Queen's Flight. The RAF Germany Battle Flight was deployed to RAF Gutersloh but there were no incidents.

1999 Operation Allied Force: NATO air operations against Serbian targets reached a peak with eighteen Harriers, operating from Gioia del Colle in Italy, and twelve Bruggen-based Tornados heavily involved.
See 10 June 1999.

28 MAY

1940 Bombing attacks against German positions around Dunkirk continued with forty-eight Blenheims attacking during the day and forty-seven Wellingtons and Whitleys bombing by night. Throughout the evacuation of Allied troops, the bombers continued their attacks, often in poor weather. The action reached a peak on 31 May when a force of 126 aircraft attacked, including the largest daylight operation so far by No. 2 Group's Blenheims when 93 of the bombers took part.

1943 The first success by an RAF aircraft firing the 3in rocket was achieved when a Hudson of No. 608 Squadron (captain Fg Off G. Ogilvie) sank *U-755* in the Western Mediterranean.

1944 The operations mounted on this day are a typical example of the wide-ranging series of air operations in support of the forthcoming Allied landings in Normandy. Bomber Command continued its attacks when 126 Lancasters and Mosquitos bombed the railway yards at Angers and another force of 201 bombers attacked three coastal gun positions. Other aircraft laid mines off the Dutch, Belgian and French coasts, others flew night intruder missions and twenty-four aircraft flew arms and supplies to the Resistance.

An air gunner boards his No. 264 Squadron Defiant wearing a combined parachute harness. *(IWM. CH 874)*

29 MAY

1919 The War Cabinet approved the gifting of 100 surplus aircraft from RAF stocks to each Dominion and to India. Small numbers of aircraft were also made available to any colonial government or protectorate requiring them. The 'Imperial Gift' paved the way for the establishment of air forces by Australia, Canada and South Africa.

1940 During morning engagements over Dunkirk, Defiants of No. 264 Squadron claimed to have shot down seventeen Messerschmitt fighters and a Junkers Ju87. A further eighteen Ju87s and a Junkers Ju88 were claimed during an afternoon battle. The aircraft never achieved the same success again and during the Battle of Britain it suffered very heavy losses and had to be withdrawn from its role as a day-fighter.

The first fighter operations using Very High Frequency (VHF) radio telephone control took place during the air battle over Dunkirk.

1941 The observer (radio) flying badge was introduced. The pattern was the same as the air gunner badge with 'RO' inside the laurel. It was made redundant following the introduction of the navigator badge in September 1942, but was reintroduced briefly in 1956 for AI operators flying in Meteor and Javelin night-fighters (AMO A.402/1941).

See 17 September 1942, 8 August 1956.

1982 Operation Corporate: eight Rapier fire units of No. 63 Squadron RAF Regiment landed at San Carlos.

Operation Corporate: an Army Air Corps Gazelle helicopter rescued Sqn Ldr R.D. Iveson of No. 1 Squadron who had evaded capture for two days after his Harrier had been shot down over Goose Green.

30 MAY

1927   No. 2 Squadron equipped with Bristol F2Bs arrived in Shanghai to reinforce RAF China Command. Following the easing of tension, RAF China Command was disbanded in August and the squadron departed for the United Kingdom, arriving in October.

1942   Operation Millennium: the first 'Thousand Bomber Raid'. The target was Cologne when 1,046 aircraft drawn from Bomber Command squadrons and Operational Training Units (OTUs) dropped more than 2,000 tons of bombs in 90 minutes.

Shanghai Racecourse, used by No. 2 Squadron as an airfield. (P.H.T. Green Collection)

OPERATION MILLENNIUM

In 1942, with the future of Bomber Command in doubt, the new Commander-in-Chief, AM A.T. Harris, approached the Prime Minister and the Chief of the Air Staff with the bold idea of assembling a force of 1,000 bombers and sending them out in one massive raid on a single German city. They approved. Harris supplemented his main bomber force with aircraft and crews drawn from Operational Training Units, some of the latter flown by pupil crews. Altogether, 1,047 bombers were gathered at 53 airfields; unfavourable weather prevented an attack against Harris's preferred target, Hamburg, and the secondary, Cologne, was attacked instead.

The major innovation was the introduction of the 'bomber stream' designed to saturate the enemy air defences. All aircraft flew the same route at the same speed and with an allotted height band. Each aircraft was given a time over the target and in this way the attack was compressed into just ninety minutes when 2,000 tons of bombs fell on Cologne. Forty-one bombers were lost.

The first Thousand Bomber Raid was a major success but the second, on Essen, was less successful. A third was mounted at the end of June against Bremen. These raids changed the tactics and effectiveness of Bomber Command for the rest of the war and they confirmed the Command's future as a major force.

Cologne Cathedral survives the devastating bombing raids. *(ACA Archives)*

VC: Fg Off Leslie Thomas Manser, pilot of a No. 50 Squadron Manchester bomber, for his selfless efforts to enable all his crew to escape their burning aircraft after attacking Cologne. (*London Gazette*, 20 October 1942, posthumous award).

1946 AM Sir Alec Coryton, Controller of Supplies (Air) at the Ministry of Supply, said at a press conference that the only future fighters and bombers in which the Air Ministry was interested were those powered by jet engines.

31 MAY

1935 An earthquake devastated the RAF station at Quetta, India, and the nearby settlement. Most of the station's buildings, apart from the hangars, collapsed and fifty-five RAF personnel and dependants and sixty-six local employees were killed. Of the two squadrons based at Quetta, only three of No. 31 Squadron's Wapiti aircraft remained serviceable and all No. 5 Squadron's Wapiti aircraft were damaged. More than 30,000 of the 65,000 population of Quetta lost their lives.

Devastation of the lines of Nos 5 and 31 Squadrons after the earthquake at Quetta. *(RAFM)*

1937 Lord Willingden, former Viceroy of India, unveiled a memorial at Halton in memory of the RAF personnel who lost their lives in the Quetta earthquake of 1935.

1940 GC (ex-EGM): Cpl Daphne Mary Pearson, who saved a pilot from a burning and bomb-laden aircraft at RAF Detling, subsequently using her body to shield the injured pilot from splinters following the detonation of a bomb on board the aircraft. (*London Gazette*, 19 July 1940)

1941 The Iraqi Revolt: after a period of attacks by Blenheims and Hurricanes against Iraqi airfields used by Luftwaffe aircraft, and an advance by British ground forces towards Baghdad, an armistice was signed and German forces withdrew. The Luftwaffe suffered the loss of all nineteen fighter and bomber aircraft deployed to Iraq in addition to a number of transport aircraft. Although only a minor involvement, it was the first defeat suffered by the Luftwaffe in the Mediterranean and Middle East area.

Flt Lt H. Burton (later AM Sir Harold Burton) reached Trelleborg in Sweden after

RAF armoured cars wait outside Baghdad after hostilities had ceased. *(IWM. CM 923)*

making the first successful escape from a German POW camp by a member of the RAF. He had escaped from Stalag Luft II, Barth, three days earlier. He was awarded the DSO for his escape.

1943 No. 2 Group carried out the last operation under the control of Bomber Command prior to transfer to the Second Tactical Air Force (2nd TAF), which formed the following day under the command of AM J.H. D'Albiac.

1957 The RAF airfield at Mafraq was handed over to the Jordanian government, marking the end of the RAF's presence in Jordan.

1992 HM the Queen Mother unveiled a statue to MRAF Sir Arthur Harris at St Clement Danes Central Church of the Royal Air Force.

2007 The RAF's last Jaguar squadron, No. 6 Squadron (Wg Cdr J. Sullivan) was disbanded at RAF Coningsby.

1 JUNE

1918 The RAF Nursing Service was created. In November Miss Joanna M. Cruikshank was appointed as Matron-in-Chief.
See 14 June 1921.

1940 A Joint Air Training Plan in the Union of South Africa was initiated. Known as the 'van Brookham agreement', the scheme was administered by the South African authorities with all training facilities pooled. All aircrew training was conducted on a joint basis with no segregation. A permanent Air Mission was established in Pretoria.

Several seaplanes of the Royal Netherlands Naval Air Service escaped from Holland as their bases were overrun and flew to RAF Pembroke Dock where they were formed into No. 320 Squadron, the first Dutch squadron within the RAF.

1942 Operation Millennium: Essen was the target for the second 'Thousand Bomber Raid'.

Wg Cdr Spry of *Air Clues. (G.R. Pitchfork Collection)*

1943 Army Co-operation Command was disbanded on the formation of the Tactical Air Force (AM J.H. D'Albiac) within Fighter Command.
See 15 November 1943.

1944 A Combined Air Transport Operations Room (CATOR) was established at RAF Stanmore to control the whole organisation and use of USAAF and RAF transport aircraft for supply by air.

The RAF's Balkan Air Force (AVM W. Elliot) was formed to provide support for Marshal Tito's Yugoslav partisans, particularly by attacking lines of communication. Mustangs and Spitfires claimed 262 locomotives destroyed in the first month of operations.

1949 Air Command Far East (ACFE) was redesignated RAF Far East Air Force (FEAF) (AM Sir Hugh Lloyd), with three subordinate Air Headquarters (AHQ) at Ceylon (Negombo), Malaya (Changi) and Hong Kong (Kai Tak).

Headquarters RAF MEDME was redesignated Headquarters Middle East Air Force (MEAF).

RAF Flying College (Air Cdre A. McKee) was formed at Manby from the Empire Air Navigation School, Empire Air Armament School and Empire Flying School.

1951 The RAF Flying College became the third RAF establishment to receive a grant of arms.
See 19 December 1929, 9 December 1931.

1952 No 591 Signals Unit formed at RAF Wythall to monitor all RAF-owned and -controlled radio networks for communications security (COMSEC). The unit moved to RAF Medmenham in July 1953 before settling at RAF Digby in July 1955.

1956 Wg Cdr S.H.P. Spry DSO, DFC, AFC, DFM joined the staff of *Air Clues*. The fictitious fighter pilot had a reputation for his forthright views, which 'did not necessarily represent the unanimous opinions of those

Air gunners training at a South African Air Force Gunnery School. *(IWM. SAF 197)*

killed and three others wounded, Walker flew it to base safely and was later awarded the DSO.

1944 Operation River: a Sunderland (captain Flt Lt J. Rand) of No. 230 Squadron operating off the River Brahmaputra landed behind Japanese lines on Lake Indawgyi in northern Burma to commence the evacuation of casualties of the 3rd Indian Division of the Chindit Force. Over the next nine days, 269 men were evacuated. A second Sunderland (captain Fg Off E.A. Garside) arrived on 6 June and evacuated a further 119 before the aircraft was wrecked at its moorings during a gale. Rand and his crew returned on 30 June and evacuated 120 casualties during three sorties from the lake in very bad weather. The operation was terminated on 4 July. Rand, and his navigator Fg Off V.N. Verney, were awarded the DFC.

1946 The Air Ministry announced that the Auxiliary Air Force was to be re-formed with thirteen day-fighter, three night-fighter and four light bomber squadrons.

1953 Following the Coronation of HM Queen Elizabeth II, four RAF bands and a large RAF detachment were among the 10,000

in authority'. His career with the magazine spanned over forty years.

1968 Flying Training Command and Technical Training Command were merged into a revived Training Command.

A Sunderland of No. 230 Squadron evacuates the walking wounded from Lake Indawgyi. *(AHB. CI 754)*

2 JUNE

1917 **VC**: Capt William Avery Bishop of No. 60 Squadron, a Canadian serving in the RFC, for his one-man raid on Estourmel Airfield near Cambrai in France in a Nieuport. (*London Gazette*, 11 August 1917)
See 11 September 1956.

1943 Eight Junkers Ju88s attacked a Sunderland of No. 464 (RAAF) Squadron (captain Flt Lt C.B. Walker) over the Bay of Biscay. The ensuing combat lasted forty-five minutes during which the aircraft's gunners shot down three of the Ju88s. Although the Sunderland was badly damaged, with one of its crew

The RAF Central Band marches in the Coronation procession. *(AHB. X 45969)*

troops, in a 2-mile column that marched in the procession from Westminster Abbey to Buckingham Palace.

1976 Operation Heliotrope: following the conclusion of an agreement between United Kingdom and Icelandic government negotiation teams ending the Third Cod War, RAF maritime reconnaissance sorties in support of the Royal Navy ceased. A total of 158 Nimrod and 20 Hastings sorties were flown in support of the Royal Navy between 24 November 1975 and 2 June 1976. The Hastings were drawn from the Bomber Command Bombing School at RAF Scampton and affectionately known as '1066 Squadron'.
See 17 May 1973, 24 November 1975.

1985 Four new stained-glass windows were dedicated at St George's Chapel of Remembrance, RAF Biggin Hill, com-

memorating the service of groundcrew during the Battle of Britain.

1994 A Chinook helicopter flying from RAF Aldergrove to Inverness crashed on the Mull of Kintyre. The crew of four and twenty-five passengers, including some of the UK's top anti-terrorism experts, were killed.

A Hastings of '1066 Squadron' displays its Cod War missions. *(RAFM)*

3 JUNE

1918 The Distinguished Flying Cross, Air Force Cross, Distinguished Flying Medal and Air Force Medal were instituted for gallantry in the air.

1940 The HQ of No. 71 Wing, Advanced Air Striking Force, moved to the Marseilles area to prepare two airfields for use by Bomber Command aircraft for attacks on Italian targets, should Italy enter the Second World War.

1942 A Wellington (captain Sqn Ldr J.H. Greswell) of No. 172 Squadron carried out the first attack on a surfaced submarine at night using a Leigh-Light searchlight. The target was the Italian Navy Marconi Class submarine *Luigi Torelli*. When illuminated, the submarine initially remained on the surface and fired recognition flares, believing the aircraft to be friendly. The Wellington dropped Mk 8 depth charges, damaging the submarine.

1967 MRAF The Lord Tedder, former Chief of the Air Staff who commanded the Mediterranean Allied Air Forces and was Air Commander-in-Chief and Deputy

The powerful Leigh-Light searchlight. *(IWM. CH 13998)*

Aid for Bosnia is loaded onto a Hercules of No. 47 Squadron. *(MOD)*

Supreme Allied Commander, Allied Expeditionary Force during the Second World War, died.
See 1 January 1946.

1982 Operation Corporate: after launching two Shrike anti-radar missiles at a radar near Stanley, a Vulcan (captain Sqn Ldr N. McDougall) was forced to divert to Rio de Janeiro after the in-flight refuelling probe broke during a crucial fuel transfer on the return flight to Ascension. The aircraft landed with insufficient fuel to complete an overshoot. The Brazilian authorities released the aircraft on 10 June.

4 JUNE

1925 An Air Ministry Order announced that 'parachutes will be issued immediately they become available to all squadrons . . . officers and airmen will wear them at all times when flying'. The first two squadrons to receive them were Nos 12 and 25 (AMWO 359/1925).

See 17 June 1926.

1940 Operation Dynamo: the evacuation of Dunkirk was completed with 338,226 Allied troops brought back to the UK. Prime Minister Winston Churchill said, 'Wars are not won by evacuations. But there was a victory inside this deliverance, which should be noted. It was gained by the Air Force.' In the fierce air-to-air fighting during the evacuation, the RAF lost 177 aircraft over Dunkirk, including 106 fighters; the Luftwaffe lost 132 aircraft of all types.

See 26 May 1940.

1944 The bombing campaign against the coastal gun batteries on the northern coast of France continued when 243 heavy bombers and 16 Mosquitos bombed four

This Mosquito PRXVI of No. 544 Squadron displays the D-Day recognition stripes. The wartime censor has deleted sensitive aerials. *(IWM. CH 14264)*

1983 MRAF Sir Thomas Pike, former Chief of the Air Staff, died.

See 1 January 1960.

1993 Operation Cheshire: Hercules of No. 47 Squadron completed 600 sorties to deliver 19 million lb of humanitarian aid to Bosnia-Herzegovina. By the end of the operation in January 1996 the RAF had delivered 26,577 tons of supplies in 1,977 sorties.

1997 Six Wessex helicopters of No. 28 Squadron marked the ending of the RAF's presence in Hong Kong with a final flight around the city.

See 19 June 1997.

sites. Three of these were deception targets in the Pas de Calais but the fourth battery, at Maisy, was in Normandy between what would become known as Omaha and Utah Beaches, where American troops would land in less than thirty-six hours.

A signal was sent that all aircraft participating in D-Day operations were to carry the black and white recognition stripe markings on the rear fuselage and wings from first light on 5 June.

5 JUNE

1944 Operation Tonga: just before midnight, the Allied invasion of north-west Europe

---

AIRBORNE ASSAULT

RAF and USAAF transport forces took off to deliver the British 6th Airborne Division and United States 82nd and 101st Airborne Divisions to dropping zones in Normandy prior to the amphibious landings. The first aircraft, piloted by Sqn Ldr C. Merrick, and with AVM L.N. Hollinghurst, AOC 38 Group, on board, took off from Harwell at 2303hr. The pathfinder aircraft, six Albemarles of No. 295 Squadron, carried the 22nd Independent Parachute Company to set up Eureka beacons and illuminations on the three main dropping zones (DZs) in the neighbourhood of the River Orne. Six Horsa gliders, towed by Halifax aircraft of Nos 298 and 644 Squadrons, carried troops to seize the two bridges over the River Orne and Canal de Caen at Benouville and Ranville. The remainder of the advance party were lifted in twenty-one Albemarles taking transport, guns and equipment to prepare for the main landings. The main body of Nos 3 and 5 Parachute Brigades were dropped from 139 Dakotas, 91 Stirlings and 30 Albemarles. Seventeen gliders carried the heavy equipment.

Eight Lancasters of No. 617 Squadron and six Stirlings of No. 218 Squadron flew a complex deception plan off Cap d'Antifer and Boulogne using window, and enhanced by nine naval and air-sea rescue launches towing balloons, to simulate a convoy approaching the French coast. Halifax and Stirlings of Nos 90, 138, 149 and 161 Squadrons dropped dummy parachutists and firework devices in a dummy airborne landing at Yvetot, some 30 miles north of Le Havre. German radar units reported a large fleet between Boulogne and Etretat so naval units put to sea and all units in the Pas de Calais were put on alert.

A Stirling dropped thirty-five troops of the SAS in Brittany to link up with the French Maquis.

Allied bombers dropped 5,000 tons of bombs on enemy coastal batteries in France and, throughout the night, Stirlings of No. 199 Squadron jammed enemy radar units.

Sqn Ldr C. Merrick, his crew and men of the 22nd Independent Parachute Company board their Albemarle of No. 295 Squadron. (*R. Nesbit Collection*)

commenced (Operation Overlord) with a parachute assault.

1956 A search and rescue Whirlwind of No. 22 Squadron was sent to the aid of the crew of a yacht foundering in heavy seas off Hayling Island. The part-time crewman, 18-year-old National Serviceman AC2 R. Martin, was lowered, unhitched himself from the winch cable and rescued an unconscious man. As the helicopter rushed the man to hospital, he remained on the yacht to protect a female survivor from being washed overboard before both were recovered. Martin was awarded the George Medal, the first to a member of the search and rescue force.

6 JUNE

1918 The Independent Force of the RAF (Maj Gen Sir Hugh Trenchard) of three day and two night squadrons, formed the previous day for conducting war without reference or subordination to the Army or Navy Commands, flew its first operational sorties; ten DH4s of No. 55 Squadron attacked Coblenz and five DH9s of No. 99 Squadron attacked Thionville.

1940 The first enemy air attack against a decoy site – a Q site simulating the night lighting of an airfield – was carried out. By the end of the month thirty-six similar attacks had been undertaken. By the end of night attacks in May 1944, 443 assaults had been made against Q sites.

1942 The Ottawa Agreement was signed after a major review and evaluation of the Empire Air Training Scheme. The name was changed to the British Commonwealth Air Training Plan (BCATP) and the review agreed to place much greater control with the RCAF since the bulk of the training was carried out in Canada.
See 19 May 1942, 27 March 1945.

A Catalina of No. 210 Squadron (captain Flt Lt D.E. Healy) landed at Spitsbergen to deliver supplies and evacuate six members of an Allied reconnaissance party who had

been wounded in an engagement with German forces. The same crew returned on 16 June to evacuate three members of the stranded party. For these and other Arctic flights, Healy was awarded the DSO.

1944 Operation Tonga: at 0320hr the third stage of the initial operation was completed when sixty-eight Horsas and four Hamilcars, towed by Halifax and Albemarle aircraft, delivered the 6th Airborne Division HQ troops and the 4th Anti-Tank Battery.

Allied ground forces began landing in Normandy at dawn. The RAF flew 5,656 sorties in support for the loss of 113 aircraft.

Operation Mallard: the final phase of the airborne assault commenced at 1840hr, when the remainder of 6th Airborne Division took off from seven airfields. The operation was an almost unqualified success with 246 gliders out of a total of 256 that took off landing on their correct landing zones.

Operation Rob Roy: the first resupply missions by fifty Dakotas were flown during the evening.

Over 700 observers of the Royal Observer Corps served as 'seaborne' observers with Allied ships to aid in aircraft recognition.

1946 Provision of aircrew for the peacetime RAF was announced. The only aircrew categories to be retained were pilot, navigator, signaller, engineer and gunner. New titles for non-commissioned aircrew were introduced. (The badges of rank to be used were promulgated in AMO A.498/47.) Equivalence with traditional ranks was as follows:

- Master Aircrew   Warrant Officer
- Aircrew I   Flight Sergeant
- Aircrew II   Sergeant
- Aircrew III   Corporal
- Aircrew IV   Corporal

(Arabic numerals were adopted shortly after publication of the AMO)

The words Pilot, Navigator, Signaller, Engineer, Gunner were used in place of the generic 'Aircrew'. Basic training was

The much-maligned NCO aircrew rank badge worn by P3 J. Shaw, a Spitfire pilot of No. 208 Squadron. *(B. Horten)*

undertaken as a Cadet and operational training as Aircrew IV (AMO A.492/46). See 31 August 1950.

1950 A Dragonfly of the Far East Air Evacuation Flight made the first casualty evacuation by helicopter when a wounded policeman was flown from an isolated police station in south Johore to hospital. Twenty-six casualties had been evacuated by helicopter from the Malayan jungle by the end of 1950.

1955 ASR 1136 for a thermonuclear bomb was issued (Yellow Sun Mk 1).

1963 At RAF Ballykelly, HRH Princess Margaret presented three Squadron Standards – a record for one occasion – to Nos 203, 204 and 210 Squadrons.

1972 The last Canberra squadron to serve in Germany, No. 16 Squadron, was disbanded.

7 JUNE

1915 VC: Flt Sub-Lt Reginald Alexander John Warneford RNAS for downing Zeppelin LZ 37 near Bruges, Belgium. He was killed on 17 June 1915. (*London Gazette*, 11 June 1915)

1941 The first contingent of 550 pilots for the RAF began flying training at eight civilian flying training schools in the USA.

Two Canberra B(I)8s of No. 16 Squadron take off from RAF Laarbruch. *(Gp Capt T. Eeles)*

A 40mm Bofors gun manned by men of the RAF Regiment in Normandy. *(AHB. CL 336)*

1944 Operation Cooney: nine Albemarles dropped fifty-six SAS troops in parties of three in a line across Brittany. Their task was to sever railway lines at eighteen chosen points in order to cut off Brest and western Brittany from the rest of France.

HQs 1304 and 1305 Wings, RAF Regiment, with five LAA Squadrons, went ashore on Juno Beach, Normandy.

Two RAF Servicing Commando Units (Nos 3207 and 3209) and an Airfield Construction Wing went ashore in Normandy to prepare emergency landing strips and advance airfields.

No. 6225 Bomb Disposal Flight sailed for Normandy but the landing craft was attacked and sunk with six killed, six wounded and one airman taken prisoner, and 90 per cent of the equipment lost. No. 6220 (BD) Flight landed two days later when they merged with the survivors of No. 6225 Flight.

1949 The first Armament Practice Camp (APC) was held at RAF Sylt when Vampires of No. 3(F) Squadron arrived for a two-week intensive period of training.

1952 AVM D.F.W. Atcherley, AOC No. 205 Group, disappeared over the eastern Mediterranean en route from Egypt to Cyprus flying a Meteor.

1954 Vampires of No. 8 Squadron commenced bombing and rocket attacks in the western Aden Protectorate against dissident Rabizi tribesmen who were receiving support from the Yemeni government. Air action continued for the rest of the year, albeit at a reduced rate from November.

8 JUNE

1940 The surviving Gladiators of No. 263 Squadron and Hurricanes of No. 46 Squadron left Bardufoss in Norway and landed on the aircraft carrier HMS *Glorious*, the first time Hurricanes had ever attempted to land on an aircraft carrier.

179

Gladiators of No. 263 Squadron in Norway. *(RAFM)*

That afternoon *Glorious* was sunk by the German battle-cruisers *Scharnhorst* and *Gneisenau*; 1,207 men were lost including the forty-one RAF groundcrew and eighteen pilots. Sqn Ldr K.B.B. Cross (OC No. 46 Squadron, (later ACM Sir Kenneth Cross) and Flt Lt P.G. Jameson (later Air Cdre) survived on a life raft in the Arctic waters and were the only two RAF survivors.

GC (ex-EGM): Plt Off Edward Donald Parker of No. 49 Squadron successfully crash-landed his Hampden bomber when an engine failed immediately after take-off. He rescued the wireless operator despite the presence of four 500lb bombs in the aircraft. (*London Gazette*, 6 August 1940)

1941 The main offensive commenced against the Vichy French in Syria. Hurricanes of Nos 80 and 208 Squadrons with Tomahawks of No. 3 (RAAF) Squadron were in action in support of the ground forces. Blenheims of No. 11 Squadron joined in the attacks a few days later. The brief campaign ended with a ceasefire on 12 July.

1944 The first 12,000lb DP 'Tallboy' bombs were dropped by No. 617 Squadron (Wg Cdr G.L. Cheshire) on a railway tunnel near Saumur on the River Loire in an effort to block the tunnel and stop German reinforcements reaching the invasion area in Normandy. One bomb scored a direct hit, blocking the tunnel for months.

A Liberator crew (captain Fg Off K. Moore) of No. 224 Squadron on patrol in the English Channel to prevent U-boats interfering with the Normandy landings sank *U-629* and *U-413* in the space of twenty-two minutes. Moore was awarded the DSO for this unique action.

Four Auster Mk IVs of B Flight, No. 652 Squadron, were the first RAF aircraft to land in France when they arrived at 0815hr, flown by their Army pilots, at a landing ground secured under enemy fire. The squadron's RAF and Army groundcrew had been among the first men to land on the Normandy beaches on D-Day. No. 652 Squadron was in action later in the day and by nightfall it had conducted seven artillery shoots.

1946 The Victory Parade and Flypast to commemorate the end of the Second World

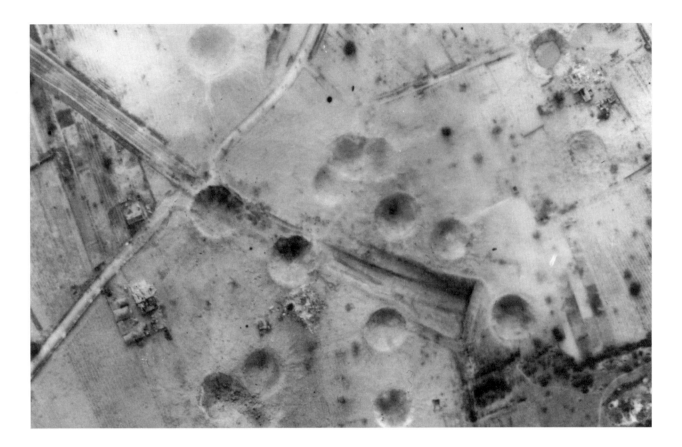

War were held in London with HM King George VI taking the salute in The Mall. A marching column, 4,562yd long, of over 20,000 men and women marched past the saluting point. A lone Hurricane, symbolising the many that had flown in the Battle of Britain, led the flypast of 306 aircraft drawn from 35 squadrons.

1950 ACM Sir John Slessor, the Chief of the Air Staff, was promoted to MRAF.

The Saumur railway tunnel after an attack by Lancasters dropping the 12,000lb 'Tallboy' bombs. *(IWM. CL 80)*

1964 Operation Nutcracker: waves of Hunters of the Khormaksar Strike Wing provided close support as troops captured Jebel Huriyah, the decisive operation that ended the intensive period of operations in the Radfan campaign. Sporadic operations continued before the final tribe sued for peace in November 1964.

See 18 November 1964.

A Belvedere delivers supplies to a mountain post during the Radfan campaign. *(AHB)*

1982 Operation Corporate: Flt Lt D.H.S. Morgan flying a Sea Harrier of No. 800 Naval Air Squadron shot down two A-4B Skyhawks with Sidewinder AIM 9L missiles over Choiseul Sound, the first RAF pilot since the Second World War to destroy two aircraft during one sortie. He was awarded the DSC.

9 JUNE

1938 The British Purchasing Commission placed orders for United States-manufactured military aircraft on behalf of the RAF: 200 Lockheed 14s (given the name Hudson in RAF service), which were initially intended for service as navigation trainers, but were subsequently used in the maritime reconnaissance role, and 200 North American Harvard advanced trainers.

1944 The main headquarters of No. 83 Group (Air Cdre A.D. Boyle) was established in an orchard in Creuilly to supervise the construction and defence of airfields, liaise with 21st Army Group and provide and control close air support operations.

1947 Flt Sgt J. Hannah **VC**, the youngest airman ever to receive the Victoria Cross, died.
See 15 September 1940.

1959 The RAF's first turbo-propeller aircraft, the Bristol Britannia, entered operational service with No. 99 Squadron (Wg Cdr J.O. Barnard) at RAF Lyneham.

10 JUNE

1940 Italy declared war on Great Britain and France.

1943 The Combined Chiefs of Staff issued a supplementary directive to their 'Combined Bomber Offensive Plan', called 'Pointblank', the destruction of the German fighter force and the industries that supplied it.

Men of the RAF Airfield Construction Branch and Royal Engineers build an airstrip in Normandy. *(IWM. CL 710)*

RAF Servicing Commandos refuel a Spitfire on an airstrip in Normandy. *(AHB. CL 76)*

1944 Typhoons of No. 124 Wing carried out a rocket attack on the HQ of the Panzer Gruppe West at Chateau-la-Caine, south-west of Caen, followed by Mitchells bombing from 12,000ft. The Chief of Staff, Gen von Dawans, and several of his senior staff were killed and the HQ put out of action until 28 June.

The first airfield in the Normandy beachhead – B3 at St Croix-sur-Mer, constructed by the RAF Airfield Construction Wings – received its first aircraft when twelve Spitfires of No. 222 Squadron (Sqn Ldr D.G.S.R. Cox) landed after a beachhead patrol. They were rearmed and refuelled by RAF servicing commandos and took off again two and a half hours later. By 14 June, No. 144 Wing (Wg Cdr J.E. Johnson) was operating three RCAF Spitfire squadrons from the airfield. B3 was one of thirty-one airfields constructed in the British zone in Normandy.

1999 Operation Allied Force: bombing was suspended after the Serbian President Milosevic accepted NATO's conditions to withdraw Serb forces from Kosovo. The RAF contributed almost fifty aircraft. Harriers of No. 1 Squadron undertook 870 bombing missions and Tornados of Nos 9 and 31 Squadrons carried out 129 attack sorties. Hercules and support helicopters were heavily involved in the campaign. One Hercules, which was supporting special forces, was lost on 11 June taking off from Kukes airstrip in Albania.

See 24 March 1999.

11 JUNE

1940 A Flamingo of No. 24 Squadron took Prime Minister Winston Churchill from RAF Hendon to France to find out 'what the French were going to do'.

Thirty-six Whitleys of Nos 10, 51, 77 and 102 Squadrons made the first attack on Italy. The aircraft based in Yorkshire

Whitley bombers at RAF Dishforth being prepared for a raid. *(No. 51 Squadron records)*

refuelled in the Channel Islands. Due to bad weather, only thirteen attacked Turin and Genoa. Two aircraft failed to return.

The Italian Air Force (the Regia Aeronautica) carried out its first operation of the Second World War against the RAF. Thirty-five Savoia Marchetti SM79 bombers, escorted by Macchi MC200 fighters, attacked the airfield at Hal Far and the seaplane base at Kalafrana. Defending Sea Gladiators of the island's Fighter Flight damaged one Italian aircraft.

One of the Gladiators that defended Malta. *(IWM. ZZZ 3915E)*

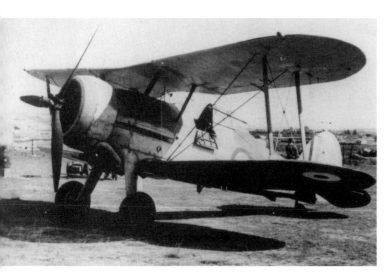

Twenty-six Blenheims from Nos 45, 55 and 113 Squadrons, operating from Egypt, carried out the first RAF attack in the North African campaign when they attacked the Italian airfield at El Adem in Libya.

1943 British troops landed on the island of Pantelleria, which lies between Tunisia and Sicily. The island had been subjected to a massive air bombardment since May and when the garrison of 11,000 Italian troops laid down its arms without firing a shot, it was the first time a heavily defended target had been overwhelmed by air power.

12 JUNE

1942 Flt Lt A.K. Gatward and Sgt G. Fern of No. 236 Squadron took a Beaufighter at low level to Paris where they flew along the Champs Elysées before dropping a large French tricolour over the Arc de Triomphe and strafing the Gestapo HQ in the city.

1944 Sisters Mollie Giles and Iris 'Fluff' Ogilvie of the PMRAFNS were the first women to arrive in Normandy when they landed on the beaches from an LST with No. 50 Mobile Field Hospital. By the end of the war they had reached the gates of Belsen Concentration Camp days after it was liberated.

Sixty-eight LAA Squadrons of the RAF Regiment reinforced Army AA units in the 'Diver' gun belt to intercept V-1 attacks on south-east England.

Bomber Command commenced a new bombing campaign against German oil targets when 303 aircraft attacked a synthetic oil plant at Gelsenkirchen. During the following months, Bomber Command and US 8th Air Force raids on oil refineries and production facilities crippled German fuel production, severely limiting the fighting ability of the German armed forces, particularly the Luftwaffe.

VC: Plt Off Andrew Charles Mynarski RCAF, a Lancaster mid-upper gunner on No. 419 (RCAF) Squadron, gave his life in an attempt to save a fellow crew member during a low-level attack on marshalling yards at Cambrai. (*London Gazette*, 11 October 1946, posthumous award)

Wg Cdr A.K. Gatward RCAF on his return from his final operational sortie. *(G.R. Pitchfork Collection)*

An RAF Mobile Field Hospital in Normandy with Sister Iris 'Fluff' Ogilvie on the right. *(RAFM)*

1953   The Queen's Medal for Champion Shots of the Royal Air Force was instituted. It is competed for at the annual RAF Small Arms Meeting at Bisley.

Damage to the Bohlen Synthetic Oil Plant. *(AHB)*

1968   To mark the 50th Anniversary of the formation of the RAF, sixty members of the Queen's Colour Squadron shared guard-mounting duties with the Brigade of Guards at Buckingham Palace, the Tower of London, St James's Palace and the Bank of England – the first time in the RAF's history. The guard was completed on 9 July. See 1 April 1943.

1999   Operation Allied Force: the success of the Allied air campaign over Serbia and Kosovo

Chinooks land reinforcements on a bridge during the opening phase of operations in Kosovo. *(MOD)*

and intense international diplomatic pressure forced the Serbian leadership to begin to withdraw Serb forces from Kosovo without a NATO ground assault. NATO forces entered the Kosovo region at daybreak, although Russian troops entering Kosovo via Serbia had already occupied part of the province. In Operation Agricola, elements of the RAF Support Helicopter Force, including six Pumas and eight Chinooks, assisted in the rapid deployment of British troops into Kosovo. Operation Agricola marked the largest support helicopter deployment since Operation Granby.

13 JUNE

1930 **GC** (ex-EGM): LAC Robert Ewing Douglas rescued the air gunner and attempted to rescue the pilot from a burning aircraft at Kohat, India. (*London Gazette*, 27 March 1931)

1940 Flg Off G. Haywood, flying a Gladiator of No. 94 Squadron, scored the RAF's first success against an Italian aircraft when he shot down an S.81 bomber off Imran Island near Aden.

1941 Just after midnight, fourteen Beauforts of Nos 22 and 42 Squadrons flew a search from Wick and Leuchars for the German pocket battleship *Lutzow*. Flt Sgt R.H. Loviett carried out a successful torpedo attack which caused serious damage, forcing the battleship to return to Kiel for major repairs. Loviett was awarded the DFM.

1944 The first *Vergeltungswaffe* No. 1 (the V-1 flying bomb) launched against Britain fell on Swanscombe at 0418hr. By the end of the war, 8,892 flying bombs had been launched from ramps and approximately 1,600 were air-launched from Heinkel 111s.
See 29 March 1945.

The first three WAAF nursing orderlies flew on operational duty in Dakotas of No. 233 Squadron during the first air evacuation of casualties from Normandy. The press christened them 'The Flying Nightingales', a name that stuck for the rest of the war.

1967 MRAF Sir Edward Ellington, former Chief of the Air Staff, died.
See 22 May 1933.

A Mk XII airborne torpedo is loaded onto a Beaufort. *(RAFM)*

Three of the RAF 'Flying Nightingale' nurses. An RAF Servicing Commando greets LACW Edna Birkett.
(Mrs Edna Morris)

1977 Support and Training Commands were merged to form RAF Support Command (AM Sir Rex Roe) at RAF Brampton.

1982 Operation Corporate: first operational use of a precision guided munition (PGM) when Wg Cdr P.T. Squire (later ACM Sir Peter Squire) dropped two Paveway laser-guided bombs (LGB) from his Harrier onto Argentinian positions on Mount Tumbledown, achieving one direct hit.

14 JUNE

1919 Capt J. Alcock and Lt A.W. Brown made the first non-stop flight across the Atlantic Ocean, from St John's, Newfoundland, to Clifden, Co. Galway in Eire, in a modified Vickers Vimy bomber. The 16 hours 12 minutes flight also established a world distance record of 1,890 miles. Both men were knighted in recognition of the achievement.

1921 HRH Princess Mary bestowed her patronage on the RAF Nursing Service, which became 'Princess Mary's Royal Air Force Nursing Service' (PMRAFNS). At the time, the sixty qualified nurses in the Service were the only women in the RAF.

1940 Fg Off E.H. Dean, flying a Gladiator of No. 33 Squadron, scored the first RAF success in North Africa when he shot down an Italian Air Force CR.42 fighter near Bardia.

1941 Operation Battleaxe: Commonwealth forces launched an attack to drive Axis forces out of Cyrenaica and relieve the siege of Tobruk. No. 253 Wing Hurricanes, Blenheims and Tomahawks supported the offensive. The offensive was a costly failure and pointed to the need for improved ground/air co-operation.

1944 The first V-1 destroyed by the RAF fell to a Mosquito VI of No. 605 Squadron crewed by Fg Off J.F. Musgrave and Flt Sgt Samwell, who went on to destroy twelve V-1s.

1968 A Royal Review of the RAF was conducted by HM Queen Elizabeth II at RAF Abingdon to mark the 50th anniversary of the formation of the Service.

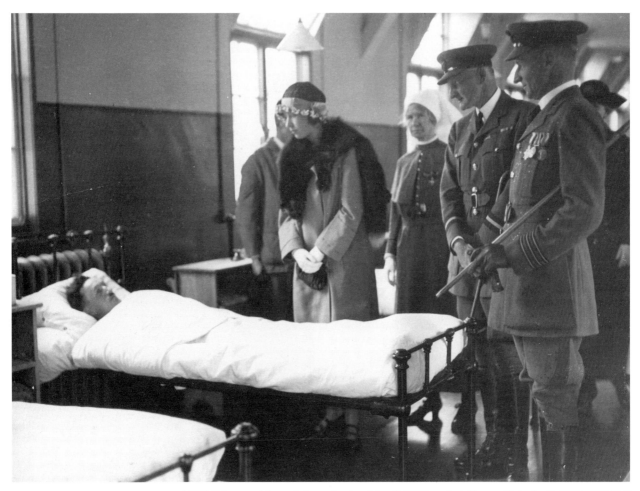

HRH Princess Mary visits patients at the RAF Hospital, Cranwell, in April 1925. *(RAFM)*

Balloons formed an important element of the defence against the V-1 flying bombs and this was the first to bring one down. The crater is visible and the blast destroyed a farm outbuilding in Kent. *(AHB. CH 13766)*

1982 Operation Corporate: Argentinean forces surrendered.

1991 Flt Lt Julie Gibson became the first female regular RAF officer to be awarded her pilot wings when she graduated at No. 6 FTS, RAF Finningley.

15 JUNE

1936 The prototype Vickers Wellington (K4049) made its first flight from Brooklands. A total of 11,461 of the twin-engine bombers were built.

1940 The Allied Air Striking Force (AASF) made its last attacks before its evacuation from France, when Battles attacked trains and transports near Evreux.

1942 The Italian heavy cruiser *Trento* was crippled and set on fire by a torpedo dropped by a Malta-based No. 217 Squadron Beaufort (captain Flt Lt A.H. Aldridge).

1943 The RAF's first autogyro squadron – No. 529 Squadron equipped with the Rota I – was formed at RAF Halton from No. 1448 Flight.

1945 Liberators of No. 159 Squadron, led by Wg Cdr L.B. Ercolani, were despatched on a 2,500-mile round trip in appalling weather to carry out a low-level attack against the last major Japanese supply ship in the South-East Asia theatre, the 10,000-ton *Toho Maru*. Several hits were scored and the tanker was

Liberators being prepared at an airfield in Ceylon for long-range sorties over South-East Asia. *(AHB. CI 1013)*

set on fire and later sank. Ercolani was awarded a DFC to add to his DSO & Bar.

Balloon Command was disbanded. The Balloon Training Unit had closed down in 1943, having trained over 10,000 RAF and WAAF balloon operators and some 12,000 operator drivers. The flying of balloon barrages had finished in the United Kingdom in autumn 1944.

An autogyro being wheeled out for take-off. *(AHB. CH 1426)*

surface communication with the city was halted and eight RAF Dakotas flew in to Wunstorf. The Berlin Airlift began on the 26th with the first RAF participation commencing on the following day.

See 28 June 1948.

1967 Five RAF parachutists, led by Sqn Ldr J. Thirtle, created a British record for a delayed drop when they jumped from 41,383ft over Boscombe Down, Wiltshire, and opened their parachutes at 2,200ft.

1968 With the handing over of RAF Labuan to the RMAF, the RAF presence in Borneo was ended.

1974 No. 63 Squadron, RAF Regiment, became the first operational Rapier SAM unit when it deployed to RAF Gutersloh.

16 JUNE

1940 The Night Interception Committee decided to form a ground radio interception unit to work in collaboration with specialist aircraft in order to investigate German navigation aids, with a view to developing radio counter-measures (RCM). This decision marked the beginning of RCM development in the UK, eventually leading to the formation of a specialist group, No. 100 Group, within Bomber Command.

See 7 October 1940, 23 November 1943.

1944 Bomber Command opened an intensive period of attacks against the 'Noball' targets (flying-bomb and rocket sites). It continued until 6 September.

See 3 August 1944.

1948 Operation Firedog: following the declaration of a state of emergency in Malaya, the RAF began air operations against the Communist Terrorist Organisation (CTO).

See 6 July 1948, 31 July 1960.

The Soviets walked out of the Allied Kommandatura in Berlin. On 24 June, all

A 'Noball' site in the Pas de Calais region after an attack by Bomber Command. *(AHB. X 75248)*

17 JUNE

A DH9A of No. 30 Squadron over Iraq. *(RAFM)*

1926 Following an attempt by Sheikh Mahmud's followers to re-establish themselves in Iraq, severe fighting led to Nos 1 and 30 Squadrons carrying out intensive air action against the Sheikh's stronghold. His followers dispersed, and Mahmud retired into Persia, taking with him a pilot and gunner of No. 30 Squadron captured after their aircraft was forced down by engine trouble; they were released in October 1926.

Plt Off Eric Pentland, a pilot under training at No. 5 FTS, RAF Shotwick, became the first RAF officer to bale out of an aircraft in an emergency when he failed to recover from an inverted spin in his Avro 504K. He became the first European member of the Caterpillar Club, formed by the parachute manufacturer Leslie Irvin for those who were forced to bale out.

1933 HM The King approved the formation of pipe bands for the two Scottish auxiliary squadrons and the wearing of kilts with their uniform. The tartan chosen was the Grey Douglas tartan in honour of a former Commanding Officer, and later Honorary Air Commodore, of No. 602 (City of Glasgow) Squadron, the Marquess of Douglas and Clydesdale, whose brothers served in No. 603 (City of Edinburgh) Squadron. The two pipe bands were the first in the RAF and remained in existence until the auxiliary squadrons were disbanded in 1957.

See 31 July 1936.

1940 Luftwaffe dive-bombers sank the troopship *Lancastria* off St Nazaire. Of the 549 RAF personnel on board, 199 were lost.

The pipe band of No. 602 Squadron. *(Cameron/Carlaw Collection)*

18 JUNE

1936 An Order was published announcing that HM The King had approved the first unit badges and mottoes for Nos 4, 15, 18, 22, 33, 201, 207 and 604 Squadrons (AMO A.142/1936).
See 16 January 1936.

1940 RAF Hurricane squadrons, having covered the evacuation of the last British ground forces from the ports of western France, were ordered back to the United Kingdom. The last out were the first in, with Nos 1 and 73 Squadrons having been based in France since September 1939.

The campaign in France and the Low Countries had cost the RAF 1,029 aircraft and over 1,500 killed, wounded or missing.

The first attempted clandestine pick-up operation ended in failure when a Walrus crashed in north Brittany with the loss of the crew and a British agent.

1942 Plt Off H. Mahn (RCAF), the pilot of a No. 415 Squadron Hampden, was rescued from his dinghy in the North Sea by an RN motor gunboat. He had survived for fourteen days with little water and no food. The rest of his crew had died of exposure.

1982 Flying from Ascension, a Hercules of No. 70 Squadron (captain Flt Lt T. Locke) set an endurance record of 28 hours 4 minutes during a supply drop to a Rapier battery close to Port Stanley.

The squadron badge of No. XV (Bomber) Squadron was among the first group to be authorised. *(G.R. Pitchfork Collection)*

19 JUNE

1912 The Central Flying School (CFS) (Capt G.M. Paine RN) officially opened at Upavon to train pilots for the Naval and Military Wings of the RFC. The first course commenced on 17 August 1912.

1943 A serious explosion occurred in the bomb dump at RAF Snaith killing eighteen airmen. A bomb disposal team, led by Wg Cdr J.S. Rowlands, had cleared the site of damaged and unexploded bombs by 29 June. Rowlands was subsequently awarded the **GC**.
See 10 August 1943.

The first course assembled at the Central Flying School. Capt G.N. Paine RN is seated in the centre and Maj H. Trenchard is on the extreme right of the centre row. *(C. Morris Collection)*

1957 Operation Grapple: the third and final thermonuclear weapon was dropped from a Valiant (captain Sqn Ldr A. Steele) of No. 49 Squadron, completing Britain's first series of megaton weapons trials.
See 8 November 1957.

The test of Britain's megaton nuclear weapon during the Operation Grapple series of trials. *(AHB)*

1997 The last RAF personnel departed Hong Kong.

20 JUNE

1923   Following the release of the Interim Report of the Salisbury Committee on the manner in which RAF operations should be integrated with those of both the Army and the Royal Navy, and on the optimum strength of the RAF at home and overseas, Prime Minister Stanley Baldwin announced in the House of Commons that: 'British air power must include a Home Defence Force of sufficient strength adequately to protect us against air attack by the strongest air force within striking distance of this country. . . . In the first instance the Home Defence Force should consist of fifty-two squadrons to be created with as little delay as possible.'

Of the projected fifty-two squadrons, thirty-five were to be equipped with bombers and seventeen with fighters.

1928   **GC** (ex-EGM): LAC Walter Arnold was a passenger in an aircraft that crashed and caught fire at Digby. He went into the wreckage and rescued the unconscious pilot despite sustaining burns. (*London Gazette*, 9 November 1929)

1929   **GC** (ex-EGM): Flt Cdt William Neil McKechie rescued a fellow cadet from a burning aircraft at RAF Cranwell. (*London Gazette*, 18 October 1929)

1961   A Vulcan (captain Sqn Ldr M.G. Beavis later ACM Sir Michael Beavis) of No. 617 Squadron made the first non-stop flight from the United Kingdom to Australia. The aircraft flew 11,500 miles in 20 hours 3 minutes at 573mph, in-flight refuelling over Cyprus, Karachi and Singapore.

1990   The Red Arrows departed for a six-day tour of Russia and Hungary, their first visit to countries of the former Warsaw Pact.

THE RED ARROWS

The Red Arrows, known as the Royal Air Force Aerobatic Team, were officially formed in 1965, and in recent years have been based at RAF Scampton. Each display pilot flies with the Red Arrows for three years, ensuring that expertise is passed on from year to year. On completion of their three-year tour of duty, pilots return to their primary RAF role with front-line or instructional squadrons. Therefore, each year three new pilots join the team and, with the exception of the leader, Red 1, all the pilots change the position they fly within the formation.

The seven-month training period commences as soon as the season finishes and continues until the new season starts in late May. Each pilot flies three times a day, five days a week, and each sortie is debriefed in minute detail with video footage. During the winter months, the Red Arrows fleet of thirteen Hawk aircraft is given an extensive overhaul by the team's dedicated ground crew. Renowned throughout the world as ambassadors for both the RAF and the United Kingdom, the team have displayed in fifty-two countries and given over 4,000 displays.

Hawks of the Red Arrows stream smoke. *(MOD)*

21 JUNE

1918 The Air Council approved the appointment of Sir Walter Raleigh, Professor of English Literature at Oxford University, as the Air Historian. By November, the Air History Section had been established and by 1921 it had changed its name to the Air Historical Branch (AHB), a title that has remained unchanged since.

1921 Capt A.F.W.B. Proctor **VC**, DSO, MC & Bar, DFC was killed in an air accident at RAF Upavon practising an air display for the annual RAF Display.
See 8 August 1918.

1928 The Air Ministry announced the findings of an inquiry into the future requirements for officers for the RAF. This resulted in a new Constitution for the General Duties Branch, allowing the creation of a more structured career for permanent officers, the provision of specialists, and the introduction of a new class of officers to be known as Medium Service officers.

1940 The first two Hurricanes arrived at Malta to reinforce the Malta Fighter Flight. The following day six more arrived from a group of twelve that had left RAF Aston Down on 17 June. They had transited through France and Tunisia but six had been lost en route for various reasons.

The RAF formed the Parachute Training School (Sqn Ldr L.A. Strange) at Ringway. This later became a component of the Central Landing School. Subsequently, the Central Landing Establishment (CLE) was formed from the School on 19 September 1940.

The first RCAF squadron to operate in the UK, No. 1 Squadron, arrived at RAF Middle Wallop and flew Canadian-built Hurricanes in the Battle of Britain. It was later renumbered No. 401 (RCAF) Squadron.

Hurricanes arrive at RAF Takali for the defence of Malta.
(R. Nesbit Collection)

22 JUNE

Paratroopers practise landings from a mock fuselage at No. 1 Parachute Training School. (*R. Nesbit Collection*)

1918 The North Russian Expeditionary Force, comprising British Army units and supported by a Royal Air Force flight equipped with de Havilland DH4 day bombers, landed at Murmansk.

1938 An 'invasion force' of Pathan tribesmen under the leadership of Sayid Muhammed Sadi, dubbed 'Shami Pir', a Syrian with pronounced pro-Nazi sympathies, began to move towards the India–Afghanistan border to mount an invasion of Afghanistan. Three Audax aircraft of No. 20 Squadron, on an armed reconnaissance sortie, sighted and immediately attacked Sadi's lashkar, which subsequently dispersed. The leader, Sqn Ldr B.E. Embry,

Sunderland L2160 of No. 230 Squadron being 'christened' *Selangor* at Port Swettenham by the Sultan of Selangor. (*AHB. H 277*)

was awarded an immediate DSO, the first of an eventual quadruple DSO.

No. 230 Squadron at RAF Seletar, Singapore, became the first squadron to receive the Sunderland flying-boat when the first aircraft arrived at the end of a ferry flight from the United Kingdom.

The British Air Commission to the USA and Canada (RAF member Air Cdr A.T. Harris) placed a contract for 200 advanced trainer aircraft (Harvards) and 200 navigation training aircraft (Hudsons). This marked the first of thousands of US-built aircraft that were acquired for the RAF and the RN.
See 3 December 1938.

1940 Flt Lt G. Burge, flying a Sea Gladiator nicknamed 'Faith', claimed the first Italian bomber shot down over Malta. The aircraft was one of three left on Malta by the Fleet Air Arm. For some time, 'Faith', 'Hope' and 'Charity' provided the only fighter defence on Malta.

1941 The first *Gee* chain ground stations at Daventry, Ventnor and Stenigot were

completed. *Gee* was a medium-range radio navigation aid, which employed ground transmitters and an airborne receiver. The navigator plotted values derived from a CRT display as position lines on a special *Gee* chart, which had a lattice overprint corresponding to time delays from the various ground stations.

1943 The 3in rocket projectile (RP) was used operationally for the first time when Beaufighters of Nos 143 and 236 Squadrons of the North Coates Wing attacked a convoy off the Dutch coast. The rockets turned out to be a devastating anti-ship weapon.

1944 The siege of Imphal was lifted after three months of fierce fighting during which the large Army and RAF garrison was entirely resupplied by air with almost 15,000 sorties flown by transport aircraft. Hurricanes and Vengeance aircraft flew over 25,000 sorties in close and indirect support. Five squadrons of Spitfires maintained the air superiority that allowed the support operations to be so effective.

1955 A Canberra B2 *Aries IV* of the RAF Flying College (captain Wg Cdr M.D. Lyne) completed the first jet trans-Polar flight

A Beaufighter X of No. 236 Squadron is armed with rocket projectiles. *(G.R. Pitchfork Collection)*

Rocket projectiles fired from a Beaufighter head for a merchant ship off the Norwegian coast. *(AHB)*

flying from Bardufoss in Norway to Fairbanks, Alaska.

1999 Operation Allied Force: following the termination of the operation, the Harrier and Tornado detachments returned to their home bases in the United Kingdom. A force of six Harrier GR7s remained in the theatre to support NATO ground forces if required.

23 JUNE

1919 DH9s and Camels of No. 47 Squadron (Maj R. Collishaw) flew the first operations in support of Gen Denikin's White Russian forces when they attacked a railway bridge at Tsaritsin on the River Volga. Operations continued until 7 October when the squadron became 'A' Squadron, RAF Mission. This Mission left south Russia from Novorossisk in March 1920. In one year of

A Camel of No. 47 Squadron in south Russia. *(Andrew Thomas Collection)*

almost non-stop operations over southern Russia the men of No. 47/'A' Squadron were awarded four DSOs, two OBEs, two MBEs, sixteen DFCs and one Bar, three AFCs, thirteen MSMs, and seventy-five Russian orders and decorations.

1921 The RAF began a weekly mail service from Cairo to Baghdad, a distance of 840 miles. The route had been surveyed and tracks ploughed across the desert to assist navigation. Nos 30, 47 and 216 Squadrons initially operated the service, which was taken over by Imperial Airways in 1927.

1938 The Secretary of State for Air (Sir Kingsley Wood) announced that the RAF was engaged in the greatest expansion scheme that any defence Service had been faced with in peacetime. This included the need to recruit over 31,000 men in the current year. These included 2,100 pilots, 550 observers, 26,000 men and 3,000 boys.

1943 Photographic reconnaissance by a Mosquito (captain Flt Sgt E.P.H. Peek) of No. 540 Squadron revealed that rockets with an estimated range up to 130 miles –

Officers of No. 47 Squadron in south Russia. The CO, Maj R. Collishaw, is seated in the centre surrounded by his officers wearing a wide variety of RNAS, RFC, Army and RAF uniforms with a Russian officer seated on the left. *(RAFM)*

Vernon transport aircraft used on the Cairo to Baghdad mail service. *(AHB. H 1665)*

A Vickers Vimy of No. 216 Squadron used on the Cairo to Baghdad mail service. *(RAFM)*

later known as the V-2 – were being developed at the German research facility at Peenemunde on the Baltic coast.

See 17 August 1943, 28 November 1943.

Operation Voodoo: a Waco CG-4A (Hadrian), carrying 3,360lb of freight, was the first glider towed across the Atlantic. A Dakota of RAF Transport Command towed it from RCAF Dorval in Canada to Prestwick in Scotland. The combination routed via Goose Bay, Bluie West One (Greenland) and Iceland, arriving at Prestwick on 30 June. The total flying time was 28 hours. The Dakota pilot, Flt Lt W.S. Longhurst, and the two glider pilots, Sqn Ldrs R.G. Sey and F.M. Gobeil RCAF, were each awarded the AFC.

1944 A Spitfire XIV pilot (Fg Off K.R. Collier) of No. 91 Squadron destroyed a 'Diver' (V-1) by using the wing of his aircraft to tip up the flying bomb after he had run out of ammunition. This was the first of a number of similar incidents.

1956 The Comet C2, the RAF's first jet transport aircraft, completed its first operational flight with No. 216 Squadron when it took the Secretary of State for Air (Rt Hon Nigel Birch) to Moscow for the Russian Air Display at Vnukovo.

1994 The Secretary of State for Defence (Malcolm Rifkind) announced that the Queen's Flight would disband on 1 April 1995 and merge with No. 32 Squadron at RAF Northolt to form No. 32 (The Royal) Squadron.

24 JUNE

1943 India Command adopted blue–white roundels on aircraft to eliminate the red, which could be interpreted as the red rising sun marking on Japanese aircraft.

1944 **VC**: Flt Lt David Ernest Hornell RCAF, captain of a No. 162 (RCAF) Squadron Canso, sank a U-boat 120 miles north of the Shetland Islands. His aircraft was set on fire and Hornell was forced to ditch. He dived into the sea to rescue a crew member and he sacrificed some of his clothing to assist others. After twenty-four hours in a dinghy, the crew were rescued, but three died of exposure including Hornell. (*London Gazette*, 28 July 1944, posthumous award)

1993 With the graduation of No. 155 Entry of apprentice engineering technicians at RAF Halton, the last entry of apprentices left No. 1 School of Technical Training. The Reviewing Officer was HRH The Duke of Gloucester.

See 7 October 1993.

The Queen's Flight Insignia. *(AHB)*

HRH The Duke of Gloucester inspects the last entry of aircraft apprentices at No. 1 School of Technical Training at RAF Halton. *(Halton Aircraft Apprentice Association)*

THE RAF APPRENTICE SCHEME

MRAF Lord Trenchard's aim in setting up the Apprentice Scheme in the early 1920s was to produce an elite corps of highly skilled airmen who would provide the backbone of the newly formed RAF. When the training scheme ceased in 1993, more than 50,000 had graduated, mostly from Halton. Over 20 per cent were commissioned, with 120 attaining Air rank and several serving on the Air Force Board. MRAF Sir Keith Williamson, 50th Entry, became Chief of the Air Staff in October 1982. ACM Sir Michael Armitage, 56th Entry, was the Chief of Defence Intelligence and was appointed to the Air Force Board as AMSO in 1985.

During the Second World War, in which several thousands of ex-apprentices gave their lives, over 900 were awarded gallantry medals, including Sgt T. Gray, 20th Entry, who was awarded the Victoria Cross posthumously. A total of 116 apprentices flew as pilots in the Battle of Britain including Gp Capt F.R. Carey CBE, DFC & 2 Bars, AFC, DFM, 16th Entry and Flt Lt S. Allard DFC, DFM & Bar, 20th Entry, who was Halton's top-scoring pilot in the Battle with twenty-three confirmed victories. Among many distinguished bomber pilots was Gp Capt T.G. Mahaddie, DSO, DFC, AFC*, 17th Entry, of Pathfinder Force fame.

Many apprentices achieved sporting fame including Gp Capt D. Finlay DFC, AFC, 12th Entry, who won a silver and bronze medal in the 110yd hurdles at the 1932 and 1936 Olympic Games.

Gp Capt The Earl of Ilchester, 33rd Entry, sat in the House of Lords and Sir John McGreggor, 41st Entry, became the Head of Hong Kong Administration in 1997. Among distinguished apprentices from overseas was AM M. Younis, 63rd Entry, who became President of Pakistan Airlines.

Perhaps the most famous ex-apprentice was Air Cdre Sir Frank Whittle, 8th Entry, the inventor of the jet engine.

A painting depicting a Passing Out Parade of aircraft apprentices. *(AHB. LA 5677)*

25 JUNE

1928 Following the breakdown of the truce between the Zeidi tribesmen and the British administration in Yemen, No. 8 Squadron resumed bombing operations. This also encouraged other tribes friendly to Britain to attack the Zeidi who withdrew from Aden in August 1928.

1942 Operation Millennium: the third 'Thousand Bomber Raid'. The target was Bremen and the raid marked the last operational sortie of the Manchester, the unsuccessful forerunner of the outstanding Lancaster bomber.

1945 A convoy of men and vehicles of No. 2848 Rifle Squadron, RAF Regiment, arrived at Gatow Airfield in the British Sector of Berlin to relieve Soviet forces and stake the RAF's claim to the airfield.

1948 HM The King gave approval for ocean-going ships and sea-going craft of the 68ft high-speed launch class, which fly the RAF ensign, to be designated 'His Majesty's Air Force Vessel' (HMAFV).

1950 North Korean forces invaded South Korea and United Nations forces came to the aid of the South. Sunderlands of the Far East Flying Boat Wing (Wg Cdr D.H. Burnside) deployed to Iwakuni, Japan, for anti-submarine and maritime reconnaissance operations. The first successful operational patrol was flown over the Yellow Sea on 4 August by an aircraft of No. 88 Squadron (captain Fg Off R.S. Brand). By the end of the war, Sunderland crews had flown 1,647 operational sorties.

Fairey IIIFs of No. 8 Squadron over Aden.
(G.R. Pitchfork Collection)

HM King George VI meets bomber crews who took part in the Thousand Bomber Raids. *(AHB. CH 5809)*

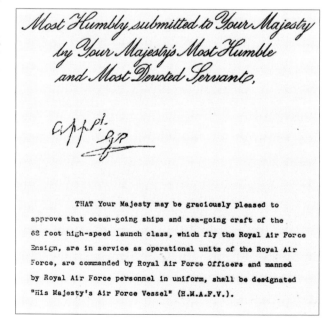

Most Humbly submitted to Your Majesty by Your Majesty's Most Humble and Most Devoted Servants,

appt. gr

THAT Your Majesty may be graciously pleased to approve that ocean-going ships and sea-going craft of the 68 foot high-speed launch class, which fly the Royal Air Force Ensign, are in service as operational units of the Royal Air Force, are commanded by Royal Air Force Officers and manned by Royal Air Force personnel in uniform, shall be designated "His Majesty's Air Force Vessel" (H.M.A.F.V.).

Royal approval for certain RAF marine craft to be referred to as 'His Majesty's Air Force Vessel'.
(Gp Capt S. Fosh)

Sunderlands of the Far East Flying Boat Wing at Iwakuni, Japan. *(AHB)*

26 JUNE

1918 The Royal Warrant instituting the Meritorious Service Medal (MSM) appeared in the *London Gazette* '. . . for the recognition of valuable services rendered by Warrant Officers, Non-Commissioned Officers and Men as distinct from flying duties . . . '. The award was discontinued in 1928.

See 1 December 1977.

The mode of saluting in the RAF and the occasions on which it is used was promulgated in AMWO 517/18.

1939 The Secretary of State for Air (Sir Kingsley Wood) announced that in time of war British civil aircraft would be used by the RAF for transport purposes whenever possible.

1940 The Air Council was reconstituted following the formation of the Ministry of Aircraft Production. The Air Member for Training joined the Council and the Air Member for Development and Aircraft Production was excluded.

1944 Eight temporary airfields constructed since 6 June were operational in the Normandy bridgehead.

The Queen's Colour for the Central Flying School

205

A Mustang III of No. 19 Squadron is serviced near the village of Ellon in Normandy. *(IWM. CL 571)*

1969 A Queen's Colour was presented to the RAF Central Flying School, Little Rissington, by HM The Queen, accompanied by the Duke of Edinburgh, the Queen Mother and Prince Charles.

27 JUNE

1919 The Air Council approved in principle an education scheme for personnel of the RAF, to be administered by a civilian education staff. The scheme was based on a paper prepared for the RAF, which concluded: 'Education, it must be remembered, is not merely a matter of teaching certain subjects but far more, especially in the case of a combatant force, of developing certain qualities of mind and of character, power of concentration,

accurate observation, orderly thinking, clear and commonsense reasoning, precise expression, with initiative, energy, self reliance and decision. . . .'

See 1 October 1920.

1941 The British Mission to the Soviet Union arrived in Moscow five days after the German invasion of that country. AVM A.C. Collier was the Head of the RAF Section.

1976 Flt Lt G.D. Lee, a Phantom pilot on No. 111 Squadron, became Britain's first world gliding champion since 1952, flying an ASW17 sailplane of the RAF Gliding and Soaring Association at Rayskala, Finland. He retained his title at the next two world championships to become the only person to be world champion three times in succession.

1989 The Air Force Board Standing Committee agreed that 'women aircrew could be employed on all aircrew specialisations in non-combatant roles'. The policy was made public on 20 July 1989. The SH and LRMP roles were opened to female aircrew in July 1991.

1995 Two Wessex of No. 84 Squadron helped to fight the biggest fire in Cyprus for 100 years. The helicopters flew firebombing sorties using 'rainmaker' buckets, delivering 80,000 gallons of water in 43 hours.

28 JUNE

1939 The Women's Auxiliary Air Force (WAAF) was formed (Director, Miss J. Trefusis-Forbes – as from 1 July 1939) from the RAF Companies of the Auxiliary Territorial Service (ATS). The Director wore the rank badges of an Air Commodore and was given the rank title of Senior Controller.

See 28 August 1939.

1940 A Sunderland of No. 230 Squadron (captain Flt Lt W.W. Campbell) operating from RAF Kalafrana, Malta, sank the Italian submarine *Argonauta*, the first since Italy had declared war. The following day he sank a second submarine, the *Rubino*. He landed on the sea and picked up survivors. Campbell was awarded the DFC.

York transport aircraft at RAF Gatow during the Berlin Airlift. *(AHB. R 1821)*

A formation of Ansons of the Southern Communications Squadron marks the retirement from RAF service of the long-serving aircraft. *(P.H.T. Green Collection)*

1944 **GC**: Air Cdre Arthur Dwight Ross RCAF who rescued an air gunner from a burning Halifax at RAF Tholthorpe despite a bomb exploding and virtually severing his arm. (*London Gazette*, 27 October 1944)

1948 Operation Knicker: Dakotas of No. 46 Group began to airlift supplies from Wunstorf Airfield in the British Zone of Germany to the British garrison in Berlin following the Soviet implementation of a blockade on surface travel. The following day the airlift was widened in scope to include supplies for the civilian population of West Berlin. On 19 July the

name of the operation was changed to Plainfare.

See 12 May 1949.

1966 Lord Shackleton, Minister of Defence, officially opened the RAF Supply Control Centre (SCC) at RAF Hendon.

1967 A Vulcan B1a (captain Flt Lt R.L. Beeson) was delivered from Waddington to Halton, landing on a 3,400ft grass runway.

1968 The retirement of the RAF's last Anson was marked by a flypast of six machines of the Southern Communications Squadron at RAF Bovingdon. A total of 8,138 Ansons were produced in the UK in addition to 2,882 built in Canada. With thirty-two years' service, the Anson was the longest-serving aircraft in the RAF at the time.

USAAF IN BRITAIN

Prior to the United States' entry into the Second World War many Americans volunteered for service in the RAF and RCAF. They suffered their first casualty when Plt Off W.M.L. Fiske, a Hurricane pilot of No. 601 Squadron, died of his wounds and burns on 17 August 1940. From October 1940, three fighter squadrons, Nos 71, 121 and 133, which became known as the 'Eagle' squadrons, were formed, and 244 American pilots flew with these squadrons before they were disbanded and incorporated in the USAAF in September 1942.

In February 1942, Brig Gen Ira C. Eaker and his staff arrived in Britain to establish a strategic bomber force to work alongside the RAF's Bomber Command. Initially, Eaker and his staff were stationed at RAF Bomber Command Headquarters near High Wycombe where Eaker established a close relationship with AM Sir Arthur Harris. The area selected for basing the first US bomber units was Huntingdonshire where airfields were under construction for the RAF. Later, well-established RAF airfields in East Anglia were made available. Many RAF procedures were adopted by the USAAF's 8th Air Force including training, intelligence, air-sea rescue procedures, and a great deal of use was made of operational airfields, maintenance and storage facilities.

B-17 Flying Fortresses of the 91st Bomb Group, 8th Air Force based at RAF Bassingbourn. *(RAF Museum)*

29 JUNE

1942 A US 8th Air Force crew (captain Capt Kegelman) operated in a No. 226 Squadron Boston in a daylight raid on Hazebrouck marshalling yards by twelve aircraft – the first operational action by USAAF in Europe. Five days later, six USAAF crews flew in a formation of RAF Bostons attacking airfields in Holland.

30 JUNE

1936 A new altitude record for an aeroplane was established when Flt Lt M.J. Adam took a Bristol 138 to 53,937ft at Farnborough.

1941 ACM Sir Robert Brooke-Popham, the C-in-C Far East, outlined his grave concerns to Whitehall about the deficiencies of the RAF in his command and the need for reinforcements. He signalled, 'At present, not only is our ability to attack shipping deplorably weak, but we have not the staying power to sustain even what we could now do. As our air effort dwindles. . . . so will the enemy's chance of landing increase. I have no doubt what our first requirement here is. We want to increase our hitting power against ships and our capacity to go on hitting.' He sent further urgent signals in August and September

The Siebe-Gorman high-altitude suit worn by Sqn Ldr F.R.D. Swain and Flt Lt M.J. Adam during their record climbs to height. *(AHB. H 1388)*

Halifax II W1048 is recovered from Lake Hoklingen, Norway. *(G.R. Pitchfork Collection)*

reiterating his concerns but pressures in other theatres prevented any significant reinforcements.

See 10 December 1941.

1948 The departure of the High Commissioner and the Army and RAF headquarters staff from the enclave at Haifa marked the RAF's final withdrawal from Palestine.

1954 The runway at RAF North Front, Gibraltar, was extended to 2,000yd allowing modern, high-performance aircraft to use the airfield.

1969 The V-Force QRA was terminated at midnight when the responsibility for Britain's strategic nuclear deterrent

passed to the Polaris submarines of the Royal Navy.

1973 An RAF diving team, led by Sgt D.A. Walker, and assisted by Norwegian divers, raised Halifax W1048 from Lake Hoklingen, Norway. The bomber of No. 35 Squadron had crash-landed on the frozen lake after attacking the German battleship *Tirpitz* on 27 April 1942. The aircraft is displayed at the RAF Museum, Hendon.

1977 The South-East Asia Treaty Organisation (SEATO) was disbanded.

1988 AHQ Cyprus ceased to operate as an independent formation, its function being subsumed by HQ British Forces Cyprus.

1 JULY

1914 The Naval Wing of the Royal Flying Corps was reorganised to become the Royal Naval Air Service (RNAS).

1916 **VC**: Maj Lionel Wilmot Brabazon Rees of No. 32 Squadron RFC, for gallantry displayed while on patrol over the Double Crassieurs zone. He disrupted a major German bombing attack on Allied positions in a de Havilland DH2, despite being wounded. (*London Gazette*, 5 August 1916)
     See 28 September 1955.

1918 HM King George V directed that the Royal Air Force take precedence after the Navy and Army (AMO 470/18).

1919 The Royal Air Force Long Service and Good Conduct Medal (LS&GC) was instituted. Awarded to NCOs and other ranks of the RAF for eighteen years' exemplary service, reduced in 1977 to fifteen years. Provision for bars for further periods of service was made from 1944 onwards.

1922 The Central Trade Test Board was established with its headquarters at RAF Uxbridge. The tests given by the examination boards consisted of a written examination and practical tests.

1928 Control of the Iraq Levies passed from the Colonial Office to the RAF. The force had its origins in 1915 and was reconstituted as the Iraq Levies in 1919. The RAF had assumed operational command in Iraq in October 1922 as part of the policy of air control.
     See 15 March 1943.

1930 The Dental Branch was formed and administered as part of RAF Medical Services.

1937 The Indian government sanctioned the RAF to attack any village suspected of harbouring the Fakir of Ipi who, since the beginning of the year, had been making repeated attempts to stir up unrest against the British. RAF squadrons in India mounted a wide-ranging campaign of air attacks against the Fakir, who continued to be a thorn in the flesh of

Iraq Levies form a guard at Wing Headquarters, Mosul, Iraq. *(AHB)*

the Indian government, although his influence declined during the Second World War.

1940 The first Polish squadron, No. 300, was formed within the RAF. It initially operated as a bomber squadron with Battles before being re-equipped in October with the Wellington. A further nine Polish squadrons were formed by mid-October 1940.

1943 The WAAF reached its peak strength of 181,835 women of all ranks.

1944 The RAF reached a peak strength of 1,185,833 (1,011,427 men and 174,406 women).

1947 The first of six squadrons of the RAF Regiment (Malaya), No. 91 Squadron, was formed at Changi. On 17 July 1961 No. 94 Squadron was the last squadron to disband.

1961 Operation Vantage: two Hunter ground-attack squadrons (Nos 8 and 208), plus

WAAFs work on the Bristol Pegasus engine of a Sunderland. *(AHB. CH 13659)*

Men of the RAF Regiment Malaya under training at RAF Catterick. *(Gp Capt K.M. Oliver)*

troops, were sent to Kuwait following a request from the Ruler for assistance in response to threats from the Iraqi Prime Minister (Gen Kassim) and to Iraqi troop movements towards the border. Shackletons of No. 37 Squadron deployed to Bahrain, Canberra bomber and photo-reconnaissance squadrons (Nos 13, 88 and 213) concentrated in the Persian Gulf area and V-bombers were brought to readiness in Malta. RAF Transport Command and the Royal Rhodesian Air Force deployed troops and equipment from the United Kingdom, Cyprus and Kenya.

1962 The Royal Air Force Flying College at Manby was renamed the RAF College of Air Warfare.

1969 UK-based V-bombers were transferred to the tactical strike and attack roles as the RN Polaris force became operational and assumed the responsibility for providing the UK strategic deterrent.

1979 Three Royal Auxiliary Air Force Regiment Field Squadrons were formed. Over the next ten years, three further Field Squadrons were formed, in addition to two in the SHORAD role.

1991 The Air Warfare Centre (Air Cdre J.G. Lumsden) was established with its headquarters at RAF High Wycombe.

2 JULY

1918 The RAF School of Music opened at Hampstead with a staff of two officers and three SNCOs.

1919 The RAF airship R34 made the first airship crossing of the Atlantic. Sqn Ldr G.H. Scott

and a crew of thirty RAF and US Navy personnel flew the airship from East Fortune in Scotland, arriving in New York on 6 July. The crew made the return journey between 9 and 13 July, thus completing the first double crossing.

The R34 airship shed at Beardmore Works, Inchinnan. *(AHB. Q 27475)*

The poster for the 1924 Hendon Aerial Pageant. *(RAFM)*

3 JULY

1919   A Royal Warrant authorised the Secretary of State for Air to issue Warrants to Warrant Officer Class I and Class II in the Royal Air Force (AMWO 845/19).

1920   The first RAF Tournament, which later became known as the RAF Pageant and later still as the RAF Display, took place. Some 60,000 people were present and saw the finest display of flying ever given in the country. The RAF Benevolent Fund benefited by some £7,000.

1940   For the first time, the targets attacked by RAF Bomber Command included invasion barges being massed for a possible invasion of Britain.
See 7 September 1940.

1948   The York aircraft commenced operations on the Berlin Airlift. By the end of the operations, Yorks had transported 233,145 tons of coal and food; almost 60 per cent of the RAF airlift effort.

1964   HM The Queen presented a new Queen's Colour for the Royal Air Force in the United Kingdom at Buckingham Palace to replace that first presented in 1951 by Her Majesty, then the Princess Elizabeth, acting on behalf of King George VI.

215

1992 Operation Cheshire: Hercules of the Lyneham Wing commenced the airlift of humanitarian supplies into Sarajevo, Bosnia. The operation lasted until early January 1996 by which time the RAF had delivered 26,577 tons of supplies in 1,997 sorties. The airlift came to symbolise the commitment of the international community to the survival of Sarajevo and its people.

4 JULY

1918 RE8 aircraft of No. 9 Squadron parachuted ninety-three boxes of small arms ammunition to attacking Australian troops on the opening day of the Battle of Hamel. The drops were conducted from an altitude of 800ft and two of the twelve aircraft involved were shot down by German ground fire.

Sidewinder-armed Harrier GR3s of No. 1(F) Squadron over the Falkland Islands. (*AM I.D. Macfadyen*)

1941 VC: Wg Cdr Hughie Idwal Edwards DFC, the commanding officer of No. 105 Squadron, led a daylight bombing raid by fifteen Blenheims on Bremen. (*London Gazette*, 22 July 1941)

1943 A No. 511 Squadron Liberator (captain Flt Lt E.M. Prchal) crashed on take-off from Gibraltar. Among those killed was Gen Sikorski, Prime Minister of the Polish Government in Exile and Commander-in-Chief of the Polish Forces in the United Kingdom.

1951 It was announced that the British Air Forces of Occupation (BAFO) in Germany were to be placed under the operational control of HQ Allied Air Forces Central Europe (AAFCE).

1982 Four Harriers of No. 1 Squadron disembarked from HMS *Hermes* and landed at Stanley Airport, Falkland Islands, to provide an air defence QRA capability. Four more Harriers arrived on 7 July.

Supplies are unloaded from a Sunderland on the Havel See, Berlin. *(AHB. R 1830)*

5 JULY

1912   Capt E.B. Loraine and his passenger Staff Sgt R.H.V. Wilson of No. 3 Squadron became the first fatalities of the Royal Flying Corps when their Nieuport monoplane crashed near Stonehenge.

1939   The Treasury gave approval for the formation of a Flying Personnel Research Committee and the provision of a physiological laboratory for medical research purposes at RAE Farnborough.
     See 12 October 1943.

1941   **GC**: Sqn Ldr Revd Herbert Cecil Pugh, who was travelling on HMT *Anselm* when it was torpedoed off West Africa. He insisted on being lowered into the hold to comfort those trapped despite the certainty that he would not be able to escape from the stricken vessel. A total of 175 RAF personnel were lost. (*London Gazette*, 1 April 1947, posthumous award)

1942   The Prime Minister called for an all-out effort on the development of *H2S* radar navigation and bombing aid. Permission was given for the magnetron valve – not previously permitted – to be flown over enemy territory.

1948 Sunderland flying-boats of Nos 201 and 230 Squadrons joined the Berlin Airlift, flying between Finkenwerder (Hamburg) and the Havel See in Berlin.

1983 The first ex-British Airways Lockheed L-1011-500 TriStars converted to air-to-air refuelling tanker/transports entered service with No. 216 Squadron at RAF Brize Norton.

6 JULY

1935 King George V reviewed the service at RAF Mildenhall, where a ground display of 350 aircraft was mounted, before moving to RAF Duxford to view a flypast of almost 200 of them. This was the first Royal Review since the formation of the RAF.

1940 The 450lb Mk VII depth charge was used operationally for the first time by an RAF anti-submarine aircraft. The depth charge gradually replaced the earlier, considerably less effective, anti-submarine bombs used by Coastal Command.

1942 A Wellington (captain Plt Off W.B. Howell) of No. 172 Squadron sank *U-502* in the Bay of Biscay, the first occasion a successful sinking had been achieved with the aid of the powerful Leigh-Light searchlight.

1948 Operation Firedog: the first RAF air strikes in the twelve-year campaign were carried out by two Spitfires of No. 60 Squadron, which destroyed a terrorist camp in the Perak region.

1949 HM King George VI presented his Colour to the RAF College Cranwell.
See 27 December 1947.

The Royal Review at RAF Mildenhall. *(RAFM)*

A Sea King approaches RAF Lossiemouth. *(RAFM)*

1965 A Hastings of No. 36 Squadron (captain Flt Lt J. Aiken), engaged on parachute training, crashed near RAF Abingdon after the elevators suffered metal fatigue. The crew of five and thirty-five TA parachutists and members of an air quartermaster course were killed.

1988 Sea King search and rescue helicopters from RAF Boulmer and RAF Lossiemouth played a major role in the rescue of survivors of the *Piper Alpha* oil rig disaster in which 167 people died. The rig, 120 miles off the north-east coast of Scotland, caught fire after a series of explosions. Nimrods from RAF Kinloss remained in the area co-ordinating rescue attempts.

7 JULY

1938 Four Wellesleys of the Long Range Development Unit (LRDU) left RAF Cranwell to fly non-stop to Ismailia, Egypt, covering the 4,300 miles in 32 hours' flying time – the longest non-stop formation flight at the time. The aircraft were positioned in Egypt

for an attempt on the Russians' world distance record of 6,306 miles.

See 5 November 1938.

1941 **VC**: Sgt James Allen Ward RNZAF, the second pilot of a No. 75 Squadron Wellington climbed onto the wing of his aircraft in flight to extinguish a fire while returning from an attack on Munster, Germany. (*London Gazette*, 5 August 1941)

See 15 September 1941.

Wellesleys of the Long Range Development Unit. *(G.R. Pitchfork Collection)*

1944 Operation Charnwood: Bomber Command mounted its first attack against enemy troop positions in support of Allied forces in Normandy. A total of 467 bombers attacked German positions in front of the Canadian 1st and British 2nd Armies north of Caen, causing the destruction of much of the northern suburbs of the town.

1955 The Air Ministry announced the reorganisation of the Middle East Air Force Command Headquarters. A Northern Group, under Air Headquarters Levant, was formed to control units in Iraq, Jordan, Cyprus and Libya. A Southern Group, under Headquarters British Forces in Aden, was responsible for units in Aden, the South Arabian coast and Kenya, and for the staging posts in the Persian Gulf. AHQ Levant and HQ British Forces Aden continued to be subordinate to HQ Middle East Air Force.

1962 The Founder's Medal of the Air League (given for outstanding contributions to British aviation) was presented to the

A Victor of the Marham Wing deploys the centre hose to refuel a Harrier GR3 of No. 1(F) Squadron.
(J. Falconer Collection)

Central Flying School on the 50th anniversary of the latter's formation.

1977 Following the breakdown of negotiations between the UK and Guatemala, the Guatemalan armed forces mobilised. In response, the British garrison was strengthened and six Harrier GR3s of No. 1(F) Squadron (Wg Cdr J.G. Saye) flew to Belize via Goose Bay with the support of Victor tankers. Although the threatened invasion of Belize did not take place, RAF assets remained in Belize as part of BRITFORBEL. During March 1981, the Harrier detachment was designated No. 1414 Flight and three Puma helicopters deployed in support of the British garrison became No. 1563 Flight.

1988 Air Cdre F.M.F. West, the last surviving air **VC** of the First World War, died.
See 10 August 1918.

220

8 JULY

1936 HM King Edward VIII inspected new types of aircraft at RAF Martlesham Heath. These included the prototype Hurricane and Spitfire and the Battle, Blenheim, Lysander, Wellesley and Whitley.

1943 Sqn Ldr T.M. Bulloch, flying a No. 224 Squadron Liberator, sank *U-514* in the Bay of Biscay. It was the fourth U-boat he had destroyed, having damaged three others, making him the most successful and most decorated anti-U-boat pilot in Coastal Command. He was awarded a DSO & Bar and a DFC & Bar.

HM King Edward VIII inspects new RAF aircraft types at RAF Martlesham Heath. *(G.R. Pitchfork Collection)*

THE U-BOAT WAR

The RAF waged a continuous war against the *Unterseeboot* (U-boat) from the first days of the Second World War until a few days after the cessation of hostilities in western Europe. Absolute figures reflecting the RAF's success against the U-boats are difficult to determine since the precise reason for the loss of some of the submarines will never be known. Undoubtedly, some would have been due to air action. It is generally accepted that aircraft of Coastal Command sank at least 192 and about 19 others in conjunction with ships of the Royal Navy. The RAF's strategic bombers destroyed over 20 and others were lost as a result of mining operations by aircraft of the RAF. However, success cannot be measured by statistics alone. It will never be known how many attacks by U-boats were thwarted by the presence of Coastal Command aircraft flying their ceaseless patrols and convoy protection sorties.

Crew members escape from a sinking U-boat in the Bay of Biscay. *(IWM)*

9 JULY

1918   Maj James McCudden **VC**, DSO & Bar, MC & Bar, MM was killed in a flying accident at Aix-le-Chateau, France.
   See 29 March 1918.

1936   RAF Cranwell and RAF Halton ceased to have the status of independent commands and were placed under the newly formed RAF Training Command.

1941   The Air Ministry issued a new directive to Bomber Command to concentrate on the dislocation of the German transportation system and to destroy the morale of the civil population as a whole and of the industrial workers in particular.

Above: HM Queen Elizabeth and HRH Princess Elizabeth meet bomber crews. *(AHB. CH 13467)*

Left: Maj James McCudden **VC** and his dog Butch. *(AHB. H 1175)*

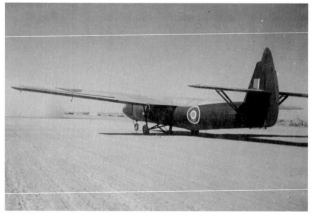

A Horsa glider about to take off from a desert airstrip. *(AHB. CNA 1664)*

1993 HM Queen Elizabeth the Queen Mother unveiled a National Memorial to the aircrew who fought in the Battle of Britain. The site chosen was on the clifftops at Capel le Ferne in the area of Kent known in 1940 as 'Hellfire Corner'.

10 JULY

1919 Dress regulations for officers were promulgated with three patterns of distinctive uniform authorised. Owing to the transition from the RNAS, RFC and Army patterns, authority was given to continue wearing the former service's patterns until RAF patterns were generally available. Badges of the RAF were to be worn on whatever pattern was used but in many cases this was ignored (AMWO 783/1919).

1940 The Battle of Britain: the first phase – the *Kanalkampf*, or Channel battle – began with German attacks on Channel convoys and the ports on the south coast.

The first Czechoslovak squadron, No. 310, was formed within the RAF equipped with Hurricanes at RAF Duxford. It flew with distinction during the Battle of Britain.

1943 Operation Husky: the Allied invasion of Sicily opened with an airborne assault mounted from airfields in North Africa. Poor weather and high winds, combined with the inexperience of many of the USAAF transport aircraft crews, resulted in only 250 of the 3,000 US paratroopers reaching designated drop zones. The glider operation fared worse, with 69 out of 137 landing in the sea with heavy loss of life. Only twelve gliders, all towed by RAF aircraft with crews more experienced in night air landing operations, reached the correct landing zone. Fortunately, the seaborne landings fared better.

1959 A Valiant (captain Wg Cdr M.J. Beetham) of No. 214 Squadron completed the first non-stop flight from the UK to Cape Town. With two air-to-air refuellings, the 6,060 miles was covered in 11hr 28min at an average speed of 528.5mph.

Wg Cdr M.J. Beetham, OC, No. 214 Squadron, and his valiant crew. *(AHB. PRB 16957)*

1942 **GC**: LAC Albert Matthew Osborne of RAF Malta for aircraft fire-fighting and rescue operations under enemy air attack. (*London Gazette*, 10 July 1942, posthumous award)

1943 Operation Husky: Nos 2855 and 2925 LAA Squadrons RAF Regiment landed with the invading forces on the beaches of Sicily. Six more squadrons joined them during the next two weeks.

1946 The Air Ministry announced that the RAF Regiment was to continue as an integral part of the RAF. It would maintain rifle, armoured and light anti-aircraft squadrons, and some units would be trained as airborne and parachute troops.

1947 The East Chapel of Westminster Abbey was rededicated as the Battle of Britain Chapel in the presence of HM King George VI, although it has come to be called the Royal Air Force Chapel. A large window of strikingly complex design is dedicated to the aircrew lost in the Battle of Britain. The badges of sixty-three squadrons that took part and flags of the Allied nations are incorporated. At the foot of the window are the words from Shakespeare's *Henry V*: 'We few, we happy few, we band of brothers.' Nearby is the roll of honour of those aircrew killed in the Battle.

Hurricanes fly in the close vic formations favoured during the Battle of Britain. *(R. Nesbit Collection)*

The Battle of Britain Memorial Window in Westminster Abbey. *(AHB)*

11 JULY

1939 Some 240 aircraft of Bomber Command participated in a series of navigational exercises, including training flights over central and southern France. These sorties served as a show of strength; they also provided valuable training in long-range overseas operations.

1940 The Photographic Development Unit was renamed the Photographic Reconnaissance Unit (PRU) and the interpretation element was formed as the Photographic Interpretation Unit (PIU) (Wg Cdr H. Hemming), the latter established at Beresford Avenue, Wembley. The PIU was from its inception a joint service organisation and it became the foundation of the Joint Air Reconnaissance Intelligence Centre (JARIC).
See 23 September 1939, 17 December 1953.

1942 Forty-four Lancasters made the longest-range daylight raid to date when they attacked shipyards at Danzig in Poland – a round trip of 1,750 miles.

1957 The Historic Aircraft Flight was formed at RAF Biggin Hill. It was redesignated the Battle of Britain Flight on 21 February 1958 and the Battle of Britain Memorial Flight on 20 November 1973.

12 JULY

1943 Wg Cdr J.D. Nettleton **VC** was declared missing in action when his No. 44 Squadron Lancaster failed to return from an attack on Turin. He and his crew have no known graves, and are commemorated on the Runnymede Memorial.
See 28 April 1942.

1944 The RAF's first operational jet aircraft – the Gloster Meteor – entered service with No. 616 (South Yorkshire) Squadron based at RAF Manston, Kent.

A Meteor F1 of No. 616 Squadron, the RAF's first jet squadron. *(L.H. Casson)*

A USAF ceremonial parade at Mitchell Field to welcome No. 54 Squadron after the first crossing of the Atlantic by jet aircraft. *(AHB. CHP 1129)*

1948 Six RAF Vampire F3s of No. 54 Squadron (Sqn Ldr R.W. Oxspring) made the first Atlantic crossing by jet aircraft taking off from RAF Odiham and flying via Stornoway, Iceland and Greenland to Goose Bay in Labrador, a distance of 2,202 miles in a flight time of 8 hours 18 minutes. They continued to the USA and undertook a number of air show appearances, including the grand opening of Idlewild Airport.

1979 MRAF Sir John Slessor, former Chief of the Air Staff and who commanded Coastal Command and the RAF Mediterranean and Middle East Command during the Second World War, died.
    See 1 January 1950.

13 JULY

1920 The first permanent and short service commissions were granted to medical officers and antedated for permanent officers to 1 October 1918.

1941 The first operational Mosquito was delivered to No. 1 Photographic Reconnaissance Unit (PRU) at RAF Benson. It flew its first photo-recce operation on 17 September when Brest was the target.

1943 No. 244 Wing, Desert Air Force (Gp Capt B. Kingcome) equipped with three Spitfire squadrons (Nos 92 and 145 and 1 SAAF),

A Spitfire Vc of No. 145 Squadron arrives from Malta at the hastily cleared airfield at Pachino in Sicily. *(R. Nesbit Collection)*

landed at Pachino, Sicily, from Malta. RAF servicing commandos of No. 3230 SCU provided ground support for the aircraft.

1944 As the Soviet Army began a rapid westerly advance, the first POW camp, Stalag Luft VI at Heydekrug, close to the Soviet border in East Prussia, was evacuated and prisoners transferred to other camps in the west.
    See 19 January 1945.

1947 Operation Diagram: following a threat of unrest in Trieste on the Italian/Yugoslav border, Mosquitos of No. 21 Squadron and Tempests of No. 135 Wing deployed to airfields in Austria and remained there for four weeks.

2001 Some 200 RAF personnel provided emergency cover in north-west England during a firemen's national strike.

RAF firemen, with a Green Goddess, under training for Operation Fresco. *(AHB)*

226

1940 An advance party of twenty-four officers and men (Gp Capt H.K. Thorold) arrived at the port of Takoradi, Gold Coast, to establish the reception area for crated aircraft to be delivered before being reassembled and ferried across Africa to reinforce the RAF in Egypt.

See 19 September 1940.

1946 The RAF airfield at Halfar on the island of Malta was handed over to the Royal Navy.

1969 The first detachment of RAF support helicopters was despatched to Northern

Hurricanes are removed from crates at Takoradi, West Africa, where they are rebuilt before being ferried to the Middle East. *(AHB. CM 3014)*

High Speed Launch 100 on acceptance trials on the Solent. *(D. Smith)*

14 JULY

1936 The Metropolitan RAF was reorganised to reflect the demands of expansion and was organised into four Commands:
- Bomber Command (AM Sir John Steel) at Uxbridge.
- Fighter Command (AM Sir Hugh Dowding) at Stanmore.
- Coastal Command (AM Sir Arthur Longmore) at Lee-on-Solent.
- Training Command (AM Sir Charles Burnett) at Ternhill.

The RAF's first High Speed Launch (HSL), the 64ft British Powered Boat Company, RAF 100, completed sea trials in the Solent and was handed over to the RAF and based at RAF Manston. Twenty-one of the sea-going 'Class 100' boats were built before improved HSLs were introduced into service with the RAF Marine Branch for air-sea rescue duties.

Wessex helicopters of No. 72 Squadron on patrol over Northern Ireland. *(AHB)*

Ireland to assist British Army units attempting to control inter-communal violence between Protestant and Catholic communities. Four Wessex of No. 72 Squadron were despatched to RAF Ballykelly; the detachment was relieved in March 1970 by a detachment from No. 18 Squadron. Support helicopters have remained based in Northern Ireland.

See 15 August 1969.

15 JULY

1945 The RAF's Second Tactical Air Force (2nd TAF) was redesignated British Air Forces of Occupation (BAFO). The RAF in Germany was initially tasked with assisting the British Army in maintaining order within the British Zone and supervising the dissolution of the Luftwaffe. The first AOC of BAFO was ACM Sir Sholto Douglas.

See 1 September 1951.

1953 The Coronation Review of the RAF by HM The Queen was held at RAF Odiham. Over 300 aircraft were inspected and 1,125 officers and other ranks drawn from all RAF Commands took part in the parade. The flypast of 640 aircraft, which included 446 jets, took thirty minutes to fly overhead. The Review was under the command of AVM The Earl of Bandon.

The Coronation Review of the Royal Air Force at RAF Odiham. *(AHB)*

16 JULY

1940 Hitler's War Directive No. 16 was issued for the invasion of Great Britain. As part of the preparations, the Directive decreed 'the English Air Force must be so reduced morally and physically that it is unable to deliver any significant attack against the German crossing [of the English Channel].' The assault was codenamed Seelowe (Sealion).

1958 Operation Fortitude: following the overthrow and assassination of King Feisal of Iraq, the UK received an appeal for assistance from HM King Hussain of Jordan. RAF transport aircraft flew No. 16 Parachute Brigade Group from Cyprus to Jordan and Hunters of No. 208 Squadron deployed to Amman to provide air support. British forces were withdrawn by 2 November 1958.

1978 No. 66 Squadron RAF Regiment, the last to be equipped with the L40/70 Bofors anti-aircraft gun, was disbanded.

A Hunter F6 of No. 208 Squadron arrives at Amman with Hastings transports on the flight line. *(AHB)*

17 JULY

1938 The first United Kingdom Air Defence Cadet Corps squadron – the forerunner of the Air Training Corps – was formed at Leicester.

1944 **VC**: Flt Lt John Alexander Cruikshank, captain of a No. 210 Squadron Catalina, sank U-boat *U-347* north-west of Norway. Despite sustaining over eighty wounds, he supervised the return flight and beached the badly damaged aircraft at base in the Shetland Islands before collapsing through loss of blood. (*London Gazette*, 1 September 1944)

AIR TRAINING CORPS

The Air Cadet Movement owes its existence to Air Cdre J.A. Chamier, known as the father of the air cadet movement. With war looming he decided to start an aviation cadet corps, and in 1938 the Air Defence Cadet Corps (ADCC) was formed to recruit and train young men in aviation skills. The ADCC was organised and run by local people in many towns and cities. The idea captured the mood of the British people and, in their eagerness to help the nation in preparation for war, young men rushed to join in their thousands. Each squadron's aim was to prepare cadets for joining the RAF or the Fleet Air Arm. They provided training in flying, military skills and instructed them in drill, dress and discipline. Physical fitness was also very actively promoted with PT and sporting activities prominent, in addition to long route marches, shooting practice and camping skills.

Cadets also played an active part in the early days of the war carrying messages, helping with clerical duties, assisting in handling aircraft and in the movement of stores and equipment. They filled thousands of sandbags and loaded miles of belts of ammunition. The government soon asked the ADCC to begin training the young men who were waiting to be called into service, and very soon thousands of well-qualified individuals passed through basic training.

In 1940 the British government took control of the ADCC, which resulted in a number of changes in the birth of a completely new organisation, called the Air Training Corps (ATC). On 5 February 1941 the ATC was officially established, with King George VI agreeing to be the Air Commodore-in-Chief, and issuing a Royal Warrant setting out the Corps' aims. The number of young men responding to this new ATC was spectacular. Within the first month the size of the old ADCC had virtually doubled to more than 400 squadrons and within twelve months it was almost eight times bigger.

Training programmes were adapted to prepare young men for entry to the RAF. Visits were arranged to RAF and Fleet Air Arm stations where cadets were given air experience flights whenever possible. To supplement flying in RAF aircraft, gliding was introduced and this allowed cadets to be initiated into basic flying training. In 1943 a special ATC Flight of ten aircraft, Oxfords and Dominies, was established.

In due course the Combined Cadet Forces' RAF sections and the ATC merged their HQ functions to form the Air Cadet Organisation as an umbrella organisation. Both still retain their individual identities and working practices at headquarters and local level. Today the Air Cadet Organisation, through its Volunteer Gliding Schools, is the largest gliding school in the world. Today, there are over 60,000 cadets, volunteer staff and civilian committee members.

HM King George VI meets cadets of the Air Defence Cadet Corps. (*AHB. CH 3072*)

18 JULY

1918 The Air Construction Service was formed within the RAF to carry out technical duties under the direction of the Administrator of Works and Buildings, Air Ministry (AMWO 661/18).

1943 RAF Woodbridge, a specialised airfield built to receive damaged aircraft returning from operations, received its first emergency landing when a USAAF B-17 bomber landed short of fuel. This was the first of 4,120 emergency landings at the airfield by the end of June 1945. Woodbridge was one of three such airfields built on the east coast (the others were at Catfoss and Manston), with a runway 3,000yd long and 250yd wide and with specialised aircraft recovery and medical facilities.

1944 The 2nd Army began its breakout from the Normandy beachhead with the greatest weight of air support given to any army. No. 83 Group flew 1,289 sorties when 140 tons of bombs and 70 tons of rockets were used. The Visual Control Post (VCP), consisting of a RAF controller in a tank fitted with VHF/RT, controlled airborne close support aircraft for the first time.

Operation Goodwood: Bomber Command mounted a very large daylight raid of 942 aircraft to drop 5,000 tons of bombs on five fortified villages in the area east of Caen in support of the 2nd Army preparing for an armoured attack. Mosquitos of No. 8 (PFF) Group marked the target using *Oboe* and Master Bombers controlled the attack. It was considered one of the most successful raids in direct support of the Allied armies.

Nos 2825 and 2932 Squadrons, RAF Regiment, were assigned to Land Forces Adriatic with Royal Marine units for amphibious operations on the Yugoslav coast and as boarding parties on RN vessels in the Adriatic.

The RAF Test Pilots School was renamed the Empire Test Pilots School.

The emergency runway built at RAF Woodbridge just south of RAF Bentwaters. *(IWM. C 5483)*

19 JULY

1917 A Cabinet Committee (the Smuts Committee), set up following two heavy attacks on London by Gotha bombers, released an interim report examining the air defence of the United Kingdom. Among the Committee's recommendations were the establishment of a London Air Defence Area to encompass all of the United Kingdom within Gotha bomber range and the acceleration of plans to form additional day-fighter squadrons for home defence.

1918 The first ever carrier-borne air strike took place when seven Camels, each carrying two 50lb bombs, were launched at dawn from HMS *Furious* to attack the German dirigible airship sheds at Tondern at the mouth of the Elbe. The strike, led by Capt W.D. Jackson, destroyed the German Navy Zeppelins L54 and L60 in their sheds. Jackson was awarded the DFC.

1924 Sulaimaniya was reoccupied by Iraqi troops, supported by RAF armoured cars and aircraft. This effectively marked the end of the Jihad called by Sheikh Mahmud in May 1924.

1934 Prime Minister Stanley Baldwin announced an expansion of the Home Defence Air Forces from fifty-two to seventy-five squadrons, and for other additions to the RAF to bring its worldwide strength to 128 squadrons in five years. This became known as Expansion Scheme 'A', which provided for the growth of the RAF to a strength of 111 front-line squadrons at home and overseas (1,252 aircraft) together with 16½ Fleet Air Arm squadrons (213 aircraft) by 31 March 1939. This was seen as a 'shop window force' to deter

A Rolls-Royce armoured car on patrol in northern Iraq.
(AHB. B 834)

American-built bombers for the RAF at Dorval waiting to be ferried across the Atlantic. *(AHB. CAN 4330)*

Germany, and so little provision was made for reserves. Over the years leading up to the Second World War this first scheme was revised/replaced numerous times until Scheme 'M' was announced on 10 November 1938. One of the most significant was Scheme 'F', which eliminated the light bombers in favour of medium and heavy bombers, and for the first time it provided for adequate reserves.

See 25 February 1936, 10 November 1938.

1940 **GC**: Cpl Joan Daphne Mary Pearson of RAF Detling was awarded the Empire Gallantry Medal (EGM) for saving the pilot of a bomb-laden aircraft following the detonation of a bomb on board. She shielded the pilot with her body from flying shrapnel. After the institution of the George Cross, recipients of the EGM were ordered to exchange it for the new award. (*London Gazette*, 6 August 1940; subsequent George Cross awarded on 23 September 1941)

2006 Two Chinooks evacuated seventy-six passengers from Beirut to RAF Akrotiri after Israel launched a series of attacks against the Lebanese capital.

20 JULY

1941 RAF Ferry Command (AM Sir Frederick Bowhill) was formed and took over the work of the Atlantic Ferry Organisation (ATFERO).

A group of badly burned aircrew being treated by Mr A. McIndoe (later Sir Archibald) at East Grinstead Hospital decided to form the Guinea Pig Club. The secretary had suffered burns to his hands, excusing him from writing many letters, and the treasurer's legs were burned, ensuring that he could not abscond with the funds! There were 649 Guinea Pigs by the end of the Second World War.

1974 Turkish forces invaded northern Cyprus. Although the Sovereign Base Areas (SBAs) were not threatened, 10,132 dependants and tourists were evacuated from RAF Akrotiri to RAF Lyneham and RAF Fairford over the period 21–30 July.

1989 A statement in the House of Commons announced that the RAF's policy had been revised to permit female aircrew to be employed in all specialisations in non-combat roles.

See 14 June 1991.

2007 Sea King helicopters mounted the biggest rescue operation of its kind from flood-

A Chinook evacuates British personnel from the dockside at Beirut alongside HMS *Bulwark*. *(MOD)*

ravaged Gloucestershire and the south-west Midlands. At the peak of activity, six helicopters were involved lifting more than 250 people to safety. On the afternoon of 23 July, in a series of sorties 87 people were lifted in one single incident by a Sea King of 'E' Flight, No. 202 Squadron. Heavy moving equipment and personnel from No. 2 MT Squadron at RAF Wittering gave support in the Cheltenham area and other RAF personnel were drafted in to a major operation to stop the flooding of a crucial electricity sub-station at Gloucester.

21 JULY

1936 The King's Flight was formed, with Flt Lt E.H. Fielden (later AVM Sir Edward Fielden) appointed as captain in the rank of Wing Commander.

1944 A Catalina (captain Sqn Ldr F.J. French) of No. 210 Squadron landed on the sea 200 miles north of the Arctic Circle to rescue six survivors from a No. 86 Squadron Liberator shot down by a U-boat. The six men had been in three one-man dinghies for forty-eight hours when they were rescued. This was the most northerly air-sea rescue mounted from the United Kingdom.

1945 The Japanese made a final desperate attempt to escape the advancing 14th Army and cross the Sittang river in southern Burma. Every available RAF aircraft was sent in to attack with 3,045 sorties flown and 750 tons of bombs dropped over the following nine days. The end of the battle signified the end of the war in Burma.

Thunderbolts of No. 30 Squadron are serviced at an airfield in Burma. *(AHB. CI 1055)*

1966 As part of the long-standing dispute over the sovereignty of Gibraltar, Spain informed the UK government that military aircraft would no longer be allowed to overfly Spanish territory.
See 12 April 1967.

22 JULY

1940 A Blenheim of the Fighter Interception Unit (Fg Off G. Ashfield) became the first aircraft to shoot down an aircraft using its own Air Interception (AI) radar when it destroyed a Dornier Do 17 at night off Selsey Bill.

No. 1 Air Ministry Works Area (Field) formed at Bristol from units returning from France. The rapid expansion of commitments led to the formation of the Airfield Construction Service in March 1941 with four squadrons commanded by RAF officers with civil engineering qualifications.
See 15 March 1940, 1 April 1944.

1950 Reserve Command was renamed Home Command.

1959 Sqn Ldr C.G. Maughan, commanding officer of No. 65 Squadron, won the *Daily Mail* Bleriot Anniversary Air Race between London and Paris. He completed the course between Marble Arch and the Arc de Triomphe in a time of 40 minutes 44 seconds, travelling by RAF Police motorcycle, Sycamore helicopter and Hunter T7. The prize money of £6,500 was donated to charity. Flt Lt Williams was second but was disqualified when his motorcycle driver failed to notice a red traffic light in London when he cruised past it at 80mph.

1966 During engine runs on a Lightning at RAF Lyneham, the CO of No. 33 MU, an engineering officer (Wg Cdr W.T. Holden) inadvertently applied reheat and he was forced to take off. The ejection seat was unarmed and after two abortive attempts he managed to land the aircraft.

1975 The Mobile Catering Support Unit was formed at RAF Benson.

Sqn Ldr C.G. Maughan and his RAF despatch rider have refreshments after arriving in Paris. *(AHB. PRB 17092)*

23 JULY

1923 HRH The Prince of Wales unveiled the RAF Memorial on the Victoria Embankment, London. MRAF Lord Trenchard unveiled an additional inscription commemorating the fallen of the Second World War on 15 March 1946. In the nearby gardens outside the old Air Ministry (now the Main Building, Ministry of Defence) stand statues to MRAF Lord Trenchard and MRAF Lord Portal.

1935 The first report on radio direction finding, later renamed radar, was made to the Air Defence Research Committee in the United Kingdom.

1940 The first RAF squadron to move to Iceland, No. 98 Squadron equipped with Battles, left RAF Gatwick for Reykjavik.

1944 Bomber Command mounted the first major raid on a German city for two months with an attack by 629 aircraft on Kiel. The majority of the Command's effort

The RAF Memorial on the Victoria Embankment, London. *(AHB. X 39983)*

A crew of No. 9 Squadron relax after returning from a raid on Stettin. *(AHB. CH 11972)*

continued to be directed against French targets in support of operations in Normandy.

See 16 August 1944.

1974   Following the Turkish invasion of Cyprus, Phantoms of Nos 6 and 41 Squadrons and No. 228 OCU arrived at RAF Akrotiri to provide tactical reconnaissance support for British forces. Further Phantoms arrived to provide an air defence capability and to escort Nimrod reconnaissance sorties. The detachment was withdrawn on 13 September.

A Phantom FGR2 of No. 228 OCU at RAF Akrotiri. *(MOD)*

24 JULY

1918 The first 1,650lb 'SN' bomb – the largest bomb to be used by the RFC/RAF during the First World War – was dropped on Middelkirke by a Handley Page 0/400 (captain Sgt L.A. Dell) of No. 214 Squadron.

1941 A major daylight raid was mounted against the German capital ships berthed in the French Biscay ports. One hundred Wellingtons, Hampdens and Fortresses bombed *Gneisenau* and *Prinz Eugen* at Brest. Fifteen unescorted Halifaxes bombed *Scharnhorst* at La Pallice causing sufficient damage for the pocket-battleship to be moved to Brest where repairs took four months. Seventeen aircraft were lost to enemy fighters and flak, 11.3 per cent of the force.

1943 Operation Gomorrah: Bomber Command mounted the first of four attacks against the city of Hamburg. The command flew 3,091 sorties and dropped 8,623 tons of high explosives and incendiaries. Much of Hamburg was devastated and the firestorm that followed the attack on the night of 27/28 July is estimated to have killed approximately 45,000 German civilians. Some 87 bombers were lost and 522 British and Allied airmen also lost their lives.

The first attack of Operation Gomorrah saw the first use of *Window* – tinfoil strips dropped from aircraft to simulate aircraft echoes and confuse ground search and night-fighter radars. The forerunner of modern 'chaff', *Window* proved very successful and only 12 of the 700 bombers that attacked on the night of 24/25 July were lost.

1946 The first live ejection test in the United Kingdom was made when Mr Bernard Lynch successfully completed an ejection using a Martin-Baker seat fired from a Meteor flying at 8,000ft and a speed of 320mph.

Officers of No. 207 Squadron pose with the 1,650lb 'SN' bomb at Ligescourt. *(AHB. Q 9971)*

Left: Andrée de Jongh, who led the 'Comète' Escape Line. *(IWM)*

Above: A Venom FB1 of No. 8 Squadron with improvised sun canopy. *(AHB)*

Dakotas of No. 267 Squadron flew on Operation Wildhorn from Foggia *(AHB. CNA 3334)*

ACM The Lord Dowding at the laying of the foundation stone at St George's Chapel of Remembrance at RAF Biggin Hill. *(AHB)*

Andrée de Jongh (Dedée), born in 1916, of the Belgian Resistance, who master-minded the 'Comète' escape line and personally escorted 118 airmen across the Pyrenees, received the first 'helper certificate', awarded as a token of gratitude, at a ceremony at the Palais des Sports, Brussels. She was also awarded the George Medal and the American Medal of Freedom with Golden Palm for gallantry.

1957 Operations commenced in central Oman against dissidents who threatened the Sultan of Oman's authority. Throughout the eighteen months of operations, Venoms of Nos 8 and 249 Squadrons and Shackletons of No. 37 Squadron provided the main offensive force with rockets and bombs.
See 9 February 1959.

25 JULY

1915 **VC**: Lt Lanoe George Hawker of No. 6 Squadron RFC, for his actions during an offensive patrol over France and in recognition of the continuous courage he demonstrated while flying a Bristol Scout with a hastily fitted cavalry carbine. (*London Gazette*, 24 August 1915)
See 23 November 1916.

1927 The first annual tactical exercise to give practice to the Home Defence staffs and squadrons was held over four days and nights involving the whole of Fighting and Bombing Areas and the ground forces of London Defences.

1943 Spitfires of No. 322 Wing foiled a Luftwaffe attempt to reinforce Sicily by air. Twenty-four Junkers Ju 52 transport aircraft and four escorting Messerschmitt Bf 109s were shot down.

1944 Operation Wildhorn III: a Dakota (captain Flt Lt S.G. Culliford) of No. 267 Squadron left Foggia, Italy, and landed in a field 200 miles south of Warsaw to collect vital parts of a German V-2 rocket, acquired by Polish partisans, for technical analysis in the UK. The Dakota became bogged down in the soft ground and took off as German troops closed in on the field. The nine-hour sortie was later described as 'one of the most outstanding and epic flights of the war by an unarmed transport aircraft'.

1951 ACM The Lord Dowding laid the foundation stone of St George's Chapel of Remembrance, RAF Biggin Hill, at a Service of Dedication. A memorial chapel had been dedicated in a disused Army hut in September 1943 but had mysteriously been gutted by fire in 1946. The new chapel

HM Queen Elizabeth II presents her Colour to No. 1 School of Technical Training, RAF Halton. *(AHB)*

faithfully reproduced the original and the names of 453 aircrew killed while flying from the Biggin Hill Sector are inscribed on the oaken reredos on each side of the altar.

1952 HM Queen Elizabeth II presented her Colour to No. 1 School of Technical Training, RAF Halton, in the presence of MRAF Lord Trenchard. Receiving the Colour was Sgt App F.M.A. Hines, thus establishing a unique custom since the School's Colour is the only one to be carried by a SNCO instead of an officer.
See 27 December 1947.

26 JULY

1918 **VC**: Maj Edward Mannock, CO of No. 85 Squadron, was shot down by ground fire at low level and killed after shooting down his sixty-first confirmed kill. The citation concluded, 'his outstanding example of fearless courage, remarkable

The No. 1(F) Squadron aerobatic team at the Zurich International Aviation Meeting with the leader, Flt Lt E.M. Donaldson, on the right. *(G.R. Pitchfork Collection)*

THE RAF'S FIRST JET SQUADRON

For reasons that have never been fully explained, in July 1944 a fighter squadron of the Auxiliary Air Force – No. 616 (South Yorkshire) Squadron – gained the distinction of being the RAF's first jet squadron. It has been claimed that a former flight commander of the squadron, who was serving in the plans division of Fighter Command at the time, cheekily nominated the squadron and, to his surprise, it was never challenged.

No. 616 Squadron was equipped with Spitfires at the time and all the pilots were converted in small groups to fly the Gloster Meteor. To gain some asymmetric flying experience before flying the new twin-engine jet, each pilot flew two sorties in an Oxford. After reading the pilot's notes and receiving a cockpit briefing from the Meteor test pilot at Farnborough, the first familiarisation sortie was flown in the jet fighter. After completing five flights each, the pilots returned to the squadron 'qualified' to fly the Meteor and operations against the V-1 flying bombs began almost immediately.

An extract from the log book of Fg Off J.S. Kirkstruk, one of the first of No. 616 Squadron's pilots to convert to the Meteor. The entries show that he flew two sorties in the Oxford followed by his first five flights in the Meteor before returning to the squadron to continue operations on the Spitfire VII. (ACA Archives)

YEAR 19.44. MONTH / DATE	AIRCRAFT Type	No.	PILOT, OR 1ST PILOT	2ND PILOT, PUPIL OR PASSENGER	DUTY (INCLUDING RESULTS AND REMARKS)
—	—	—	—	—	— TOTALS BROUGHT FORWARD
JUNE 21	DOMINI		G/C HAWTREY	SELF	CATFOSS — KIRTON LINDSEY
22	DOMINI		G/C HAWTREY	"	KIRTON LINDSEY — HENDON.
24	OXFORD	HM 950	F/LT ENDERSEY	"	CIRCUITS + BUMPS.
25	SPITFIRE VII	V	SELF	—	AIR TEST
26	" "	P	"	—	AIR TEST
27	" "	W	"	—	RANGER
29	OXFORD	HM 950	F/O MILLER	SELF	CULMHEAD TO FARNBOROUGH
30	METEOR I	EE214	SELF	—	EXPERIENCE ON TYPE
30	" "	EE 214	"	—	LOCAL FLYING
30	" "	EE 214	"	—	LOCAL FLYING
	O/C 616 Sqdn.		S/LDR	SUMMARY FOR JUNE CGS SPIT. II MASTER II	
				UNIT 616 Sqdn SPITFIRE VII	
				DATE 30/6/44 METEOR I	
				SIGNATURE JSKirstruck OXFORD.	
JULY 1	METEOR I	EE 213	SELF	—	LOCAL FLYING
4	" "	EE 213	"	—	LOCAL + ONE ENGINE APPROACH
4	OXFORD	L 4637	F/O MILLER	SELF	FARNBOROUGH TO CULMHEAD
5	SPITFIRE VII	MD 105	SELF	—	RANGER – LOIRE VALLEY. RETURNED WEATHER
6	" "	MD 178	"	—	RANGER – PARIS AREA. LANDED TANGMERE
6	" "	MD 178	"	— .	FROM TANGMERE
8	" "	MD 178	"	—	SHIPPING RECCO – ST. PETER PORT ST. HELIER – GRANVILLE – ST. MALO.

GRAND TOTAL [Cols. (1) to (10)]
......911......Hrs......10.......Mins.

TOTALS CARRIED FORWARD

skill, devotion to duty, and self-sacrifice, which has never been surpassed'. (*London Gazette*, 18 July 1919, posthumous award)

1937 The No. 1(F) Squadron aerobatic team (leader Flt Lt E.M. Donaldson), flying Fury biplane fighters, in weather conditions that grounded other teams, were the acclaimed stars of the Zurich International Aviation Meeting. General Erhard Milch, Chief of Staff of the Luftwaffe, met the team and told them that 'he had never in his life seen flying like it'.

A Handley Page 0/400 of the Communications Squadron with wings folded. *(AHB. H 1858)*

Canberra PR9s of No. 39 (1 PRU) Squadron taxi in after their final sortie, marking the end of fifty-five years' service of the Canberra. *(RAFM)*

27 JULY

1918   A Communications Squadron (Capt C. Patterson) was formed at RAF Hendon for the exclusive use of Cabinet Ministers, Members of Air Council and other VIPs travelling by air on urgent business.

See 13 December 1918.

1944   A Meteor F1 of No. 616 Squadron patrolled a line from Ashford to Robertsbridge in Kent on an anti-Diver sortie at 1430hr. This was the first RAF (and Allied) jet operation. Five further patrols were flown later in the day.

1953   An armistice was signed at Panmunjon that brought about a complete cessation of hostilities in Korea.

28 JULY

1918   A Handley Page 0/400 (captain Maj A.S.C. MacLaren) left RAF Manston on the first England to Egypt flight. The 2,592 miles were completed in 36 hours 13 minutes' flying time.

See 29 November 1918.

1943   The *Empire Darwin* and *Empire Tide*, homeward bound from Gibraltar, each launched their Hurricane of the MSFU to engage three Focke-Wulf FW200 Condor reconnaissance aircraft shadowing the convoy. Fg Offs P.J.R. Flynn and J.A. Stewart shot two down, despite their aircraft being hit by return fire. They baled out near the convoy and both were subsequently awarded the DFC.

1955   The last Lincoln detachment to Kenya (No. 49 Squadron) used in support of ground forces involved in the Mau Mau campaign departed for the UK.

2006   The disbandment parade for No. 39 (1 PRU) Squadron at RAF Marham marked the end of the Canberra's fifty-five years of RAF operational service – the longest for any aircraft in RAF history.

See 25 May 1951.

1938   No. 11 Squadron became the first squadron based in India to convert to the Blenheim I, the first monoplane to fly operations over the North-West Frontier of India.

1974   No. 15 Squadron RAF Regiment was sent to RAF Akrotiri to bolster the ground defence of RAF installations on Cyprus following the Turkish invasion.

1978   Fg Off P. Warren-Wilson landed his Piper Cherokee Six at RAF Cranwell after completing a 29,000-mile round-the-world flight in 118 days, having landed at forty-six different airfields. He had taken off on 31 March 1978 to mark the 60th anniversary of the formation of the RAF.

Lt E.T. Strever (right) and his Beaufort crew, photographed at Malta after their successful hijack of an Italian rescue aircraft. *(R. Nesbit Collection)*

29 JULY

1942   After being shot down and captured off the coast of Greece, a Beaufort crew (captain Lt E.T. Strever SAAF) of No. 217 Squadron hi-jacked the Italian Cant Z 406 floatplane transporting them to Italy and flew it to Malta. Hence it was their captors who were made POWs.

1977   The Silver Jubilee Review of the RAF was conducted by HM The Queen at RAF Finningley.

30 JULY

1919   A joint RAF and RN force successfully attacked Kronstadt, a major Russian naval base on the Baltic Sea, firing a dry dock and damaging the depot ship *Pamyat Azova*. See 17 August 1919.

An Osprey I of No. 407 Flight is catapulted. *(G.R. Pitchfork Collection)*

1936 The RAF Volunteer Reserve (RAFVR) was formed to recruit 800 reservists a year for pilot training between 1936 and 1938; provision was also made for recruiting 2,500 observer trainees and 3,200 wireless operator (air gunner) trainees.

1937 Prime Minister Neville Chamberlain announced the transfer of the Fleet Air Arm from the RAF to the Admiralty.

1943 By a strange twist of fate, Sunderland U/461 (captain Flt Lt D. Marrows RAAF) sank *U-461* as it transited the Bay of Biscay on the surface in company with two other U-boats. A Halifax of No. 502 Squadron (captain Fg Off A. van Rossum) sank another, and surface vessels that had been called to the scene sank the third.

The first occasion when the officers of No. 602 (City of Glasgow) Squadron wore the Grey Douglas tartan kilts during a guest night at RAF Rochford in 1937. *(No. 602 Squadron Association Archive)*

1993 RAF Upavon, the oldest RFC/RAF airfield, was closed and handed back to the Army.

31 JULY

1915 **VC**: Capt John Aidan Liddell of No. 7 Squadron RFC, for his actions during a reconnaissance patrol over Ostend in Belgium when he was severely wounded. He died of his wounds on 31 August 1915. (*London Gazette*, 23 August 1915)

1919 HRH Captain Prince Albert (later King George VI) completed a flying course at Croydon and was awarded his RAF pilot's badge and, the following day, a permanent commission as a squadron leader.

1936 The Air Ministry approved the wearing of kilts with mess kit by auxiliary officers of the Scottish Auxiliary Squadrons.
See 17 June 1933.

Hunter F1s of No. 43(F) Squadron. *(MOD)*

1945 A Liberator (captain Flt Lt J.A. Muir) of No. 160 Squadron, based at Minneriya, Ceylon, made a round trip of 3,735 miles to drop two British officers and supplies to clandestine forces near the Kota Tingii–Johore Baru road just north of Singapore. Muir was forced to orbit for over an hour until the correct ground signals were displayed. The aircraft was airborne for 24 hours 10 minutes, believed to be the longest combat operation by a landplane during the Second World War.

1954 The Hunter entered squadron service with No. 43(F) Squadron (Sqn Ldr R. Lelong) at RAF Leuchars.

1960 Operation Firedog: the emergency campaign against terrorists in Malaya ended. From the beginning of the

operations in 1948, FEAF aircraft flew 375,849 sorties and 361,442 flying hours.
    See 16 June 1948.

1964 After eighteen years of unbroken operations, a Hastings of No. 202 Squadron flew the last Bismuth meteorological reconnaissance flight. Five flights were flown every week from RAF Aldergrove whatever the weather. These flights were unique in being the only RAF unit routinely cleared to fly over Eire while on operational duty in peacetime.

1992 Gp Capt G.L. Cheshire, Baron Cheshire of Woodhall **VC**, OM, DSO & 2 Bars, DFC died.
    See 8 September 1944.

1993 The withdrawal of British forces from Belize, including the Harrier and Puma detachments, was completed.

1 AUGUST

1919 The first list of officers awarded permanent commissions in the RAF was included in the *London Gazette*.

1940 Hitler's War Directive No. 17 ordered the Luftwaffe to destroy the RAF and its supporting infrastructure in the shortest possible time, while maintaining its combat effectiveness for Operation Sealion, the seaborne invasion of England.

1941 A Sunderland of No. 230 Squadron became the first RAF maritime reconnaissance aircraft to be shot down during an attack on an enemy submarine by the submarine under attack. While searching in the Gulf of Sollum, the crew sighted the Italian submarine *Delfino* on the surface. During the attack, machine-gun fire from the submarine damaged the aircraft so severely that it subsequently crashed. The *Delfino* rescued four survivors from the twelve-man crew of the Sunderland.

No. 651 Squadron was formed at RAF Old Sarum as the first Air Observation Post (AOP) Squadron. The squadrons were RAF units, each one commanded by a Royal Artillery gunner major (pilot) with an RAF adjutant. The RAF provided the aircraft (Auster) and the airmen to maintain them; the Army supplied the support services and the soldiers to man them; all the pilots were artillery officers, trained to fly by the RAF. The Army commanded the squadrons in the field with the RAF responsible for technical flying matters.

1945 The wartime command structure in the Mediterranean and Middle East was reorganised to meet the peacetime situation with the establishment of HQMEDME (ACM Sir Charles Medhurst). Control was exercised through a number of subordinate headquarters and the area covered comprised the central Mediterranean, North Africa, the Middle East, Levant, Iraq, Sudan, Aden and East Africa.

See 1 June 1949.

1950 Reserve Command was renamed Home Command.

1952 The King's Flight was renamed the Queen's Flight.

1953 The Bomber Command Armament School (BCAS) (Wg Cdr J.S. Rowlands **GC**) was formed at RAF Wittering for the training and support of nuclear weapons.

1962 The first RAF Regiment personnel completed parachute training and No. 2 Squadron, RAF Regiment was categorised as an airborne unit.

1967 Transport Command was renamed Air Support Command (AM Sir Thomas Prickett), and given greatly increased responsibility for the long-range strategic, and tactical, air support/assault role.

A Harrier GR7 at Gioia del Colle, Italy. *(MOD)*

1968   WRAF officers assumed RAF ranks.

1976   The Security Branch, consisting of the RAF Regiment and Police Branches, was formed under a Commandant General (RAF).

1995   Operation Deliberate Force: twelve Harrier GR7s of No. 4 Squadron were deployed to Gioia del Colle, Italy, to undertake ground-attack and reconnaissance tasks against Serbian targets in Bosnia-Herzegovina.

1997   The Chinooks of No. 18 Squadron left RAF Laarbruch, marking the end of RAF helicopters based in Germany.

2003   ACM Sir Jock Stirrup was appointed Chief of the Air Staff.

2 AUGUST

1918   RAF aircraft provided support for elements of the North Russian Expeditionary Force to occupy the port of Archangel.

An Air Ministry Weekly Order announced approval for the designs of distinguishing

A Hurricane aboard the aircraft carrier *Argus* shortly before taking off for Malta. *(Andrew Thomas Collection)*

flags and lamps to be used by officers commanding RAF units. The privilege of flying the flags and displaying the lamps rested with the officer and not with the unit (AMWO 782/1918).

1940   The RAF's first four-engine bomber, the Stirling, entered service with No. 7 Squadron at RAF Leeming.

Operation Hurry: the first delivery of Hurricane fighters to Malta was made. Twelve aircraft were flown off from the aircraft carrier HMS *Argus* east of Gibraltar. All arrived safely and, together with the Sea Gladiators, formed No. 261 Squadron, the first fighter squadron to participate in the air defence of Malta. By October 1942, 346 Hurricanes and 396 Spitfires had been delivered to Malta by aircraft carriers with 28 lost en route.
See 9 May 1942.

1941   Desert camouflage of a disruptive pattern of dark earth and middle stone was introduced on aircraft in the Middle East.

1955   Following the nationalisation of the Suez Canal by Egypt on 26 July 1956, preparations to take the canal by force began. It was announced that Canberras would deploy from the United Kingdom to Cyprus and reservists would be called up.

A Stirling of No. 7 Squadron. *(G.R. Pitchfork Collection)*

1977 Ten Buccaneers of No. 208 Squadron and two Vulcans of the Waddington Wing arrived at Nellis AFB, Nevada, to become the first non-US participants in Exercise Red Flag.

3 AUGUST

1916 The interim report of the Committee of Inquiry chaired by Mr Justice Bailhache into the administration of the Air Services (the Bailhache Committee) was released. The Committee recommended that there should be one Department charged with the equipment of both flying services.

1944 Since the opening attack on 16 June, Bomber Command had continued to mount a series of heavy raids against the V-1 launching sites and their storage and support sites in the Pas de Calais. The heaviest involved 1,114 bombers against three flying-bomb storage sites on the Bois de Cassan, Forêt de Nieppe and Trossy-St-Maxim. All raids were successful but six Lancasters were lost.

1955 Fg Off H. Molland of No. 263 Squadron became the first RAF pilot to eject at a speed in excess of the speed of sound. He abandoned his Hunter F5 at 25,000ft over the North Sea at an indicated Mach number of 1.1. He was rescued from the sea by a passing tug.

4 AUGUST

1919 New RAF rank and appointment titles were introduced (AMO 973/19).

1932 Aviation suits and overalls with rank badges were to be regarded as uniforms (AMO A.209/32).

1944 **VC**: Sqn Ldr Ian Willoughby Bazalgette DFC, captain of a Lancaster of No. 635 Pathfinder Squadron, for his action during a daylight bombing raid on the V-1 storage depot at Trossy-St-Maxim. After four of his crew baled out, he attempted a crash landing to save the lives of the two remaining men who were wounded and unable to bale out. They died when the aircraft exploded. (*London Gazette*, 17 August 1945, posthumous award)

The first success by an Allied jet when WO D. Dean of No. 616 Squadron used the wing of his Meteor jet fighter (after the cannons had jammed) to tip up a V-1 flying

bomb, which crashed and exploded harmlessly near Tonbridge.

1967 MRAF Sir Charles Elworthy was appointed Chief of the Defence Staff, a post he held until 8 April 1971. He was created Baron Elworthy of Timaru on 9 May 1972.

1981 No. 18 Squadron re-formed at RAF Odiham as the first RAF heavy transport helicopter unit equipped with Chinook HC1s.

5 AUGUST

1918 German airships raided the United Kingdom for the last time, when five Zeppelins of the German Navy headed for targets in the Midlands, but the raid was a

WO 'Dixie' Dean of No. 616 (South Yorkshire) Squadron, who used the wing of his Meteor to tip up a V-1 flying bomb. *(R. George)*

Maj E. Cadbury. *(RAF Museum)*

failure. Two de Havilland DH4s from Yarmouth attacked one airship, Zeppelin L70, flying at 17,500ft just north of Wells-next-the-Sea on the Norfolk coast. On board the L70 was the commander of the German Naval Airship Division, Fregattenkapitan P. Strasser. It fell into the sea in flames, killing all of the crew. Subsequently, a de Havilland DH4 flown by Maj E. Cadbury and Capt R. Leckie (later Air Marshal) was credited with destroying L70. RAF aircraft also damaged a second airship; the L65 and the surviving airships dropped their bombs into the sea and returned to base. Cadbury and Leckie were awarded the DFC.

1982   Air Cdre Sir Hughie Edwards **VC**, KCMG, CB, DSO, OBE, DFC died in Australia.
      See 4 July 1941.

6 AUGUST

1939   Nine Blenheims of No. 39 Squadron left Risalpur for Singapore. In very severe monsoon weather, six aircraft and three crews were lost, including the squadron commander, Wg Cdr B. Ankers, whose aircraft was struck by lightning and caught fire.

1942   The first offensive radio counter-measure (RCM) radar jammer to enter service with the RAF – *Moonshine* – was used operationally for the first time when eight Defiant II aircraft transmitted from a holding pattern south of Portland. The jammers produced spurious returns on the enemy's early-warning radar.

1945   The first atom bomb was dropped on Hiroshima. Gp Capt G.L. Cheshire **VC** and Dr W. Penney, an atomic scientist, had expected to fly on one of the accompanying B-29 bombers, but Washington vetoed this at the last minute. When the second bomb was dropped on Nagasaki three days later, both men observed the detonation from

another aircraft. After the attack, Cheshire was convinced that the two atomic bombs had stopped the war and he commented, 'Japan could do nothing to stop the bombers, so she stopped the fighting. The alternative was atomic extinction.'

1948   The first of the newly re-formed Royal Auxiliary Air Force fighter squadrons were rearmed with jet fighter aircraft. No. 500 (County of Kent) Squadron at RAF West Malling, near Maidstone, received Meteors, and No. 605 (County of Warwick) Squadron at RAF Honiley, near Kenilworth, received Vampires.

7 AUGUST

1930   The Royal Aircraft Establishment commenced a series of trials for in-flight refuelling using a DH9 as tanker aircraft and a Virginia as the receiver. The observer in the receiver attempted to catch a weighted cable suspended from the tanker flying above, using the curved head of a walking stick. The first public demonstration was given at the 1931 RAF Display at Hendon.
      See 7 February 1924.

1939   Headquarters Coastal Command moved to Eastbury Park, Northwood, Middlesex.

1944   Seventeen Typhoon squadrons, operating from advanced landing grounds in

Rocket projectiles being fitted to a Typhoon of No. 609 (West Riding) Squadron. *(AHB. CH 113345)*

Normandy, attacked German columns and tanks threatening to cut off the US 30th Infantry Division near Mortain as it advanced rapidly southwards after the breakout from the Cherbourg peninsula. Throughout the whole day, German armoured columns came under attack from relays of Typhoons during 458 sorties when 2,088 rockets and 80 tons of bombs were expended, causing the German attack to stall. The day became known as 'The Day of the Typhoon'. By 11 August Typhoons had flown 2,193 sorties, fired 9,580 rockets and dropped 398 tons of bombs.

1966 The first of fourteen VC10 strategic transports arrived at RAF Brize Norton for service with No. 10 Squadron. The first operational flight was flown a year later on 4 August 1967.

1976 ACM Sir Neil Cameron was appointed Chief of the Air Staff.
See 31 August 1977.

8 AUGUST

1918 **VC**: Capt Andrew Frederick Weatherby Beauchamp-Proctor (South Africa) of No. 84 Squadron, whose flying record was described as being 'almost unsurpassed in its brilliancy'. (*London Gazette*, 30 November 1918)
See 21 June 1921.

1939 The last major British peacetime exercise and full-scale rehearsal of the air defence system started, with over 1,300 aircraft taking part in the three-day exercise over the south-east of England. At the end of the practice, a civilian 'blackout' was ordered.

1940 The Battle of Britain: the second phase began with intense fighting over the English Channel, particularly off the Isle of Wight, in support of Convoy CW9, and heavy Luftwaffe attacks against radar sites and airfields.

1944 Following the start of an uprising against German forces in Warsaw by the Polish Home Army on 1 August, the Chiefs of Staff despatched a signal to AM Sir John Slessor, Air Commander-in-Chief Mediterranean Allied Air Forces and Commander-in-Chief RAF Mediterranean and Middle East, requesting that he comply with Polish appeals for assistance if operationally practicable. Supply-dropping operations

Pilots of No. 19 Squadron scramble to their Spitfire Is at RAF Duxford. (*R. Nesbit Collection*)

began on this night, and continued until 21–22 September. The majority of resupply operations were flown by Polish and RAF special duties units, together with RAF and South African Air Force heavy bomber squadrons, operating from Italian bases. Operations by the Halifax and Liberator aircraft were hampered by the full moon period, prevailing weather conditions and the refusal of the Soviet authorities to permit the use of Soviet-controlled forward airfields by Allied supply aircraft before 10 September 1944. Allied casualties were heavy. Between 8/9 August and 21/22 August, 31 aircraft were lost, together with 248 aircrew, of whom 203 were killed. Polish resistance in Warsaw ceased on 2 October 1944 with the surrender of the Home Army units.

1955 Sqn Ldr R.L. Topp flew a Hunter from Edinburgh to Farnborough covering 335 miles in 27 minutes 45 seconds, averaging 724mph.

1956 The observer (radio) 'RO' flying badge was reinstated for AI radar operators flying in Meteor and Javelin night-fighters. After ten courses, it ceased to be awarded in 1957 (AMO A.192/1956).

9 AUGUST

1934 The reintroduction of the trade of air observer was announced. The first course began at RAF Eastchurch on 29 October 1934 (AMO A.196/1934).
See 21 October 1937.

1941 Wg Cdr D.R.S. Bader, the legless fighter pilot and leader of the Tangmere Wing, failed to return from a sweep over France. He was made a POW and later imprisoned in Colditz Castle where inveterate escapers and the most troublesome prisoners were incarcerated.

1946 Air Staff Requirement (ASR) OR 1001 was issued for an atomic bomb to be suitable for carriage in the next generation of bombers.

1990 Operation Granby: following the invasion and occupation of Kuwait by Iraqi forces on 2 August, the Secretary of State for

Wg Cdr D.R.S. Bader at Westhampnett a few days before he was shot down. On his right are Fg Offs J.E. Johnson and H.S.L. 'Cocky' Dundas of No. 616 Squadron.
(AVM J.E. Johnson)

Defence (Tom King) announced that British forces would join coalition forces and deploy to Saudi Arabia and the Gulf region. An advance party left for Dhahran, Saudi Arabia, to prepare for the arrival of an RAF detachment. ACM Sir Patrick Hine, AOC-in-C Strike Command, was appointed the Joint Force Commander who worked from his headquarters at RAF High Wycombe. On 11 August he appointed AVM R.A.F. Wilson as Air Commander, British Forces Arabian Peninsula, with a headquarters at Riyadh, Saudi Arabia.

10 AUGUST

1918 **VC**: Capt Ferdinand Maurice Felix West of No. 8 Squadron for a low-level attack on German troops far over enemy lines during which he was severely wounded but crash-landed over Allied lines and saved the life of his observer. (*London Gazette*, 8 November 1918).
See 7 July 1988.

1943 **GC**: Wg Cdr John Samuel Rowlands for work on bomb disposal activities over more than two years. He repeatedly displayed the most conspicuous courage and unselfish devotion to duty in circumstances of great personal danger.
See 19 June 1943.

1977 ACM Sir Michael Beetham was appointed Chief of the Air Staff.

11 AUGUST

1942 The Chief of the Air Staff (ACM Sir Charles Portal) gave instructions to the Commander-in-Chief of Bomber Command (AM Sir Arthur Harris) to form a 'Target Finding Force'. Harris, who had always opposed the idea, objected to the name and selected the title 'Pathfinder Force'.
See 15 August 1942.

1943 **VC**: Fg Off Lloyd Allan Trigg DFC, captain of a No. 200 Squadron Liberator, sank the U-boat *U-468* off Dakar, West Africa. He

released the depth charges accurately despite the aircraft being on fire and crashing immediately after the attack. The **VC** was awarded after the debriefing of the surviving captain of the U-boat, the only occasion the supreme award has been awarded exclusively on the evidence of the enemy. (*London Gazette*, 2 November 1943, posthumous award)

1966 Indonesian Confrontation: with the signing of a peace treaty between Malaysia and Indonesia, Confrontation was formally ended after three years and eight months. The AOC No. 224 Group (AVM C.N. Foxley-Norris) stated, 'The Borneo campaign was a classic example of the lesson that the side which uses air power most effectively to defeat the jungle will also defeat the enemy.'

1990 Operation Granby: following the government's decision to commit British forces in support of a request for security assistance from King Fahd of Saudi Arabia to friendly governments, RAF combat aircraft began to deploy to the Gulf. Twelve Tornado F3s drawn from Nos 5 and 29 Squadrons attending an Armament Practice Camp at RAF Akrotiri were deployed to Dhahran in Saudi Arabia. This composite deployment was subsequently designated No. 5 (Composite) Squadron (Wg Cdr E. Black). Twelve Jaguar GR1As drawn from Nos 6,

A Belvedere of No. 66 Squadron over Krokong during the Indonesian Confrontation. *(AHB. T 5309)*

41 and 54 Squadrons (Wg Cdr J. Connolly) left RAF Coltishall for Thumrait in Oman. Two VC10 tankers of No. 101 Squadron left for Seeb in Oman and were later positioned at Bahrain. No. 20 Squadron, RAF Regiment, left Cyprus with Rapier air defence missiles and later transferred to Bahrain.

12 AUGUST

1915 The first sinking of a ship by a torpedo launched from the air was achieved by Flt Cdr C.H.K. Edmonds, flying a Short Type 184 sea plane from the Gulf of Xeros from the sea plane carrier *Ben-My-Cree* during the Dardanelles Campaign. A Whitehead 14in 810lb torpedo was launched at a range of 300yd, sinking the ship.

1938 An order was issued imposing major restrictions for officers and airmen applying for leave to Greater Germany (AMO A.314/38).

A Chain Home Low aerial array on the south coast of England. *(AHB. CH 15183)*

1940 The Battle of Britain: the Luftwaffe commenced a systematic assault on the RDF (radar) sites and coastal fighter airfields.

VC: Flt Lt Roderick Alastair Brook Learoyd, a pilot of No. 49 Squadron flying a Hampden, successfully bombed the Dortmund–Ems canal against fierce ground fire. (*London Gazette*, 20 August 1940)

1941 Blenheims of No. 2 Group, with a strong fighter escort as far as the Dutch coast, carried out a low-level attack on two power stations near Cologne – the Goldenberg plant at Knapsack, and the Fortuna plant at Quadrath. This was the deepest penetration to date in a daylight raid from the United Kingdom. Fifty-four Blenheims, each carrying two 500lb bombs, were despatched and almost 1,500 fighter sorties were flown in support of these and other bomber formations on diversionary operations. Ten Blenheims failed to return (18.5 per cent of the force).

1943 **VC**: Flt Sgt Arthur Louis Aaron DFM, the pilot of a No. 218 Squadron Stirling who bombed Turin and despite grievous wounds flew on to North Africa and saved his crew. The following day he died of his wounds. (*London Gazette*, 3 November 1943, posthumous award)

13 AUGUST

1912 Maj H. Trenchard, a Boer War veteran, was posted to the Central Flying School as an instructor after gaining his aviation certificate at Larkhill.

1914 Following mobilisation, Headquarters RFC (Brig Gen Sir David Henderson) deployed to France. Nos 2, 3 and 4 Squadrons flew from Dover to Amiens, and on the following day No. 5 Squadron flew from Southampton to Boulogne. Subsequently, all of the RFC squadrons were concentrated at Amiens in support of the British Expeditionary Force (BEF). The flying squadrons were later transferred to Maubeuge aerodrome.

Airmen of No. 3 Squadron RFC with a Leyland transport. *(AHB. H 1907)*

Dogfights over Kent. *(R. Nesbit Collection)*

1925   The Air Council decided that it was undesirable that officers and airmen should belong to the 'British Fascisti' or any similar organisation.

1940   The Battle of Britain: *Adler Tag* (Eagle Day). The Luftwaffe commenced massive attacks to eliminate Fighter Command's squadrons and airfields. During the course of the day, the Luftwaffe generated over 1,500 sorties and shot down thirteen RAF fighters for the loss of forty-seven of their own. A further forty-seven RAF aircraft were destroyed on six Fighter Command airfields.

A force of eleven Blenheims of No. 82 Squadron attacked the German-held airfield at Aalborg in northern Denmark. All were shot down and twenty aircrew were killed with the remaining thirteen captured. This was the second occasion on which No. 82 had been wiped out in three months.
See 17 May 1940.

1951   **GC**: Flt Lt John Alan Quinton, the navigator of a Wellington of No. 228 OCU involved in a mid-air collision clipped the only parachute in reach to an ATC cadet flying as a passenger enabling him to escape, thus forfeiting his own life. (*London Gazette*, 25 October 1951, posthumous award)

Bomber Command participated in the USAF Strategic Air Command (SAC) Bombing Competition for the first time. Two Washington B1 crews joined forty-five SAC crews taking part in the competition, which was held at MacDill Air Force Base in Florida.

1961   Early in the morning the German Democratic Republic (GDR) began to block off East Berlin and the GDR from West Berlin by means of barbed wire and anti-tank obstacles. Streets were torn up, and barricades of paving stones were erected. Tanks gathered at crucial places. The subway and local railway services between East and West Berlin were interrupted. Inhabitants of East Berlin and the GDR were no longer allowed to enter West Berlin, among them 60,000 commuters who had worked in West Berlin so far. In the following days, construction brigades began replacing the provisional barriers by a solid wall. Over the coming years, RAF Chipmunks based at RAF Gatow flew surveillance sorties over West Berlin.

See 10 November 1989.

1990 Operation Granby: three Nimrods arrived at Seeb to support coalition naval forces in the Persian Gulf.

August and was followed by Spitfires of Nos 251, 322 and 324 Wings.

1945 The Japanese formally accepted the surrender terms of the Potsdam Proclamation. The following day Emperor Hirohito broadcast to the Japanese people when Allied forces in the Pacific received orders to cease offensive operations.

1947 The independence of India was proclaimed. All RAF squadrons had departed except Nos 10 and 31, which remained briefly at RAF Mauripur (Karachi), which had by then become part of Pakistan.

1974 Following the failure of peace talks between Greece and Turkey, a further evacuation of 9,989 dependants from RAF Akrotiri began.
See 20 July 1974.

14 AUGUST

1944 Operation Dragoon: the Allied invasion of the south of France began with a parachute assault at night, in thick fog, to the west of St Raphael. The following morning, Spitfires of No. 225 Squadron flew spotting duties for naval guns and tactical reconnaissance sorties. The squadron landed at Ramatuelle on 20

15 AUGUST

1930 Notification was given that RAF aircraft were to have rudder striping changed from blue, white, and red from the rudder post to red, white and blue, to be effective from 29 September.

1940 The Battle of Britain: *Luftflotte* 5 in Scandinavia attacked targets in the north-

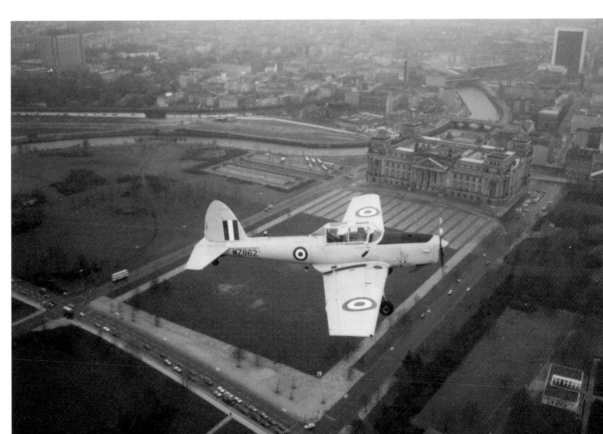

A Chipmunk operating on intelligence-gathering duties over Berlin. *(AHB)*

east of the United Kingdom. Due to the distance, Messerschmitt Bf109s were unable to escort the bombers which suffered heavily at the hands of the RAF fighter squadrons based in the north. Such were their losses that targets in the north were never attacked again in daylight. Very heavy attacks were mounted against the south of England, co-ordinated with those in the north. The Luftwaffe suffered heavy losses with the RAF and anti-aircraft defences claiming to have shot down 180 enemy aircraft. In the event, the Luftwaffe lost 76.

1942 The Pathfinder Force (PFF) was formed within No. 3 Group under the command of Gp Capt D.C.T. Bennett, with headquarters at RAF Wyton.
See 25 January 1943.

1943 All WAAF recruit training was centralised at RAF Wilmslow.

1947 The RAF School of Aeronautical Engineering, RAF Henlow, was renamed the RAF Technical College.

RAF police dogs were used for the first time in a search for victims of a coal-mine accident at Whitehaven, Cumbria.

1956 A RAF/USAF meeting was held at the Air Ministry to establish co-ordination of nuclear strike plans.

1963 The closure of the Thor missile site at RAF Feltwell brought an end to RAF involvement with strategic ground-based missiles.

1969 Operation Banner: Hercules airlifted the first large-scale troop reinforcements to Northern Ireland.
See 31 March 2002.

THE PATHFINDER FORCE

The role of the force was to guide the main force of Bomber Command by identifying the target precisely and then illuminating it, so that 'marker' aircraft could drop incendiaries, or sky-marker flares above cloud, as aiming points for the main force. Starting life with five squadrons – one drawn from each Bomber Group – it achieved group status as No. 8 (PFF) Group in January 1943 and eventually became equipped with Lancasters and Mosquitos, the most suitable aircraft for this demanding task.

AVM D.C.T Bennett (1910–86). *(AHB. CH 13646)*

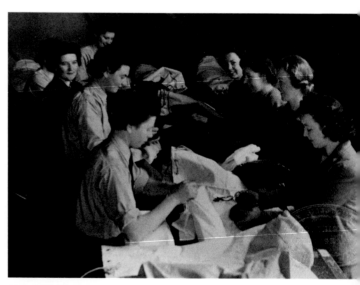

New WAAF recruits draw clothing at RAF Bridgnorth. *(AHB)*

16 AUGUST

1918 The first massed low-level attack by the RAF on an enemy airfield was carried out, when sixty-five SE5s, Camels, DH4s and Bristol F2B fighters attacked the German aerodrome at Haubourin. No RAF aircraft were lost.

1935 Following an attempt by dissident Upper Mohmand tribes on the North-West Frontier to destroy the Gandab military road and its outposts, Wapitis and Harts provided air support for ground forces attempting to regain control of the region.

1940 **VC**: Fighter Command's only Victoria Cross was awarded to Flt Lt Eric James Brindley Nicolson of No. 249 Squadron for an engagement near Southampton, when he shot down an enemy fighter despite his Hurricane being on fire and being badly burned himself. He was killed in action on 2 May 1945 flying over the Bay of Bengal. (*London Gazette* 15 November 1940)
See 2 May 1945.

1944 Bomber Command's main offensive against Germany was resumed, after its diversion to support Allied operations in support of the Normandy landings, with the opening attacks against Stettin and Kiel.

1960 Cyprus became a Republic: administration of the Sovereign Base Areas of Akrotiri and Dhekelia passed to AOC-in-C Middle East Air Force.

BOMBER COMMAND'S EFFORT AFTER THE D-DAY LANDINGS

In the period from the Allied landings on 6 June until the main strategic bomber offensive against Germany was resumed, Bomber Command aircraft flew 46,844 sorties and suffered the loss of 727 aircraft (1.6 per cent). Some 17,580 of the sorties were flown in daylight, which exceeded the total number of Bomber Command's daylight sorties flown between September 1939 and the departure of No. 2 Group in May 1943 – at about a tenth of the cost in aircraft casualties.

A Bristol F2B fighter on the Western Front. *(ACA Archives)*

Lancasters bomb Trossy-St-Maxim in northern France. *(IWM)*

A Hart of No. 39 Squadron en route to Gilgit on the North-West Frontier of India. *(AHB. H 760)*

259

17 AUGUST

1917 The Cabinet Committee Report on Air Organisation (the Smuts Report) was presented to the War Cabinet. It recommended the creation of an Air Ministry 'to control and administer all matters in connection with air warfare of every kind and that the new ministry should proceed to work out the arrangements for the amalgamation of the two [Air] services and for the legal constitution and discipline of the new Service'. The Report stated that 'the day may not be far off when aerial operations with their devastation of enemy lands and destruction of industrial and populous centres on a vast scale may become the principal operations of war, to which the older forms of military and naval operations may become secondary and subordinate'. The Smuts Report laid the foundations for the creation of the RAF.

See 16 October 1917, 29 November 1917.

1919 Eight DH9s of No. 47 Squadron carried out bombing and strafing attacks on gun and searchlight crews protecting the Kronstadt naval base in southern Russia, suppressing the defences and thereby enabling RN motor torpedo boats to attack naval vessels in the base. Two battleships and the depot ship *Pamyat Azova* were sunk.

1940 Germany proclaimed a complete blockade of the British Isles and threatened to sink any neutral vessel on sight.

Due to the heavy casualties in Fighter Command, the length of training for replacement pilots at the fighter OTUs was reduced and pupils received as little as ten to twenty hours on Hurricanes or Spitfires before joining front-line squadrons.

Plt Off W.M.L. (Billy) Fiske became the first American citizen to die while serving with the RAF during the Second World War. Flying a Hurricane of No. 601 Squadron he crash-landed in flames after engaging a German bomber over Bognor and he died the following day.

1942 Blenheim aircraft of Bomber Command flew their last operational sorties when No. 18 Squadron carried out night intruder attacks against airfields in Holland and Germany.

Spitfires of No. 11 Group escorted the first operation mounted by the US 8th Air Force when twelve B-17 Fortress bombers attacked Rouen railway centre.

A reconnaissance photograph of the Peenemunde air research and experimental station after the heavy attack by Bomber Command.
(ACA Archives)

A Hunter F6 of No. 20 Squadron over Pulau Tioman, Malaysia. *(J. Falconer Collection)*

A Royal Warrant instituted the Air Efficiency Award for long and meritorious service in the Auxiliary Air Force or the RAF Volunteer Reserve.

1943 Operation Hydra: the first RAF attack was carried out on the Peenemunde air research and experimental station where the V-1 and V-2 rockets were being developed. Of the 597 heavy bombers despatched, 40 failed to return. Some 1,938 tons of bombs were dropped. This was the first occasion using the 'master of ceremonies' (Gp Capt J. Searby of No. 83 Squadron) technique applied to a large-scale target, a role retitled 'master bomber' thereafter. This was also the first occasion when a 'red spot fire' marker bomb was used operationally. The latter comprised a 250lb case packed with impregnated cotton wool, which burst and ignited at 3,000ft and burned as a vivid crimson fire for about ten minutes. The raid was successful and the Germans were forced to transfer the development of the V-2 elsewhere, causing at least two months' delay in the programme.

1948 Operation Plainfare: the RAF lifted 1,735.6 tons of aid to Berlin, the highest achieved in a single day throughout the airlift.
See 6 October 1949.

1960 The Air Council introduced the Trenchard Memorial Awards Scheme to encourage service personnel to carry out worthwhile projects.

1964 Indonesian Confrontation: a party of Indonesian regular troops landed at three separate points in west Malaysia. Two weeks later, a force of paratroopers was dropped in north central Johore. All FEAF attack aircraft were placed on high alert. Hunters of No. 20 Squadron fired rockets and cannons into the area of the landings.
See 23 December 1964.

18 AUGUST

1940 The Battle of Britain: dubbed 'The Hardest Day', this day saw the fiercest fighting of the Battle of Britain when both the RAF and the Luftwaffe suffered the highest number of aircraft destroyed or damaged in the air and on the ground for any day

A wartime drawing of Sgt E. Mortimer and Cpl E. Henderson who were each awarded the Military Medal for bravery during attacks against RAF Biggin Hill. *(AHB. LD 1283)*

A Typhoon rocket attack against enemy transports in Normandy. *(IWM. C 4571)*

during the Battle. Throughout the course of the day, the Luftwaffe launched three major attacks against airfields and radar stations in southern England. The RAF airfields at Biggin Hill, Croydon and Kenley suffered extensive damage, but continued to operate their squadrons. The Luftwaffe lost sixty-seven aircraft against the thirty-one fighters lost by the RAF.

1941 Mr D.M. Butt of the War Cabinet Secretariat issued his report on Bomber Command's bombing accuracy. He concluded that of all the aircraft recorded as having attacked their targets, only one-third had got within 5 miles of them. The report showed the need for the development of scientific aids to navigation and bomb aiming, and the development of revolutionary tactics.

1942 The Pathfinder Force flew its first operation when the target was Flensburg.

1943 The RAF School of Firefighting and Rescue was established at RAF Sutton-on-Hull.

1944 Air attacks by the Tactical Air Force in France reached a peak after German ground forces trapped in the Falaise pocket attempted to flee eastwards. Scores of armoured vehicles and transports blocked the narrow lanes and were subjected to devastating attacks by fighter-bombers. The German Situation Report for the period stated, 'enemy air activity rose to immense proportions this week, and in many cases rendered it impossible to move our troops'.

The U-boat threat to the sea communications of the Expeditionary Force was considered to have come to an end. During the period Coastal Command aircraft had sunk thirty U-boats and shared in the destruction with naval forces of a further five.

19 AUGUST

1915 Col H. Trenchard assumed command of the RFC in France on promotion to Brigadier General in succession to Sir David Henderson. He requested another squadron by the middle of September and he further

262

suggested that one squadron be provided for each Army Corps (for artillery work, photography and close reconnaissance), and that there should be a further squadron for each Army for special work such as bombing.

1942 Operation Jubilee: over seventy squadrons of aircraft drawn from Fighter, Coastal and Bomber Commands gave extensive support to the amphibious assault to seize temporarily the Channel port of Dieppe.

OPERATION JUBILEE

During the operation, 2,614 sorties were flown with fifty-six fighter squadrons of Hurricanes, Spitfires and Typhoons, as well as four squadrons of Mustang reconnaissance aircraft. Five Blenheim and Boston squadrons were used for close support and smoke-laying but preliminary night bombing was refused for fear of causing French civilian casualties and alerting the enemy. Considerable resistance was encountered after the landing and bombers were called in to attack enemy gun positions – with limited success – and smoke screens were laid to cover the operation.

The air fighting was the fiercest since the Battle of Britain with the RAF losing 106 aircraft, and three RAF high-speed launches (HSL) on air-sea rescue duties were also lost. Although the operation was unsuccessful, a number of vitally important lessons were learned which were subsequently applied in the planning and conduct of landings in the Mediterranean and the invasion of north-west Europe (Operation Overlord).

HSL 122 was destroyed on rescue operations during Operation Jubilee and HSL 123 picked up survivors before it too was destroyed by enemy fire. *(ACA Collection)*

---

20 AUGUST

1940 The Battle of Britain: Prime Minister Winston Churchill declared in the House of Commons that, 'The gratitude of every home in our island, in our Empire and indeed throughout the world, except in the abodes of the guilty, goes to every British airman who, undaunted by odds, unwearied in their constant challenge and mortal danger, are turning the tide of world war by their prowess and by their devotion. Never in the field of human conflict was so much owed by so many to so few.'

1944 It was announced that Transport Command had flown 20,000 casualties from France to Britain since the liberation of France had begun.

1945 Mosquitos of No. 110 Squadron carried out the RAF's last bombing operation of the Second World War when they attacked Japanese troops still engaging a Force 136 Unit near Shwegyin in Burma. By coincidence, No. 110 had carried out the first bombing operation of the war when Blenheims attacked the German battleship *Admiral Scheer* on 4 September 1939.

1946 **GC**: Sqn Ldr Hubert Dinwoodie of No. 5140 Bomb Disposal Squadron for making safe eleven unstable bombs following the accidental explosion of a twelfth being unloaded from a train. (*London Gazette*, 4 February 1947)

1959 The Central Treaty Organisation (CENTO) was formed to replace the Baghdad Pact.

1968 Following the Soviet invasion of Czechoslovakia the forces of RAF Germany were placed on a high state of readiness to guard against the possibility of a Soviet assault on West Germany.

1971 Flt Lt HRH The Prince of Wales graduated from the RAF College Cranwell and was awarded his pilot's badge by Chief of the Air Staff, ACM Sir Denis Spotswood.
See 8 March 1971.

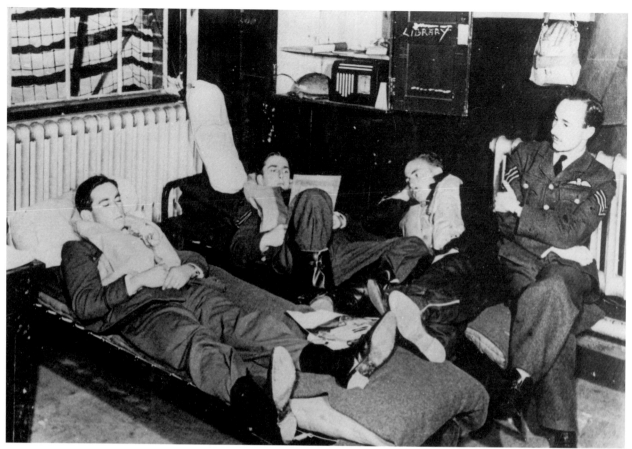

Pilots of No. 17 Squadron at readiness at RAF Martlesham Heath. *(AHB. H 1971)*

HRH The Prince of Wales with HRH The Duke of Edinburgh after receiving his 'wings' at RAF College Cranwell. They are accompanied by AVM D. Hughes (Commandant), ACM Sir Denis Spotswood (CAS) and AM Sir Leslie Mavor (C-in-C Training Command). *(RAF College Cranwell)*

264

1984 A Sea King of No. 202 Squadron (captain Flt Lt I. MacFarlane) rescued an injured crew member from the Liberian container ship *Kormoran* 360 miles west of Land's End. Operating from RAF Brawdy, the helicopter refuelled at Cork Airport and from the Glomar Arctic 2 oil rig, arriving at the ship at 2300hr. MacFarlane and his crew arrived back at Brawdy after a nine-hour flight, the longest RAF helicopter rescue at the time.

1987 The body of Rudolf Hess, who had died in Spandau Prison and was the last surviving Nazi war criminal convicted at the Nuremburg War Crimes Trial, was flown out of Berlin in a Hercules to be handed over to his family.

1940 The first unit established to support the activities of the Special Operations Executive (SOE) and other clandestine operations – No. 419 (Special Duties) Flight – was formed at RAF North Weald. The flight was subsequently redesignated No. 1419 (SD) Flight on 1 March 1941 and No. 138 Squadron on 25 August 1941 before moving to RAF Tempsford.
See 19 October 1940.

1941 British fighter aircraft camouflaged upper surfaces changed to a disruptive pattern of ocean grey and dark green to reflect the change from defence over the homeland to the offensive across the Channel to enemy-occupied France.

21 AUGUST

1918 Two Handley Page 0/400 bombers of No. 216 Squadron dropped over a ton of bombs on Cologne railway station at night, causing a large explosion. They were airborne for seven hours.

A Lysander of No. 161 Squadron at RAF Tempsford and used to support clandestine operations. *(RAFM)*

Armourers fuse 112lb RL bombs at an airfield in northern France. *(AHB)*

22 AUGUST

1941 A meeting at the Air Ministry recommended that glider pilots should be Army volunteers.

1950 The introduction of the new trade structure for airmen and airwomen in ground trades was announced. The review acknowledged the need for substantial changes in the current structure and to bring the training and employment of airmen more into line with industrial practice without damaging the principles of command and control essential to service needs. The rank of senior aircraftman was introduced, together with specialist technician ranks and the three classifications of airmen below NCO rank were abolished as classifications and became ranks instead (AMO A.515/1950).
See 2 January 1919, 6 March 1963.

1954 In the fight against the Mau Mau, air operations were given priority over ground operations in the Aberdare Mountains.

23 AUGUST

1915 A distinguishing badge – single-winged 'O' – was introduced for air observers. Irreverently called 'the flying arsehole', the badge remained until 1942 when it was superseded by a range of flying badges for non-pilot aircrew. Those already qualified to wear the observer's badge were allowed to continue wearing it.

1921 HM Airship R38 – which had been sold to the US Navy while under construction – broke up in the air over Hull during an acceptance test flight. Air Cdre E.M. Maitland, Cdr L.H. Maxwell USN, twenty-seven officers and men of the RAF and fifteen officers and men of the US Navy were killed. The captain of R38, Flt Lt Wann, and three crew members survived.

1943 Bomber Command opened the preliminary phase of the 'Battle of Berlin' with the first of a series of three raids against the German capital. The Command despatched 1,652 sorties on these three raids and lost 125 aircraft.

THE BOMBER BATTLE OF BERLIN

The Battle of Berlin was the longest and most sustained bombing offensive against one target in the Second World War. The 'Big City' was deep in the heart of Germany and heavily defended by anti-aircraft batteries and night fighters, which had reached a peak of efficiency. Bomber Command's Commander-in-Chief, AM Sir Arthur Harris, hoped to produce 'a state of devastation in which German surrender is inevitable'. It was the RAF's supreme effort to end the war by strategic bombing. After the preliminary phase of three raids in August, the main battle commenced on the night of 18/19 November. To take advantage of the longer nights, sixteen further major raids were mounted and, by the time

Bomber Command turned its attention to lesser German cities in March 1944, more than 10,000 sorties had dropped over 30,000 tons on Germany's sprawling capital city. The cost was high with 620 aircraft and their crews lost.

WO Lauren and his No. 166 Squadron crew relax after returning from Berlin.
(ACA Archives)

1944   Dakota transport aircraft of No. 267 Squadron and USAAF 60th Troop Carrier Group evacuated 1,059 Yugoslav partisans and 16 Allied aircrew from a hastily prepared landing strip near Brezna, Yugoslavia. Mustangs of No. 213 Squadron provided a fighter escort.

Girl partisans in local costume and battledress meet the arrival of a Dakota at a clandestine airstrip in Yugoslavia. *(AHB. CNA 3069)*

24 AUGUST

1934   The RAF's first rotary wing aircraft, a Cierva autogyro, was delivered to the RAF School of Army Co-operation at Old Sarum.

1939   Readiness State 'C' and general mobilisation was declared, placing the RAF on a war footing. Aircraft were put on twelve-hour standby and personnel on leave were recalled to duty. Auxiliary Air Force and

A Cierva autogyro on trials at the School of Army Co-operation. *(RAFM)*

An Anson of No. 502
(Ulster) Squadron
patrols over a convoy
in the Western
Approaches.
(R. Nesbit Collection)

Volunteer Reserve personnel were ordered to report to their mobilisation centres. The Observer Corps was called out for standing duty.

Coastal Command Ansons of No. 48 Squadron began to fly regular North Sea reconnaissance patrols.

1940 The Battle of Britain: the third phase commenced and saw the beginning of heavy attacks against fighter airfields near London and an intensifying of German night attacks.

1942 A specially converted Spitfire Vc, flown by Fg Off G.W.H. Reynolds, from Alexandria intercepted a Junkers Ju86P-2 high altitude reconnaissance aircraft approaching the Egyptian city. The combat took place at 42,000ft, and was the first success against

these very high-flying aircraft. Reynolds had no pressurised protection against operating at that extreme height. He was awarded the DFC.

1958 The Far East Jungle Rescue Team (Sqn Ldr R.D. Mullins) completed their first rescue when they parachuted into the Malayan jungle to rescue the crew of a Valetta transport aircraft. Four of the seven-man crew had survived. A landing zone was cut in the jungle and a Sycamore helicopter landed during the afternoon of the 26th and evacuated the first injured survivor. The remaining survivors were airlifted to safety the following day. On the 28th a short service was conducted in a Valetta orbiting the crash site when wreaths were thrown onto the wreck in memory of the three aircrew who had died.

25 AUGUST

1914 The first British aerial victory of the First World War was achieved when a German Taube aircraft was forced to land by three aircraft of No. 2 Squadron. One of the British aircraft also landed, and the crew chased the German crew into nearby woods. They then set fire to the German aircraft before taking off again.

1939 The first two RAF Mobile Receiving Stations (MRS), later renamed Mobile Field Hospitals (MFH), were formed. No. 1 MRS arrived in France on 25 September and was based at Nantes. During the Second World War, twenty-four MFHs were formed and served worldwide.

1940 Following German raids on London on the previous evening, the War Cabinet sanctioned the first RAF attack against Berlin. Eighty-one bombers were despatched but thick cloud hampered the attack.

1942 Gp Capt The Duke of Kent was killed in a Sunderland of No. 228 Squadron, which crashed near Dunbeath, Caithness, in Scotland en route to Iceland.

1944 With guides from the French Maquis, No. 2798 Rifle Squadron, RAF Regiment, became one of the first Allied units to enter Paris when it secured Longchamps racecourse near Paris as a radar site and possible landing site.

1954 The first Canberra squadron to be based in Germany, No. 149 Squadron, arrived at RAF Ahlhorn. The Canberra remained in service in Germany until 1972.

HRH The Duke of Kent about to board a Liberator. *(AHB. CH 3161)*

Walking wounded have refreshments at No. 1 Casualty Air Evacuation Unit. *(RAFM)*

26 AUGUST

1939 Readiness State 'D' was put into force. Aircraft were dispersed on their airfields, and all personnel were recalled. E-class reservists were ordered to report to their units.

1944 **GC:** Fg Off Roderick Borden Gray RCAF of No. 172 Squadron was severely wounded when his Wellington ditched but he gave his dinghy to two injured crew members. He eventually lost consciousness and died. (*London Gazette*, 13 March 1945, posthumous award)

Gale & Polden Ltd., Aldershot.

PRIZE WINNERS, R.A.F. CADET COLLEGE, CRANWELL
JULY, 1928

F/C. W. R. Worstall
The Aeronautical Engineering Prize

F/C. F. Whittle
The Abdy Gerrard Fellowes Memorial Prize

F/C. Sgt. H. J. Pringle
The Humanistic Subjects Prize

F/C. U/O. N. E. White
The Sword of Honour

F/C. Cpl. G. N. E. Tindal-Carill-Worsley
The R.M. Groves Memorial Prize

Flight Cadet F. Whittle (centre rear) with fellow prize winners on graduation from the RAF College Cranwell, July 1928. (*RAF College Cranwell*)

1948 Air Cdre Frank Whittle, inventor of the jet engine, retired from the RAF on medical grounds. Shortly afterwards he was appointed KBE, the first Halton aircraft apprentice and graduate of the RAF College Cranwell to be knighted.

27 AUGUST

1914 The first Royal Naval Air Service (RNAS) unit arrived on the Continent. The East-church Squadron (Cdr C.R. Samson) was transferred to Ostend and the squadron subsequently redeployed to Dunkirk. The squadron was renamed No. 3 Squadron RNAS on 1 September 1914.

1918 The Air Council decided that medical officers would wear the same badges of rank as the rest of the RAF but that they would wear a distinctive collar or lapel badge and a maroon instead of a black band round the hat. The latter was short-lived. The badge, based on the winged caduceus of Mercury, was approved in its final form in June 1920.

1919 HM King George V approved the title 'Chief of the Royal Air Force'. The most senior rank was given as 'Marshal of the Air' but it is said that King George V objected to this saying that this applied to God only and the title was changed to 'Marshal of the Royal Air Force'. The familiar titles for the commissioned ranks of the RAF were introduced when military rank titles were dropped. Officers of General rank adopted the title 'Air Officers' (AMWO 973/19).

1936 An announcement was made that HM King George VI had approved the institution of the Royal Air Force Volunteer Reserve (RAFVR) (AMO A.204/1936).

1940 The RAF was made responsible for the disposal of unexploded bombs on Air Force property and all bombs found on or adjacent to crashed aircraft. Initially known as Demolition Sections, of which there were eighty, they were manned by station armourers. In September 1940, Mobile Bomb Disposal Squads were formed at twenty-five strategically located RAF stations with additional BD Squads formed throughout the war.
See 21 April 1943.

GC: Sqn Ldr Eric Lawrence Moxey, an Air Ministry technical officer who volunteered to attempt to defuse two unexploded bombs

Air Cdre Sir Frank Whittle (1907–96) as a Group Captain.
(AHB. CH 11867)

at RAF Biggin Hill. One weapon exploded and he was killed. The citation concluded 'on many occasions Sqn Ldr Moxey has exhibited similar complete disregard for his personal safety'. This was the first award of the George Cross to a member of the RAF. (*London Gazette*, 17 December 1940, posthumous award)

1941 Two Hudsons of No. 269 Squadron attacked the Type VIIC U-boat *U-570* off Iceland, damaging it sufficiently to prevent it from submerging. It then surrendered to Hudson S/269 (captain, Sqn Ldr J.H. Thompson), which remained until relieved by a Catalina. Naval forces towed the U-boat to Iceland. It was eventually repaired and became HM Submarine *Graph*.

1944 The first major raid by heavy bombers of Bomber Command against Germany in daylight was undertaken when 243 aircraft attacked the synthetic-oil refinery at Homberg. Sixteen Spitfire squadrons provided an escort.

The climax was reached in the campaign against the pilotless V-1 rockets when eighty-seven of the ninety-seven launched

were destroyed: sixty-two by guns, nineteen by fighters, two by balloons and four by a combination of balloons and guns.

1990 Operation Granby: the first twelve Tornado GR1s arrived at Muharraq, Bahrain. Subsequently Tornado GR1 detachments were established at Tabuk on 8 October and Dhahran on 3 January 1991.

28 AUGUST

1919 HM King George V approved the violet and white alternate diagonal striped ribbons for the DFC and DFM, and a similar red and white for the AFC and AFM, thus replacing the horizontal striping used for a brief period.

1939 The WAAF was mobilised and the Air Ministry authorised their recruitment for specific trades.

1945 Operation Birdcage: following the signing of the preliminary surrender document by Japanese delegates in Rangoon, the

A Royal Navy party prepares to board the Type VIIC U-boat *U-570*, which had surrendered off Iceland to two Hudsons of No. 269 Squadron. *(AHB. C 2069)*

pre-planned operation for the Release of Allied Prisoners-of-War and Internees (RAPWI) was launched with leaflet-dropping Liberators flying to known POW camps. The operation was completed on the 31st by which time 150 tons of leaflets had been dropped on fifty-eight sorties. Drops of food and medical supplies immediately followed this.
See 30 August 1945.

1952 Fg Off M.O. Berg became the RAF's only prisoner of war during the Korean War when he was forced to eject from his Meteor F8, which had been crippled by anti-aircraft fire. He was shot down while serving with No. 77 Squadron, Royal Australian Air Force.

1945 Operation Mastiff: the first RAF team parachuted into Singapore Island to negotiate and safeguard the release of POWs. Over the next few days other RAF and Force 136 teams were dropped to camps in Burma, Siam and Malaya. By 5 September teams had also reached camps in French Indochina and Sumatra.
See 8 September 1945.

Dakotas landed at Bangkok and the first POWs were released and flown to Rangoon.

1950 The government announced a number of initiatives to raise the strength of the defence forces including the extension of the period of National Service from eighteen months to two years, and the restoration of flying pay.

29 AUGUST

1944 Operation Blockade: air attacks on road and rail communications to isolate northern Italy by medium bombers of the Mediterranean Allied Tactical Air Force commenced. Baltimore, Boston, Marauder and Wellington bombers of the RAF and SAAF were heavily engaged. The operation ended on 8 April 1945.

GC: Sgt Arthur Banks, a pilot of No. 112 Squadron, who fought with the Italian partisans after being shot down. Later he was captured, tortured and executed by Italian Fascists. (*London Gazette*, 5 November 1946, posthumous award)

30 AUGUST

1942 Battle of Alam el Halfa: this little-known week-long battle was the climax of army/air co-operation in the Western Desert and one in which the seal was set on the procedure and organisation for air support. The battle was a classic of its kind, exemplifying the use of air power on efficient and economical grounds, when used in direct support of an army in the field.
See 30 September 1941.

AVM P. Maltby (left), the highest-ranking RAF officer to be a prisoner of the Japanese, is greeted after his release from a POW camp. *(AHB)*

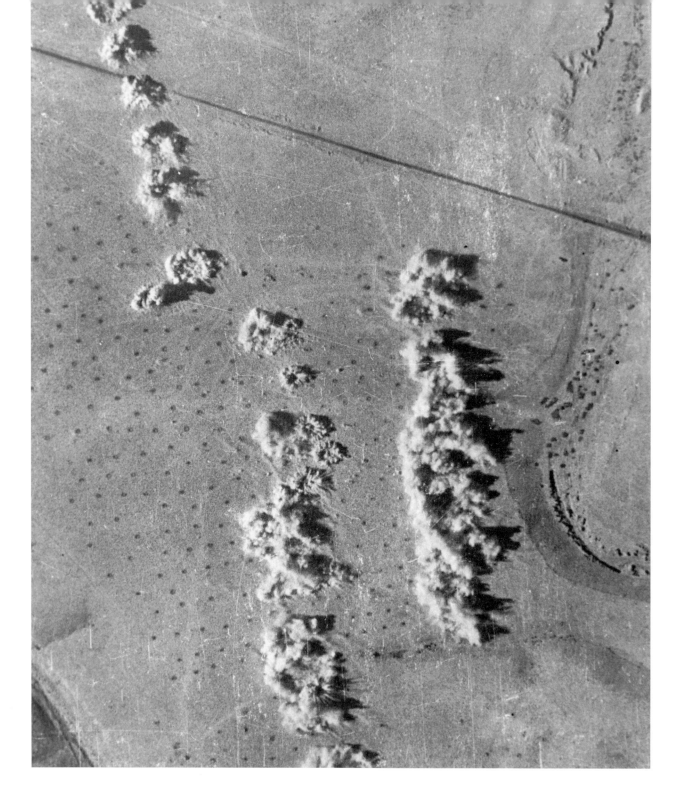

RAF bombers attack a German fuel dump in the Western Desert. *(R. Nesbit Collection)*

31 AUGUST

1995 Operation Deliberate Force: following a Serbian mortar attack on Sarajevo, Harrier GR7s of No. 4 Squadron, supported by laser-marking Jaguars, attacked military targets in Bosnia in support of the UN Protection Force (UNPROFOR). Attacks continued at intervals until 14 September when Bosnian-Serb heavy weapons began to be moved from around Sarajevo.

1943 Wg Cdr K.H. Burns of No. 97 Squadron was the Master Bomber on a raid on Berlin. Over the target his Lancaster was severely damaged by a night-fighter and he ordered his crew to bale out. As he prepared to jump the aircraft exploded and he was knocked unconscious and thrown clear at 22,000ft. He regained consciousness three hours later under some pine trees to find the ripcord of his parachute had not been pulled and there

The body of HRH Diana, The Princess of Wales, arrives at RAF Northolt. *(No. 32 (The Royal) Squadron Archives)*

was so little of it open that it could have cut down his speed only fractionally. He walked to a police station and was taken to hospital where he was cared for by German doctors. His right arm had been blown off, he had a collapsed lung and his back was broken. He recovered, was repatriated and returned to bomber operations, ending the war with a DSO and two DFCs.

1950 The very unpopular non-commissioned aircrew ranks introduced in June 1946 were abandoned in favour of the traditional ranks with the minimum aircrew rank restored to that of sergeant. Aircrew were to wear a gilt eagle in the vee of the chevrons (AMO A.545/50).
See 6 June 1946.

1953 Operation Cyclone: the RAF in Malaya undertook the first crop-spraying operation. Modified Sikorsky S51 and S55 helicopters were used to spray herbicide on jungle clearings used by the terrorists to cultivate food. During Cyclone I, over thirty clearings were sprayed and one terrorist killed in

associated ground-force operations. A second series of crop-spraying sorties (Operation Cyclone II) quickly followed and by the end of 1953 a total of eighty-eight clearings had been sprayed. However, due to the paucity of helicopters, spraying operations were held in abeyance after 1954.

1973 Maintenance Command was disbanded and absorbed into RAF Support Command, which formed the following day.

1977 MRAF Sir Neil Cameron was appointed Chief of the Defence Staff. He held the appointment until 31 August 1979 and was created Baron Cameron of Balhousie on 14 March 1983.

The Inspectorate of Flight Safety (Air Cdr K.W. Hayr) was formed.

1997 A BAe146 (captain Sqn Ldr G. Laurie) of No. 32 (The Royal) Squadron returned to RAF Northolt from Paris with the body of HRH Diana, The Princess of Wales, who had been killed in a motoring accident. Her coffin was borne from the aircraft by members of the Queen's Colour Squadron of the RAF Regiment.

1 SEPTEMBER

1937 ACM Sir Cyril Newall was appointed Chief of the Air Staff.

1939 A Royal Proclamation called out the RAF Reserve (including the RAFVR) for permanent service. The Auxiliary Air Force was embodied.

The Air Transport Auxiliary (ATA) (Director Gerald d'Erlanger) was formed to deliver new and repaired aircraft to RAF units.
See 30 November 1945.

1944 The first and most destructive phase of the V-1 campaign, the bombardment of the United Kingdom from bases in the Pas de Calais, came to an end with the launch of the final weapon at 0400hr. Between 13 June and 1 September 1944, no fewer than 8,617 V-1s had been fired at the United Kingdom from northern France. Aircraft of Fighter Command shot down 1,846 with the Tempest accounting for 663.

Women pilots of the Air Transport Auxiliary. *(AHB. C382)*

ACM Sir Cyril Newall (1886–1963). *(AHB)*

1946 RAF Regiment officers began to replace seconded Army officers in the Aden Protectorate Levies.
See 1 February 1957.

1950 The first RAF B-29 (Washington) squadron, No. 115 Squadron, was formed at RAF Marham.

1951 The highest RAF command formation within Germany, British Air Forces of Occupation (BAFO), reverted to its earlier wartime designation of Second Tactical Air Force (2nd TAF), a name more closely representing the role of the formation as a tactical air force within NATO.

1958 The RAF's first Thor Intermediate-Range Ballistic Missile squadron, No. 77 (SM) Squadron, RAF Bomber Command, was formed at RAF Feltwell.
See 22 February 1958.

1963 ACM Sir Charles Elworthy was appointed Chief of the Air Staff.

A Thor IRBM on the launch pad during an exercise.
(AHB. T 2616)

1966 The first lay-down nuclear weapons (WE 177B) were delivered to RAF Cottesmore.

1972 Strike Command absorbed Air Support Command, whose assets were grouped in No. 46 Group, which formed with effect from this date.

1973 Support Command was formed (AM R.E.W. Harland).

1983 The first Germany-based Tornado squadron, No. 15 Squadron, started to form at RAF Laarbruch.

2 SEPTEMBER

1916 The first German airship was destroyed over Britain. Sixteen airships of the German Army and Navy had been despatched to attack London, the largest airship raid of the First World War. One airship was forced to return early. Of the remaining fifteen, SL11 (Hauptmann W. Schramm) was shot down in flames by Lt W. Leefe Robinson in a BE2c of No. 39 (Home Defence) Squadron.

VC: Lt William Leefe Robinson for shooting down Zeppelin SL11. (*London Gazette*, 5 September 1916)
See 31 December 1918.

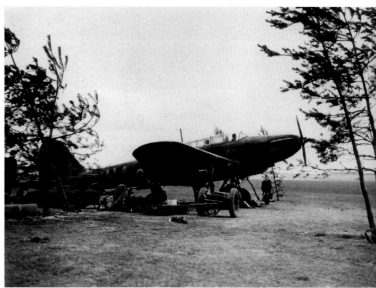

A Battle of No. 218 Squadron at an aerodrome in France.
(AHB)

The twenty-two Hunter loop by No. 111 Squadron. *(AHB. PRB 15707)*

1939 The first echelon of the Advanced Air Striking Force (AASF) (AVM P.H.L. Playfair) deployed to France. The ten squadrons of Battles of the AASF had all arrived in France by 15 September.

1943 The term 'radar' was officially adopted by the RAF in preference to the abbreviation 'RDF' (AMO 863/43).

1945 The Second World War war ended at 1030hr Tokyo time (0130hr GMT), when the unconditional surrender of Japan was signed on board the battleship USS *Missouri*, at anchor in Tokyo Bay.

1958 Twenty-two Hunter F6 fighters (leader Sqn Ldr R.L. Topp) completed two looping manoeuvres during an aerobatic sequence at the 19th SBAC Farnborough Air Show. Twelve aircraft were drawn from No. 111 Squadron – the Black Arrows – with the remaining ten drawn from other Fighter Command Hunter squadrons. An air correspondent described it as 'the most wonderful aerobatic manoeuvre ever witnessed, a performance transcending all others'.

3 SEPTEMBER

1939 Great Britain, Australia, New Zealand and France declared war on Germany. South Africa entered the war on 5 September and Canada declared war on Germany on 10 September.

As a result of the various Expansion Schemes leading up to the outbreak of war, the RAF's strength had grown to 11,753 officers and 163,939 other ranks.

A Blenheim of No. 139 Squadron was the first British aircraft to cross the German frontier in the Second World War when it photographed units of the German Fleet leaving Wilhelmshaven. The aircraft crew were Fg Off A. McPherson, Cdr Thompson RN and Cpl V. Arrowsmith.

Plt Off John Noel Isaac of No. 600 Squadron became the first Briton to die in the Second World War when his Blenheim crashed into Heading Street in Hendon at 1250hr, 1 hour 50 minutes after the British declaration of war.

Ten Whitleys of Nos 51 and 58 Squadrons flew the first *Nickel* (leaflet) raid on Germany. Six million leaflets were dropped on Hamburg, Bremen and over the cities of the Ruhr. There were no losses but three aircraft were forced to land at airfields in France.

1945 Sqn Ldr F. McKenna of the Special Investigation Branch (SIB) of the RAF arrived in Germany to investigate the murder of the fifty RAF officers executed after the Great Escape. A larger SIB team

151

Achtung!

Deutsche! Vergeßt nicht!

Deutsches Blut ist im polnischen Krieg in Strömen geflossen.

Aber:

1. Aus dem siegreichen Blitzkrieg ist nichts geworden. Beweis: — Das englische Kriegskabinett beschloß seine Politik auf einer **Kriegsdauer von drei oder mehr Jahren** aufzubauen.
2. Die französische Armee überschritt am 6. September **die deutsche Grenze**, aber erst 4 Tage später gaben es die amtlichen deutschen Stellen zu. Im Westen stehen englische Truppen Schulter an Schulter mit ihren französischen Verbündeten.
3. Vor der englischen und französischen Kriegsflotte ist **die deutsche Handelsflagge** vom Weltmeer verschwunden. Infolgedessen habt Ihr eine ganze Reihe wesentlicher **Kriegsrohstoffe**, wie Benzin, Kupfer, Nickel, Baumwolle, Wolle und Fett fast nicht mehr. Auf Einfuhr aus neutralen Ländern könnt Ihr Euch diesmal nicht verlassen, weil Eure Regierung nicht dafür bezahlen kann.
4. Tagtäglich zeigt die englische Luftwaffe ihre Macht durch **Flüge weit ins deutsche Land** hinein.

Deutsche! Vergeßt nicht!

Weitergeben! 151

EH. 151 (No. 7).

(Revised English Version).

ACHTUNG!!   ACHTUNG!!

TO THE GERMAN PEOPLE.

Germans, note that, in spite of the German blood which has been shed in the Polish war:

1. Your Government's hope of successful Blitkrieg has been destroyed by the British War Cabinet's decision to prepare for a three years' war.

2. The French Army crossed the frontier into Germany on the 6th September, or four days before the German official sources admitted it.

   In the West, British troops are already standing shoulder to shoulder with their French Allies

3. The British and French fleets have swept German merchant shipping from the oceans. Therefore your supplies of a whole range of essential war war materials, such as petrol, copper, nickel, rubber, cotton, wool, and fats are almost gone. You can no longer rely, as you did in the last war, upon neutral supplies, because your Government cannot pay for them.

4. Night after night the British Air Force (Englische Luftwaffe) has demonstrated its power by flights far into German territory.

GERMANS NOTE.

Above: The first propaganda leaflet dropped by the RAF during the Second World War (with translation). *(RAFM)*

Below: Jaguars of the Coltishall Wing on patrol over Iraq during Operation Warden. *(RAFM)*

279

(Wg Cdr W. Bowes) joined the investigation in December. After a painstaking operation, gradually piecing together enough evidence to identify the culprits, they were placed on trial. The Court pronounced its verdict on 3 September 1947, and in early February 1948 thirteen of the perpetrators were hanged at Hamelin Gaol, Hamburg, two were sentenced to life imprisonment and two received ten-year sentences. Bowes and McKenna were appointed OBEs.

See 24 March 1944.

1948 Exercise Dagger: the first full-scale UK air defence exercise since the end of the Second World War, it included USAF B-29 bombers.

1980 The first course for the development of leadership and command skills for junior NCOs assembled at the Airman's Command School at RAF Hereford.

1991 Operation Warden: Jaguars of No. 54 Squadron began to patrol northern Iraq in an effort to reassure Kurdish refugees sheltering in 'safe havens'.

4 SEPTEMBER

1937 In very poor weather, an Anson from RAF Martlesham Heath detected a naval surface force at a distance of 9 miles with the aid of a very short wavelength airborne radar, which was eventually developed into an air-to-surface vessel (ASV) radar.

1939 In a message to the RAF, HM King George VI stated: 'The RAF has behind it a tradition no less inspiring than those of the other Services and in campaigns which we have been compelled to undertake you will have to assume responsibilities far greater than those your Service had to shoulder in the last War. One of the greatest of them will be the safeguarding of the Island from the menace of the air. I can assure all ranks of the Air Force of my supreme confidence in their skill and courage and their ability to meet whatever calls may be made upon them.'

The first British bombing raids of the Second World War were conducted. Blenheims of Nos 110 and 139 Squadrons attacked German shipping in the Schillig Roads, near Wilhelmshaven; three bombs hit the pocket battleship *Admiral Scheer* but failed to detonate. Wellingtons of Nos 9 and 149 Squadrons attacked – or tried to attack – similar targets off Brunsbuttel with 500lb bombs. The first to attack was Flt Lt K.C. Doran of No. 110 Squadron. Five Blenheims and two Wellingtons were shot down.

Sgt G. Booth and AC 1 L.J. Slattery, the observer and WOP/AG of No. 107 Squadron, became the first British POWs of the Second World War when their Blenheim was shot down over the German coast.

1942 Operation Orator: two squadrons of torpedo-carrying Hampdens, Nos 144 and 455, flew from RAF Sumburgh to Vaenga in north Russia to provide support for convoy PQ 18. Twenty-three of the thirty-two aircraft arrived safely at airfields in the area. They flew one patrol on 13 September before the aircraft were handed over to the Soviet Air Force.

1943 The first RAF servicing commandos to reach Italy, No. 3232 Squadron, landed a day after the 8th Army from an LST at Reggio before driving their vehicles and equipment to the nearby airfield.

1944 Authority was given to form the Central Fighter Establishment (CFE) at RAF Wittering. The Fighter Interception Unit and the Air Fighting Development Unit were absorbed on 1 October and the Fighter Leaders School on 27 December.

1945 Three RAF Airfield Construction Squadrons (Nos 5024, 5026 and 5207) of No. 5358 Wing (Wg Cdr P. Morter), on their way to construct airfields for RAF use in the Pacific, were diverted to Hong Kong to provide guards, assist in POW repatriation and to restore the major services and utilities in the territory. Over 3,000 men of the Wing disembarked to assist in guarding 18,000 Japanese prisoners and in the restoration of Hong Kong before leaving for home in April 1946.

A Hampden is refuelled on its 'airfield' at Vaenga, north Russia. *(RAFM)*

1957 The last ab initio air signallers to be awarded their 'S' flying badge graduated from No. 1 Air Signaller's School at RAF Swanton Morley. They were the last of 30,000 signallers, wireless operators and WOP/AGs trained since the beginning of the Second World War.

2001 The departure from RAF Bruggen of the last Tornado marked the end of a continuous period of fifty-six years of RAF aircraft based in Germany and a permanent RAF presence on the European mainland.

5 SEPTEMBER

1922 The first RAF evacuation airlift was mounted when Turkish irregular forces and militia working with local Kurdish tribes infiltrated into northern Iraq and occupied Rowanduz. They mounted probes towards Sulaimaniya and forced a column of Imperial troops to retreat. Sixteen DH9As and two Vernons, the latter having just arrived in theatre, evacuated sixty-seven women, children and a number of Levies

from Sulaimaniya to Kirkuk over the next few days.

1939 An Anson of No. 500 Squadron made the first attack on a German submarine, 10 miles north of Ostend. The damage claim made by the crew was not accepted.

1944 Nos 2771 and 2871 Armoured Car Squadrons, RAF Regiment, were with the leading elements of the Army, which liberated Brussels.

A Vernon ambulance over Hinaidi, Iraq. *(AHB. H 1149)*

6 SEPTEMBER

1939 A technical fault at the Chain Home RDF (radar) station at Canewdon, compounded by a series of mistakes within RAF Fighter Command's fighter control system, led to friendly aircraft being plotted as an incoming air raid. Hurricanes of No. 56 Squadron were scrambled to intercept this 'phantom raid', only to be plotted as hostile in their turn. Further squadrons were scrambled; tragically, a section of No. 72 Squadron (Spitfire) misidentified two Hurricanes as Messerschmitt Bf 109s and shot both down; one pilot, Plt Off M.L. Hutton-Harrop, was killed. The 'Battle of Barking Creek', as the events of 6 September were later to become known, led to a wholesale review of RAF Fighter Command's plotting system.

1945 Wg Cdr J.R.H. Merrifield and Flt Lt J.H. Spires flying a Mosquito PR 34 took off from RAF St Mawgan and landed at Torbay, Newfoundland seven hours later to create a new east-west transatlantic record.

1951 Special uniforms were introduced for established RAF and WRAF bands (AMO A.512/51).

7 SEPTEMBER

1929 Fg Off H.R. Waghorn, flying a Supermarine S.6, won the Schneider Trophy over seven laps of a quadrilateral course over the Solent at an average speed of 328.63mph, the RAF's second success.

See 13 September 1931.

1940 The Battle of Britain: the fourth phase opened with the Luftwaffe switching its attention to the bombing of London. Almost 1,000 bombers were despatched during the afternoon to carry out an all-out onslaught against London. Over succeeding days heavy night attacks were mounted against the capital.

Invasion Alert No. 1 was promulgated. Bomber Command's major effort was concentrated against German invasion preparations, including the Channel ports.

1942 The crew of a No. 70 Squadron Wellington crash-landed in the North African desert

The Supermarine S.5 flown into second place during the 1929 competition for the Schneider Trophy. *(G.R. Pitchfork Collection)*

German invasion barges being assembled at Dunkirk.
(R. Nesbit Collection)

The Meteor F4 flown by Gp Capt E.M. Donaldson along
the coast of Sussex. *(RAFM)*

after the aircraft had been damaged by flak over Tobruk. Over the next twenty-eight days five of them trekked 400 miles through enemy lines and were eventually picked up by a patrol of the Long Range Desert Group. The sixth man was captured and became a POW.

1946 Gp Capt E.M. Donaldson, flying a Meteor F4 of the RAF High Speed Flight, established a world speed record of 615.81mph over a course off the Sussex coast.

1994 RAF Gatow, Berlin, was closed and handed over to the Luftwaffe.

8 SEPTEMBER

1936 Three Welsh intellectuals made a symbolic protest against the building of a bombing school at RAF Penrhos near Pwllheli by setting fire to offices and workshops. They immediately gave themselves up to the police. On the fiftieth anniversary in September 1986 a plaque commemorating the event was unveiled on the spot. There can be no other airfield that boasts a memorial to those who tried to burn it down!

1943 The armistice between the Allies and Italy was made public.

1944 The attack on Le Havre marked the last bombing operation by the Stirling when four of No. 149 Squadron's aircraft joined a force of Lancasters. The aircraft remained in Bomber Command, serving with the Heavy Conversion Units. It continued to give excellent service in the airborne, SOE and transport roles.

Wg Cdr G.L. Cheshire (1917–92). *(AHB. CH 12667)*

VC: Wg Cdr Geoffrey Leonard Cheshire DSO & 2 Bars, DFC of No. 617 Squadron awarded in recognition of an extended period of operational flying and out-standing prowess. The citation included, 'In four years of fighting against the bitterest opposition he has maintained a record of outstanding personal achievement, placing himself invariably in the forefront of the battle'. (*London Gazette*, 8 September 1944)

Eight Beaufighters of No. 272 Squadron, of the Balkan Air Force, attacked the ocean-going 51,000-ton Italian liner the *Rex*, anchored off Trieste. The liner capsized after being hit by 123 rockets, thus preventing her from being used as a block-ship in Trieste harbour.

1945 Operation Mastiff: a reinforced RAF team (Wg Cdr T.S. Tull) parachuted into central Java to locate POW camps and assume command. Operations became dangerous when Indonesian nationalist forces attacked the camps. Japanese troops were used as guards but bitter fighting broke out and some Allied personnel, POWs and Japanese were killed by the nationalists. The camps were held until ground forces arrived and took over. Tull was awarded the DSO.

9 SEPTEMBER

1938 A Royal Warrant established the Auxiliary Territorial Service (ATS) for women. One company was usually to be an RAF Company distinguished by an RAF armband.
See 28 June 1939.

1939 Squadrons of the Air Component of the British Expeditionary Force (BEF) (AVM C.H.B. Blount) commenced deployment to France. Hurricanes of Nos 1 and 73 Squadrons arrived at Le Havre and by the 15th Nos 85 and 87 had arrived at Rouen. Four Lysander squadrons for army co-operation duties, and four squadrons of Blenheim bomber/reconnaissance aircraft had arrived in France by the middle of October.

Pilots of No. 87 Squadron scramble to their Hurricanes at an airfield in northern France. *(AHB)*

1943 Operation Avalanche: the Allies launched an amphibious landing at Salerno with air cover. The first RAF Regiment unit to reach Italy was No. 2906 Squadron, which landed with the Army on the beaches at Salerno.

1945 Advance elements of No. 224 Group (AVM The Earl of Bandon) landed in Malaya and established a headquarters on the airfield at Kalanang. Twenty-four Spitfires of Nos 11 and 17 Squadrons arrived shortly afterwards, having flown off two Royal Navy escort aircraft carriers.

No. 909 Wing (Gp Capt D.O. Finlay) moved to Don Muang Airfield near Bangkok to become AHQ Siam. Men of No. 2945 Squadron, RAF Regiment, defended the airfield. Within days, Spitfires of No. 20 Squadron and Mosquitos of No. 211 Squadron arrived. Mosquitos of No. 685 (PR) Squadron located and photographed remote POW camps. Resupply RAF Dakotas

carried repatriated POWs on their return flights.

Spitfires of No. 132 Squadron flew off the aircraft carrier HMS *Smiter* and landed at Kai Tak, Hong Kong, to provide air defence for the colony when HQ RAF Hong Kong (Air Cdre W.A.D. Brook) was established.

1956 Operation Tasman Flight: the first Vulcan B1 to be taken on charge by the RAF, XA897, departed from Boscombe Down en route to Melbourne via Aden and Singapore. The aircraft was flown by Sqn Ldr D.R. Howard, with AM Sir Harry Broadhurst, AOC-in-C Bomber Command, as a member of the crew. The aircraft arrived at Melbourne on 11 September after a total flight time of 23 hours 15 minutes. The aircraft subsequently toured Australia and New Zealand and took part in the Battle of Britain commemorations planned by each country.

See 1 October 1956.

Spitfire XIVs of No. 132 Squadron arrive at Hong Kong. *(AHB. CF 881)*

A Buccaneer S2B of No. 208 Squadron on readiness at RAF Akrotiri. *(G.R. Pitchfork Collection)*

1983 Operation Pulsator: six Buccaneers drawn from Nos 12 and 208 Squadrons arrived at RAF Akrotiri, Cyprus, to provide support for British troops in Beirut. Two aircraft made a series of very low passes over the city to announce their presence. Subsequently they remained on alert in Cyprus until the operation ceased on 26 March 1984. Chinook helicopters provided an air transport link to the city and internal support to the British troops.

10 SEPTEMBER

Men of the RAF Regiment examine bombs abandoned on the edge of Taranto. *(R. Nesbit Collection)*

1942   The first 4,000lb incendiary was dropped during a raid on Düsseldorf.

1943   No. 2856 LAA Squadron, RAF Regiment, landed in Italy at Reggio, followed by ten more squadrons.

1953   As the campaign against the Mau Mau in Kenya intensified, Army reinforcements were required. Transport Command Hastings, supplemented by civil transport aircraft, carried HQ No. 49 Brigade and two infantry battalions to RAF Eastleigh, Nairobi. The extensive use of the airfield's red 'murram' dirt runways by an increasing number of very heavy aircraft, in addition to the locally based aircraft, provided a formidable task for the Air Ministry Works Directorate which deserves great credit for keeping the runway available almost continually throughout the four-year campaign.

2000   Chinook helicopters played a major part in the rescue operation of British soldiers held by the 'West Side Boys', a group of rebels fighting in Sierra Leone.

11 SEPTEMBER

1939   With the possibility that Italy might enter the war, London flying-boats of No. 202 Squadron left Malta to be based in Gibraltar to provide anti-submarine patrols and reconnaissance in the Straits of Gibraltar and the western Mediterranean.

A London flying-boat of No. 202 Squadron at Kalafrana, Malta. *(No. 202 Squadron Records)*

1941 No. 151 Wing RAF (Nos 81 and 134 Squadrons), equipped with Hurricanes, and under the command of Wg Cdr H.N.G. Ramsbottom-Isherwood, carried out the first operational flights from Vaenga near Murmansk. The Wing arrived by sea on 1 September at Archangel, Russia, where the aircraft were assembled and air-tested over the next ten days. Additional aircraft arrived on the aircraft carrier HMS *Argus* on 7 September and flew off to Vaenga. One of the pilots was Plt Off N. Cameron (later MRAF Lord Cameron). Air defence operations for the defence of Murmansk port and escort sorties for Russian bombers continued until 10 October. The Wing was credited with destroying fifteen enemy aircraft. Russian pilots were then converted to the Hurricane and the aircraft were handed over to the Soviet Naval Air Arm. The Wing withdrew to the United Kingdom on 29 November.

1945 Following an agreement at the Potsdam Conference that the United Kingdom would accept the Japanese surrender in French Indochina south of the 16th Parallel, prior to the resumption of French colonial control, Dakotas of No. 62 Squadron began to airlift the leading elements of the 80th Brigade, 20th Indian Division, into Saigon. On the following day, the first French troops flew into Saigon. In practice, British troops concentrated on disarming Japanese forces in the country, allowing French troops to deal with local nationalist movements affiliated to the Viet Minh.

1956 Hon. AM W.A. Bishop **VC**, CB, DSO & Bar, MC, DFC, RCAF died.
See 2 June 1917.

Russian soldiers building revetments for Hurricanes of No. 151 Wing at Vaenga Airfield near Murmansk. *(AHB. CR 184)*

12 SEPTEMBER

1925 The first Auxiliary Air Force squadron, No. 602 (City of Glasgow) Squadron was formed at Renfrew. A month later, No. 600 (City of London) Squadron formed at RAF Northolt.

    See 9 October 1924, 10 March 1957.

1929 Sqn Ldr A.H. Orlebar of the RAF High Speed Flight, piloting a Supermarine S.6 seaplane, established a new world speed record of 357.75mph at Calshot.

1942 Operation Orator: nine Catalinas of No. 210 Squadron deployed to the Kola Peninsula, north Russia, to fly patrols in support of convoys PQ 18 and QP 14 to and from Murmansk. Coastal Command's contribution to the protection of these convoys involved over 100 aircraft from squadrons based in the UK, Iceland and Russia.

A Charles Cundall painting of a No. 210 Squadron crew returning from an operation in their Catalina.
(AHB. LD 1409)

1944 **GC**: Assistant Section Officer Noor Inayat-Khan WAAF, SOE radio operator (codename 'Madeleine'), who was betrayed and captured by the Gestapo in Paris. She refused to co-operate and twice tried to escape. She was eventually transferred to Dachau concentration camp and shot. (*London Gazette*, 5 April 1949, posthumous award)

Air and ground crews of No. 602 (City of Glasgow) Squadron at RAF Renfrew with a DH9A.
(No. 602 Squadron Association Archive)

1944 The first operational use was made of *Loran* (Long Range Navigation) – a navigation and bombing aid with 1,200 miles' range – during a raid on Frankfurt.

1945 A ceremony marking the formal surrender of Japanese forces was held in Singapore. Six of the recently arrived Sunderlands of No. 209 Squadron (Gp Capt G. Francis) carried out a flypast.

1987 MRAF Sir William Dickson, former Chief of the Defence Staff and Chief of the Air Staff, died.
    See 1 January 1953, 1 January 1956.

THE SCHNEIDER TROPHY

The Schneider Trophy Contest was first held in Monaco in April 1913 for the award presented by Jacques Schneider – a patron of French aviation. It was to assume the greatest significance and exert a profound influence on the design and development both of aircraft and engines in addition to claiming the attention and resources of several nations. Great Britain first won the trophy in 1914 but it was not until 1926 that the Air Ministry was finally persuaded that the RAF should compete, and an embryo High Speed Flight was formed at RAF Felixstowe with Sqn Ldr L.H. Slatter in command. The team gathered in 1927 in preparation for the tenth Schneider Trophy to be held at the Lido, Venice. With Flt Lt S.N. Webster at the controls, a Supermarine S.5 (N220) won the event. The next event two years later was flown over the Solent and Flt Lt H.R. Waghorn flying a Supermarine S.6 (N247) was the winner. Flt Lt J.N. Boothman flying a Supermarine S.6B (S1595) gained the RAF's third victory in 1931, allowing it to keep the Schneider Trophy in perpetuity.

The great Schneider Trophy contests were over, but their influence on the development of airframes and engines for high-speed flight was profound. The brilliant Supermarine designer R.J. Mitchell used the experience gained by the success of the winning aircraft to design a high-speed monoplane fighter, which became the Spitfire. In addition, the Rolls-Royce engineers had learned a great deal in developing the engine for the Supermarine aircraft and the further development led to the Merlin engine, which ultimately powered world-beating aircraft including the Hurricane, Spitfire, Lancaster, Mosquito and the North American Mustang.

Lady Houston with the 1931 Schneider Trophy team. Standing on the right in the rear row is R.J. Mitchell, the designer of the Spitfire. *(RAFM)*

13 SEPTEMBER

1931   The RAF won the Schneider Trophy for the third successive time. Flt Lt J.N. Boothman, at the controls of a Supermarine S.6B of the RAF High Speed Flight, took the trophy with an average speed of 340.08mph. This third victory enabled the RAF to permanently retain the Schneider Trophy. The trophy and the S.6B in which it was won for the final time are in the collection of the Science Museum.

1940   The first enemy aircraft brought down by the balloon barrage, a Heinkel HeIIIP of 8/KG27 returning from a raid on Ellesmere Port, was brought down near Newport, South Wales, by a balloon of No. 966 Squadron.

14 SEPTEMBER

1924   In response to urgent warnings received on 13 September that Turkish troops would attempt to seize Zahko, a town north of Mosul, nine Bristol Fighters of No. 6 Squadron mounted a series of offensive patrols over the town. They located and attacked Turkish cavalry approaching the town, forcing them to retreat.

1942   Bomber Command Hampdens flew their last operation when aircraft of No. 408 (RCAF) Squadron attacked Wilhelmshaven. The aircraft continued to serve with Coastal Command.

1943   Spitfires of No. 324 Wing, together with Seafires of the Fleet Air Arm and Lightnings of the USAAF, deployed ashore to provide land-based fighter cover over the Salerno landings. During this day 1st Tactical Air Force flew 700 sorties.

Operation Microbe: six Dakotas of No. 216 Group, led by Sqn Ldr C.R.A. Forsyth, took off from Nicosia at 2240hr to drop 122 paratroopers on the Greek island of Cos in the Dodecanese. Nos 2909 (LAA) and 2901 (Field) Squadrons, RAF Regiment, were transported by air and sea to Cos on the following day to provide defence of the airfield at Antimachia. Spitfires of No. 74

Bullock power at Serretelle airfield, near Naples, assists the men of No. 232 Squadron and their Spitfire IXs.
(R. Nesbit Collection)

Squadron RAF and No. 7 Squadron SAAF provided air defence. Further landings were subsequently made on the neighbouring islands of Leros and Samos. However, by late November all three islands had been retaken by German forces, with heavy Allied ground, air and naval losses.

1964 Indonesian Confrontation: No. 65 (SAM) Squadron, armed with Bloodhound Mk 2 at RAF Seletar, was ordered to bring one section to immediate readiness to defend Singapore.

1994 Following the removal of cruise missiles by the USAF from RAF Greenham Common, the RAF police detachments were withdrawn after six years of policing the Campaign for Nuclear Disarmament (CND) peace camps.

15 SEPTEMBER

1919 Coastal Area was formed to control all units working with the Royal Navy. The remaining portion of the RAF at home was organised into Southern Area and Northern Area.

English and Czech pilots of No. 310 (Czech) Squadron at RAF Duxford. *(G.R. Pitchfork Collection)*

A new pattern of service uniform for officers was approved standardising the uniform colour as blue/grey. Rank lace was changed to black with a bright, pale blue central stripe replacing the gold braid. A silk flying badge replaced the gold badge. The Service Dress has remained in use ever since and is still worn as the No. 1 uniform (AMWO 1049/19).

1940 **VC**: Sgt John Hannah, a wireless operator/air gunner of No. 83 Squadron, for his actions when his Hampden was set on fire during an attack on Antwerp. He was the youngest airman ever to be awarded the Victoria Cross. (*London Gazette*, 1 October 1940)

The Battle of Britain: the Luftwaffe mounted its biggest daylight attack on London with 1,020 sorties flown over England. Fighter Command flew 705 sorties and in the course of these operations the Luftwaffe lost fifty-six aircraft. The Battle ran for a few more weeks but this day proved decisive and made it clear to the German High Command that reports of Fighter Command's impending demise had been greatly exaggerated. This date has since been recognised as 'Battle of Britain Day'.

1941 Sgt J.A. Ward **VC** was killed in action when his No. 75 Squadron Wellington was shot down over Hamburg. He and three

members of his crew are buried in Hamburg Cemetery. Two of his crew survived to become POWs.

See 7 July 1941.

1943 Eight Lancasters of No. 617 Squadron dropped the first 12,000lb HC bomb during an attack against the Dortmund–Ems Canal. Five aircraft were lost.

See 23 September 1944)

1945 AHQ Hong Kong was formed.

1949 For the first time, an official description of the RAF badge was published (AMO A.666/49) as: 'In front of a circle inscribed with the motto, "Per Ardua Ad Astra", and ensigned with the Imperial Crown, an eagle Volant and affronte, the head lowered and to the sinister.' The order also disposed of the lengthy controversy about the identity of the bird in the badge.

1952 Following the occupation of the village of Hamasa by a Saudi Arabian party during a dispute concerning the border between Oman and Saudi Arabia, three Vampire FB5s from No. 6 Squadron at RAF Habbaniya, and accompanied by a Vickers Valetta, deployed to RAF Sharjah from where they carried out demonstrations and leaflet drops over the village.

1960 The RAF Germany Canberra force was declared to SACEUR with a full nuclear delivery capability.

See 1 October 1959.

1971 RAF Tengah was handed over to the Singapore Air Defence Command at a formal parade, thirty-two years after the RAF opened the airfield.

The RAF badge with King's Crown. *(AHB)*

Javelin FAW9s of No. 60 Squadron fly over RAF Tengah, Singapore. *(J. Abell)*

293

16 SEPTEMBER

1942 **GC**: Sgt Graham Leslie Parish, a navigator on a delivery flight who helped to rescue passengers from his burning aircraft after it had crash-landed near an airfield in Sudan. (*London Gazette*, 2 April 1943, posthumous award)

1952 A Hastings (captain Flt Lt M.A. Clancy) of No. 24 Squadron crashed in a whiteout on the Greenland ice cap. The twelve men on board survived for nine days in the fuselage in temperatures as low as -40°C before being rescued by a Grumman Albatross and a ski-equipped Dakota of the USAF.

1963 Indonesian Confrontation: Malaysia came into existence with the full support of the British government. Following the unsuccessful attempt to depose the Sultan of Brunei on 8 December 1962, President Sukarno of Indonesia, driven by the desire

The crashed Hastings on the Greenland ice cap. (*AHB. PRB 5447*)

to unite Malaya, the Philippines and Indonesia within an Indonesian empire, began to support insurgents in attacks across the 970-mile border between Kalimantan, Sarawak and Sabah on the island of Borneo. Between the declaration of the Federation of Malaysia and 1966, Indonesian insurgents and troops were also inserted into Singapore and Malaya by aircraft. In response, the British armed forces mounted an intensive counter-insurgency operation in order to guarantee the security of the states making up the new Malaysian Federation. RAF transport aircraft and helicopters supported the British Army presence in Sarawak and Sabah. An Air Defence Identification Zone (ADIZ) was established over Sarawak and Sabah, policed by the Hunters of No. 20 Squadron and Javelins of Nos 60 and 64 Squadrons from RAF stations Kuching and Labuan. Eventually, hostilities came to an end following the conclusion of a peace treaty on 11 August 1966.

1970 HRH The Princess Anne presented the Queen's Colour of the Royal Air Force Germany.
See 31 March 1993.

A Whirlwind picks up Gurkha troops in Borneo. (*AHB. CFP 1187*)

17 SEPTEMBER

1930 Sheikh Mahmud crossed into southern Kurdistan from Persia and triggered another uprising in Iraq. Over the next three months there were constant periods of action and skirmishes. Aircraft of Nos 30, 55 and 70 Squadrons mounted air attacks and troop reinforcement flights. RAF armoured cars supported them. By the end of December, the RAF had flown 1,496 hours in support of Iraqi Army operations.

1932 Wapitis of Nos 27 and 60 Squadrons carried out intensive bombing operations against the Shamozai Mohmands who were attacking the Chitral Relief Column. Operations continued until 16 October when the tribe submitted and withdrew.

1936 The first full-scale trial of an RDF (radar) system was carried out at Bawdsey Research Station to track Coastal Command Ansons and flying-boats. Although the results of the trial were mixed, the Chief of the Air Staff concluded that the concept had been proved and justified the development of RDF as part of the air defences of the UK.

1937 Two severe thunderstorms struck RAF Cardington. Eleven unmanned balloons were flying at 600ft. Four were struck by lightning and set on fire and six others were brought down and destroyed. One survived and remained flying.

1940 A Beaufighter of No. 29 Squadron flew the first operational patrol by a night-fighter fitted with Air Interception radar (AI Mk IV). The Beaufighter was the first truly effective radar-equipped night-fighter to be operated by the RAF.

1942 Flying badges for the navigator (N), air bomber (B), and flight engineer (E) were introduced. All were to the same design as the air gunner badge with the appropriate letter in the laurel. The air bomber badge ceased to be issued in 1945 and the flight engineer badge in 2004 (AMO A.1019/1942).

Wapitis of No. 27 Squadron over the North-West Frontier of India. (*G.R. Pitchfork Collection*)

Airborne forces prepare to embark on Stirlings of No. 620 Squadron at RAF Fairford. *(IWM. CL 1154)*

1944 Operation Market: a mass parachute and glider assault by three divisions of the First Allied Airborne Army took place to seize bridges in the area of Eindhoven (United States 101st Airborne Division), Nijmegen (United States 82nd Airborne Division) and Arnhem (British 1st Airborne Division). A simultaneous ground assault by 30 Corps, British 21st Army Group, was intended to relieve the parachute troops and create a bridgehead from which the German West Wall defensive line could be outflanked. However, this plan was frustrated by the presence of the 9th and 10th SS Panzer Divisions in the area selected for the assault. Elements from these formations slowed the attack by 30 Corps to a crawl and drove much of 1st Airborne Division into a pocket some distance from its drop zones and its objectives, the road and rail bridges at Arnhem. Attempts to reinforce and resupply the airborne divisions were also badly disrupted by poor weather. Eventually, on 25 September, the survivors of 1st Airborne Division were withdrawn across the Rhine.

See 25 September 1944.

1963 The Ballistic Missile Early Warning System (BMEWS) at Fylingdales was declared operational.

1993 A Hercules (captain Flt Lt T. Collins) of No. 1312 Flight, based in the Falkland Islands, searched the South Atlantic in appalling weather for the crew of a Russian cargo vessel that had sunk. Wreckage, dead and two survivors were located and survival aids dropped. One seaman survived. The Hercules was airborne for eighteen hours.

The BMEWS radars at RAF Fylingdales on the Yorkshire Moors. *(J. Falconer Collection)*

18 SEPTEMBER

1944 No. 2721 Squadron, RAF Regiment, was detached to X Corps to provide infantry support for armoured car regiments leading the advance towards the Gothic Line in Italy.

1971 The final parade of the Queen's Colour for the Far East Air Force took place at RAF Changi. The Reviewing Officer was the Commander Far East Air Force, AVM N.M. Maynard, and No. 63 Squadron, RAF Regiment, provided the Guard of Honour.

1985 During Exercise Cold Fire, Harriers of Nos 3 and 4 Squadrons operated for the first time from a German autobahn using one lane as a landing strip, with an operations centre in a lay-by.

1994 With the lack of official sponsorship, the RAF Police Dog Demonstration Team was disbanded.

2005 HRH The Prince of Wales unveiled the Battle of Britain London Memorial on the Victoria Embankment. The names of 2,936 aircrew who flew during the Battle are recorded.

19 SEPTEMBER

1918 The first 'trade' badge to be authorised in the RAF was the wireless operator's arm badge, which has remained unchanged to this day although renamed the tele-communications badge in 1951. The design, centrally a right fist clutching six lightning flashes, is worn by all qualified ground crew below the rank of Warrant Officer who are employed in the radio engineering ground trades (AMWO 1066/18).

1940 The first of the RAF's 'Eagle Squadrons', No. 71 Squadron, was formed. The aircrew were predominantly drawn from United States citizens enrolled in the RAF. Subsequently, two further Eagle Squadrons (Nos 121 and 133 Squadrons) were formed.
See 29 September 1942.

The Takoradi–Khartoum–Egypt ferry route was initiated when a Blenheim escorted six Hurricanes to Abu Sueir in Egypt, arriving on 26 September. One of the great air supply lines of the Second World War had been opened. By December the output from Takoradi was between 120 and 150 aircraft per month.
See 14 July 1940.

RAF Police training with their dogs. *(AHB. R2457)*

The first group of Eagle Squadron pilots. The pilot in uniform in the centre wears the 'ES' badge of the Squadron. *(AHB. CH 2403)*

1942 Bomber Command mounted the first Allied daylight raid on Berlin. Six Mosquito BIVs of No. 105 Squadron took off from RAF Horsham at 1230hr for a high-level raid on the city. However, due to poor weather over the target, only one aircraft bombed Berlin, through cloud. Two aircraft bombed the alternative target (Hamburg), two returned with mechanical problems and one failed to return.

1944 **VC**: Flt Lt David Samuel Lord DFC, captain of a Dakota of No. 271 Squadron, for his action during an airdrop of supplies at Arnhem, during Operation Market Garden. Despite his aircraft being on fire, he made a second supply drop over the dropping zone before the aircraft crashed. He was the sole Transport Command recipient of the supreme award for valour. (*London Gazette*, 13 November 1945, posthumous award)

Operation Market Garden: Air Sea Rescue launches rescued ninety-two airmen and soldiers from ditched gliders and tug aircraft in the North Sea. During the four-day operation, RAF launches saved 144 lives and naval launches rescued a further 79.

Wg Cdr G.P. Gibson **VC** DSO & Bar, DFC & Bar, and his navigator, Sqn Ldr J.B. Warwick, were killed in action when their Mosquito crashed over Holland when returning from a bombing sortie to Rheydt. They were buried in the local cemetery at Steenbergen, Holland.
See 16 May 1943.

1945 Spitfire IXs of No. 273 Squadron deployed to Tan Son Nhut Airfield in French Indochina. Following its arrival, the Squadron flew armed reconnaissance sorties in support of British troops in the French colony. Subsequently, No. 273 Squadron was joined at Tan Son Nhut by Dakotas of No. 267 Squadron and a flight of Mosquito PR34s of No. 684 Squadron engaged on photo-mapping duties. The airfield was also occupied by the Gremlin Task Force – a unit consisting of Japanese aircrew under British command, formed to operate Japanese transport aircraft in support of British and French forces.

1963 The formation of the state of Malaysia on 16 September 1963 resulted in an upsurge of hostility towards United Kingdom nationals living and working in Indonesia. Three Argosys of No. 215 Squadron, together with a Hastings of No. 48 Squadron, began to airlift any British citizens who wished to leave Indonesia to Singapore. Some 400 passengers were flown out over the next few days.

20 SEPTEMBER

1938 The Hampden bomber entered operational service; the first unit to receive it was No. 49 Squadron at RAF Scampton.

1939 The first engagement between the RAF and the Luftwaffe took place. Three Messerschmitt Bf109s of *Jagdgruppe* 152 attacked three No. 88 Squadron Battles of the Advance Air Striking Force west of Saarbrucken. Two Battles were shot down.

GC (ex-EGM): Fg Off Reginald Cubitt Graveley of No. 88 Squadron, the pilot of a Battle shot down over France. He displayed 'great gallantry' in rescuing the air observer and attempting to rescue the air gunner. (*London Gazette*, 11 November 1939)

WAAF plotters on duty in the Fighter Command Operations Room at RAF Bentley Priory. *(R. Nesbit Collection)*

RAF Regiment gunners guarding an airstrip in Burma.
(AHB. CF 342)

21 SEPTEMBER

1939 The first WAAF plotters stood watch in the Fighter Command filter room at RAF Stanmore.

1945 Five RAF Regiment Wings, comprising fourteen squadrons, landed in Malaya to occupy airfields on the mainland and the islands of Penang and Singapore.

1948 Operation Firedog: RAF Kuala Lumpur was established as the main RAF base for air operations during the Malayan Emergency.

1952 Plt Off Jean Lennox Bird WRAFVR, of No. 15 Reserve Flying School, was the first woman to be awarded the RAF pilot's badge; thirty-nine WRAFVR officers served as pilots by the time the last one left the service in January 1957. Jean Lennox-Boyd may not have been the first female to wear the RAF pilot badge since it is known that Mrs Jane Wynne-Eyton, a sergeant pilot with the Kenya Auxiliary Air Force, flew with the East Africa Communications Flight when she was mentioned in despatches.

1918 RAF aircraft operating in support of Gen Allenby's campaign in Palestine attacked and destroyed the retreating Turkish 7th Army at Wadi el Far'a. T.E. Lawrence wrote of this attack: 'It was the RAF which had

The recovery of the Loch Ness Wellington.
(ACA Archives)

converted the Turkish retreat into a rout, which had abolished their telephone and telegraph connections, had blocked their lorry columns, and scattered their infantry units.'

1920 Two Handley Page 0/400s of No. 70 Squadron carried a 1,176lb mountain gun, with ninety-eight rounds and six men, from Heliopolis to Almaza where the gun was reassembled and the first round fired seven minutes after unloading. This was the first demonstration to the Army of a tactical heavy airlift.

1984 The remains of a Wellington bomber were raised from Loch Ness. The aircraft (N2980) of No. 20 OTU had taken off from RAF Lossiemouth on 31 December 1940 and ditched in the loch. It was transported to the Brooklands Museum, partially restored and put on display.

Ground crew repair a damaged DH9A of No. 31 Squadron on India's North-West Frontier. *(J.M. Bruce/S. Leslie Collection)*

22 SEPTEMBER

1922 The Air Ministry received from the Viceroy of India a damning report from AVM Sir John Salmond on the state of the RAF in India. Salmond concluded: 'The RAF as a whole is in the depressed state natural to a neglected service and its morale and power of work have consequently decreased.' After identifying the causes, he recommended:
- A reorganisation of the present RAF units in India.
- The despatch of fifty Rolls-Royce aircraft engines home for repair.

- The expedition of the building programme for the RAF in India to the benefit of both the health of personnel and the efficiency of material.
- The introduction of a separate budget or section of the budget showing all expenditure, including works, on the RAF in India.
- An improvement in the status of the AOC India.
- The return of Group Headquarters RAF in India to Simla in the proximity of the Army Headquarters and the government of India.
- An addition of two squadrons to the strength of the RAF in India.
- Consequent on this increase the utilisation of the RAF as the sole punitive weapon for the control of the tribesmen in Waziristan with resultant economy in both the numbers and cost of maintenance of troops of occupation, and in the cost of punitive operations.
- The adoption of a definite policy for the utilisation of the RAF for an active offensive against Afghanistan, a policy, which should result in great economies both in peace and war.

1943 Bomber Command carried out the first 'spoof' raid technique when the primary target was Hanover. Twenty-one Lancasters and eight Mosquitos of No. 8 Group carried out a diversionary raid dropping much *Window* and many flares and target indicators to simulate a larger force attacking Oldenburg.

23 SEPTEMBER

1938 Authority was given to build an underground operations block at HQ Fighter Command, RAF Bentley Priory.

1939 The RAF's first dedicated photographic reconnaissance unit – the Heston Flight – formed at Heston. The commander of the Flight was Wg Cdr Sidney Cotton, who as a civilian in the late 1930s had conducted a series of clandestine photographic sorties

The Dortmund–Ems Canal breached after an attack by Bomber Command aircraft. *(AHB)*

over Germany on behalf of the Secret Intelligence Service (SIS). The Heston Flight was renamed No. 2 Camouflage Unit on 1 November in an effort to disguise its activities. Later it became the Photographic Development Unit.

See 11 July 1940.

1940 In a unique raid for this stage of the war, Bomber Command carried out a concentrated attack on just one city. A force of 129 Hampdens, Wellingtons and Whitleys attacked Berlin.

1944 The Dortmund–Ems Canal was breached north of Munster by two 12,000lb 'Tallboy' bombs dropped by Lancasters of No. 617 Squadron.

See 15 September 1943.

1945 No. 1331 Wing, RAF Regiment, with three squadrons, occupied Kai Tak airfield, Hong Kong.

1949 The last RAF Dakota sortie of the Berlin Airlift flew into Gatow. The aircraft (KN652) bore the following inscription: 'Positively the last load from Lübeck – 73,705 tons. Psalm 21, Verse 11. For they

intended evil against thee. They imagined a mischievous device which they were not able to perform.'

24 SEPTEMBER

1938 In response to the Munich crisis, RAF emergency routine was brought into force including the formation of Mobilisation Pools, which was ordered on 27 September.

1940 The George Cross (**GC**) and the George Medal (GM) were instituted by HM King George VI for acts of the greatest heroism or of the most conspicuous courage in circumstances of extreme danger. The **GC** was intended for civilians and members of the fighting services for actions where purely military honours were not normally granted. It replaced the Empire Gallantry Medal and existing holders of that medal were able to exchange it for the **GC**. The GM was primarily introduced to reward civilians, but the King extended the award to service personnel on 29 January 1941.

1944 Following the liberation of Araxos Airfield on 23 September by No. 2908 Squadron, RAF Regiment, Spitfires of No. 32

Squadron flew into the airfield to become the first RAF units to return to Greece.

1987 A Tornado F3 completed the first unrefuelled transatlantic crossing by a British fighter, covering the 2,200 nautical miles from Canada in 4 hours 45 minutes.

2004 Operation Veritas: a detachment of six Harrier GR7As of No. 3(F) Squadron, the first British combat aircraft committed to the operation, flew out from RAF Cottesmore to Kandahar in southern Afghanistan. The Harriers were to provide a close air support and reconnaissance capability to coalition forces and the International Security Assistance Force (ISAF).
See 18 March 2002.

A Blue Steel air-launched missile being loaded onto a Vulcan. *(AHB)*

A Harrier GR9 at Kandahar, Afghanistan. *(MOD)*

25 SEPTEMBER

1944 Operation Market: six Dakotas of No. 575 Squadron flew the final resupply mission to Arnhem. Transport aircraft of Nos 38 and 46 Groups flew 1,340 sorties including 698 glider sorties during the operation. In attempting to drop reinforcements and supplies to the British paratroopers at Arnhem, the RAF lost fifty-seven transport aircraft shot down or destroyed in crashes.

Seventy Halifax bombers started a series of flights to carry petrol in jerricans from England to airfields in Belgium, in order to alleviate a severe fuel shortage being experienced by Allied ground forces. Aircraft of No. 4 Group flew 435 such sorties during an eight-day period. Each Halifax carried about 165 jerricans, approximately 750 gallons, on each flight.

1962 Controller Aircraft (CA) Release was given for the Blue Steel stand-off missile to be carried on Vulcans with an operational warhead in the case of national emergency. No. 617 Squadron was the first to be declared 'emergency operational' with Blue Steel.

1991 Officer Cadet Kate Saunders became the first woman to eject from an RAF aircraft. She was flying in the rear seat of a No. 233 OCU Harrier T4 (pilot Sqn Ldr A.D. Stevenson), which crashed near Driffield. She suffered serious injuries after ejecting at low level and descending into the fireball. Stevenson, who was uninjured, pulled her clear. It was his second ejection in fourteen months.

26 SEPTEMBER

1927 A Supermarine S.5 seaplane flown by Flt Lt S.N. Webster won the Schneider Trophy competition, with an average speed of 281.49mph. The aircraft also set a 100km closed-circuit record of 283.67mph. Flt Lt O.E. Worsley flying another Supermarine S.5 gained second place. The race was held at Venice.

1938 Following the German threat of annexation of the Sudetenland in Czechoslovakia, a state of national emergency was declared in Great Britain and all RAF operational units were ordered to war stations. They returned to peace stations on 6 October.

1997 Sqn Ldr A. Green, a Tornado F3 pilot, created a new land speed record of 714mph driving the Thrust supersonic car in the Nevada Desert.

27 SEPTEMBER

1922 Following threats by Mustapha Kemal Bey (more commonly called Kemal Ataturk) to occupy Constantinople, the first RAF squadron arrived to support the British Army of Occupation positions at Chanak, which had been surrounded by Turkish forces. No. 203 Squadron Nightjars commenced reconnaissance patrols over Turkish positions. The following day, HQ Constantinople Wing (Gp Capt R.M. Fellowes), with three squadrons (Nos 4, 25 and 207), embarked for Turkey. No. 208 Squadron and a detached flight of No. 56

Wg Cdr J.E. 'Johnnie' Johnson. *(AVM J.E. Johnson)*

The airfield at San Stephano, the home for No. 208 Squadron's Bristol F2B Fighters. *(RAFM)*

Squadron had been transferred from Egypt to join the force on 25 September. The squadrons of the Wing remained at San Stefano and Kilia until a peace treaty was signed on 23 August 1923. The 'Chanak Crisis' was the first postwar test of the RAF's capability to mobilise and transfer a fighting formation to any foreign trouble spot in a short time, and at virtual overnight notice.

1937   Squadron code letters began to appear on RAF aircraft. They were displayed on each side of the fuselage roundel.

1944   Wg Cdr J.E. Johnson, Wing Leader of No. 127 Spitfire Wing, shot down a Messerschmitt Bf109 over Germany. It was his thirty-fourth confirmed victory (plus seven shared) making him the RAF's official top-scoring fighter pilot. (Note: It is believed that Sqn Ldr M.T.StJ. Pattle of No. 33 Squadron shot down 'around fifty' enemy aircraft before he was killed in Greece in April 1941.)

1962   Exercise Falltrap: the largest RAF peace-time air armada took place when No. 38 Group Argosy, Beverley and Hastings aircraft dropped 1,610 men and forty platforms during the NATO exercise in northern Greece. Hunters and Whirlwind helicopters provided support.

28 SEPTEMBER

1928   The Under-Secretary of State for Air (Sir Philip Sassoon) and the Director of Equipment RAF (Air Cdre A. Longmore) began a 9,900-mile flight from Felixstowe to Karachi and back by Blackburn Iris flying-boat in order to inspect RAF units in Malta, Egypt, Iraq and India. The party returned to Felixstowe on 14 November 1928.

1936   Sqn Ldr F.R.D. Swain flew a Bristol 138A from RAF Farnborough to 49,944ft to establish a new world aircraft altitude record.
See 30 June 1937.

The Iris flying-boat carrying the Under-Secretary of State for Air at Aboukir en route to Karachi.
(G.R. Pitchfork Collection)

Sqn Ldr F.R.D. Swain after creating a new world height record. *(G. Tyak)*

1939 The RAF Staff College yearly courses and qualifying examination were suspended after the 17th Course for the duration of the war.

1943 HQ Desert Air Force (AVM H. Broadhurst) occupied the complex of airfields around Foggia, southern Italy, following their capture the previous day by the 8th Army. These large airfields proved admirably suitable for the heavy bomber force and the air transport force. Operations from the airfields commenced on 1 October.

1955 Gp Capt L.W.B. Rees **VC**, OBE, MC, AFC died.
   See 1 July 1916.

1970 No. 101 Entry entered the RAF College Cranwell as the final flight cadet entry. No. 1 Graduate Entry had reported to the College on 1 September.

RAF Halifax and Liberator bombers at Foggia Airfield, Italy. *(AHB. CM 5477)*

The Supermarine S.6B flown by Flt Lt G.H. Stainforth. *(ACA Archives)*

29 SEPTEMBER

1931 Flt Lt G.H. Stainforth of the RAF High Speed Flight established a new world speed record of 407.5mph, flying a Supermarine S.6B at Lee-on-Solent.

1942 The three American-manned RAF 'Eagle' Squadrons (Nos 71, 121 and 133) were transferred to Fighter Command of the US 8th AAF at a ceremony at Bushey Hall. They formed the 4th Fighter Group, 'The Eagles', becoming the 334th, 335th and 336th Squadrons and were equipped with Spitfires.

See 19 September 1940.

1945 Air Headquarters, Netherlands East Indies (AHQNEI) (Air Cdre C.A. Stevens) was formed at Batavia, Java.

See 28 November 1946.

1971 The Puma helicopter entered service with No. 33 Squadron at RAF Odiham.

30 SEPTEMBER

1918 The Allied armies, with the aid of substantial air support, broke the German's final defensive line in France, the Hindenburg Line.

1935 Scapa and Singapore flying-boats of Nos 204 and 230 Squadrons were detached to Egypt to monitor Italian shipping following the start of the Abyssinian crisis.

Scapas of No. 204 Squadron at Alexandria. *(RAFM)*

British and Dutch refugees evacuated from Java by Dakotas of No. 31 Squadron. *(AHB)*

1940   **GC**: Wg Cdr Laurence Frank Sinclair for rescuing the air gunner aboard an aircraft that had burst into flames while taking off from RAF Wattisham. (*London Gazette*, 21 January 1941)

1941   The Middle East Directive on Direct Air Support was issued. This was an important milestone in the development of Army/Air co-operation and became the basis of air support control in the Western Desert, Italy and north-west Europe.
     See 30 August 1942.

The first operational patrol by a Liberator was flown by an aircraft (captain Flt Lt S.J. Harrison) of No. 120 Squadron. With an operational range of 2,000 miles, the Liberator became Coastal Command's very long range (VLR) aircraft, capable of 'eliminating' the notorious Atlantic Gap where German U-boats had operated without a threat from the air.

1946   No. 31 Squadron disbanded at Kemajoram and re-formed in India. During the year that the squadron's Dakotas were based in the Netherlands East Indies, they flew over 11,000 sorties, carrying 127,800 passengers and 26,000 tons of freight. The commanding officer, Wg Cdr B. Macnamara, was awarded the DSO, a rare 'peacetime' award.

1949   The RAF Missing Research and Enquiry Service, established in 1945 to trace the 41,881 aircrew missing during the Second World War, disbanded at RAF Bad Eilsen. To date, 23,881 of the missing personnel had been found, and all but 2,445 of these had been positively identified.

1955   No. 1340 Flight was disbanded in Kenya. During the course of the Mau Mau emergency, the Flight's Harvards dropped 21,936 20lb bombs and lost eight aircraft in accidents.

1970   The air loadmaster flying badge was introduced. The badge was the same design as the air gunner badge with 'LM' in the laurel (DCI (RAF) S159).

1991   The Royal Observer Corps stood down after sixty-six years of service.

1997   RAF flying operations ceased at the Air Weapons Training Installation (AWTI) at Decimomannu, Sardinia. The RAF Support Unit closed on 1 April 1998.

1 OCTOBER

1920 Col I. Curtis was appointed Educational Adviser to the RAF, a civil appointment, on a salary of £1,200 per annum. The duties of the appointment included:

- Advice on all matters affecting education, and liaison with service and civilian education authorities.
- Control of civilian education staff.
- Questions concerning educational supplies.
- Arrangements in connection with RAF personnel attending courses at the universities.
- Arrangements for educational, as apart from professional, examinations other than at the Cadet College.
- General and vocational education of all ranks in preparation for educational certificates and for their return to civil life.

1922 The RAF assumed military control of Iraq. Throughout the winter of 1922/23, irregular posts were located and attacked from the air; these attacks formed the first effective check on Turkish aspirations. Air supply operations were conducted to support RAF squadrons operating from Kirkuk.

1925 The first University Air Squadron (UAS) was formed at Cambridge, followed by Oxford UAS on 11 October 1925.

1939 The first British aircraft to fly over Berlin following the outbreak of the Second World War were three Whitleys of No. 10 Squadron, tasked to drop leaflets.

1940 The Battle of Britain: the opening of the final phase when daylight raids by long-range bombers were replaced by fighter-bomber attacks and heavy night attacks against London.

1945 No. 1307 Wing HQ, RAF Regiment, and No. 2963 LAA Squadron landed at Tan Son Nhut Airfield outside Saigon for internal security duties.

1946 The RAF Education Branch was formed comprising RAF officers holding permanent, temporary or short-service commissions.
See 18 October 1927.

Tutor trainers of Cambridge University Air Squadron. *(G. Tyak)*

Barrage balloons over central London during the Battle of Britain.
(AHB. HU 3725)

1948 The Directorate of RAF Legal Services was formed following the recommendations of the 1946 Lewis Committee on Army and Air Force Courts Martial. The first Director was Air Cdre J.B. Walmsley, who was later appointed Queen's Counsel.

1955 The Royal Air Force Levies (Iraq) were disbanded.
See 1 July 1928, 15 March 1943.

1956 Vulcan B1 XA897 departed Aden on the final leg of its return journey from Australia to the United Kingdom, captained by Sqn Ldr D.R. Howard and with ACM Sir Harry Broadhurst flying as co-pilot. Unfortunately, the aircraft encountered extremely poor weather conditions while attempting to land at Heathrow Airport and crashed on approach. The pilot and co-pilot ejected successfully, but the four crew members in the rear of the aircraft were killed.
See 8 September 1956.

1959 An interim nuclear capability was declared to SACEUR for all RAF Germany light bomber/interdictor squadrons and Exercise Cenovite was introduced to test the generation capabilities in the nuclear (strike) role. The four Canberra interdictor squadrons each had a single aircraft on fifteen-minute Quick Reaction Alert (QRA), a task that was to remain with RAF Germany for the next thirty years.
See 15 September 1960.

1964 Technician and Craft Apprentice Schemes replaced those for (Aircraft) Apprentices, initiated in February 1920, and Boy Entrants, initiated in September 1934, respectively.

1966 The Technical Branch was renamed the Engineer Branch. Individuals continued to be commissioned into the Technical Branch until 27 September 1966 but by 4 October they were gazetted into the Engineer Branch.

1968 RAF Brize Norton became the main passenger terminal for long-range transport flights of Air Support Command.

The first surface-to-air missiles (SAMs) entered service with the RAF Regiment

A Tigercat air defence missile launcher of the RAF Regiment. *(AHB. TN 6269)*

The first RAF Buccaneers arrive at RAF Honington with No. 12 Squadron. (*G.R. Pitchfork Collection*)

when No. 48 Squadron re-equipped with the Tigercat short-range missile.

1969 The first Harrier squadron – No. 1 Squadron – formed at RAF Wittering as the first operational fixed-wing VTOL squadron in the world. Squadron pilots had been converting to the aircraft since July.

The first RAF Buccaneer squadron – No. 12 Squadron (Wg Cdr G.G. Davies) – formed at RAF Honington.

1980 A Sea King (captain Flt Lt M. Lakey) from RAF Lossiemouth rescued twenty-two people from the Swedish container ship *Finneagle*, which was carrying a dangerous cargo. The ship was on fire and in danger of exploding. The helicopter hovered in severe turbulence for forty minutes, and rescued all those on board, including women and children. A senior officer of the Coastguard service commented, 'the rescue by Michael Lakey and his crew was the most outstanding in my experience'. Lakey was awarded the George Medal. The four other members of his crew were also decorated for gallantry.

2 OCTOBER

1918 DH4s of No. 224 Squadron and DH9s of No. 226 Squadron co-operated with the combined Allied fleets in an attack against Durazzo, Albania, and dropped 5 tons of bombs on the railway sidings and dumps.

1969 The first Nimrod maritime reconnaissance aircraft entered service with the Maritime Operational Training Unit at RAF St Mawgan.

1990 The British Commanders-in-Chief Mission to Soviet Forces (BRIXMIS) based in Berlin was deactivated, so removing the need for intelligence-gathering flights by the two Chipmunks based at RAF Gatow.

The Berlin Air Safety Centre ceased to operate, having been manned continuously since its formation on 12 December 1945.

1991 The end of RAF Germany's QRA(I) (Battle Flight) commitment was marked by a practice scramble by a pair of Phantoms drawn from Wildenrath's two resident squadrons, Nos 19 and 92. Over a period of twenty-five years, there had been 250 operational and 1,500 training scrambles.

A Phantom FGR2 of No. 92 Squadron scrambles from RAF Wildenrath. (*J. Falconer Collection*)

3 OCTOBER

1918   Aircraft of Nos 82 and 218 Squadrons (DH 9s and FK8s) resupplied French and Belgian troops in the Houlthorst Forest, whose reserves were exhausted. Some 15,000 rations were air-dropped in bags of earth to prevent damage.

1944   A large force of Lancasters attacked the sea walls of Walcheren Island. Coastal gun batteries on the island dominated the approaches to the port of Antwerp, whose facilities were crucial to the advancing armies. A gap 100yd wide was forced and the island was flooded.

4 OCTOBER

1939   A Mission to Canada, led by Lord Riverdale, was appointed to secure Dominion governments' agreement to the establishment of the proposed Empire Air Training Scheme. The Mission arrived in Ottawa on 14 October.
See 17 December 1939.

The breach blasted by Lancasters in the dykes at Walcheren Island. *(AHB)*

312

DECEPTION AND DECOYS

To co-ordinate a strategy to defeat German bombing by deception, a secret department was formed in 1939 at the Air Ministry. Under the leadership of the charismatic Col J.F. Turner, and with the help of leading technicians in the film industry, almost 800 sites were constructed and occupied by decoys of various types. Dummy aircraft and buildings, artificial fires and deceptive lighting were deployed to these sites. Postwar analysis suggests that some 2,220 tons of bombs were dropped against the decoy sites during 815 Luftwaffe attacks, the majority at night. Because of the secret nature of the work, the full extent of the value of this programme, and the protection it provided to Britain's forces and civilians, has only become fully realised many years after the end of the Second World War.

A Spitfire decoy in its two carry bags and in place after inflation. *(AHB)*

A meeting at HQ Bomber Command led to the formation of a special branch of the air staff to organise a system of day and night dummy airfields to protect RAF airfields against air attack.

See 6 June 1940.

1943 Air Cdt Lady Mary Welsh, former Inspector of the WAAF, was appointed Director of the WAAF and was later promoted to Air Chief Commandant. She retired at the end of 1946 and her rank was never used again.

1992 RAF Biggin Hill, immortalised for the part its aircrews played during the Battle of Britain, closed.

5 OCTOBER

1930 The largest airship in the world, the R101, encountered gusting wind and crashed into a hillside near Beauvais, north of Paris. It had departed the previous day for its intended destination in India via a refuelling stop at Ismailia in Egypt under the command of Flt Lt C. Irvin. The passengers included Lord Christopher

Airship R101. *(AHB H 1437)*

Thomson, Secretary of State for Air, and Sir Sefton Brancker, Director of Civil Aviation. Forty-six of the fifty-four passengers and crew were killed. According to survivors, the top layers of the outer cover and some of the forward gas bags had been torn in the wind, thus causing a loss of the flammable lifting gas hydrogen, which was ignited by the hot engine exhausts and electrical sparking from torn wiring. The loss of the R101 spelled the end of the British attempt to create lighter-than-air aircraft.

1944 Five Spitfires of No. 401 (RCAF) Squadron, operating near Nijmegen, combined to become the first aircraft to shoot down a Messerschmitt Me262 jet fighter in aerial combat.

1999 The Joint Helicopter Command, a tri-service force encompassing the RAF's Support Helicopter force, the Army Air Corps and those Fleet Air Arm squadrons equipped with Commando assault helicopters, formed (AVM D.M. Niven).

6 OCTOBER

1949 Operation Plainfare: a Hastings flew the last RAF sortie for the Berlin Airlift.
See 28 June 1948, 12 May 1949.

THE BERLIN AIRLIFT

The Berlin airlift was initiated in response to a land and water blockade of the city that had been instituted by the Soviet Union in the hope that the Allies would be forced to abandon West Berlin. The massive effort to supply the 2 million West Berliners with food and with fuel for heating began in June 1948, and lasted until September 1949, although the Russians lifted the blockade in May of that year. During the round-the-clock airlift some 277,000 flights were made, many at three-minute intervals. The RAF contribution was 49,733 flights carrying 394,509 tons of aid to Berlin and 167,654 passengers in both directions. By spring 1949, an average of 8,000 tons was being flown in daily. More than 2 million tons of goods – of which coal accounted for about two-thirds – were delivered.

Hastings of No. 47 Squadron wait to be loaded at Schleswigland as German workmen build new dispersal areas. (*Andrew Thomas Collection*)

7 OCTOBER

1940 No. 80 (Signals) Wing formed at Radlett for radio/radar intelligence and radio counter-measures work. It transferred to No. 100 Group on 8 November 1943.

1943 Lancasters of No. 101 Squadron attacking Stuttgart made the first operational use of *Airborne Cigar (ABC)*, an aid for jamming night-fighter communications.

1944 A force of Lancasters of No. 617 Squadron attacked the Kembs Dam on the River Rhine just north of Basle, Switzerland. Seven aircraft attacked from 8,000ft, and to draw the flak, six aircraft, led by Wg Cdr J.B. Tait, dropped delayed-action Tallboys from 600ft, which destroyed the lock gates. Two of the low-level force were shot down.

1948 Training of composite medical teams to drop by parachute to attend to casualties began with four nursing sisters and four nursing orderlies at RAF Upper Heyford.

1993 With the graduation of No. 155 Entry from RAF Cosford's No. 2 School of Technical Training, the apprentice scheme that was a pillar on which Lord Trenchard founded the RAF ended.
See 24 June 1993.

2001 Operation Veritas: the UK commenced operations as part of the International Security Assistance Force (ISAF) against the Al Qaida terrorist organisation and the Taliban regime. RAF tanker aircraft provided air-to-air refuelling support to US carrier-based aircraft, and RAF reconnaissance and surveillance aircraft flew operational sorties. This heralded a long period of RAF involvement in operations over Afghanistan.
See 18 March 2002.

RAF nursing sisters ready to make their parachute drop. *(RAFM)*

A C-17 Globemaster of No. 99 Squadron lands at Kabul. *(MOD)*

8 OCTOBER

1918 **VC**: Capt Andrew Frederick Weatherby Beauchamp Proctor of No. 84 Squadron for fifty-four 'victories' as a fighter pilot. His CO described him as 'that little man who had the guts of a lion'. (*London Gazette*, 30 November 1918)

See 21 June 1921.

1919 No. 86 (Communication) Wing completed its last cross-Channel flight prior to disbanding. Between December 1918 and October 1919 the Flight had flown a total distance of 350,000 miles.

1939 During a patrol over the North Sea, three Hudsons of No. 224 Squadron sighted a Dornier Do18 of *2/Kustenfliegergruppe 506* flying low over the sea 20 miles north-east of Aberdeen. The leader (Flt Lt A. Womersley) attacked it with his forward-firing gun, forcing it to alight. The German crew abandoned the aircraft, which was then destroyed by the gunfire of the three Hudsons. This was the first enemy aircraft claimed by the RAF in the Second World War.

1943 The Portuguese authorities allowed the RAF to establish an airbase at Lagens, Azores, to be used for anti-submarine operations.

See 20 October 1943.

Having been used continuously since April 1940, Wellingtons operated for the last time under Bomber Command control when they attacked Hanover. Nos 303 (Polish) and 432 (RCAF) Squadrons provided the twenty-six aircraft.

1953 The London to New Zealand Air Race started. An RAF Canberra PR3 flown by

Flt Lts R.L.E. Burton and D.H. Gannon (right), the winning crew of the London–New Zealand Air Race. *(AHB)*

The winning Canberra PR3 takes off from the Cocos Islands en route for the next stop in Australia. *(AHB. CFP 784)*

Flt Lt R.L.E. Burton and Flt Lt D.H. Gannon won the speed section: 12,270 miles in 23 hours 50 minutes, establishing a London to Christchurch record at 514.8mph. Another Canberra (captain Wg Cdr L.M. Hodges, later ACM Sir Lewis Hodges) established a London to Colombo record, 10 hours 25 minutes at 519.5mph.

9 OCTOBER

1919 The RAF took over control of its own police from the Army and authority was given for the appointment of the first Provost Marshal of the RAF (Wg Cdr G.T. Brierley).

AUXILIARY AIR FORCE

Provisions for an Air Force Reserve and Auxiliary Air Force were made in 1917 and in his 1919 Memorandum, AM Sir Hugh Trenchard said that a reserve Air Force should be organised on a territorial basis. In 1922 a Bill was drafted, but it did not become law until 1924 when Sir Samuel Hoare was Secretary of State for Air. He was a staunch advocate of the Auxiliary Air Force and would later comment:

Trenchard envisaged the Auxiliaries as a corps d'elite composed of the kind of young men who earlier would have been interested in horses, but who now wished to serve their country in machines. He conceived the new mechanical yeomanry with its aeroplanes based on the great centres of industry. Esprit de corps was to be the dominating force in the squadrons and each, therefore, was to have a well-equipped headquarters, mess, and distinctive life of its own. Social meetings were to be encouraged and on no account was any squadron to be regarded as a reserve for filling up regular units. The experiment was successful from the beginning.

The forebodings of the doubters and critics were soon proved groundless. So far from the non-regular units damaging the reputation of the regular squadrons they actually added some of the most glorious pages to the history of the Royal Air Force during the Second World War.

Altogether, twenty-one squadrons were formed and during the Second World War they were credited with some of the RAF's most memorable achievements. The first enemy aircraft to be shot down over Britain fell to Nos 602 and 603 Squadrons. Of the sixty-six RAF squadrons in the Battle of Britain, fourteen were Auxiliary Air Force squadrons. The first U-boat sunk by ASV radar was credited to No. 502 Squadron. Mosquitos of No. 605 Squadron were the first to destroy a V-1 flying bomb and No. 613 Squadron Mosquitos carried out the pinpoint attack on the Gestapo headquarters in The Hague. No. 616 Squadron was the first RAF squadron to be equipped with jets. When, in January 1957, it was announced that the Royal Auxiliary Air Force was to be disbanded, an outstanding contribution to the Royal Air Force's history ended.

An Avro Tutor of No. 616 (South Yorkshire) Auxiliary Squadron at RAF Doncaster in 1938.
(G.R. Pitchfork Collection)

AVM A. Coningham (1895–1948). (AHB)

1924 An Order in Council established the Auxiliary Air Force (AAF).
See 12 September 1925, 10 March 1957.

1941 Air Force Headquarters Western Desert, the Desert Air Force (DAF), formed at Maaten Bagush in Libya (AVM A. Coningham).

1944 Operation Frugal: Mosquito PRIXs of No. 544 Squadron commenced direct flights from RAF Northolt to Moscow carrying mail for the Summit Conference attended by Prime Minister Winston Churchill. The flights continued until 20 October.

The plaque mounted on a hangar wall at RAF Wyton to commemorate the award of the first DFCs in the Second World War. (AHB)

10 OCTOBER

1938 The Wellington entered operational service with No. 99 Squadron at RAF Mildenhall.

1939 The award of the first DFCs – the first of any British gallantry awards of the Second World War – were announced in the *London Gazette* to Fg Off A. McPherson of No. 139 Squadron and to Flt Lt K.C. Doran of No. 110 Squadron. Doran was the first to be awarded a Bar to the DFC (30 January 1940) for services in the Second World War.

1941 The first of two Greek squadrons, No. 335, was formed within the RAF. Equipped with Hurricanes, it operated in the Western Desert.

1980 RAF police deployed to civilian prisons to enhance security during a strike by national prison officers.

11 OCTOBER

1917 The 41st Wing of the RFC was formed at Ainville-sur-Madon under the command of Lt Col C.L.N. Newall (later MRAF Sir Cyril Newall), with the task of bombing industrial targets in Germany.

1918 The Revd H.D.L. Weiner was appointed the first RAF Chaplain-in-Chief.
See 21 March 1920.

The Prince of Wales inspects flight cadets on the occasion of the opening of the new RAF College, Cranwell, building. *(RAF College Cranwell)*

The Prince of Wales addresses dignitaries following the opening of the RAF College, Cranwell, building. On the right of the stage is MRAF Lord Trenchard and third from the left is AM Sir Hugh Dowding. *(RAF College, Cranwell)*

1934   AM HRH The Prince of Wales officially opened College Hall, Cranwell.

1942   The Luftwaffe resumed all-out attacks on Malta. During the period to 19 October, Axis forces flew 2,400 sorties against the island. However, none of the airfields on Malta were put out of action for more than thirty minutes and only two aircraft were destroyed on the ground. The Luftwaffe lost forty-six aircraft and the RAF thirty Spitfires. After 20 October enemy raids tapered away as Luftwaffe units were transferred to North Africa to sustain Rommel's Afrika Korps.

1943   No. 38 Wing was expanded to Group status to become No. 38 (Airborne) Group, with

its Headquarters at RAF Netheravon, equipped with nine squadrons of Albemarles, Halifax and Stirling aircraft. AVM L.N. Hollinghurst assumed command on 6 November.

1956   The first British 'live' atomic weapon drop from an aircraft took place at Maralinga, Australia. A Valiant (captain Sqn Ldr E.J.G. Flavell) of No. 49 Squadron flying at 30,000ft released a Blue Danube round modified to produce a yield of 3–4 kilotons.

1977   Following the massing of Guatemalan troops on the border with the British colony of Belize, the British Army garrison was reinforced by three Pumas of No. 33 Squadron transported to Belize aboard Belfasts of No. 53 Squadron.

12 OCTOBER

1940   Hitler postponed Operation Sealion (the invasion of Britain) until the spring of 1941.

1941   Stirling bomber N6086 (captain Fg Off P. Boggis) of No. 15 Squadron, and named 'MacRobert's Reply', flew its first operational sortie when it attacked Nuremberg. After the death in a Blenheim over the North Sea of her third son, Sir Iain, Lady

One of the 'MacRobert' Hurricanes of No. 94 Squadron. The pilot is Flt Sgt D. Wood of Wolverhampton. *(AHB)*

Flt Lt P. Boggis and crew aboard the 'MacRoberts Reply' Stirling of No. 15 Squadron. *(ACA Archives)*

MacRobert of Douneside, Aberdeenshire, donated £25,000 to purchase a Stirling bomber in memory of her three sons who had all been killed flying. She also presented four Hurricane fighters to serve with No. 94 Squadron, the former squadron of her second son, Sir Roderic, who had been killed in action over Iraq in April 1941.

1943 The Air Council approved a proposal to found an Institute of Aviation Medicine at RAE Farnborough.
See 5 July 1939.

13 OCTOBER

1939 Wg Cdr H.M.A. 'Wings' Day, the Officer Commanding No. 57 Squadron, was shot down in his Blenheim during a daylight reconnaissance over Germany. For almost three years afterwards he was the senior RAF officer among POWs in Germany. He made escape his own first interest but ensured it became the primary interest of those under his command in various POW camps. He made six escapes himself, including getting free from the tunnel during the 'Great Escape' from Stalag Luft III on 24 March 1944. He was captured five days later in Stettin, but was one of the few who escaped execution. He was sent to Sachenhausen concentration camp under sentence of death if he escaped. Undaunted, he successfully escaped and reached Allied lines in north Italy on 15 April 1945. Inspiring though his own efforts were, he will be remembered as an outstanding Senior British Officer (SBO) in successive camps, and for his organising skill. It was he who laid the foundations of the escape organisation, the pattern of which spread to every Air Force camp in Germany with results which at times seriously embarrassed the German High Command. He was awarded the DSO and appointed OBE for his services as a POW.
See 24 March 1944.

14 OCTOBER

1927   Agreement was reached to form an RAF Education Officers' Association, independent of all other organisations, to represent the views of civilian education officers to the Air Ministry.

1944   Operation Hurricane: at first light 957 bombers were despatched to Duisburg. Later that night the Command carried out its largest raid of the war when 1,576 aircraft were despatched, and it was during this raid that the greatest tonnage of bombs (5,453 tons) was dropped on German territory by the RAF. This included the largest tonnage (4,547) on a single target at night (Duisburg). The total effort for the 24-hour period was 2,589 sorties with twenty-four aircraft lost. Total tonnage of bombs dropped in the period was approximately 10,050 tons. These record totals were never exceeded in the war.

1954   The first jet flight over the North Pole was made by a Canberra B2 'Aries IV' (captain Wg Cdr A.H. Humphrey – later MRAF Sir Andrew Humphrey) of the RAF Flying College. The aircraft flew from Bardufoss in Norway to the Pole, returning to Bodø in Norway after a flight lasting 6 hours 43 minutes.

1982   ACM Sir Michael Beetham was promoted to MRAF on relinquishing the post of Chief of the Air Staff.

15 OCTOBER

1941   The Air Landing School (India) was formed at Willingdon Airport, New Delhi, with Valentia and Hudson aircraft, to train paratroopers and supply-dropping personnel.

1944   Air Defence of Great Britain was renamed RAF Fighter Command.

1948   The RAF and USAF airlifts into Berlin were merged in a Combined Airlift Task Force (CALTF), commanded by Maj Gen William

Wg Cdr A.H. Humphrey returns from his flight to the North Pole in Aries IV. *(AHB)*

Indian troops practise parachute drills at the Air Landing School (India). *(AHB. CM 5675)*

H. Tunner of the USAF. Air Cdre J.W.F. Mercer of the RAF was appointed deputy commander.

1951   The Egyptian government abrogated a 1936 treaty relating to the presence of British forces in the Suez Canal Zone. As fighting broke out around the British bases in the Canal Zone, No. 16 Independent Parachute Brigade was flown from Cyprus aboard Valettas of Nos 70, 78, 114, 204 and 216 Squadrons to support the units stationed in the Canal Zone.

1953   Operation Hotbox: following the detonation of a 10-kiloton atomic weapon at 0700hr, the UK's second atomic test, a Canberra B2 (captain Wg Cdr G.H. Dhenin, later AM Sir Geoffrey Dhenin) entered the atomic cloud six minutes after the explosion at Emu Field, South Australia, to assess the behaviour of the aircraft and the effects of the cloud on the crew. Subsequently, between 1952 and 1958, RAF squadrons operating modified Canberras were called upon to conduct extensive sampling sorties

A Sycamore in support of ground forces against EOKA terrorists in Cyprus. *(AHB. CMP 921)*

in support of the UK's atmospheric nuclear test programme. Dhenin, a medical officer trained as a pilot, was awarded the AFC.

1955   No. 308/5 Air Task Force (Gp Capt S.W.B. Menaul), later redesignated 308.5 Task Group, was formed at RAF Weston Zoyland to participate in the British atomic test at Monte Bello Island, off the northern coast of Australia.

1956   The last Lancaster in RAF operational service, an MR3 of the School of Maritime Reconnaissance, departed from RAF St Mawgan after a brief ceremony and address by the AOC-in-C Coastal Command (AM Sir Brian Reynolds).

The Nicosia Helicopter Flight became No. 284 Squadron. The squadron was equipped with Sycamore helicopters, and tasked with supporting British Army units conducting internal security operations against EOKA terrorists seeking the union of Cyprus with Greece. In the words of Field Marshal Lord Harding, the Governor and Commander-in-Chief, 'No. 294 Squadron contributed more to fighting terrorism on the island than any other single unit.'

Kestrels of the Tripartite squadron at RAF West Raynham. *(P.H.T. Green Collection)*

1964 The Kestrel (P.1127) Tripartite Evaluation Squadron (Wg Cdr D.McL. Scrimgeour) formed at RAF West Raynham to investigate vertical and short take-off and landing (VSTOL) operations. The Kestrel was developed into the Harrier, which entered service with the RAF in 1969.

See 1 October 1969.

1979 At a ceremony held at the British Aerospace factory at Bitteswell, Leicestershire, the Red Arrows aerobatic team (Sqn Ldr B. Hoskins) received the team's ninth Hawk aircraft to complete the replacement of the Gnat aircraft used by the team since its formation in 1965.

1982 ACM Sir Keith Williamson was appointed Chief of the Air Staff and became the first former aircraft apprentice to fill the highest appointment in the Service.

1985 ACM Sir David Craig was appointed as Chief of the Air Staff in succession to ACM Sir Keith Williamson who was promoted to MRAF.

1993 With the disbandment of No. 55 Squadron, the last of the V-bombers, the Victor, retired from RAF service after thirty-six years.

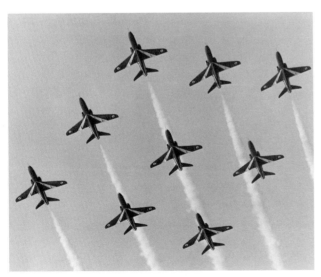

The Red Arrows aerobatic team with their new Hawk aircraft. *(J. Falconer Collection)*

16 OCTOBER

1917 It was announced in Parliament that a Bill had been prepared with the title 'The Air Force (Constitution) Act'. This Bill received the Royal Assent on 29 November with the altered title 'The Air Force Act'.

See 29 November 1917.

1939 The first enemy aircraft to be shot down over British territory – a Junkers Ju88 of *Kampfgeschwader 30* – was intercepted by Spitfires of No. 602 Squadron and came down near Crail in the Firth of Forth. The pilot was the only survivor and became a

An E-3D Sentry of No. 8 Squadron on patrol over the Adriatic. *(RAFM)*

Sqn Ldr Nicky Smith, the RAF's first female helicopter pilot. *(AHB)*

POW. Shortly afterwards, a second bomber from the same formation was shot down by pilots of No. 603 Squadron.

1992 Operation Sky Monitor: E-3D Sentry aircraft of No. 8 Squadron, operating as part of the NATO Airborne Early Warning (NAEW) Force, commenced monitoring flights of Bosnia-Herzegovina airspace in support of UN Resolution 781. Orbits were flown over the Adriatic. On 31 October an additional NAEW orbit was commenced over Hungary, following an agreement with the Hungarian government.

Flt Lt Nicky Smith graduated from No. 2 FTS, RAF Shawbury, as the first female RAF helicopter pilot.

17 OCTOBER

1927 Four Southampton flying-boats of the RAF's Far East Flight (Gp Capt H.M. Cave-Brown-Cave) left RAF Mountbatten (Plymouth) for the 9,500-mile flight via Marseille, Naples, Cairo, Aboukir, Baghdad, Karachi, Bombay, Calcutta, Madras and Rangoon to Singapore, which was reached on 28 February 1928. The objectives of the flight were primarily to 'show the flag' and to collect information on possible seaplane bases and harbours and on local conditions.

See 21 May 1928, 1 November 1928.

1940 A Standing Committee was set up by the Air Council to consider the substitution of WAAF for RAF personnel.

1945 No. 904 Wing (Gp Capt D.J. Lee), the air component of Air Headquarters, Netherlands East Indies (Air Cdre C.A. Stevens) landed at Batavia, Java. This included an advance party of Nos 60 and 81 Squadrons, Nos 2739 and 2962 Squadrons of the RAF Regiment and RAF servicing commandos.

1953 The Queen unveiled the RAF memorial at Runnymede, Coopers Hill, which commemorates 20,389 airmen and women who were lost in the Second World War during operations from bases in the United Kingdom and north-west Europe, and who have no known grave. The names of 3,187 airmen who operated from the Middle East and Mediterranean, and have no known grave, are commemorated on the Alamein Memorial. Those who have no known grave following operations in the Far East are recorded on the Singapore Memorial, which stands within the Kranji War Cemetery.

Southampton flying boats at Hinaidi, Iraq, en route to Singapore. *(AHB. H328)*

EPITAPH

Written by an anonymous author and adapted for Runnymede by John Paul DFM, pilot of No. 37 Squadron.

Do not stand at this shrine and weep,

We are not here, we do not sleep.

We are the thousand winds that blow,

We are the diamond glints on snow,

We are the sunlight on ripened grain,

We are the gentle autumnal rain.

When you waken in the morning's hush,

We are the swift uplifting rush

Of quiet birds in circled flight,

We are the bright stars that shine at night.

Do not stand at this shrine and cry –

We are not here – we did not die.

Wreaths laid at the dedication of the Runnymede Royal Air Force Memorial, 1953. *(AHB)*

1955 Plt Off R.T. Foster became the first RAF pupil pilot to fly solo on a jet aircraft without any previous flying experience. He made his five-minute solo flight in a Jet Provost T1 at No. 2 FTS, Hullavington, after 8 hours 20 minutes' instruction.

1982 The first Phantom FGR2 of No. 29 Squadron landed at RAF Stanley, Falkland Islands, after a ferry flight from Ascension Island. Flown by the CO, Wg Cdr I.D. Macfadyen, it was the first of nine that arrived over the next three days to assume the air defence role.
See 30 March 1983.

2006 The Defence Secretary (Des Browne) opened the RAF's new Headquarters at RAF High Wycombe, marking the collocation of Strike Command and Personnel and Training Command.
See 1 April 2007.

18 OCTOBER

1927 The Air Ministry rejected the proposal to brigade the civilian education staff as a corps to be known as 'The Royal Air Force Educational Corps', but accepted the designation 'The Royal Air Force Educational Service'.
See 1 October 1946.

2005 Following a devastating earthquake in Pakistan, the RAF provided the first international aid when a Hercules carried supplies and the first personnel to provide assistance. These included engineers, UKMAMS, police and a team from the Tactical Air-Land Coordination Element (TALCE). On 22 October the first of three Chinook helicopters of No. 27 Squadron were flown to Islamabad in a C-17 Globemaster II of No. 99 Squadron. The helicopters flew the first aid mission four days later.

19 OCTOBER

1923 It was announced that the Air Ministry had been given authority to proceed with an airship programme.

A P-40 Kittyhawk of No. 112 Squadron (Shark Squadron) negotiates the scrub at a desert landing ground in North Africa. *(IWM. CM 2730)*

The reconsecration of the RAF church of St Clement Danes. *(AHB)*

1930 A flight of Fairey IIIDs of No. 47 Squadron left from Khartoum for West Africa, returning on 25 November.

1940 A Lysander of No. 419 (Special Duties) Flight, flown by Flt Lt W.J. Farley, landed in a field near Montigny in France to pick up an RAF agent, Philippe Schneidau, thus completing the first of many successful pick-ups from France.

1942 Squadrons of the Middle East Air Force (ACM Sir Arthur Tedder) started a full offensive against Axis air and ground forces in the Western Desert in support of the British 8th Army operations to break out from its position at El Alamein, which opened on the night of 23 October.

1943 **VC**: Flt Lt William Ellis Newton RAAF, a Boston pilot of No. 22 (RAAF) Squadron for displaying 'great courage and an iron determination to inflict the utmost damage on the enemy' during his service in Salamaua, New Guinea. His aircraft was shot down on 16 March 1943 and he was captured. Fourteen days later a Japanese naval officer beheaded him. (*London Gazette*, 19 October 1943, posthumous award)

1958 St Clement Danes, Strand, London, was reconsecrated as the Church of the Royal Air Force in the presence of the HM The Queen.

20 OCTOBER

1921 A badge was approved for wear on the breast pocket of the RAF blazer by those officers who had represented the RAF at sport or games against the Royal Navy and Army. The badge consisted of an eagle and crown in gold lace mounted on a dark blue shield with an edging of RAF colours (AMWO 826/21).

1930 The first formal instrument flying course began at CFS. On 1 September 1931 'E' Flight was established at CFS solely for instrument flight training.

1934 The Air Fighting Development Establishment (later Unit) was formed at RAF Northolt. The establishment later became part of the Central Fighter Establishment (CFE), which was later absorbed by the Central Trials and Tactics Organisation (CTTO) on its formation. In July 1991, CTTO became a major element of the newly formed Air Warfare Centre.

See 1 October 1944, 1 July 1991.

1936 The Air Ministry announced the 'Shadow Scheme', which was evolved to increase the output of aeroplanes and aero-engines as part of the RAF expansion programme. The firms involved were the Austin, Daimler, Rootes-Securities, Rover and Standard Motor Companies and the Bristol Aeroplane Company.

1943 No. 247 Group (AVM B.G. Bromet) was established at Lagens, Azores. Fortresses of Nos 206 and 220 Squadrons flew the first anti-submarine patrols from the airfield.

See 8 October 1943.

1952 Four No. 12 Squadron Canberras and two supporting Hastings left Binbrook on a 24,000-mile goodwill tour of South America led by AOC No. 1 Group (AVM D.A. Boyle).

21 OCTOBER

1919 Air Ministry Weekly Order 1158/19 announced the formation of a Stores Branch for 'accounting and dealing with all stores for the RAF'. The first officer, Flt Lt F.E.J. Coates, was appointed to the branch on 8 June 1920. In 1936 the name was changed to Equipment Branch and to Supply Branch on 1 July 1970.

The Air Depot at Alexandra. *(G. Tyak)*

The first RAF Fortress arrives at Lagens, Azores. *(AHB. CA 4)*

1929 **GC** (ex-EGM): Plt Off Sidney Noel Wiltshire for demonstrating 'conspicuous gallantry' as a pilot under training, by re-entering a burning aircraft to rescue his flying instructor. (*London Gazette*, 31 January 1930)

1937 The observer badge of the First World War period was reinstated, initially for tradesmen dual-qualified as observers who flew on a part-time basis in the rank of corporal (AMO A.347/1937).

See 1 May 1918, 9 August 1934.

1945 Twenty-six P-47 Thunderbolts of Nos 60 and 81 Squadrons flew into Kemajoran Airfield near Batavia to provide support for SEAC forces. They flew the first operational task over the Netherlands East Indies three days later when a full-scale demonstration flight was made over Soerabaya, Sumatra.

See 30 October 1945.

1952 A State of Emergency was declared in Kenya following the murder of Chief Waruhui by the Mau Mau. Hastings of No.

A pilot climbs into the cockpit of his Thunderbolt at an airstrip in Burma. *(AHB. CI 1058)*

511 Squadron flew to Nairobi with troops of the 1st Battalion Lancashire Fusiliers to reinforce resident British Army units.

22 OCTOBER

1940 The Coastal Command Tactical Development Unit was formed at RAF Carew Cheriton, Pembrokeshire, to conduct service trials of, and to examine and develop tactical employment of, radio devices, primarily air-to-surface vessel radar (ASV). It was redesignated the Coastal Command Development Unit in January 1941, to avoid confusion with the Torpedo Development Unit formed in December 1939, and in January 1945 it became the Air-Sea Warfare Development Unit.

1946 Air access to Berlin, and the rules for flights in the three corridors and Berlin Zone were approved by the quadripartite nations. Known as 'The 46 Agreement' it formed the terms of reference for the Berlin Air Safety Centre.

See 2 October 1990.

The officers and airmen of No. 8 Squadron at RAF Khormaksar, Aden. *(R. Deacon)*

1962 Egyptian Air Force MiG fighters based in Yemen attacked Nuqab in Aden. In response, Hunters carried out border patrols and a subsequent retaliatory attack when they destroyed a fort in Yemen. Additionally, in a show of strength, a Valiant of No. 90 Squadron engaged on a 'Lone Ranger' exercise flew along the frontier. Canberra PR7s of Nos 13 and 58 Squadrons were detached to RAF Khormaksar in order to monitor Egyptian vessels in the Red Sea that were thought to be carrying arms to Yemen.

23 OCTOBER

1919 The Executive Committee of the Royal Air Force Memorial Fund held its first meeting and appointed Lord Hugh Cecil as chairman. The objects of the fund were:
- To build a memorial.
- To establish boarding schools for the children of deceased airmen.
- To assist the education of deceased officers' children.
- To relieve distress among officers and men and their dependants, particu-

larly through the provision of medical treatment.
In December 1933 the fund restyled itself 'The Royal Air Force Benevolent Fund'.
See 23 July 1923.

1940 AVM C.H.B. Blount, AOC No. 22 (Army Co-operation) Group, was killed in an air crash at RAF Hendon.
See 9 September 1939.

1941 No. 205 (Heavy Bomber) Group formed at RAF Shallufa, Egypt. The group became the RAF's major heavy-bomber force in the Mediterranean and Middle East theatre during the Second World War.

1942 At 2130hr the British 8th Army launched the first phase of its offensive at El Alamein. Wellingtons patrolled the area and bombed opportunity targets, and a further six Wellingtons jammed German Army tactical radio nets. The following day, aircraft of the Desert Air Force provided extensive support. The second phase of the

Wellington Ics of No. 38 Squadron over the Western Desert. *(ACA Archives)*

24 OCTOBER

battle began on 1/2 November, and resulted in the complete defeat of the Afrika Korps.

1985 Late at night, the main Headquarters, RAF Support Command at RAF Brampton, was burned down. The staff moved into vacant married quarters and set up offices. Within a month an annexe building was in use and the temporary site and married quarters were fully operational, and demolition of the main building was well under way.

1939 War courses commenced at the RAF School of Administration at Gerrards Cross.

1942 Eighty-eight Lancasters made the first daylight raid on Italy when they attacked Milan.

1944 Five squadrons of Typhoons of No. 146 Wing (Gp Capt D.E. Gillam) carried out a pinpoint attack against the Headquarters of the German 15th Army at Dordrecht, Holland, to coincide with lunchtime. Two generals, seventeen general staff officers

A rocket-armed Typhoon of No. 137 Squadron at Eindhoven. *(K. Brain)*

and many other officers and other ranks were killed.

1976 MRAF Sir Andrew Humphrey was appointed Chief of the Defence Staff.

25 OCTOBER

1938 Nearly 1,000 RAF personnel, the largest ever contingent at the time, sailed in the troop-ship *Nevassa* from Southampton for overseas stations. The first stop was Malta before calling at Port Said, Port Sudan, Aden, Basra and Karachi.

1940 ACM Sir Charles Portal was appointed as Chief of the Air Staff, a post he held for the remainder of the war.

1942 Four Focke-Wulf 190s attacked the RAF Officers' Hospital in the Palace Hotel, Torquay, on a 'tip-and-run' raid. Nineteen patients and nursing staff were killed and forty-five wounded. The hospital was extensively damaged and never returned to use.

1943 The first Typhoon rocket attack was carried out when six aircraft of No. 181 Squadron (Sqn Ldr F.W.M. Jensen) attacked a power station near Caen. Three Typhoons were

shot down including that of Jensen, who became a POW.

1960 A formal ceremony, attended by the C-in-C Far East Air Force (AM A.D. Selway) and the Deputy Prime Minister of Malaya, marked the RAF's withdrawal from RAF Kuala Lumpur and its handover to the Federation of Malaya for use by the Royal Malayan Air Force.

ACM Sir Charles Portal (1893–1971). *(AHB)*

333

26 OCTOBER

1918 The Independent Force of the RAF was created with Maj Gen Sir Hugh Trenchard as Commander-in-Chief.

1931 The de Havilland DH82 Tiger Moth made its first flight at Stag Lane Aerodrome. It entered RAF service a year later and was used as an elementary trainer for the next fifteen years. British production totalled 4,668 for the RAF, including 3,433 produced by Morris Motors Ltd. A further 2,751 were built in Canada, Australia and New Zealand for the British Commonwealth Air Training Plan. The Tiger Moth was finally retired from the RAF in February 1955.

1942 Beauforts of Nos 42 and 47 Squadrons and Bisleys of No. 15 (SAAF) Squadron attacked a convoy carrying crucial supplies to Rommel's Panzer army in North Africa. A torpedo sank the primary target, the oil tanker *Proserpina*.

1962 Following the discovery of preparations for the deployment of Soviet SS4 Sandal Medium-Range Ballistic Missiles to the island of Cuba, on 22 October, President John F. Kennedy announced the imposition of a quarantine (blockade) of that island. In light of the rapidly worsening relationship between the USA and the Soviet Union, and the assumption of Defence Condition 2 (DEFCON 2) alert status by the US Air Force's Strategic Air Command, eleven Bomber Command and RAF Germany nuclear strike squadrons and Thor missile squadrons were placed on alert, but not dispersed, between 26 October and 2 November. The Soviet Union began to dismantle the missile bases on Cuba from 2 November and the US blockade was terminated on 20 November.

A Mark XII Torpedo is loaded on to a Beaufort at RAF Luqa, Malta. *(AHB)*

27 OCTOBER

1918   **VC**: Maj William George Barker (Canadian) of No. 201 Squadron destroyed four enemy aircraft in a dogfight over the Fôret de Mormal, France. (*London Gazette*, 30 November 1918)

See 12 March 1930.

1925   Three DH9As of No. 47 Squadron, led by Sqn Ldr A. Coningham (later Air Marshal), began the first trans-Africa flight. The detachment flew from Helwan, Cairo, to Kano in Nigeria via Khartoum and Fort Lamy, arriving at Kano on 1 November after a flight of 5,268 miles. The Flight arrived back at Cairo on 19 November.

1931   A non-stop flight left RAF Cranwell in Lincolnshire for Abu Sueir in Egypt, in a Fairey Long-Range Monoplane crewed by Sqn Ldr O.R. Gayford and Flt Lt D.L.G. Bett, a distance of 2,857 miles. This was the first non-stop flight from England to Egypt.

1944   A force of fifteen Liberators of No. 159 Squadron, each carrying six mines, took off from an advanced base near Calcutta to mine the approaches to Georgetown harbour off Penang Island. Led by Wg Cdr J. Blackburn, the operation involved a round trip of over 3,000 miles. Photographic reconnaissance showed some ships sunk. This type of operation was repeated again in November and January. Blackburn was awarded a Bar to his DSO.

See 26 March 1945.

The Fairey Long Range Monoplane at Abu Sueir. *(AHB. H 1053)*

28 OCTOBER

1925   The first entry of apprentice clerks enlisted for training at RAF Ruislip. The final entry was No. 61, which commenced training on 28 April 1941. On completion of their training, 2080 apprentices had graduated.

1939   Spitfires of Nos 602 and 603 Squadrons brought down a Heinkel He111 of *Stab/ Kampfgeschwader 26* near Haddington, Lothian. This was the first enemy aircraft brought down on mainland Britain during the Second World War.

1940   Italian forces invaded Greece from Albania. By the end of December the RAF had deployed three light bomber squadrons equipped with Blenheims (Nos 30, 84 and 211 Squadrons) and two fighter squadrons equipped with Gladiators (Nos 80 and 112 Squadrons) to Greece. The Gladiator squadrons succeeded in achieving a degree of air superiority over the Italians.

A Chinook of No. 27 Squadron lifts aid to deliver to the refugees of the earthquakes in Pakistan. *(MOD)*

1944 The Empire Air Navigation School (Air Cdre P.H. Mackworth) was formed at RAF Shawbury for advanced navigation instruction and the development of new techniques.

2005 Chinook helicopters of No. 27 Squadron, based at Chaklala near Islamabad, commenced delivery of relief aid to mountain villages following a devastating earthquake in northern Pakistan.

29 OCTOBER

1925 The Observer Corps was formed.

1943 Flt Lts O.S.L. Philpot and E.E. Williams, with Lt R.M.C. Condor RA, escaped from Stalag Luft III, Sagan, after tunnelling under the compound wire. A vaulting horse, which carried the three men from their hut to the vaulting site, was used daily for gymnastics. For ten weeks the men had constructed a tunnel from a disguised trapdoor beneath the 'Wooden Horse'. Philpot reached Sweden on 3 November and Williams and Condor arrived in Sweden via Denmark on 11 November. All three men were awarded the MC.

1944 A force of thirty-six Lancasters of Nos 9 and 617 Squadrons led by Wg Cdr J.B. Tait took off from RAF Lossiemouth to attack the battleship *Tirpitz*. As the bombers approached the ship moored near Tromsø in northern Norway, cloud obscured the ship. The 'Tallboy' bombs were dropped blind and no direct hits were scored.

See 12 November 1944.

1969 MRAF The Lord Douglas, who commanded Fighter Command, RAF Middle East and Coastal Command during the Second World War, died.

Members of the Royal Observer Corps at their post. *(AHB. CH 2477)*

30 OCTOBER

1918 Viscount Cowdray donated £100,000 to provide a permanent building to house the Royal Air Force Club. The buildings at 128 Piccadilly were acquired the following year.
See 24 February 1922.

1939 A service operational trial of Very High Frequency (VHF) Radio Telephone was held at RAF Duxford.

A Hurricane, piloted by Plt Off P.W. Mould of No. 1 Squadron, based at Vassincourt in France, shot down a Dornier Do17P reconnaissance aircraft – the RAF's first air combat victory over the Continent during the Second World War.

The first WAAF Recruit Depot was established at RAF West Drayton.
See 15 August 1943.

1945 Following the outbreak of widespread and fierce conflicts between Indonesian nationalists and British troops attempting to occupy the Netherlands East Indies, AHQNEI was reinforced. Additional combat assets included elements of Nos 47, 81 and 110 Squadrons (Mosquito FBVI), No. 27 Squadron Beaufighter Xs and photo-reconnaissance by No. 681 Squadron Spitfire PRXIX. Additionally, No. 31 Squadron Dakotas provided transport support to British troops in the colony. RAF aircraft were regularly called upon to fly armed reconnaissance and close air support sorties.

1956 As the international situation in the Middle East deteriorated, the RAF was ordered to leave RAF Amman, Jordan, and relocate the force of 850 men to Mafraq where Venoms of No. 32 Squadron were fully armed and combat ready at five-minutes' notice. No. 19 LAA Wing, RAF Regiment, provided airfield defence. RAF Mafraq was vacated and handed to the Jordanian authorities on 31 May 1957, marking the end of the RAF's presence in Jordan.
See 16 July 1958.

1988 HM Queen Elizabeth the Queen Mother unveiled a statue of ACM Lord Dowding at St Clement Danes, the central Church of the Royal Air Force in The Strand.

An RAF Regiment patrol prepares to search a village in Java. *(AHB. CF 1070)*

31 OCTOBER

1927   HRH Princess Mary opened the modern hospital and nursing staff quarters at RAF Halton, which was given the name of Princess Mary's RAF Hospital Halton.

1940   The Battle of Britain was officially regarded as having come to an end on this date. The aircrew who flew under the operational control of Fighter Command, and who flew an operational sortie during the battle, have since become immortalised as 'The Few', and 2,917 were awarded the 'Battle of Britain' clasp to the 1939–45 Star. Of these, 544 lost their lives during the official period of the battle – 10 July to 31 October 1940. On 15 May 1947, Secretary of State for Air, Mr Philip Noel-Baker, announced official German statistics for Luftwaffe aircraft casualties during the Battle of Britain, which are accepted to be accurate: 1,733 aircraft destroyed and 643 damaged.

1943   Five Dakotas of No. 216 Group dropped 100 paratroopers of the Greek Sacred Squadron on the island of Samos. A further 100 troops were dropped the following night.

1945   With the end of the war in the Far East, Tiger Force – the bomber force created for operations against Japan – was disbanded without being deployed.

See 24 February 1945.

1956   Operation Musketeer: following the Egyptian government's rejection of an ultimatum presented by Britain and France and its closure of the Suez Canal, British and French forces commenced military operations with an air offensive against twelve Egyptian airfields. RAF Valiant and Canberra bombers operated from airfields in Malta and Cyprus.

HRH Princess Mary opens the RAF Hospital at Halton. She is accompanied by Sir Samuel Hoare MP, Secretary of State for Air, AVM Sir David Munroe CIE, Director General RAF Medical Services, and Dame Joanna Cruickshank DBE RRC Matron-in-Chief. *(Halton Aircraft Apprentice Association)*

Armourers prepare 1,000lb bombs before loading onto a Canberra B2 for operations over Suez. *(AHB)*

1957 Operation Profiteer: intermittent detachments of Valiant and Vulcan bombers from RAF Bomber Command squadrons to RAF Changi began. Aircraft were detached to the Far East for periods of two weeks every three months between this date and 26 June 1960. The detachments also operated from RAF Butterworth from 6 June 1958. 'V-force' detachments did not fly offensive sorties in support of internal security operations in Malaya (Operation Firedog), but undertook practice attacks on the Song Song and China Rock ranges and 'flag-waving' sorties with the aim of demonstrating the RAF's capability to project power in defence of the Commonwealth.

1971 With the withdrawal of the RAF from most of its former stations in the Far East, the Far East Air Force disbanded at Changi, Singapore. By 1972, and after forty-three years' presence, the once powerful RAF in the Far East had been reduced to RAF Hong Kong with No. 28 Squadron at Kai Tak, the staging post at Gan, and a small contribution to ANZUK in Singapore.

1 NOVEMBER

1924 The RAF Meteorological Flight was formed at RAF Eastchurch; it was equipped with Snipe aircraft.

1928 The Far East Flight left on the third stage of their cruise to Hong Kong, returning to Singapore on 11 December 1928. The cruise had lasted fourteen months and covered 27,000 miles without any serious incidents. The contemporary press hailed it 'the greatest flight in history'. On 8 January 1929 the flight was retitled No. 205 Squadron and based at RAF Seletar.
See 17 October 1927, 21 May 1928.

1938 RAF Balloon Command formed (AVM O.T. Boyd). By early 1939 a total of forty-seven squadrons were in existence, Nos 901 to 947 inclusive, organised basically on a county territorial system of affiliation.

The handling and winch party prepare to launch a barrage balloon. *(AHB. CH 1519)*

1941 The RAF assumed full responsibility for the training of parachute troops. Instructors were drawn from RAF physical training instructors. No. 1 Course arrived for training at RAF Ringway two days later.

1946 Approval was given for the formation of twenty RAuxAF Regiment Squadrons, of which only twelve were raised.

1949 The fighter squadrons of the RAuxAF were transferred from Reserve Command to Fighter Command.

1954 The headquarters of RAF forces in Germany was transferred to the Joint Headquarters at Rheindahlen, where it remained for the next forty years.

1956 Anglo-French air operations against Egypt entered a second phase aimed at destroying the Egyptian Air Force on the ground in order to prepare the way for an amphibious assault on Port Said.

1959 The first RAuxAF Maritime Headquarters was formed at Edinburgh. Similar units

HRH The Duchess of Gloucester inspects the Queen's Colour Squadron mounted by the RAF Regiment. Sqn Ldr P. Hutchins is the escorting officer. *(Gp Capt K.M. Oliver)*

were later established at Northwood, Plymouth and Belfast to provide specialist staff to supplement the manning of the HQs.

1960 The Queen's Colour Squadron of the RAF (Sqn Ldr P. Hutchins) was established at RAF Uxbridge with responsibility for RAF ceremonial duties. It was manned by RAF Regiment officers and airmen.

1967 The military withdrawal from Aden commenced with the largest airlift conducted by the RAF since the Berlin Airlift of 1948–9. Some 5,800 men of the British Army were flown out to Muharraq in Hercules of No. 36 Squadron, Britannias of Nos 99 and 511 Squadrons and Belfasts of No. 53 Squadron. The remaining RAF units in Aden, Nos 8, 21, 37, 43, 78, 84 and 105 Squadrons and No. 1417 Flight, were either withdrawn to other stations in the Gulf region or disbanded. British forces completed their withdrawal on 29 November when the last 875 men were flown out.

See 29 November 1967.

1981 The RAF Electronic Warfare Operational Support Establishment (EWOSE) was formed at RAF Benson.

1990 Operation Granby: an RAF Air Transport Detachment (ATD) of Hercules drawn from the Lyneham Wing (Nos 24, 30, 47 and 70 Squadrons and No. 242 Operational Conversion Unit) was established at King Khalid International Airport in Riyadh. The first of fifteen Puma helicopters of No. 230 Squadron left in a USAF C-5 Galaxy for Ras Al Ghar, Saudi Arabia.

2 NOVEMBER

1948 MRAF Lord Tedder unveiled the Polish Air Force Memorial on the edge of RAF Northolt Airfield. Engraved on the reverse of the memorial are the names of 1,241 Polish airmen killed on operations.

1961 Operation Sky Help: following the devastation of much of British Honduras by Hurricane 'Hattie', transport aircraft, including those of the RAF, began to ferry supplies to Belize. A special Air Transport Operations Centre was established at Kingston, Jamaica, to co-ordinate aid and evacuation. Shackletons, Hastings, Britannias and chartered British airliners airlifted 329,854lb of freight and 746 passengers. An RAF Medical Relief Team (Sqn Ldr B.A.J. Barrow) remained in the ruins of the city for twelve days and set up an emergency hospital.

AVM F.H. McNamara **VC**, CB, CBE, RAAF died.
See 20 March 1917.

3 NOVEMBER

1940 Following the Italian attack on Greece on 28 October, eight Blenheim 1Fs of No. 30 Squadron flew to Eleusis to provide air defence cover for Athens. By the end of the month Nos 84 and 211 Squadrons, equipped with Blenheims, and No. 80 Squadron with Gladiators, had arrived in

MRAF The Lord Tedder lays a wreath after unveiling the Polish Air Force Memorial outside RAF Northolt. *(AHB)*

Greece. AVM J.H. D'Albiac commanded the RAF component.

GC: Sgt Raymond Mayhew Lewin, the captain of a Wellington that crashed shortly after take-off from Malta. Despite being injured he rescued the second pilot from the burning aircraft. (*London Gazette*, 11 March 1941)

1943 Thirty-eight Lancasters carried out the first large-scale operational test of the blind-bombing device *G-H* during an attack against the Mannesmann tubular-steel works on the northern outskirts of Dusseldorf. The accuracy achieved exceeded expectations.

VC: Flt Lt William Reid, a pilot on No. 61 Squadron who pressed on to his target at Düsseldorf despite severe damage to his Lancaster and suffering serious wounds. Later, on 31 July 1944, a falling bomb hit his Lancaster and he baled out to spend the rest of the war as a POW. (*London Gazette*, 14 December 1943)

1958 Signals Command (AVM L. Dalton-Morris) was formed at RAF Medmenham from No. 90 (Signals) Group.
See 1 January 1969.

1962 A Whirlwind (captain Flt Lt T. Egginton) of No. 22 Squadron went to the aid of the French trawler *Jeanne Gougy* aground off Land's End. A large wave capsized the trawler and it was feared all had been lost. A man was seen waving from the wheel-house. The helicopter winchman, Flt Sgt E. Smith, rescued two men and coastguards rescued another two. Although on the point of exhaustion, Smith insisted on being lowered again and he found a further survivor in the wheelhouse, which was being consistently submerged by waves, and rescued him. Twelve of the trawler's crew were lost. Smith was awarded the George Medal and Egginton received the AFC.

1984 Operation Bushell: six Hercules commenced relief flights to the starving population of Ethiopia. The operation continued until 16 December 1985; by then, 32,380 tons of supplies had been air-dropped and air-landed from 2,152 sorties.

A Whirlwind lifts one of the survivors from the French trawler *Jeanne Gougy*. (*G.R. Pitchfork Collection*)

Famine relief aid is unloaded from a Hercules on a makeshift airstrip in Ethiopia. (*AHB. CN 10-85*)

An Army student pilot and his RAF instructor prepare to take off for a training flight in a Hotspur glider. *(AHB)*

4 NOVEMBER

1928 Flt Lt D. D'Arcy-Greig established a world speed record of 319.57mph in a Supermarine S.5.

1941 No. 1 Glider Training School was formed at RAF Thame, marking the commencement of glider pilot training under a permanent scheme. A second school opened at RAF Weston-on-the Green on 1 December.

1944 Flt Lt J.B. Herman RAAF was the pilot of a No. 466 Squadron Halifax detailed to attack a munitions factory at Bochum. During the return flight the aircraft was hit by enemy fire and Herman gave the order to bale out. Before he could grab his parachute, the Halifax exploded and he was thrown clear. In mid-air, he collided with the mid-upper gunner, Flt Sgt M.J. Vivash and grabbed his left leg as Vivash was opening his parachute. The parachute deployed slowly, allowing Herman to maintain his grasp and the two men came down safely under Vivash's parachute. Both men became POWs.

1976 The Hawk entered RAF service with CFS at RAF Valley.

1996 RAF Sek Kong, the last RAF station in mainland Asia, closed when No. 28 Squadron moved its six Wessex helicopters to Kai Tak International Airport in Hong Kong, where it operated until British withdrawal from the colony in 1997.

5 NOVEMBER

1938 Three Wellesleys of the RAF's Long Range Development Unit (LRDU) set off from Ismailia in Egypt to Darwin in Australia to attempt to beat the world's distance record of 6,306 miles held by the Soviet Union. Two aircraft piloted by Sqn Ldr R. Kellett and Flt Lt A.N. Combe reached Darwin after a non-stop flight of 7,158.7 miles in just over forty-eight hours, creating a world distance record. The third aircraft (Flt Lt H.A.V. Hogan) had to land at Koeping in Timor with insufficient fuel to complete the non-stop flight.

See 7 July 1938.

LONG RANGE DEVELOPMENT UNIT

With a widespread empire and the threat of war in Europe, the RAF decided to examine the possibilities of extended military flights and in 1938 the Long Range Development Unit (LRDU), under the command of Wg Cdr O.R. Gayford, was formed at RAF Upper Heyford. Initially three standard Vickers Wellesley bombers were delivered to the unit and five Type 292 aircraft specially modified to obtain the maximum range possible supplemented these in due course. These aircraft had all military equipment removed and additional fuel cells installed, and were fitted with the 1010hp Pegasus XXII engine, automatic boost and engine cowlings.

Once the unit was operational plans were made for an attempt on the world's absolute distance record. On 7 July 1938 four aircraft left RAF Cranwell at the start of what was a practice run for the main attempt, and flew to Ismailia in Egypt. Preparations then began for the attempt on the distance record. The crews were as follows:

No. 1 Aircraft	Sqn Ldr R. Kellett	Pilot
	Flt Lt R.J. Gething	Navigator-Pilot
	Plt Off M.L. Gaine	W/Operator-Pilot
No. 2 Aircraft	Flt Lt H.A.V. Hogan	Pilot
	Flt Lt R.G. Musson	Navigator-Pilot
	Flt Sgt T.D. Dixon	W/Operator-Pilot
No. 3 Aircraft	Flt Lt A.N. Combe	Pilot
	Flt Lt B.K. Burnett	Navigator-Pilot
	Sgt H.B. Gray	W/Operator-Pilot

The aircraft took off at 0355hr and flew over south Arabia, the southern tip of Persia, India, Malaya and Borneo. All went well until the aircraft were approaching Lomblen Island, in the Netherlands East Indies, when Hogan's aircraft was discovered to have insufficient fuel to reach Darwin and he landed at Koepang. The other two reached Fanny Aerodrome, Darwin, at 1330hr on 7 November with only 170 and 50 litres of fuel remaining. The flight of 7,158.7 miles, completed in just over forty-eight hours, was a new world record. Hogan's aircraft arrived later that day. A week later, the three aircraft set off on a tour of Australia.

Five of the officers achieved air rank, Burnett retired as an ACM, Hogan as an AVM and Coombe, Gething and Gayford reached the rank of Air Commodore. Kellett and Musson were killed in action and Dixon died in a training accident. Herbert Gray, then a Flight Lieutenant, was executed in the Sham Shul Po POW camp in Hong Kong by the Japanese. For his activities while a POW, he was posthumously awarded the George Cross.

The aircrew of the Long Range Development Unit display a map of the route from Ismailia to Darwin.
(RAF Museum)

345

1956 Operation Musketeer: Anglo-French airborne forces seized key points in the Canal Zone as a preliminary to a major seaborne assault with the aim of gaining control of the Suez Canal. Seven hundred paratroops of No. 3 Battalion Parachute Regiment jumped onto Gamil airfield from Valettas and Hastings. One Hastings pilot, Sqn Ldr J.A. King DSO, DFC, was awarded the AFC for reaching the drop zone despite major unserviceabilities with his aircraft. It was the only decoration awarded for RAF operations although Sqn Ldr D.C.L. Kearns of the Joint Helicopter Unit and Fg Off R.C. Olding, serving on an exchange appointment with the Fleet Air Arm, were awarded the DSC.

1984 The first two Tornado F2s entered service with No. 229 OCU at RAF Coningsby.

A Blenheim I of No. 211 Squadron on a rudimentary airstrip in northern Greece. *(IWM. ME 2598)*

6 NOVEMBER

1918 Lieutenant A.A. McLeod **VC** died from an influenza virus.
See 27 March 1918.

1935 The first flight of the prototype Hawker Hurricane (K5083). A total of 14,231 Hurricanes were built.

1939 The Central Gunnery School was formed at RAF Warmwell.

The first unexploded German bombs to be recovered in the United Kingdom in the Second World War were dealt with by armourers from RAF Sullom Voe, Shetlands.

1940 Three Blenheims of No. 30 Squadron flew the first offensive sorties in the Greek campaign when they carried out a reconnaissance over Albania and dropped bombs on Valona Airfield.

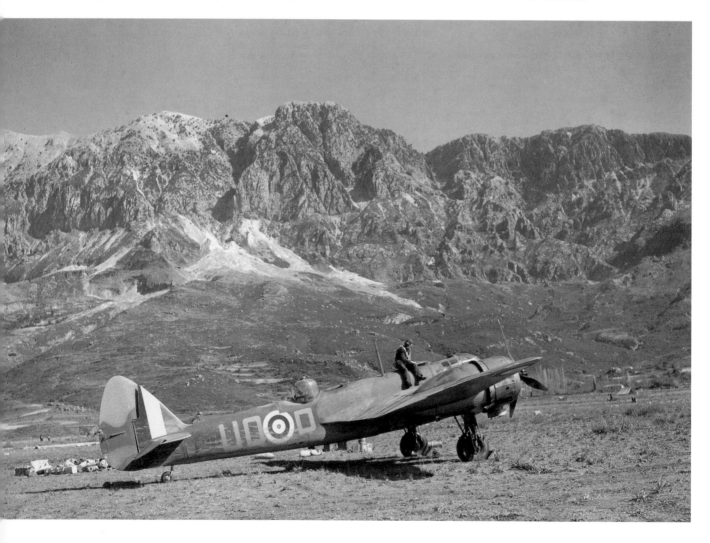

Ground crew at Gibraltar assembling Spitfire Vbs, fitted with tropical filters, in readiness for Operation Torch. *(RAFM)*

1942 After nine days of continuous work, RAF ground engineers completed the assembly of 122 Spitfires and Hurricanes, which had been sent to Gibraltar in crates.

1944 The Landing Ship Transport (LST) 420, sailing from Tilbury with reinforcements, hit a mine entering Ostend. Of the 265 RAF personnel on board, 233 lost their lives, the biggest RAF loss of life in a single incident.

1955 A memorial window to commemorate the members of Nos 2, 3, 8, and 100 Groups, Bomber Command, who gave their lives in the Second World War, was unveiled in Ely Cathedral by AVM A. McKee.

1956 Operation Musketeer: men of No. 48 (Field) Squadron, RAF Regiment, landed at Gamil Airfield to provide airfield defence. The British and French governments ordered a ceasefire to be effective at midnight following Egypt's agreement to the deployment of UN forces to protect the Suez Canal.

1975 Six Harriers of No. 1 Squadron (Wg Cdr P.P.W. Taylor) were despatched to Belize to strengthen the British garrison in an effort to deter any possible Guatemalan military action. With a reduction in the threat, the Harriers were dismantled and returned to the UK in April 1976.

See 6 July 1977.

1992 ACM Sir Michael Graydon was appointed Chief of the Air Staff.

Harrier GR3s at Belize Airport. *(J. Falconer Collection)*

7 NOVEMBER

1915 **VC**: Lt Gilbert Stuart Martin Insall of No. 11 Squadron RFC, for his actions during a fighting patrol across German lines. He retired as a group captain in July 1945. (*London Gazette*, 23 December 1915)

See 17 February 1972.

1941 The first Free French squadron, No. 340, was formed within the RAF. It initially operated Spitfires from RAF Turnhouse.

1942 Operation Torch: 650 aircraft were parked on the airfield at RAF North Front, Gibraltar, ready to take part in the landings in north-west Africa.

1943 A Mosquito of No. 248 Squadron (captain Fg Off A.J.L. Bonnett RCAF) made the first attack on a U-boat using a 6-pdr (57mm) Molins gun. Eight rounds were fired causing serious damage to *U-123*, which returned to Lorient.

1945 Gp Capt H.J. Wilson flying a Meteor F4 set a world speed record of 606.25mph at Herne Bay – the first officially confirmed record established by a jet aircraft.

1953 The first production atomic bomb was delivered to the RAF.

8 NOVEMBER

1942 Operation Torch: just after midnight British and American troops, with air support provided by the RAF and the USAAF, invaded French Morocco and Algeria. Eighteen Hurricanes of No. 43 Squadron landed on the airfield at Maison Blanche at 1000hr to be met by men of Nos 3201 and 3202 Servicing Commando Units (SCU), who had landed on beaches near Surcouf a few hours earlier and marched to Maison Blanche. This was the first time that RAF servicing commandos were used operation-

A tropicalised Hurricane IIc of No. 43 Squadron after landing at Maison Blanche in Algeria on the first day of Operation Torch. *(IWM)*

ally. Once refuelled, the Hurricanes carried out standing patrols. Later in the day Spitfires of Nos 81 and 242 Squadrons arrived to provide additional fighter cover. Five Field Squadrons and five LAA Flights of the RAF Regiment landed over the next few days.

1943 Two Spitfire pilots of No. 615 Squadron achieved the aircraft's first success in the Burma theatre when they shot down a Japanese 'Dinah' reconnaissance aircraft near Chittagong.

Sir George Thomson was appointed the first Scientific Adviser to the Air Ministry.

1945 Officers and airmen employed as parachute training instructors were granted honorary aircrew status. They were entitled to wear the appropriate aircrew badge, which followed the same design as the air gunner badge with a parachute emblem (AMO A.1079/1945).

1957 Operation Grapple X: a second series of thermonuclear weapon tests at Christmas Island commenced with the drop from a Valiant (captain Sqn Ldr B. Millett) of No. 49 Squadron over the southern end of the island. The two-stage bomb exploded with a force of 1.8 megatons exceeding the predicted yield of 1 megaton by almost 100 per cent. Three more weapons were air-dropped by No. 49 Squadron on 28 April, 2 September and 11 September 1958. The Grapple series of tests were concluded on 23 September with the detonation of a weapon suspended from a balloon. This proved to be the last atmospheric nuclear testing trial by Britain.

9 NOVEMBER

1945 With the situation in the Netherlands East Indies deteriorating, eight Thunderbolts of No. 60 Squadron and two Mosquitos of No. 110 Squadron flew into Surabaya Airfield in eastern Java as reinforcements for the support of No. 9 Brigade.
See 21 October 1945.

1971 A No. 24 Squadron Hercules (captain Flt Lt C.G. Harrison) crashed into the sea on an early morning flight from Pisa in Italy. The five crew members and forty-eight Italian paratroopers lost their lives.

1981 The first hardened aircraft shelters to be erected in the United Kingdom came into use at RAF Honington in Suffolk.

1989 The East Germans opened the Berlin Wall, and the following day work began to demolish it as Communism collapsed and the Cold War ended.
See 13 August 1961.

A Tornado GRI of No. 9 Squadron outside a new hardened aircraft shelter at RAF Honington. (J. Falconer Collection)

10 NOVEMBER

1918 The last bombing operations by the Independent Force were carried out at night by Handley Page bombers against a number of German-occupied airfields. During its five months of existence, the force dropped 543 tons of bombs on enemy industrial targets and airfields.

1938 The Secretary of State for Air (Sir Kingsley Wood) announced to Parliament the last of the pre-war expansions of the RAF. Scheme 'M' planned to raise the Metropolitan Air Force to 163 squadrons (2,549 first-line aircraft) with an all-heavy Bomber Command of 85 squadrons and Fighter Command of 50 squadrons. This new emphasis on the fighter arm was the scheme's distinguishing feature. The Secretary of State said, 'I propose to give the highest priority to the strengthening of our fighter force, that force which is designed to meet the invading bomber in the air.' So the dictum that 'the bomber will always get through' was overthrown.

1940 The first landplanes to be ferried across the Atlantic by air, seven Hudsons, were flown the 2,200 miles from Gander in New-foundland, Canada, to RAF Aldergrove in Northern Ireland by aircrew of the Atlantic Ferry Organisation (ATFERO). The flight was led by Capt D.C.T. Bennett, who later rejoined the RAF and became the AOC of No. 8 (Pathfinder) Group, Bomber Command. ATFERO had been established in July 1940 at the initiative of the Minister of Aircraft Production, Lord Beaverbrook, to ferry aircraft purchased from United States manufacturers to the United Kingdom by air, avoiding a slow and hazardous sea crossing. ATFERO aircrews comprised a mixture of civilian and military personnel. Between 1940 and 1944, 4,321 aircraft for the RAF were ferried by air across the Atlantic, in addition to the 10,468 for the USAAF.

Air gunners dressed in heavy flying clothing make final checks of their guns. *(G.R. Pitchfork Collection)*

The very unconventional, but highly successful, photographic reconnaissance pilot Adrian Warburton DSO & Bar, DFC & 2 Bars, who photographed the Italian Fleet at Taranto. *(R. Nesbit Collection)*

A Maryland (captain Fg Off A. Warburton) of No. 431 Flight based on Malta carried out a daring reconnaissance of Taranto naval base, to confirm the presence of a large Italian fleet. Warburton carried out a further reconnaissance the following day to identify the fleet's dispositions. That night, Swordfish of the Fleet Air Arm carried out a successful torpedo attack, which severely damaged three battleships.

1941 During a speech at the Mansion House, Winston Churchill stated that 'We now have an Air Force which is at least equal in size and number, not to mention quality, to the German Air Force.'

1942 The Royal Warrant for the Conspicuous Gallantry Medal (CGM) was extended to Army and RAF personnel 'while flying in operations against the enemy'. Warrant officers, non-commissioned officers and men were eligible for the medal, which ranked second to the Victoria Cross; 109 were awarded during the Second World War including one to a member of the Glider Pilot Regiment.

11 NOVEMBER

1918 The Armistice was signed to end the First World War.

On charge to the RAF, the largest air arm in the world, were 22,647 aircraft of all types, including 3,300 on first-line strength, and 103 airships. There were 133 squadrons and 15 flights overseas (on the Western Front, in the Middle East, Italy and Mediterranean District); 55 squadrons at home; 75 training squadrons and depots; 401 aerodromes at home and 274 abroad. Personnel strength was 27,333 officers and 263,837 other ranks, with approximately 25,000 WRAF. From January to November 1918 nearly 5,500 tons of bombs were dropped, 2,953 enemy aircraft destroyed, and an area of 5,000 square miles photographed by the RAF. The industry was producing about 3,500 aeroplanes a month. The RAF at home then consisted of five Area Commands:

- South-Eastern Area (Maj Gen F.C. Heath-Caldwell)
- South-Western Area (Maj Gen P.W. Game)
- Midland Area (Maj Gen J.F.A. Higgins)
- North-Eastern Area (Maj Gen Hon. Sir F. Gordon)
- North-Western Area (Maj Gen G.C. Cayley)

1948 Operation Plainfare: Hastings of Transport Command joined the Berlin Airlift operating from Schleswigland.

1953 The first detachment of Lincoln bombers arrived at RAF Eastleigh in Kenya to supplement the Harvards of No. 1340 Flight. Bomber Command squadrons based in the United Kingdom continued to furnish detachments for operations against the Mau Mau until July 1955. The Lincolns were used to pattern-bomb known terrorist camps and operating areas.

1954 The St Edward's crown replaced the Tudor crown on all official RAF badges (AMO A.274/54).

1968 After a decision to name all fourteen VC10 transport aircraft in memory of a recipient of the Victoria Cross, a ceremonial parade was held at RAF Brize Norton when the inscription on the first aircraft to be named was unveiled. The ceremony was performed by Wg Cdr P.E. Lord RAF (Retd), brother of the late Flt Lt David Lord **VC**, DFC, the only member of Transport Command to receive the supreme award.

2001 MRAF Sir Denis Spotswood, former Chief of the Air Staff, died.
See 1 April 1971.

A Lincoln over the Aberdare Forest in Kenya. *(RAFM)*

The brother of Flt Lt D. Lord **VC** unveils the first of fourteen VC10s to be named after air recipients of the Victoria Cross. *(RAFM)*

12 NOVEMBER

1914 The Royal Flying Corps and the Royal Naval Air Service adopted red, white and blue roundels as British aircraft markings.

1941 The first of two Belgian squadrons, No. 350, was formed within the RAF. Initially based at RAF Valley, the squadron operated Spitfires throughout the war.

1942 Operation Chocolate: Hudsons of Nos 117 and 267 Squadrons moved No. 243 Wing from Amriya to LG 125, well behind enemy lines in the Western Desert, and from which its Hurricanes strafed retreating Afrika Corps units, taking them totally by surprise. Over 300 vehicles were destroyed, as well as 11 aircraft on the ground. After four days the force withdrew.

1944 Operating from airfields in the north of Scotland, a force of thirty Lancasters

SINKING OF THE TIRPITZ

For four years, the powerful German battleship *Tirpitz* dominated British and American naval strategy in the European theatre. Its presence alone posed a constant threat to the convoys crossing the Atlantic and others en route to Russia, and there was great political pressure for its destruction. Over 700 RAF and Fleet Air Arm aircraft attacked 'the Beast', as Prime Minister Winston Churchill called her, in German ports and Norwegian fjords, and on one occasion at sea. So long as *Tirpitz* remained afloat, strong British and American naval forces urgently needed in the Mediterranean, and later Pacific, theatres had to be kept available. The entry into service of Barnes Wallis' 'Tallboy' bomb provided a much-improved capability to destroy her. Fleet Air Arm attacks in April 1944 and attacks by RAF Lancasters in September had damaged the ship – although the full extent was unknown by British intelligence – and it was moved to Tromsø for repairs, putting it in range of Lancasters operating from RAF Lossiemouth in the north of Scotland. On the successful attack on 12 November, her port side was ripped open and armoured decks shattered and *Tirpitz* sank in eleven minutes with great loss of life.

The leader of the attack on the *Tirpitz*, Wg Cdr J.B. Tait, OC 617 Squadron, addresses a press conference. *(IWM. CH 14145)*

drawn from Nos 9 and 617 Squadrons, and led by Wg Cdr J.B. Tait, sank the German battleship *Tirpitz* in Tromso Fjord using 12,000lb 'Tallboy' bombs.

1948 The Chief of the Air Staff wrote to the Head of Air Force Staff, British Joint Services Mission (USA) to ask him to investigate the possibility of obtaining some B-29s for the RAF. They would provide a stopgap before a new generation of V-bombers entered service. The first four arrived on 22 March 1950.

1950 The Air Ministry announced that Vampire FB5s were being flown from Britain to re-equip fighter squadrons of the Far East Air Force. These were the longest jet delivery flights undertaken by any air force to that date, covering a distance of some 8,500 miles.

1981 Wessex helicopters of No. 72 Squadron redeployed from the UK to RAF Aldergrove in Northern Ireland. Duty in the province was not new for the Squadron as it had maintained a detachment in Northern Ireland throughout the 1970s.

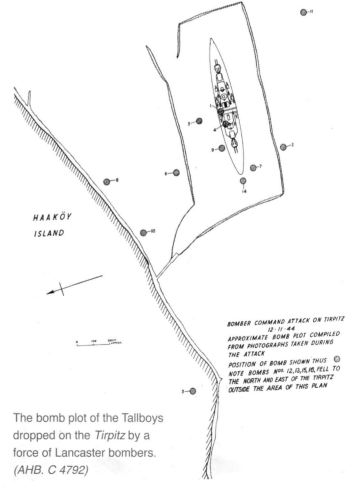

The bomb plot of the Tallboys dropped on the *Tirpitz* by a force of Lancaster bombers. *(AHB. C 4792)*

13 NOVEMBER

1940   The Halifax entered operational service with No. 35 Squadron at RAF Leeming.

1941   The Air Ministry informed Bomber Command that only limited operations were to be carried out while the whole future of the Command was debated.

1992   The famous 'golf balls' at RAF Fylingdales were replaced in service with the commissioning of the three-sided pyramid structure of the new AN/FPS-115 phased-array radar.

14 NOVEMBER

1933   The RAF's last biplane heavy bomber, the Handley Page Heyford, entered service with No. 99 Squadron at RAF Upper Heyford.

1944   ACM Sir Trafford Leigh-Mallorie was killed in an air accident in southern France while flying out to take up the appointment of Allied Air Commander South-East Asia.

1962   Three Vulcans from Nos 27, 83 and 617 Squadrons set out on a round-the-world flight during which they covered 30,000 miles in fifty hours' flying time. Stops included Perth in Australia, to coincide with the Commonwealth Games, New Zealand, to coincide with celebrations of the 25th anniversary of the Royal New Zealand Air Force (RNZAF) and the USA.

1977   Operation Burberry: following a national strike by local authority fire crews, 20,000 service personnel were provided for civil fire cover. Of these 8,750 (Army and RAF) were trained at the RAF Regiment Depot at RAF Catterick.

1988   ACM Sir Peter Harding was appointed Chief of the Air Staff in succession to ACM Sir David Craig, who was promoted to MRAF.

15 NOVEMBER

1941   The Mosquito entered full squadron service with No. 105 Squadron at RAF Swanton Morley in the low-level bombing role. The first bombing operation was carried out on 31 May 1942. A small photographic reconnaissance unit had operated the aircraft since July.
See 13 July 1941.

1943   HQ Allied Expeditionary Air Forces (AEAF) was formed (ACM Sir Trafford Leigh-Mallory). Its component forces were the Second Tactical Air Force (2nd TAF), the Air Defence of Great Britain (ADGB) and the US 9th Air Force.

Fighter Command was dissolved, the tactical elements becoming 2nd TAF (AM Sir Arthur Coningham) and the remaining squadrons coming under the command of a new organisation, ADGB (AM Sir Roderic Hill).

1946   The Air Ministry announced the formation of four new branches for the postwar RAF. The Aircraft Control, Catering, Physical Education and Provost Branches came into being on 1 January 1947.

Handley Page Heyford bombers of No. 99 Squadron. *(ACA Archives)*

Mosquito IVs of No. 105 Squadron. *(ACA Archives)*

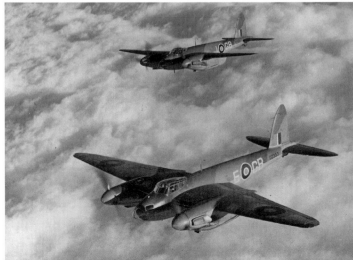

1947 The British Commonwealth Air Forces of Occupation in Japan disbanded and the RAF presence in Japan ceased officially.
See 31 January 1946.

1972 HM The Queen opened the Royal Air Force Museum on the site of the former RAF Hendon.

16 NOVEMBER

1941 Two days before the Crusader Offensive in the Western Desert, a combined Army/Air Force Headquarters was established to co-ordinate and control direct air support.
See 30 September 1941.

HM The Queen opens the RAF Museum at Hendon with MRAF Sir Dermot Boyle in attendance. *(RAFM)*

AIR–LAND CO-OPERATION

The RAF had established Army Co-operation Flights as early as 1919, followed by squadrons in 1924 and a Command in December 1940. However, it was not until the campaigns in North Africa that it was fully appreciated how vital it was that ultimate success in the land battle could only be achieved by creating a well-organised and structured organisation for air-land co-operation. The RAF architect was the new AOC-in-C of RAF Middle East, AM Sir Arthur Tedder, and it soon became clear that 'co-operation and flexibility' were the keynotes of his strategy. He appointed AVM A. Coningham to command No. 204 Group in the Western Desert and Tedder's first instruction to him was to 'get together with the Army'. Both men made a major contribution to the development of air-land warfare.

Air support depended upon command and control, which in turn depended upon communications and mobility. Coningham saw the need to establish his advanced headquarters with that of the Army and during Operation Crusader, although there were some difficulties, the Army enjoyed 'the best support it had ever had'. The arrival of Lt Gen B. Montgomery to command the British 8th Army gave even greater impetus to the development of closer air-land co-operation. He was to say later, 'any officer who aspires to high command in war must understand . . . the use of air power'. He went on to add that 'concentrated use of the air striking force is a battle-winning factor . . . it follows that control of the available air power must be centralised, and command must be exercised through RAF channels'.

The experience gained by the Desert Air Force in North Africa and Italy became the foundation for the procedures and organisation of air-land co-operation in the reconquest of North-West Europe, where the 2nd Tactical Air Force made such a huge contribution to victory.
See 27 December 1943.

Sqn Ldr R. Sutherland and Maj C. Gray man a visual control post in Normandy. *(AHB. CL 566)*

1943 ACM Sir Richard Peirse was appointed as Commander-in-Chief, Air Command South-East Asia (ACSEA), on its formation. This was an integrated allied command of RAF India Command and the 10th US Air Force. The following month, Eastern Air Command (Maj Gen G.E. Stratemeyer USAAF) was formed with headquarters in Delhi to control all air forces in eastern India.

17 NOVEMBER

1918 Following the conclusion of the armistice, Baku was reoccupied by British troops to prevent this Caspian Sea port being occupied by the Red Army. Subsequently, a Caspian Sea Flotilla consisting of captured Russian merchant vessels was formed by the Royal Navy for operations against Communist forces in the area. No. 17 Squadron and No. 47 Squadron (DH9s and Camels) on land and No. 266 Squadron (Short 184 seaplanes) deployed on seaplane carriers and supported operations by the British Army and RN.

1990 Operation Granby: AVM W.J. Wratten took over as Air Commander British Force Middle East, vice AVM R.A.F. Wilson.

18 NOVEMBER

1935 The RAF in the Middle East was strengthened by the transfer of eleven squadrons from the UK and brought to a state of readiness following Italian aggression in Abyssinia.

1941 Operation Crusader: British Commonwealth Forces launched a second offensive in the Western Desert. AM A. Tedder, AOC-in-C Middle East, assembled a formidable force of aircraft under the control of AVM A. Coningham's No. 204 Group. In all, sixteen squadrons of fighters (Hurricanes, Tomahawks and Beaufighters), eight squadrons of bombers (Blenheims and Marylands) and three tactical reconnaissance squadrons (Hurricanes and Bostons) were assembled. The RAF quickly established a measure of air superiority and although the land offensive achieved initial success it failed to push the Axis forces back to Benghazi.

1943 Bomber Command launched the main phase of the Battle of Berlin when 444 aircraft were despatched to the 'Big City'.
See 24 March 1944.

1964 All offensive action in the Radfan ceased after the Ibdali tribe, which had defied

"DESERT AIR FORCE—we presume, old man"

The unconventional dress of aircrew of the Desert Air Force did not always meet with the approval of staff officers safely established in the headquarters in Egypt.
(ACA Archives)

A Beverley of No. 84 Squadron lands on the airstrip at Thumier, 60 miles north of Aden. *(RAFM)*

government control to the end, capitulated and sued for peace.

See 29 April 1964.

1988 The RAF Fire and Rescue Training Squadron disbanded at RAF Catterick and moved to RAF Manston, where it was combined with the former civilian Air Force Department Fire School to form the RAF Fire Services Central Training Establishment (Wg Cdr J. Gritton).

19 NOVEMBER

1915 **VC**: Sqn Cdr Richard Bell-Davies of No. 3 Squadron, RNAS, for landing to rescue a downed airman after completing a bombing attack on Ferejik Junction in Bulgaria in a Nieuport 12. (*London Gazette*, 31 December 1915)

1940 A Beaufighter night-fighter of No. 604 Squadron achieved the type's first AI radar-assisted success when Flt Lt J. Cunningham and Sgt J.R. Phillipson shot down a Junkers Ju88A near Chichester.

In their first combat since arriving from Egypt, Gladiators of No. 80 Squadron, operating from Trikkala in central Greece, shot down nine Italian fighters.

1942 Operation Freshman: two Halifaxes departed from RAF Skitten in Scotland, each towing a Horsa glider carrying sixteen Royal Engineers, in an attack on the Norsk Hydro Plant at Vermørk, near Rjukan, some 60 miles due west of Oslo. A landing zone for the gliders was to be established by the Norwegian Resistance and marked

Fido burning along the runway edges to allow a Lancaster to land. *(R. Nesbit Collection)*

using a 'Eureka' transponder. Tragically, although the first glider-tug combination (captain Sqn Ldr A.B. Wilkinson) successfully managed the 340-mile crossing from the UK to Norway, the aircraft was unable to find the landing zone due to the failure of the 'Rebecca' receiver fitted to the aircraft. As the pilot attempted to find the correct site on map reading alone, the glider's towing rope snapped and the glider crashed at Fylesdalen. Eight of the seventeen men in the glider were killed and four severely injured, and all the survivors were captured before they could leave the scene of the crash. The injured men were subsequently poisoned and the Gestapo shot the uninjured men on 18 January 1943. The second tug (captain Flt Lt Parkinson) and its glider crashed immediately after crossing the Norwegian coast. All of the crew of the tug were killed and the survivors from the glider were captured and shot a few hours later. The Nørsk Hydro Plant was believed to be manufacturing heavy water for the German nuclear programme and was subsequently destroyed by Norwegian agents.

1943 Four Halifaxes of No. 35 Squadron landed at RAF Graveley with the aid of FIDO (Fog Investigation Dispersal Operation or, as it became known in the RAF, Fog Intensive Dispersal Operation), the first emergency use of the facility. In all, fifteen UK airfields were eventually equipped with FIDO, and during the war it was estimated that 2,520 aircraft were safely recovered, 1,200 of them at the emergency landing strip at RAF Woodbridge.

1948 A P-51 Mustang of No. 101 Squadron Israeli Air Force shot down a Mosquito PR34 of No. 13 Squadron conducting a reconnaissance sortie from Fayid in the Canal Zone.

20 NOVEMBER

1936 The RAF's first monoplane heavy bomber, the Fairey Hendon, entered service with No. 38 Squadron.

1940 AM O.T. Boyd, who was en route to the Middle East to become the Deputy AOC-in-C, was taken prisoner when the Wellington

THE BATTLE OF BRITAIN MEMORIAL FLIGHT

In the years immediately following the Second World War, it became traditional for a Hurricane and Spitfire to lead the Victory Day flypast over London. From that event grew the idea to form an historic collection, initially to commemorate the RAF's major battle honour, the Battle of Britain, and in later years to recognise the RAF's involvement in all the campaigns of the war. Thus, in July 1957 the Historic Aircraft Flight was formed at RAF Biggin Hill in what had become a predominantly jet-powered Air Force. The Flight, later to be called the Battle of Britain Flight, was formed with a Hurricane (LF363) and three Spitfire XIXs (PM631, PS853, PS915) and over the years, other examples of these two aircraft have been part of the Flight.

With the arrival of the Lancaster, the name was once again changed to the Battle of Britain

Memorial Flight and for years affectionately called the BBMF. PA474 was one of only two Lancasters remaining in an airworthy condition out of the 7,377 that were built. The aircraft has appeared in the markings of various Lancaster squadrons.

The Flight has been immensely popular with the general public and since 2003 they have been tasked for over 700 individual aircraft appearances during each year's display season, a tasking level that has been maintained.

Lancaster PA474 at RAF Waddington shortly before joining the Battle of Britain Flight. *(P.H.T. Green Collection)*

he was travelling in made a forced landing in Sicily.

See 24 January 1944.

1973 Lancaster B1 PA474 flew to RAF Coltishall to join the Battle of Britain Flight, which was renamed and became the Battle of Britain Memorial Flight. The Flight moved to RAF Coningsby in 1976.

21 NOVEMBER

1941 The Findlater Stewart Committee established by the Chiefs of Staff recommended the formation of a Royal Air Force Aerodrome Defence Corps under the executive control of the Air Ministry.

See 1 February 1942.

1969 The British military communications satellite, Skynet 1A, was launched on a Delta rocket from Cape Kennedy and placed in a geostationary orbit over the Indian Ocean. It provided secure voice, telegraph and fax links between UK military headquarters and ships and bases in the Middle East and Far East. No. 1001 Signals Unit, RAF Oakhangar, Hampshire, provided the satellite ground station and control centre.

See 11 December 1982.

1986 The first ever RAF air-to-air refuelling of a fully loaded passenger-carrying transport aircraft was carried out on a trooper flight to Oman as part of Exercise Saif Sareea. The receiver was a VC10 C1 of No. 10 Squadron carrying 129 troops, the tanker was a VC10K of No. 101 Squadron. The refuelling took place over Sicily as part of the 4,200-mile, 9½-hour flight.

22 NOVEMBER

1913 Capt C.A.H. Longcroft (later AVM Sir Charles Longcroft) of No. 2 Squadron flew non-stop between Montrose, Portsmouth and Farnborough in a Royal Aircraft Factory BE2. His flight covered a distance of 445 miles in a time of 7 hours 20 minutes. In recognition, Capt Longcroft received the Royal Aero Club's Britannia Challenge Trophy.

1939 The first successful photographic reconnaissance sortie was made by a Spitfire PRIA (Flt Lt M.V. Longbottom) of the Special Survey Flight, a detachment of No. 2 Camouflage Unit operating from Coulommiers in northern France. Photographs were taken of the Eupen–Elsenborn region of northern Luxembourg.

Wg Cdr F.S. Cotton prepares to greet Fg Off M.V. 'Shorty' Longbottom after a photographic reconnaissance sortie in a pink painted Spitfire PR1A during early 1940. *(RAF Museum)*

23 NOVEMBER

1916 Maj L.G. Hawker **VC**, DSO was killed in a dogfight with Baron Manfred von Richtofen (the 'Red Baron').
See 25 July 1915.

1943 No. 100 (Special Duties) Group (Air Cdre E.B. Addison) was formed at RAF West Raynham in Bomber Command. The group was formed in an effort to draw together Bomber Command's existing Radio Counter-Measures (RCM) electronic warfare operations, and during the course of the bomber offensive against Germany No. 100 Group and its forebears pioneered the use of offensive electronic warfare.
See 16 June 1940.

1945 A No. 31 Squadron Dakota force-landed 5 miles from the airfield at Kemajoran, Java. The four crew and nineteen troops escaped but their mutilated bodies were found by a patrol eight days later, having been murdered by Indonesian terrorists.

1949 The RAF Antarctic Flight (Sqn Ldr G.B. Walford) sailed in the MV *Norsel* with the British Scandinavian Antarctic Expedition for Queen Maud Land. The Flight was equipped with two Auster VI aircraft modified to operate with skis and floats.
See 1 February 1950.

24 NOVEMBER

1947 Sqn Ldr J. Lomas flying a Meteor F4 set up a new record between Edinburgh (Turnhouse) and London (Bovingdon) in 30 minutes 25 seconds at 617.6mph.

1975 Operation Heliotrope: the Third Cod War: Two earlier Cod Wars (also called the Iceland Cod Wars) in 1958 and 1972 had occurred over Iceland's claims of authority over tracts of ocean off their coastline as being their exclusive fishery zone. Nimrod maritime patrol aircraft resumed intensive surveillance flights within the 200-mile zone announced by the Icelandic government. The sorties were mounted in order to fulfil three objectives: in support of the Royal

Nimrod MR1s at RAF Kinloss. *(J. Falconer Collection)*

Navy to locate British and Icelandic vessels; to provide a British military presence in support of UK trawlers; and to demonstrate to the Icelandic government the UK's resolve to protect British fishing interests. Nimrod patrols were subsequently supplemented by a small number of sorties flown by Hastings T5 aircraft of No. 230 OCU.

See 2 June 1976.

1990 Operation Granby: the first three Chinook helicopters of No. 7 Squadron were flown to Ras Al Ghar in USAF C-5 Galaxy transports. Others were transported by sea.

25 NOVEMBER

1919 AM Sir Hugh Trenchard, Chief of the Air Staff, issued his Memorandum on the Permanent Organisation of the Royal Air Force. The scheme established the peacetime basis of the Service within the financial provision approved by the Cabinet (£15million per year). The governing

The motor transport section at the Air Depot, Alexandria, in 1919. *(G.Tyak)*

principle was 'to concentrate on providing for the needs of the moment as far as they can be foreseen and on laying the foundations of a highly-trained and efficient force which, though not capable of expansion in its present form, can be made so without any drastic alteration should necessity arise in years to come'. The Memorandum also stressed the extreme importance of training, noting that 'to make an Air Force worthy of the name, we must create an Air Force spirit, or rather foster this spirit that undoubtedly existed in a high degree during the war, by every means in our power'.

See 11 December 1919.

1940 ACM Sir Hugh Dowding was replaced as AOC-in-C Fighter Command by AM Sholto Douglas.

26 NOVEMBER

1955 Following a widespread campaign of terrorist bombings and activities in Cyprus, the Governor declared a State of Emergency.

1972 Operation Deep Freeze: a Hercules of No. 30 Squadron (captain Sqn Ldr E. Waddingham) flew from Christchurch, New Zealand, and landed on the snow runway at Williams Field, McMurdo Sound in Antartica to resupply the scientific party at the research base. Six sorties were flown onto the snow runway during the annual resupply operation.

27 NOVEMBER

1918 No. 29 (Operations) Group (Headquarters, Edinburgh) was formed with command status, to administer units in Scotland under the operational control of the Commander-in-Chief Grand Fleet. The Group included RAF personnel aboard the Grand Fleet's aircraft carriers and aboard the ships of the Battle Cruiser Force, together with shore-based supporting units. It was also responsible for No. 28

(Operations) Group, which comprised all stations in the Orkneys and the Shetland Isles.

1962 Fg Off D. Bennett, the last RAF National Service officer, was demobbed from RAF Scampton.

See 23 January 1963.

1978 Twelve Buccaneers of No. 809 Naval Air Squadron and ten Phantoms of No. 892 Naval Air Squadron launched from the Royal Navy's HMS *Ark Royal*, and landed at RAF St Athan for conversion and allocation to RAF squadrons earmarked to provide tactical air support of maritime operations (TASMO) following the paying off of the RN's last fixed-wing aircraft carrier.

1980 The RAF General Purposes Telephone Network (GPTN) opened when D Sigs (Air) (Air Cdre P. Owen) made a telephone call from the Zone Switching Centre at RAF Brampton to the Station Commander at RAF Carlisle.

28 NOVEMBER

1942 **VC**: Flt Sgt Rawdon Hume Middleton RAAF, pilot of a No. 149 Squadron Stirling, for saving the lives of his crew after his bomber was severely damaged over Turin and he sustained major wounds. He managed to return to England where his crew baled out, but he died when the bomber crashed. (*London Gazette*, 13 January 1943, posthumous award)

1943 Photographs taken at Zinnovitz and Peenemunde by Sqn Ldr J.R.H. Merrifield flying a Mosquito PRIX of No. 540 Squadron disclosed a tiny cruciform shape on launch rails. This provided the connection between Peenemunde and the 'ski sites' photographed in northern France, confirming that the sites were for launching the V-1 flying bombs.

1944 The Bofors Detachment B.11 of No. 2875 LAA Squadron, RAF Regiment, shot down a Luftwaffe Messerschmitt Me262 jet

The reconnaissance photograph taken of Peenemunde showing the V-1 rocket on launching rails (arrowed). *(IWM. CL 1055)*

Wreckage of the Messerschmitt Me262 jet fighter shot down by gunners of the RAF Regiment. *(IWM. CL 1648)*

fighter at the RAF advanced airfield at Helmond, Holland. This was the first occasion a jet aircraft was shot down by ground fire.

1946 Air HQ Netherlands East Indies and No. 904 Wing were disbanded, ending British air involvement in the Netherlands East Indies. The last British ground troops also withdrew from the colony. Between September 1945 and November 1946, the RAF flew 19,533 sorties over the Netherlands East Indies.
See 29 September 1945.

1969 Coastal Command merged with Strike Command as No. 18 (Maritime) Group, thus completing the rationalisation of the RAF home command structure from eight Commands to four – Strike, Air Support, Training, and Maintenance.

2000 At a ceremony at RAF Honington, the RAF Regiment established formal links with the Commando de l'Air of the French Air Force.

2001 Flt Lt W. Reid **VC** died.
See 3 November 1943.

29 NOVEMBER

1917 The Air Force (Constitution) Act, 1917, received Royal Assent. The Act sanctioned the establishment of an Air Ministry as a Department of State. Maj Gen Sir Hugh Trenchard was appointed as the first Chief of Air Staff.

1918 A Handley Page 0/400 (captain Capt R. Smith) left Cairo for Baghdad, carrying Maj Gen G. Salmond, on a visit to units in Mesopotamia. The aircraft went on to survey the route to New Delhi and Calcutta.
See 28 July 1918.

1967 British forces completed their withdrawal from Aden, ending 128 years of British rule and, for the RAF, 48 years of occupation of Khormaksar and Steamer Point.

30 NOVEMBER

1945 As part of the restructuring of Air Command South-East Asia (ACSEA), RAF Air Command Far East was formed to control AHQs in existence or being established throughout the Far East, including those in Burma, Malaya, Hong Kong and Ceylon.

The Air Transport Auxiliary was disbanded. During the war its 1,152 men and 166 women pilots ferried 307,378 aircraft; 136 men and 15 women died in service with the ATA.
See 1 September 1939.

1963 MRAF The Lord Newall, former Chief of the Air Staff, died.
See 1 September 1937.

1966 Following the disbandment of No. 224 Squadron on 31 October – the last flying unit to be based at Gibraltar – AHQ Gibraltar was disestablished at midnight. RAF North Front was renamed RAF Gibraltar, controlled directly by Headquarters, No. 19 Group, Coastal Command.

1981 The last Whirlwind helicopters on active search and rescue duties were retired from service and replaced by the larger Wessex helicopter.

1999 RAF Laarbruch was handed over to the German authorities, leaving RAF Bruggen as the last RAF operational station in Germany.

A Hunter FR10 of No. 1417 Flight over Al Qara in the Aden Protectorate. *(Ray Deacon)*

1 DECEMBER

1937 An Air Ministry Directive was issued to Coastal Command establishing its operational role in war as 'trade protection, reconnaissance and co-operation with the Royal Navy'.

1940 RAF Army Co-operation Command (AM Sir Arthur Barrett) was formed.

No. 148 Squadron, equipped with Wellingtons, was established on Malta, becoming the first bomber squadron to be based on the besieged island.

1954 HQ Middle East Air Force moved to RAF Nicosia following disturbances in the Canal Zone.

1958 The RAF's first surface-to-air missile, Bloodhound 1, entered operational service with No. 264 Squadron at RAF North Coates.

1966 RAF Idris in Libya was closed. The bombing range at Tarhuna, used for Armament Practice Camps, had been closed in September.

1977 The Meritorious Service Medal was reintroduced into the RAF (DCI. RAF J19/78).
See 26 June 1918.

2 DECEMBER

1940 The first successful use was made of a 'Starfish' site, when sixty-six German bombs intended for Bristol were dropped on it. The 'Starfish' decoy fire was designed to light up in the path of an enemy bomber force at just the right moment to look like markers dropped by enemy pathfinders.
See 17 April 1941.

1980 The first of an initial batch of thirty-three Chinook heavy-lift helicopters were accepted into service at RAF Odiham.

1991 A decision was made to lift the restriction on the employment of female aircrew in the fast jet (FJ) force.

3 DECEMBER

1938 The first American-designed aircraft to enter service with the RAF, a North American Harvard, arrived for testing at the A&AEE, RAF Martlesham Heath. The aircraft subsequently became the RAF's

A Bloodhound Mk 1 at RAF North Coates.
(Andrew Thomas Collection)

Javelin FAW9s at Ndola, Zambia. *(AHB. PRB 32469)*

main advanced training aircraft and was in continuous use until April 1955.

1951 Four Vampires of the Gutersloh Wing were lost when the weather at base deteriorated rapidly and the four pilots were forced to bale out.

1965 Javelins of No. 29 Squadron deployed from RAF Akrotiri to Ndola in Zambia to provide air defence for that country following the announcement of a Unilateral Declaration of Independence by the Rhodesian government. Argosies of Nos 114 and 267 Squadrons flew air-defence radars and ancillary equipment into Zambia. No. 29 Squadron returned to Akrotiri in August 1966.

See 19 December 1965.

4 DECEMBER

1940 At a meeting of the Defence Council, the Prime Minister reaffirmed that Coastal Command would remain as part of the RAF.

1942 **VC**: Wg Cdr Hugh Gordon Malcolm, the commanding officer of No. 18 Squadron, led an unescorted daylight raid against a forward landing ground at Souk-el-Arba, North Africa. All eleven Blenheims failed to return with Malcolm's one of the last to fall. Malcolm was the only graduate of the RAF College Cranwell to be awarded the **VC**. Several months later, Lady Tedder, wife of the Middle East Air Commander-in-Chief, opened the first of a chain of service rest and leisure centres in North Africa, which she named 'Malcolm Clubs'. After the war, these facilities were established worldwide on RAF stations and continued to exist for almost sixty years. (*London Gazette*, 27 April 1943, posthumous award)

1944 Following growing unrest, demonstrations in Athens by the Communist-based National Liberation Front (EAM) and National Popular Liberation Front (ELAS) on 2 December resulted in British troops being forced to fire on the demonstrators. Two days later, police stations were attacked and RAF units operating from Hassani began flying sorties against EAM and ELAS targets in the Athens area.

See 19 December 1944.

1969 The RAF Staff College, Andover, was closed after forty-seven years, leaving Bracknell as the RAF's sole staff college.

See 31 December 1996.

5 DECEMBER

1944   Twelve RAF Regiment squadrons deployed on airfields in southern Greece became involved in open warfare against forces (ELAS) of the Greek Communist Party, which attempted a coup against the legitimate Greek government.

1961   Bomber Command held its first Micky Finn Command-wide no-notice readiness and dispersal exercise. During the course of the exercise, the V-Force was required to disperse to its designated wartime dispersal airfields and assume a war posture. Micky Finn exercises were conducted annually throughout the 1960s and early 1970s.

A Valiant crew scramble. *(MOD)*

6 DECEMBER

1942   Operation Oyster: a mixed force of light bombers from No. 2 Group, led by Wg Cdr J.E. Pelly-Fry, carried out an attack on the Philips radio and valve works in Eindhoven in the Netherlands. Aircraft that participated in the attack included forty-seven Venturas of Nos 21, 464 and 487 Squadrons, thirty-six Bostons of Nos 88, 107 and 226 Squadrons and ten Mosquitos of Nos 105 and 139 Squadrons. Two factories within the complex were severely damaged, and there was little destruction outside the boundaries of the works. However, nine Venturas, four Bostons and one Mosquito were lost, most to enemy fighters, and three aircraft crashed on landing in the UK. This 19 per cent loss

The operations board at HQ No. 2 Group for Operation Oyster, the attack on Eindhoven. *(G.R. Pitchfork Collection)*

AIRCRAFT & CREW STATES AT 1800 HRS	SQDN.	TIME ON TARGET	TASK	EFFORT	R.T. S.A.C.S.	TAKE OFF TIME EST.	CALL SIGN	W.T. S.A.C.S.	E.T.R. BASE	TIME LANDED	CAPT. OF A/C
MITCHELL	107	1230		6	Roamer	1113	BC1	AH5	1336		
				6							
VENTURA	226	1230		6	Illingworth	1125	8UT	FD9	1345		
				6							
BOSTON	88	1230		6	Holtby	1133	IWT	TIK	1345		
		Z21 Eindhoven		6							
MOSQUITO	21	1236		9	Fogey	1133	BJ8	3OL	1354		
		AIRBORNE		8							
BLENHEIM	464	1236		7	Eclipse	1133	N7G	8BT	1354		
				7							
SQUADRON CODE LETTERS	487	1236		8	Organ	1133	UD5	K6R	1354		
				8							
	105	1232		8	Reveille	1132	7PM	6FQ			
	139	1232	Earthquake	2		1132	7PM	LW1	1330		
	139	1250	Damage Assessment	1		1200	7PM	LW1 F	1342		
			Total -	94							

367

Bostons over the burning Philips radio and valve factory in Eindhoven. *(G.R. Pitchfork Collection)*

7 DECEMBER

rate was unsustainable, and further large daylight raids of this type were not repeated.

1944 Some 475 Lancasters and 12 Mosquitos mounted the first major attack against an oil target in eastern Germany. They attacked the synthetic-oil plant at Leuna near Leipzig, 500 miles from the bombers' bases in England. Despite extensive cloud cover, considerable damage was inflicted on the plant.

1941 Japan attacked the principal US naval base in the Pacific, at Pearl Harbor, Hawaii. Tokyo announced that it was at war with the USA and Britain.

Two Catalina flying-boats of No. 205 Squadron, based at RAF Seletar in Singapore, searched for a Japanese convoy off the coast of north-east Malaya. One aircraft (captain Fg Off E. Beddell) was lost to Japanese fighters to become the first RAF loss in the Far East war.

1950 The Reserve of Air Force Officers (RAFO) was restyled the Royal Air Force Reserve of Officers (RAFRO). It consisted of ex-regular officers with a reserve obligation.

1967 A Whirlwind helicopter of the Queen's Flight crashed in Berkshire. The Captain of the Flight, Air Cdre J.H.L. Blount, was killed, together with the crew of two and the Flight's engineering officer.

8 DECEMBER

1939 A new RAF Air Command, British Air Forces in France (BAFF) (AM A.S. Barratt), was formed to co-ordinate the operations of all RAF units in France.

1941 In the aftermath of the Japanese landings in northern Malaya, RAF and RAAF squadrons mounted an intensive series of attacks on enemy troop positions, landing areas and airfields. Such heavy losses were suffered that the RAF was virtually a spent force after the first day of operations.

1952 Operation Becher's Brook: the first twelve of 400 Canadian-built Sabres for the RAF left RCAF Baggotville on a ferry flight to England via Bluie West One (Greenland) and Keflavik, Iceland. Sixty pilots of No. 147 Squadron (formerly No. 1 Overseas Ferry Unit) were used to ferry the aircraft in ten convoys, the largest involving fifty-four aircraft. The last convoy landed in Scotland on 19 December 1953 – a year to the day after the arrival of Becher's Brook One.

1962 An Indonesian-sponsored revolt by the North Kalimantan National Army (TNKU) began with the aim of deposing the Sultan of Brunei. Four Beverleys of No. 34 Squadron deployed elements of a Gurkha battalion from Singapore to Brunei town. The first Beverley (captain Sqn Ldr M.G. Bennett) landed on an obstructed runway and the ninety-three Gurkha troops took over the airfield, allowing the other aircraft to land. A Britannia of No. 99 Squadron

Sabres arrive at RAF Abingdon after Operation Becher's Brook. *(G. Tyak)*

369

A Beverley of No. 34 Squadron lands British and Gurkha troops at Brunei. *(AHB)*

took reinforcements to Labuan. No. 48 Squadron Hastings, No. 52 Squadron Valettas and No. 205 Squadron Shackletons, supported by No. 38 (RAAF) Squadron Hercules, and No. 41 (RNZAF) Squadron Bristol Freighters, subsequently flew further reinforcements to the area. By the thirteenth day after the revolt broke out, the airlift had taken to Brunei and Labuan 3,209 passengers, 113 vehicles, assorted guns and trailers, 13 dogs, 2 Auster aircraft and 624,308lb of freight. Subsequently, No. 20 Squadron Hunters and No. 45 Squadron Canberras were detached to Labuan to provide close air support. No. 209 Squadron Twin Pioneers and No. 66 Squadron Belvedere helicopters were deployed to Brunei for local transport. Prompt action to seize areas taken by the TNKU led to the collapse of the rebellion by 17 December, although low-level operations continued for several months to mop up the remaining rebels.

See 21 December 1962.

1966   HQ Bomber Command announced that the Vulcan squadrons were changing their attack profiles from high to low level. By the end of 1967 the whole Vulcan force used the low-level free-fall weapon delivery technique.

9 DECEMBER

1931   The second grant of arms to a RAF establishment was made to the Central Flying School. The first had been made two years earlier to the RAF College, Cranwell.

See 18 December 1929.

1941   **VC**: Sqn Ldr Arthur Stewart King Scarf, a pilot of No. 62 Squadron flying a Blenheim, was the sole survivor of a formation to attack Singora Airfield, Thailand. Shortly after crash-landing on return, he died of his wounds. Due to the turmoil of the Malayan campaign, the authorities did not hear of Scarf's actions until 1946. (*London Gazette*, 21 June 1946, posthumous award)

The Armorial Bearings of the
CENTRAL FLYING SCHOOL

The Central Flying School Arms.
(G.R. Pitchfork Collection)

A line-up of No. 62 Squadron Blenheim 1s. *(IWM. K 627)*

1964 All Valiant aircraft were grounded, except in the case of national emergency, following discovery of fatigue in the rear spar.

1988 MRAF Sir David Craig was appointed Chief of the Defence Staff, a post he held during the break-up of the Warsaw Pact and the end of the Cold War. He served until 1 April 1991 when he was created Baron Craig of Radley.

10 DECEMBER

1928 **GC** (ex-EGM): Fg Off Walter Anderson and Cpl Thomas Patrick McTeague who swam from the shore to help rescue a pilot of an aircraft that had crashed in the sea off Leysdown. (*London Gazette*, 12 April 1929)

1941 Buffalos of No. 453 Squadron (Flt Lt T.A. Vigors) were scrambled too late to intercept Japanese aircraft attacking the battleship HMS *Prince of Wales* and the battle-cruiser HMS *Renown* off the east coast of Malaya. The fighters arrived to find the two warships sinking.
See 30 June 1941.

Brewster Buffaloes of No. 243 Squadron over Malaya escorting a Blenheim IV. *(IWM. K 1228)*

Two Buffalos of No. 67 Squadron flew the first operation in the Burma campaign when they escorted a No. 60 Squadron Blenheim carrying out a reconnaissance sortie.

1943 HQ Mediterranean Allied Air Forces was formed with joint Anglo-American staffs at all levels by merging the headquarters of North West Africa Air Force with those of Mediterranean Air Command.

1971 Hercules transport aircraft flew eighteen sorties between Karachi/Islamabad and Masirah, to evacuate 909 British and friendly foreign nationals from West Pakistan following serious disturbances in the country. RAF VC10s flew them on to Cyprus.

11 DECEMBER

1918 The initial meeting was held at the War Office to determine the measures to fulfil

the RAF's requirements for telephone, telegraph and W/T communications in the field. After further conferences, it was decided that the GPO and Army would retain responsibility for RAF landline and telephone services with the RAF responsible for providing its own wireless communications.

1919 The Secretary of State for War and Air, Winston Churchill, presented a White Paper to Parliament outlining the postwar development of the Royal Air Force. Drafted by the Chief of the Air Staff, AM Sir Hugh Trenchard – and often referred to as the 'Trenchard Memorandum' – the White Paper provided for:

• Home: two squadrons (increasing to four) as a striking force; one Army co-operation flight for each Army Division; one or more squadrons for artillery co-operation; one reconnaissance and spotting squadron; half a torpedo squadron; an aeroplane fighting flight, a flying-boat flight and a float seaplane flight (eventually increasing to three aeroplane and two seaplane squadrons) for Fleet co-operation.

- Overseas: eight squadrons and one Depot in India; seven squadrons and one Depot in Egypt, three squadrons and one Depot in Mesopotamia; one seaplane flight in Malta; one seaplane flight in Alexandria; one seaplane flight on an aircraft carrier in the Mediterranean.

The White Paper also provided for the foundation of a comprehensive personnel training structure in the UK – including the RAF College, the RAF Staff College and the RAF Apprentice School, Halton – and the introduction of the Short Service Commissions.

See 25 November 1919.

1936 HM King George VI was promoted to Marshal of the Royal Air Force.

1945 Spitfire IXs of No. 273 Squadron carried out strafing attacks on Viet Minh guerrillas surrounding a French force at Banme Thuet, French Indochina. Leaflets were dropped in advance to warn the Viet Minh of this action.

1982 An Ariane rocket launched the first in a series of six Skynet 4 communications satellites.
See 21 November 1969.

A Spitfire XIV of No. 273 Squadron escorting a Dakota over South-East Asia. *(A. Day)*

12 DECEMBER

1918 The formation of the Chaplain's Branch was announced.

1936 Of a formation of seven Heyford bombers of No. 102 Squadron, en route from RAF Aldergrove to RAF Finningley, four crashed in icing conditions over the Pennines.

1940 British aircraft camouflage schemes were regulated and standardised. Two main schemes of temperate land (disruptive pattern of dark green and dark earth) and temperate sea (disruptive pattern of dark slate grey and extra dark sea grey) were adopted for upper and side surfaces. Under-surfaces were standardised at matt black for night flying aircraft, and all other types, including flying-boats, had dark egg-shell blue. An exception was photographic reconnaissance aircraft, which had a pink finish.

1946 The Air Council appointment of Air Member for Technical Services was created.

1971 Following an armed revolt in East Pakistan where the population was seeking separation from West Pakistan, three Lyneham-based Hercules (Wg Cdr K.J.E. Hannah) evacuated 434 people from the bomb-cratered runway at Dacca in East Pakistan

to Calcutta and thence to Singapore in an operation described by the Foreign and Commonwealth Office as 'a miracle'.

1992 Operation Vigour: two Hercules aircraft and four crews took part in relief flights into Somalia. Based near Mombasa, Kenya, the aircraft flew missions to Mogadishu and Kismayu airports as well as to several rough fields within Somalia.

13 DECEMBER

1918 The first flight from England (Martlesham Heath) to India (Karachi) began. Maj A.S.C. MacLaren and Capt R. Halley flying a Handley Page V/1500, 'Old Carthusian', arrived at Karachi on 15 January on two of the four engines.

See 24 May 1919.

THE FIRST FLIGHT TO INDIA

The Handley Page V/1500 aircraft used for the first flight to India had a wingspan of 126ft and four Rolls-Royce engines between them developing 1,400hp. The fuel capacity was 1,000 gallons and the aircraft had a top speed of 95–100mph. Accompanying the crew and the three NCO mechanics was Maj Gen N. MacEwen, who was to take over as AOC India on arrival. As both the General and MacLaren had attended Charterhouse School, the aircraft was named 'Old Carthusian'. Another passenger for the flight was MacLaren's little Maltese terrier, Tiny.

After an abortive start on 8 December, the flight got under way from Martlesham Heath on the 13th. After seven days the crew landed on the racecourse at Malta before crossing to North Africa. After the failure of two engines they landed in the desert where the crew were collected a few days later and taken to Cairo. After repairs to the aircraft, it was moved to

Cairo on New Year's Day. On 8 January they departed for Baghdad and, after another forced landing in the desert, they arrived at Bushire on the 11th. The following day they reached Bundar Abbas and on the 13th set off for Karachi, but with 50 miles to go an engine failed and they landed on a spit of sand near a village where, miraculously, there was a representative of the Eastern Telegraph Company who made contact with the RAF Headquarters in India.

With a change in the wind, and after unloading most of the equipment, a three-engine take-off was accomplished. Soon after becoming airborne a second engine failed, but the Army at Karachi had been alerted to the expected arrival of the aircraft and a flare path had been prepared as dusk fell. A ridge was cleared with a few feet to spare and a landing with full power on the two remaining engines was made during the evening of the 15th, thus completing the first flight to India from England.

Handley Page V/1500 'Old Carthusian'.
(AHB. H 194)

Armourers wearing NBC protective clothing load a BL 755 cluster bomb onto a Jaguar during a Taceval exercise.

(RAFM)

1918 No. 86 (Communications) Wing was formed at RAF Hendon to provide rapid transport between London and Paris in connection with the Versailles Peace Conference.

1960 The first AAFCE Tactical Evaluation (TACEVAL) of RAF units was carried out on Nos 16 and 31 Squadrons at RAF Laarbruch in Germany.

North Sea. Luftwaffe Messerschmitt Bf109 fighters intercepted the Wellingtons and shot five down into the sea; a sixth crash-landed near Newmarket.

1990 Operation Granby: four Victor K2 tankers of No. 55 Squadron deployed from RAF Marham to Muharraq in Bahrain. The detachment was increased to a maximum of eight aircraft during January 1991.

14 DECEMBER

1939 Six Wellingtons of No. 99 Squadron were lost from an attacking force of twelve during an attempted raid on the German Navy cruisers *Nurnberg* and *Leipzig*, which had been damaged in a naval action in the

15 DECEMBER

1937 The first Hurricane to enter operational service was delivered to No. 111(F) Squadron at RAF Northolt. The fighter was the RAF's first eight-gun fighter.

A T.31 glider of the Western Gliding Club about to be winch-launched at RAF Cosford. (AM I.D. Macfadyen)

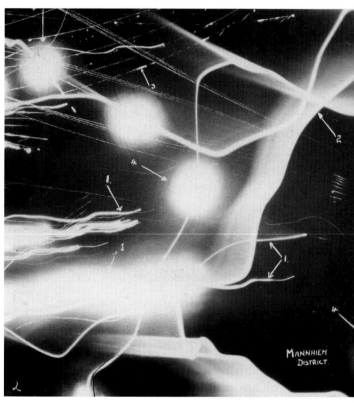

Searchlights and flak over Mannheim. (ACA Archives)

1949 Four enthusiasts, led by Air Cdre G.J.C. Paul, founded the RAF Gliding and Soaring Association as they travelled in the back of a London taxi to a reunion. Also at the birth was a policeman who tried to stop it on the grounds of overloading the cab.

1956 The first of four Type 80 radar early warning stations in RAF Germany was completed at Brockzetel and was designated No. 101 Signals Unit (SU).

1971 With the ceremonial lowering of the RAF ensign at RAF Muharraq, and the disbandment of the last RAF command formation permanently based in the Persian Gulf region, Air Forces Gulf, the RAF presence in the region finished.

1994 The first female RAF fast jet pilot, Flt Lt Jo Salter, was awarded combat-ready status on No. 617 Squadron.

16 DECEMBER

1940 Bomber Command carried out the first 'area attack' on a German industrial city when 134 aircraft attacked Mannheim in retaliation for the German attacks on Coventry and Southampton. It was the largest force sent to a single target at that stage.

1943 Bomber Command mounted the first bombing attacks against the V-1 flying-bomb launching sites in northern France. Nine Lancasters of No. 617 Squadron (Wg

Cdr G.L. Cheshire) dropped 12,000lb bombs on a site at Abbeville. The sites became known as 'Crossbow' targets.

Beaufighters and Mosquitos of No. 100 Group operated in the intruder role over Germany for the first time.

1944 The Germans launched a final and major offensive in the Ardennes. Poor weather until the 23rd prevented intervention by Allied air forces when the tactical squadrons were finally able to mount sustained support, which eventually halted and drove back the enemy columns.

A Tornado GR1 of No. 12 Squadron taxies out at a Kuwaiti air base for an Operation Southern Watch sortie. *(MOD)*

1947 The Auxiliary Air Force was granted the prefix 'Royal'.

1983 The Chiefs of Staff of the British, French, West German, Italian and Spanish air forces signed a preliminary agreement for a Future European Fighter Aircraft (EFA), later given the name Typhoon by the RAF.
See 31 March 2006.

1991 A press release was issued to announce that the restriction on female fast jet aircrew had been lifted. From this point, fast jet places became open to female pilots and navigators.
See 2 December 1991.

1998 Operation Desert Fox: with Saddam Hussein's continued obstruction of United Nations' weapons inspectors and his refusal to comply with Security Council resolutions, cruise missile attacks and air strikes by the United States Navy (USN) and air strikes by RAF Tornado GR1s on targets in Iraq commenced in an effort to degrade Iraq's ability to manufacture and use weapons of mass destruction and to diminish the military threat posed by Iraq towards its neighbours. The Tornados of No. 12 Squadron, operating from Ali al-Salem Air Base in Kuwait, attacked the airfield at Talil near Baghdad and military targets near Basra using Paveway II LGBs. The attacks continued until 19 December, the Tornados having flown twenty-eight sorties and attacked eleven targets.

17 DECEMBER

1918 The RAF's Aeroplane Postal Service Continental was officially started after a twenty-four hour delay due to poor

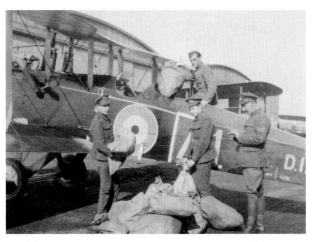

Mailbags are loaded onto a DH9 of No. 120 Squadron operating the RAF's Aeroplane Postal Services Continental. *(RAFM)*

MRAF Lord Trenchard inspecting Halton aircraft apprentices. *(AHB. H 2463)*

weather. However, Lt F.O. Thornton of No. 57 Squadron had ignored the weather the day before when he took off in a DH4 from Namur with mail for Spa. This was the first mail flight by the RAF on an organised schedule.

1924   The first 399 aircraft apprentices to complete the three-year apprenticeship, as No. 1 Entry, at No. 1 School of Technical Training, RAF Halton, passed out. The reviewing officer was ACM Sir Hugh Trenchard.

1937   The Secretary of State for Air (Lord Swinton) inspected the RAF's first mobile recruiting office manned by men of the Inspectorate of Recruiting.

1939   The formal Memorandum of Agreement to establish the Empire Air Training Scheme (renamed the British Commonwealth Air Training Plan in 1942) was signed in Ottawa by government representatives of the United Kingdom, Canada, Australia and New Zealand.

See 29 April 1940, 6 June 1942.

1953   The Joint Air Reconnaissance Intelligence Centre (JARIC) UK was established.

See 11 July 1940.

1958   The Secretary of State for Air (Mr George Ward) announced that 'it has been decided to develop a new strike/reconnaissance aircraft as a Canberra replacement. This would be capable of operating from small airfields with rudimentary surfaces and have a very high performance at all levels.' It became known as TSR2.

See 6 April 1965.

18 DECEMBER

1911 A Technical Sub-Committee of the Committee of Imperial Defence was established to examine the requirements of an Air Service for use in war on land and sea. The Under-Secretary of State for War (Col J.E.B. Seely) was appointed to chair the Technical Sub-Committee and a group led by Brig Gen D. Henderson, and including Col G. Macdonogh, Capt F.H. Sykes and Maj D. MacInnes, undertook much of the detailed work of the sub-committee.

1922 The first course of boy mechanics (later referred to as aircraft apprentices) of No. 2 School of Technical Training passed out at RAF Cranwell. ACM Sir Hugh Trenchard was the reviewing officer.

1924 Flight markings were permitted on aircraft wheel discs. 'A' Flight – red, 'B' Flight – yellow, 'C' Flight – blue.

1939 Twenty-four Wellingtons of Nos 9, 37, 38, and 149 Squadrons were despatched on a daylight armed reconnaissance against shipping in the Wilhelmshaven area.

Armourers hoist 250lb bombs into the bomb bay of a No. 149 Squadron Wellington. *(G.R. Pitchfork Collection)*

Sir David Henderson pictured as a major general. *(RAFM)*

Twelve aircraft failed to return; most, if not all, were shot down by German fighters alerted by an experimental *Freya* early warning radar installation at Wangerooge. This was believed to be the first time an air-defence radar was used operationally by the enemy. The most notorious engagement of the 'Phoney War', this engagement became known as the 'Battle of the Heligoland Bight'.

1943   GC: Flt Lt Hector Bertram Gray of RAF Kai Tak who after capture passed messages between the POW camp and the British Military Intelligence Staff until he was betrayed. The Japanese executed him. (*London Gazette*, 19 April 1946, posthumous award)

See 5 November 1938.

19 DECEMBER

1921   No. 1 Armoured Car Company formed at Heliopolis, Egypt, equipped with Rolls-Royce 'A' armoured cars.

1929   The RAF College Cranwell received a grant of arms, the first of three RAF establishments.

1944   AHQ Greece at Kifisia was attacked by ELAS troops. Despite the best efforts of No. 2933 Squadron, RAF Regiment, the head-quarters was overrun on 20 December and a large number of British prisoners were taken and marched north. Wellingtons of No. 221 Squadron dropped supplies to the column.

1962   The first RAF air quartermasters received their flying badges.

1965   The oil lift commenced to Ndola and Lusaka, Zambia, initially from Tanzania and then from Nairobi, Kenya, by Britannias of Nos 99 and 511 Squadrons following declaration of UDI by the government of Southern Rhodesia. Using 45-gallon drums, 3,500,000 gallons of fuel, 2,000,000lb of freight and 3,731 passengers were carried by the end of the operation on 31 October 1966.

See 3 December 1965.

Petrol is loaded on to a Britannia at Nairobi. *(AHB)*

A Puma over the Victoria Falls during Operation Agila.
(AHB)

20 DECEMBER

1979 Operation Agila: the deployment of a Commonwealth Monitoring Force by RAF Hercules and VC10, assisted by USAF transport aircraft, to Salisbury, Rhodesia, began. In addition to 987 passengers and 351,700lb of freight, 6 Puma, 6 Gazelle and 6 Scout helicopters were also transported by air. On 24 December forward deployment of the Force to selected areas began and was completed in three days. A ceasefire came into effect at midnight on 28 December and the anticipated trouble from Communist guerrillas did not materialise. The operation was completed by mid-March 1980 when the forces were withdrawn.

1940 Spitfires of No. 66 Squadron flew the first 'Rhubarbs' (offensive sweeps by fighters against targets of opportunity) when they operated in the Le Touquet area.

1942 During a raid on Lutterade power station, Mosquitos of No. 109 Squadron used *Oboe* – a navigation and bombing aid, with a range-measurement station indicating when bombs were to be released – operationally for the first time.

1956 Operation Musketeer: the last RAF personnel were withdrawn from Gamil Airfield after the RAF's short occupation of the Egyptian airfield.
See 31 October 1956.

1956 Operation Challenger: over five days 350 RAF and 35 French Air Force transport aircraft staged through RAF Luqa following the withdrawal of troops who had taken part in the Suez Canal operation. A total of 2,212 personnel were accommodated and despatched, necessitating the provision of 7,541 meals and 7,821 in-flight meals – the busiest time Luqa ever experienced.

21 DECEMBER

1939 The air gunner badge for air gunners, wireless operator/air gunner (WOP/AG) and wireless operator mechanics/air gunner (WOM/AG) was introduced. It superseded the brass wing bullet and was a single wing with brown laurel wreath

The air gunner's flying badge became the standard design for other non-pilot aircrew trades. *(G.R. Pitchfork Collection)*

Vulcans at readiness. *(J. Falconer Collection)*

enclosing the letters 'AG' in white. It ceased to be awarded in 1954 (AMO A.547/ 1939).

See 12 April 1923.

The Nizam of Hyderabad donated the first 'gift' squadron of the war when No. 152 Squadron was renamed No. 152 (Hyderabad) Squadron.

1962 At the end of the Kennedy–Macmillan conference in Nassau it was announced that the Skybolt programme was to be cancelled and replaced by a submarine-launched missile, the Polaris. This decision was a watershed for the RAF and Bomber Command with the responsibility for the strategic nuclear deterrent, held by the RAF since the late 1950s, handed over to the Royal Navy.

See 30 June 1969.

RAF transport aircraft had delivered to Brunei a total of 3,209 troops (including the RAF Regiment), 113 vehicles and artillery pieces, two Auster AOPs of the Army Air Corps and 64,308lb of freight.

See 8 December 1962.

1982 With the disbandment of No. 44 Squadron, the last of the 'big bomber' aircraft left RAF service. The squadron was the last to operate the Vulcan in its original bomber role – only the six air refuelling tankers of No. 50 Squadron remained in service.

22 DECEMBER

1916 It was decided to widen the role of the Air Board, under the presidency of Lord Cowdray, giving it limited executive powers. A section of the New Ministries and Secretaries Act 1916, which brought the Board into being, laid down that 'for the purpose of this Act the President of the Air Board shall be deemed to be a Minister appointed under this Act'.

See 11 May 1916.

1939 The first regulations for the WAAF, including terms of service, ranks, discipline, uniform and leave, were laid down in an Air Ministry Order (AMO 550/1939).

2004 Alice Strike, who served in the WRAF during the First World War, died in Halifax, Canada, at the age of 108.

WAAFs undertook an increasingly wide variety of tasks as the Second World War progressed. *(AHB)*

23 DECEMBER

1928 The evacuation to India of 586 civilians from the British Legation in Kabul began, following its isolation by rebel tribes led by Kabibullah Khan. Victorias of No. 70 Squadron flew 28,160 miles, much of it over very mountainous terrain and in severe weather. DH9As and a Handley Page Hinaidi also participated. A total of 28,160 miles were flown and the operation ended on 25 February 1929 after 84 sorties.

1939 Military Intelligence 9 (MI 9) was established. Among its duties was the preparation of plans to assist men to evade capture and to facilitate the escape of POWs. Later it became responsible for debriefing returning evaders and escapers, for co-ordinating escape lines, co-ordinating the training of aircrew in escape and evasion techniques and the development of escape aids.

1941 Buffaloes of No. 67 Squadron destroyed six bombers and four fighters of the Japanese invasion force over the Burmese capital, Rangoon. Five Buffaloes were lost. Two days later the Japanese launched a much stronger attack against the city.

1943 Gen D. Eisenhower was appointed Supreme Allied Commander of Expeditionary Forces in the United Kingdom with ACM Sir Arthur Tedder appointed as Deputy Supreme Commander.

1944 **VC:** Sqn Ldr Robert Anthony Maurice Palmer DFC & Bar, pilot of No. 109 Squadron and master bomber during a daylight attack by Lancasters on Gremburg marshalling yards. He continued his run-up to the target despite his bomber being on fire, in order to mark the target. (*London Gazette*, 23 March 1945, posthumous award)

1964 Indonesian Confrontation: following a serious incursion in Johore by Indonesian troops, Hunters of No. 20 Squadron and Canberras of No. 45 Squadron mounted air strikes against the infiltrators. These were repeated during the next few days when the infiltrators were eliminated.

Text visible within the montage photograph:

THE FIRST EVACUATION OF WOMEN.

LOOKING TOWARDS THE JALALABAD PLAIN FROM THE KHYBER.

A TYPICAL GROUP WAITING TO BE EVACUATED

TRUSK, HIS W/T OPERATOR AND AN AFGHAN PILOT.

A BUNCH OF WOMEN FROM THE FOREIGN LEGATIONS.

UNLOADING A NEW ENGINE FOR TRUSK'S "9A" FLOWN UP BY MAXWELL ON 8928.

SOME OF BACCHI SACHAO'S REBELS ON GUARD AT SHERPUR AERODROME

SIR FRANCIS (WITH UNION JACK)

BEESLEY, MAX, SIR FRANCIS + VARIOUS AFGHAN CUSTOMS OFFICIAL AT KABUL

SIR PERCY BOLTON, GROUP CAPTAIN MILLS AND SIR FRANCIS HUMPHRYS AT PESHAWAR ON THE DAY OF FINAL EVACUATION 25.2.29.

MAX + MRS ANDY

EMPLANING THE FIRST LOAD OF WOMEN FOLK

A montage of photographs of the evacuation of the British Legation in Kabul. *(AHB)*

Gen Dwight D. Eisenhower, Supreme Commander, with some of his senior air staff including ACM Sir Arthur Tedder (extreme left) and ACM Sir Trafford Leigh Mallory (4th from left). *(IWM. CH 18550)*

24 DECEMBER

1941 The Lancaster entered service with No. 44 Squadron at RAF Waddington.

1962 Indonesian Confrontation: a Joint Force HQ was established in Brunei with the resounding title of HQ COMBRITBOR (Commander, British Forces, Borneo).

A Lancaster B1 of No. 44 Squadron over Lincolnshire. *(P.H.T. Green Collection)*

25 DECEMBER

1914 The first enemy aircraft was intercepted over Britain. During an attempted attack on the London dock area, an RFC Vickers FB4 Gunbus (664) based at Joyce Green, and flown by 2Lt M.R. Chidson with Cpl Martin as gunner, intercepted a Friedrichshafen FF29 floatplane of *See Flieger Abteilung 1* over Erith, Kent. During the subsequent pursuit, the FF29 released two bombs, which landed in a field near Cliffe railway station. The Gunbus crew broke off their attack when the aircraft's solitary Vickers-Maxim machine gun jammed; although damaged, the FF29 succeeded in returning to base.

1923 During the summer of 1923, Sheikh Mahmud, who had fled to Persia following the arrival of a British column in May, returned to Sulaimaniya and proclaimed himself King of Kurdistan. He resumed his trouble-making. In response, his house was bombed and, once again, he 'retired'.

See 13 May 1931.

The Vickers FB4 Gunbus (664), which made the first interception of an enemy aircraft over Britain. *(Cross and Cockade)*

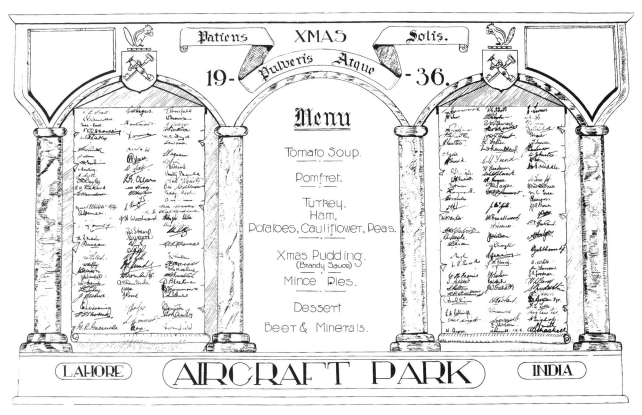

Xmas menus for airmen serving overseas in India. *(ACA Archives)*

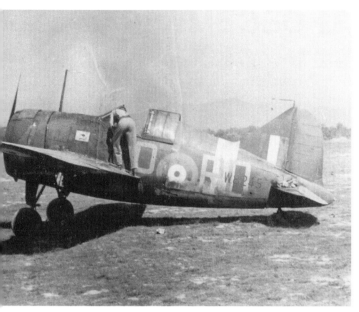

A Buffalo of No. 67 Squadron at Mingaladon, Burma.
(ACA Archives)

1941 In the second Japanese air attack on Rangoon, RAF fighters dispersed the attacking force, destroying eighteen bombers and six fighters before they reached the capital. Pilots of No. 67 Squadron claimed to have destroyed a further twelve aircraft over Rangoon itself.

26 DECEMBER

1939 The first squadron of the RAAF in England, No. 10 (RAAF) Squadron flying the Sunderland, was brought up to full strength for service with Coastal Command.

1940 Blind-approach equipment began to be introduced into operational aircraft for the first time.

27 DECEMBER

1943 Following the success of the North African campaign when air–land co-operation and joint operations were pivotal for victory, Gen Sir Bernard Montgomery said: 'First of all you must win the battle of the air. That must come before you start a single sea or land engagement. If you examine the conduct of my campaigns, you will find that we never fought a land battle until the air battle was won.'

See 16 November 1941.

1947 HM King George VI signified approval of the award of King's Colours: one for the RAF in the United Kingdom, another for the RAF College Cranwell and one for No. 1 School of Technical Training, RAF Halton. After the King's death, Queen Elizabeth II approved a fourth Colour, a Queen's Colour to the RAF Regiment.

See 6 July 1949, 26 May 1951, 25 July 1952.

1965 After Britain's first off-shore drilling platform, *Sea Gem*, capsized off the north-east coast of England, a Whirlwind (captain Sgt L. Smith) of No. 202 Squadron based at RAF Leconfield was scrambled. The helicopter crew rescued three men from the freezing water and in a snow-storm described as 'horrendous conditions'. The winchman, Flt Sgt J. Reeson, was awarded the George Medal, the navigator, Flt Lt J. Hill, received the AFC, and Sgt L. Smith the Queen's Commendation.

28 DECEMBER

1933 An Avro Tutor was allotted to the Central Flying School for trials of yellow dope, which was later adopted as the standard for RAF trainers.

1963 No. 3 Wing, RAF Regiment, established the 'Green Line' in Nicosia, Cyprus, to separate warring Turkish and Greek communities.

29 DECEMBER

1939 A captured Messerschmitt Bf109E was flown from France to England for evaluation. The aircraft was flown by Wg Cdr McKenna and was escorted by a Hudson.

1944 Flt Lt R.J. Audet of No. 411 (RCAF) Squadron flying a Spitfire IX became the only Spitfire pilot to claim five victories in a single sortie. It was the first time he had met enemy aircraft in the air, but within ten minutes he had become an 'ace', having shot down three Focke-Wulf 190s and two Messerschmitt Bf109s in the Osnabruck area. By the end of January, he had destroyed a further five aircraft in the air and two on the ground and was awarded the DFC & Bar. On 3 May he was shot down attacking a train and was killed.

A Wapiti of No. 5 Squadron is refuelled at Khanpur on the North-West Frontier of India. *(C. Morris Collection)*

31 DECEMBER

1918 Lt W.L. Robinson **VC** died of influenza after being released from a German POW camp.
See 2 September 1916.

1929 A farewell message from MRAF Sir Hugh Trenchard was published in AMWO No. 802: 'On leaving the Air Service after 17 years' work in the Royal Flying Corps and the Royal Air Force, and on ceasing to be Chief of the Air Staff after 11 years' service in that post, I wish to bid good-bye to all ranks of the Royal Air Force and to thank them all for the hard work and keenness which has been shown in the

building of this new Service and in raising it to the position which it now occupies. I am certain that the future will add still further to the reputation of the Air Force and to its importance in the defence of the British Empire.'

1936 After announcing himself as the Champion of Islam, the Fakir of Ipi declared a holy war and was engaged by Army columns in November on the edge of Mahsud territory on the North-West Frontier of India. He was forced to hide but was located in a fortress and Wapitis of No. 60 Squadron mounted a series of bombing attacks for three days and destroyed the fort. After his withdrawal towards the Afghanistan border, seven RAF squadrons were heavily involved in supporting the 45,000 troops engaged. These operations continued until May, but sporadic operations carried on until the end of 1937 before more intensive operations resumed in 1938. The Fakir of Ipi continued to spread and advocate rebellion for years to come.

1947 AHQ Burma was disbanded and the RAF's presence in Burma came to an end.

1959 The first V-bombers – Valiants of No. 207 Squadron – were assigned to SACEUR in the tactical bombing role.

1965 The RAF Technical College was merged into the RAF College Cranwell. Relocation from RAF Henlow to the RAF College was completed on 3 January 1966.

1972 The Central Band of the WRAF was disbanded. It grew from a Drum and Trumpet Band formed at RAF Stanmore in 1944 before being formally established at RAF Uxbridge in 1950.

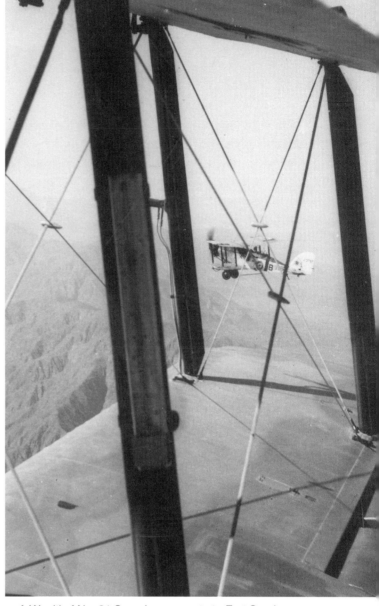

A Wapiti of No. 31 Squadron en route to Fort Sandeman on the North-West Frontier of India. *(C. Morris Collection)*

1996 The RAF Staff College Bracknell closed and a new Joint Services Command and Staff College was established at Bracknell on 1 January 1997.

BIBLIOGRAPHY

Abbott, P.E. and Tamplin, J.M.A., *British Gallantry Awards*, Nimrod Dix & Co, 1981

Air Publication 125, *A Short History of the Royal Air Force*, Air Ministry, 1936

Air Publication 736, *Signals, Radio in Maritime Warfare*, Air Ministry, 1954

Air Publication 818, *Drill and Ceremonial*, Air Ministry

Air Publication 1116, *Signals, Fighter Control and Interception*, Air Ministry, 1952

Air Publication 1136, *Signals, Aircraft Radio*, Air Ministry, 1956

Air Publication 3003, *A Brief History of the Royal Air Force*, HMSO, 2004

Air Publication 3231, *Airborne Forces*, Air Ministry, 1951

Air Publication 3232, *Air Sea Rescue*, Air Ministry, 1952

Air Publication 3234, *Women's Auxiliary Air Force*, Air Ministry, 1953

Air Publication 3235, *Air Support*, Air Ministry, 1955

Air Publication 3327, *Colours and Standards in the Royal Air Force*, Air Ministry, 1957

Air Publication 3368, *The Origins and Development of Operational Research in the RAF*, HMSO, 1963

Air Publication 3410, *The Malayan Emergency 1948–1960*, Ministry of Defence, 1970

Armitage, Michael, *The Royal Air Force*, Arms & Armour, 1993

Ashworth, Chris., *RAF Coastal Command*, Patrick Stephens, 1992

Babington-Smith, Constance, *Evidence in Camera*, Chatto & Windus, 1958

Banks, Arthur, *Wings of the Dawning*, Images Publishing, 1996

Barker, Ralph, *The Hurricats*, Pelham Books, 1978

Bishop, Edward, *The Debt We Owe*, Airlife, 1989

Bowyer, Chaz, *Royal Air Force Handbook 1939–1945*, Ian Allen, 1984

——, *RAF Operations 1918–1938*, William Kimber, 1988

——, *For Valour, The Air VC*, Grub Street, 1992

Brooks, Andrew, *V Force – The History of Britain's Airborne Deterrent*, Janes, 1982

Burns, Michael, *Queen's Flight*, Blandford Press, 1986

Carter, Nick and Carter, Carol, *The Distinguished Flying Cross*, Savannah, 1998

Christie, Carl A., *Ocean Bridge*, Midland Publishing, 1995

Crawley, Aidan, *Escape from Germany*, HMSO, 1985

Cull, Brian and others, *Spitfires over Israel*, Grub Street, 1994

Delve, Ken, *The Source Book of the RAF*, Airlife, 1994

——, *D-Day – The Air Battle*, Arms & Armour, 1994

Dobinson, Colin, *Fields of Deception*, Methuen, 2000

Dowling, John, *RAF Helicopters, The First Twenty Years*, HMSO, 1992

Dudgeon, A.G., *Hidden Victory*, Tempus Publishing, 2000

Escott, Beryl, *Women in Air Force Blue*, Patrick Stephens, 1989

Foot, M.R.D., *SOE*, BBC, 1984

Franks, Norman, *RAF Fighter Command*, Patrick Stephens, 1992

——, *Valiant Wings*, Crecy, 1994

——, *Search, Find and Kill*, Grub Street, 1995

Freeman, Roger, *The Mighty Eighth*, Macdonald & James, 1978

Golley, John, *Aircrew Unlimited*, Patrick Stephens, 1993

Gordon, L.L., *British Battles and Medals*, Spink & Son, 1971

Grey, C.G., *A History of the Air Ministry*, George Allen & Unwin, 1940

Halley, James, *The Squadrons of the Royal Air Force & Commonwealth*, Air Britain, 1988

Harris, Sir Arthur, *Despatch on War Operations*, Frank Cass & Co., 1995

Haslam, E.B., *The History of Royal Air Force Cranwell*, HMSO, 1982

Hering P.G., *Customs and Tradition of the Royal Air Force*, Gale & Polden, 1961

Hill, Roderic, *The Baghdad Air Mail*, Edward Arnold & Co., 1929

Hinsley F.H., *British Intelligence in the Second World War*, HMSO, 1988

Hobson, Chris, *Falklands Air War*, Midland Publishing, 2002

Hunt, Leslie, *Twenty-one Squadrons*, Garnstone Press, 1972

James, T.C.G., *The Battle of Britain*, Frank Cass, 2000

Jefford, C.G. *RAF Squadrons*, Airlife, 1993

——, *Observers and Navigators*, Airlife, 2001

Jones, H.A., *The War in the Air*, Oxford University Press, 1937

Kendrick, Ian, *Music in the Air*, Egon Publishers, 1986

Lacey-Johnson, Lionel, *Point Blank and Beyond*, Airlife, 1991

Lake, Alan, *Flying Units of the RAF*, Airlife, 1999

Leaf, Edward, *Above all Unseen*, Patrick Stephens, 1997

Lee, Sir David, *Flight from the Middle East*, HMSO, 1978

——, *Eastward*, HMSO, 1984

——, *Wings in the Sun*, HMSO, 1989

MacBean, John and Hogben, Arthur, *Bombs Gone*, Patrick Stephens, 1990

Macdonald, Patrick, *Through Darkness to Light*, Pentland Press, 1991

Mackersey, Ian, *Into the Silk*, Robert Hale, 1956

Mason, Francis K., *Battle over Britain*, Aston Publications, 1990

May, Carman and Tanner, *Badges and Insignia of Britain's Armed Forces*, Adam & Charles Black, 1974

Merrick, K.A., *Flights of the Forgotten*, Arms & Armour, 1989

Middlebrook, Martin and Everitt, Chris, *The Bomber Command War Diaries*, Viking, 1985

Morgan, D.R., *Short Historical Account of No. 83 Group*, Private, 1957

Moyes, Philip, *Bomber Squadrons*, Macdonald, 1965

Nesbit, Roy C., *The Strike Wings*, William Kimber, 1984

——, *Armed Rovers*, Airlife, 1995

——, *RAF in Action, 1939–1945*, Public Record Office, 2000

Nichol, John and Rennell, Tony, *The Last Escape*, Viking, 2002

Oliver, Kingsley M., *Through Adversity*, Forces & Corporate, 1997

——, *The RAF Regiment at War*, Pen & Sword, 2002

Owen, Roderic, *The Desert Air Force*, Hutchinson, 1948

Payne L.G.S., *Air Dates*, Heinemann, 1957

Pearcy, Arthur, *Berlin Airlift*, Airlife, 1997

Pitchfork, Graham, *Shot Down and on the Run*, National Archives, 2003

——, *Shot Down and in the Drink*, National Archives, 2005

Price, Alfred, *Instruments of Darkness*, William Kimber, 1967

Probert, Henry, *High Commanders of the Royal Air Force*, HMSO, 1991

——, *The Forgotten Air Force*, Brassey's, 1995

——, *The Rock and the Royal Air Force*, Gibraltar Books, 2005

Probert, H. and Gilbert, M., *'128': The Story of the Royal Air Force Club*, RAF Club, 2004

Rawlings, John, *Fighter Squadrons of the RAF*, Macdonald and Jane's, 1969

——, *Coastal, Support and Special Squadrons*, Jane's, 1982

Rexford-Welch, S.C., *The Royal Air Force Medical Services*, HMSO, 1954

Richards, D. and Saunders, H. StG., *Royal Air Force 1939–1945*, Vols 1–3, HMSO, 1953

Richards, Denis, *The Hardest Victory*, Hodder & Stoughton, 1994

Robertson, Bruce, *Aircraft Markings of the World 1912–1967*, Harleyford Publications, 1967

Ross A.E., *Through Eyes of Blue*, Airlife, 2002

Saundby, Sir Robert, *Air Bombardment*, Chatto & Windus, 1961

Saunders, Hilary St George, *Per Ardua*, Oxford University Press, 1944

Schofield, Ernest and Nesbit, Roy Conyers, *Arctic Airmen*, William Kimber, 1987

Shores, Christopher, *Fledgling Eagles*, Grub Street, 1991

——, *Dust Clouds in the Middle East*, Grub Street, 1996

——, *Air War over Burma*, Grub Street, 2005

Shores, Christopher and others, *Fighters over Tunisia*, Neville Spearman, 1975

——, *Malta: The Hurricane Years 1940–4*, Grub Street, 1987

——, *Malta: The Spitfire Year 1942*, Grub Street, 1991

——, *Bloody Shambles*, Vol. I, Grub Street, 1992

——, *Bloody Shambles*, Vol. II, Grub Street, 1993

Shores, Christopher and Thomas, Chris, *2nd Tactical Air Force*, Vols 1–3, Classic, 2004

Smith, David J., *Britain's Aviation Memorials and Mementoes*, Patrick Stephens, 1992

Streetley, Martin, *Confound and Destroy*, Macdonald and Janes, 1978

Sturtivant, Ray, Hamlin, John and Halley, James J., *RAF Flying Training and Support Units*, Air Britain, 1997

Sweetman, John, *Tirpitz – Hunting the Beast*, Sutton, 2000

Tavender, Ian, *The Distinguished Flying Medal Register*, Savannah, 2000

Taylor, John W.R., *C.F.S.*, Jane's, 1987

Taylor, Bill, *Royal Air Force Germany*, Midland Publishing, 2003

Terraine, John, *The Right of the Line*, Hodder and Stoughton, 1985

——, *Business in Great Waters*, Leo Cooper, 1989

Thetford, Owen, *Aircraft of the Royal Air Force*, Putnam, 1995

Treuenen James, A.G., *The Royal Air Force. The Past 30 Years*, Macdonald and Jane's, 1976

Tucker, Nicholas G., *In Adversity*, Jade, 1997

Verity, Hugh, *We Landed by Moonlight*, Ian Allan, 1978

Walpole, Nigel, *Seek and Strike*, Astonbridge Publishing, 2001

Webster, Sir Charles, and Frankland, Noble, *The Strategic Air Offensive against Germany*, Vols 1–4, HMSO, 1961

Wood, Derek, *Attack Warning Red*, Carmichael & Sweet, 1992

Wood, Derek, with Dempster, Derek, *The Narrow Margin*, Hutchinson, 1961

Wright, Robert, *Dowding and the Battle of Britain*, Macdonald, 1969

Wynn, Humphrey, *RAF Nuclear Deterrent Forces*, The Stationery Office, 1994

——, *Forged in War*, The Stationery Office, 1996

PAPERS, JOURNALS AND MAGAZINES

Aeroplane

After the Battle

Air Clues

Air Historical Branch Narratives

Air Ministry Orders

Air Ministry Weekly Orders

Air Power Review

Air Publications

Defence White Papers

Flight

London Gazette

Royal Air Force Historical Society Journals

RAF College Cranwell Journals

RAF News

RAF Quarterly Review

NATIONAL ARCHIVES OFFICIAL RECORDS

AIR 2/991, 2506, 5016, 8706, 8708, 10121, 10664, 11509, 14141, 14229, 18159

AIR 8/1504

AIR 14/865, 1432

AIR 20/6403, 6534, 6693, 7412, 7460, 7753, 10068, 10169, 10345, 10362, 10574, 10735, 11429, 11639

AIR 21/7

AIR 23/2679

AIR 27/288, 479, 956, 1066, 1372, 1423, 1425, 1504, 1565, 1644, 2028, 2201, 2303, 2394, 2440

AIR 28/7590

AIR 35/190

AIR 37/1153

AIR 41/8

AIR 45/2

AIR 49/389

INDEX

Page references in **bold** refer to illustrations.
Military personnel are given the highest rank that appears in the text.

McKinley, Wg Cdr D.C., 142
Mackworth, Air Cdre P.H., 336
MacLaren, Maj A.S.C., 243, 374
McLeod, Lt A.A., 79, 346
McMurdo Sound, Antarctica, 362
McNamara, AVM F.H., 71, 342
Macnamara, Wg Cdr B., 308
McPherson, Fg Off A., 278, 318
MacRobert, Lady, 319–20
McTeague, Cpl T. P., 371
Mafraq, Jordan, 170, 337
Magwe, 60, 71, **71**
Mahaddie, Gp Capt T.G., 203
Mahmud, Sheikh, 146, **147**, 157, 163, 192, 232, 295, 385
Mahn, Plt Off H. RCAF, 193
mail services, 200, **201**, 377–8, **377**
Mailly-le-Camp, 136
Maintenance Units (MUs), 1–2
  No. 32, 10; No. 33, 235
Maison Blanche, Algeria, 348, **348**
Maisy, France, 176
Maitland, Air Cdre E.M., 266
Majunga, Madagascar, 68
Malaya, 92, 143, 178, 268, 273, 275, 285, 294, 300, 369, **372**
  see also Firedog, Operation
Malaysia, 254, 261, **261**, 294, 298
'Malcolm Clubs', 366
Malcolm, Wg Cdr H.G., 366
Malden Island, 148
Mallard, Operation, 177
Malta, 39, 198, 244
  attacks on, 9, 23, 71, 116, 130, 140, 142, 184, 319; awarded George Cross, 114; units on, 22, 32, 60, 88, 131, 140, 196, 214, 224, 248, 305, 338, 365
Malta Fighter Flight, 196
Maltby, AVM P., 60, **273**
Manby, 171, 214
Manna, Operation, 128, **128**
Mannheim, 62, 376, **376**
Mannock, Maj E., 240–1
Manser, Fg Off L.T., 169
Manston, 33–4, 57, 64, 225, 227, 231, 243, 357
Maralinga, Australia, 319
Mareth Line, Battle of, 78
Margaret, HRH Princess, 94, 178
Marham, 31, 74, 243, 276, 375
Marina, Princess, 94
Marine Acceptance Depots, 108
Marine Aircraft Experimental Establishment, 91
Marine Branch, 88, 227
marine craft, 204, **204**
Marine Craft Section, 108
Maritime Operational Training Unit, 311
Market, Operation, 296, 298, 303
Marrows, Flt Lt D. RAAF, 245
Marseilles, 174
Martin, AC2 R., 177
Martin, Capt James, 66, **66**
Martin, Cpl, 385
Martin, Sqn Ldr H.B., 130

Martin-Baker ejection seats, 65, 66, 105, 237
Martlesham Heath, 71, 221, **221**, **264**, 280, 365, 374
Mary, HRH Princess, 188, **189**, 338, **338**
Masirah, Oman, 86, 372
Master Bombers, 231, 261, 274, 383
Masterman, Air Cdre E.A.D., 1, 53
Mastiff, Operation, 273, 284
Maubeuge aerodrome, 255
Maughan, Sqn Ldr C.G., 235, **235**
Mauripur, 14, 18, 257
Mavor, AM Sir Leslie, **264**
Maxwell, Cdr L.H. USN, 266
Maxwell Field AFB, **127**, 128
Maynard, AVM N.M., 297
medals and decorations
  Air Efficiency Award, 261; Air Force Cross, 174, 272; Air Force Medal, 174, 272; Conspicuous Gallantry Medal, 351; Distinguished Flying Cross, 174, 272, 318, **318**; Distinguished Flying Medal, 174, 272; Dutch Flying Cross, 108; Empire Gallantry Medal, 233, 302; Founder's Medal of the Air League, 220; India General Service Medal, 131, **131**; Long Service and Good Conduct Medal, 212; Meritorious Service Medal, 205, 365; Queen's Medal for Champion Shots of the RAF, 186; Royal Observer Corps, 22
  see also George Cross; Victoria Cross
Medhurst, ACM Sir Charles, 247, 360
Medical Relief Team, 342
Mediterranean Allied Air Forces, 372
Mediterranean Allied Tactical Air Force, 273
Mediterranean/Middle East (MED/ME), 171, 247, 360
Medium Bomber Force (MBF), 4
Medmenham, 171, 343
Meiktila, Burma, 59
Melbourne, Australia, 285
Melsbroek, Brussels, **123**
memorials
  Alamein, 325; Battle of Britain, 173, 223, 297; Bomber Command, 347; Coastal Command, 68; Polish Air Force, 342, **342**; Runnymede, 225, 325, 326, **326**; Singapore, 325; Victoria Embankment, 235, **236**
Menaul, Gp Capt S.W.B., 322
Mercer, Air Cdre J.W.F., 322
Merchant Ship Fighting Unit (MSFU), 137, 161, 243
Merrick, Sqn Ldr C., 176, **176**
Merrifield, Wg Cdr J.R.H., 282, 362
Mesopotamia, 364
Meteor drones, 127
Meteorological Flight, 340
Meteorological Office, 91
Metropolitan Air Force, 45, 227, 350
Micky Finn exercises, 366
Microbe, Operation, 291
Middelkirke, 237
Middle East Air Force (MEAF), 92, **113**, 171, 220, 328, 365
Middle Wallop, 61, 196
Middleton, Flt Sgt R.H. RAAF, 362
Miho, Japan, 122
Milage, Operation, 53

413